THE RELIGIOUS FUNCTION
OF THE PSYCHE

Traditional concepts of God are no longer tenable for many people who nevertheless experience a strong sense of the sacred. These people require an approach to religion that recognizes its actual manifestations within their own lives.

The Religious Function of the Psyche offers an examination of divinity that focuses on its unique, personal manifestations within the psyche, the body, relationships and the world at large.

Using the language and interpretive methods of depth psychology, particularly those of C. G. Jung and psychoanalytic self psychology, the author, Lionel Corbett, offers an introduction to Jung and religion and a bridge between the transpersonal and the personal levels of the psyche. Lionel Corbett suggests a psychological model for the relationship between the divine and the human, and offers an alternative approach to spirituality than that found in traditional religious systems.

Problems of evil, suffering, and the notion of human development as an incarnation of spirit, are dealt with in this book by a religious approach to the psyche that can be applied in both everyday life and within the practice of psychotherapy.

Lionel Corbett is Professor of Depth Psychology, Pacifica Graduate Institute, Santa Barbara, California, USA.

THE
RELIGIOUS FUNCTION
OF THE PSYCHE

Lionel Corbett

First published 1996
by Routledge
11 New Fetter Lane, London EC4P 4EE

Simultaneously published in the USA and Canada
by Routledge
29 West 35th Street, New York, NY 10001

Routledge is an imprint of the Taylor & Francis Group

Reprinted 1997 and 1999

© 1996 Lionel Corbett

Typeset in Times by
Ponting–Green Publishing Services, Chesham, Bucks
Printed and bound in Great Britain by
Bookcraft Ltd, Midsomer Norton, Somerset

British Library Cataloguing in Publication Data
A catalogue record for this book is available from the
British Library

Library of Congress Cataloging in Publication Data
Corbett, Lionel
The religious function of the psyche / Lionel Corbett.
p.   cm.
Includes bibliographical references.
1. Psychology, Religious. 2. Psychoanalysis and religion.
3. Jungian psychology. I. Title.
BL53.C657   1996
200´. 91– dc20   95–25778
CIP

ISBN 0–415–14400–0 (hbk)
ISBN 0–415–14401–9 (pbk)

CONTENTS

FIGURES

ACKNOWLEDGEMENTS

This book could not have been written without the support and encouragement of my wife, Cathy Rives, MD, to whom I am very grateful. My friend Kate Jones read an early version of the manuscript, and made innumerable suggestions about style and content which greatly improved the clarity and accuracy of the text. The comments and suggestions of my friend Andrew Samuels were also very useful in this regard. I am indebted to the many patients and friends who have allowed me to describe their experience of the numinosum within these pages, as well as to the innumerable people at conferences and lectures on this subject who affirmed that this approach to the psyche had personal validity. Acknowledgement is also due to Routledge for permission to reproduce material from *The Collected Works of C. G. Jung*, translated by R. F. C. Hull. I would also like to thank Eve Daintith for her meticulous copy editing.

To Zachary, Ashley and Gabriel

INTRODUCTION
The new psychological dispensation

Edward Edinger (1984) has suggested that we are beginning a new chapter in our religious history. He believes that humanity's relation to the divine mystery is no longer simply mediated by means of law or faith, as it was in the Judaeo-Christian era. We now have a new psychological dispensation, a new manner of understanding the relationship between the divine and the human. Our felt sense is that we are addressed by transpersonal levels of the psyche. This dialogue has become the 'new context, the new vessel with which humanity can be the carrier of divine meaning' (p. 90). I hope to clarify some of the ways that the idea of a new dispensation may be implemented in practice.

This book grew from two sources. The first was my personal frustration with traditional concepts of divinity. Although I have always been a religious individual, I have never been able to make much use of the ways in which traditional religious systems conceive of God. These ideas seemed to have little to do with my own experience. The second source was the realization that many of the people I work with in psychotherapy also experience the sacred in ways that have little to do with established religious systems. Many people have a deeply personal or private sense of what is really sacred to them, while they maintain an outward adherence to a traditional church or synagogue, for reasons such as family allegiance or simple sentimentality. In some such cases, I find that the individual's real spirituality has never been expressed until it emerges in the consulting room – it is like a secret life. This book is dedicated to the idea that many people with a strong sense of the sacred require an approach that recognizes its actual manifestations within their own lives.

Widespread disenchantment exists both with traditional notions about God and also with the doctrinal systems to which these ideas belong. Orthodox systems of thought are often out of harmony with individual needs for, and experiences of, the sacred. We have long had to rethink the traditional ideas about God as an Old Man in the Sky who is benevolently watching over us. The events of recent generations, such as genocides, environmental catastrophes and nuclear weapons, together with the advent of feminist thought, have forced us to abandon the traditional anthropomorphic images of the divine as an invisible Superior Being who requires a certain type of behaviour. The divine is not necessarily experienced

1

as a celestial mechanic, lawyer, caretaker, parent or any other entity that is comparable to some human concept. No concept of divinity that is not the result of personal experience will ultimately hold sway. There have been many attempts to tell people what God requires of them that are based on authority rather than personal knowledge. These are doomed to provoke reactions of disbelief, as the reality flies in the face of the theory. The illusory image of a God who is an all-good, protective but invisible spirit can no longer be maintained with a straight face. It is time to acknowledge that the divine manifests itself to individuals in unique ways, some of which cause great suffering. For an approach to divinity that has personal relevance, it is necessary to focus on its manifestations within the psyche, in the body, in relationships, in the world at large or in any other way that matters. The problem is to locate the Other in the person's life.

The availability of a usable depth psychological approach to the experience of divinity actually encourages us to define 'God' in an individually meaningful manner, rather than confining us to the worship of someone else's idea of what God means. Seen from within the depth psychological paradigm, God is always experienced in unique ways. And like the mystics, the depth psychologist, and especially the psychotherapist interested in practising with a religious sensibility, is mainly interested in the God of direct experience. Since the psyche is the essential medium for religious experience, within the psychological approach to divinity any conceptual distinction between God and the psyche's expression of the divine is purely theoretical and of little practical significance. In other words, as some of the Eastern traditions have long held, at the subjective level – which is the proper province of psychology – the divine is indistinguishable from Mind or Consciousness itself. The religious approach to the psyche avoids all specu-lation about the essence of divinity *beyond* the psyche, or at best regards this kind of speculation as merely a comment on the personal psychology of its proponents.

It is of course nothing new to focus on the radical immanence of divinity, or to suggest that the human and the divine are inextricably mixed and that both are to be found within the person. What I believe to be useful about the approach suggested here is that it allows us to describe the dynamics of this interaction in increased detail, using the language and hermeneutics of pure psychology rather than theology. For this reason it is a method that may be directly relevant to the consulting room, in which case nothing need be lost in attempting to translate between personal psychology and theology. Using what is known about the processes of the transpersonal Self in its relation to the development of a personal self, I have suggested ways in which those elements of the psyche that we label as human and divine can best be understood as belonging to an undivided continuum of consciousness. I also try to describe something of how these strands of the psyche combine to form the structures of human personality. It may be a surprise to find that, within this model, our psychopathology, rather than being considered a barrier to spiritual growth, itself becomes an important intrapsychic manifestation of the divine. Accordingly, spiritual practice becomes inseparable from introspective work on one's own psychological difficulties. But such is the inexorable conclusion: no longer is therapeutic attention to emotional distress an exclusively secular affair. Using examples from psychotherapeutic practice, I have demonstrated that an experience of the divine may be located *within* one's psychopathology.

If this sounds outrageous, it should be remembered that every religious system has a different view of divinity. There is no single, agreed-upon God, only different experiences and concepts of God or of ultimate reality. To the depth psychologist, this fact is not surprising; only the psyche itself is universal, and the psyche has an infinite capacity to produce sacred imagery. Within the religious approach to the psyche, the manifestations of transpersonal levels of the psyche are viewed as the fundamental, irreducible beginning of all personal religion that is not grounded in an existing tradition. Hence, consciousness itself, or the forms and images it assumes, becomes our focus. When the individual *is* happily immersed in a traditional religion, the psychologist cannot comment on the literal, historical truth of particular events, such as those depicted in sacred texts, and so we concentrate on their meaning or their internal resonance within the personality. This axiom of the primacy of the psyche is itself a metaphysical position, which I regard as analogous to the mythical underpinnings of all traditions; it is a postulate or commitment that is difficult or impossible to prove. The idea is located within an evolving myth of consciousness which provides a particular understanding of the individual's place in the world. For the depth psychological approach to religion, this new myth acts as a unified field theory, thereby solving some of the problems that plagued earlier religious traditions. The divine as Mind structures the world as we know it, and spirit is actually synonymous with transpersonal levels of the psyche – we use the word 'psychological' rather than 'spiritual' when we think we understand what is happening. The soul is that aspect of the psyche that feels as if it is personal, but it cannot be divorced from the totality of the larger consciousness of which it is a part. Within the psychological paradigm, religion is not a reified set of ideas and propositions; religion means attention to the manifestations of the psyche, to its images and affects.

This book is about the experience of divinity that emerges both from the practice of dynamic psychotherapy and from the principles of depth psychology which underpin this work. To articulate this view, I have relied heavily on C. G. Jung's religious writing and his particular approach to religious matters. I believe that this offers the best chance for a psychologically based re-examination of human religious yearnings. Since Jung's work is most concerned with archetypal or transpersonal levels of experience, there is a need for a bridge to more personal levels of the psyche, which Jung tended to ignore. I have used the language of psychoanalytic self psychology to bridge the divide between the archetype and everyday psychodynamics, so that spiritual concerns and the practice of psychotherapy can be integrated. I adopt a psychologically informed approach to the sacred that takes into account what we know about psychodynamics at the same time as it gives due weight to the primacy of religious experience. I hope this book will be of special use and encouragement to people who experience the sacred in ways that are very real but which are not necessarily traditional.

The book is intended to provide an introduction to a religious approach to the psyche, as this can be applied both in everyday life and also within the practice of psychotherapy. In order that the arguments can be followed by people who are not familiar with the literature in this area, I have included a summary of material that will already be well known to readers of Jung. I ask the indulgence of that group and of specialists in the area of Jung and religion. Without the inclusion of some basic concepts, newcomers to this approach will find it ungrounded and removed from its original context. I should add that the reviews of Jung's ideas are based on my own understanding of them, and readers should be aware that they may not always represent the consensus of other Jungian scholars. References to the works of C. G. Jung thus (CW 16, 395) refer to the volume number of the *Collected Works* and the paragraph numbers.

1

THE RELIGIOUS ATTITUDE IN PSYCHOTHERAPY

DEPTH PSYCHOLOGY AS A SPIRITUAL PURSUIT

My intention in this book is to advocate an approach to the psyche which will lead to the development of an individual, intensely personal spirituality. I wish to illustrate the ways in which depth psychology can address those questions and experiences which have traditionally been the exclusive province of established religions. A perspective on divinity that is rooted within the psyche allows for the description and discussion of human suffering, of evil and of transpersonal experiences, without the necessity for recourse to the tenets of established doctrinal systems. I hope to show that particular life situations and experiences can form the basis of a personalized religion when they are understood by means of depth psychological methods. This requires an approach that retains, or even enhances and releases, the full religious significance of the experience. It is important to state at the outset that this approach is open to *any* manifestation of the divine, however novel or traditional its form. Such openness is possible because we have no preconceived idea about the form in which the divine may or may not become manifest. In Jungian psychology, these manifestations are termed 'numinous'. This word, or its noun 'the numinosum', are used to refer to any such experience. (The term is discussed in detail on p. 11.)

Because the psychological approach is receptive to the many varieties of appearances of the numinosum, certain types of religious experience or solutions to spiritual dilemmas which would be discounted by some orthodoxies are here valued as of great importance to the individual, albeit not necessarily to the collective. Since we cannot dictate the form which the numinosum may take within the individual psyche, our task is to recognize and appreciate it, even – or perhaps especially – if it appears in the form of suffering or psychopathology.

Therefore the religious attitude to the psyche regards attention to introspectively obtained material, such as dreams, visions, creative products, emotional distress, fantasy or simply reflection on personal history, as a valid spiritual pursuit if the transpersonal or archetypal underpinnings of such events are recognized. This attitude relies on a contentious axiom of the depth psychological approach, which is that the raw material for a religious approach to the psyche is mediated by levels of the psyche that extend beyond the personal. (The problem here is whether there is anything such as a God that is beyond the psyche itself.) Jung described these transpersonal levels of the psyche as objective or autonomous. They seamlessly interact with, and are the ground of, more personal material. Practically speaking, and in the consulting room, this interaction is illustrated by the following example, which shows the inherence of emotional difficulty and transpersonal experience. A young man was in the midst of considerable emotional turmoil, feeling as if he could not cope, and that he was entirely alone with his difficulties. Looking aimlessly out of his window, he suddenly saw an enormous face in the sky, looking down at him. He was terrified at this vision, which lasted only a few seconds. (Here the reader is asked to accept my clinical assessment that the event was accompanied by no other phenomena which could be interpreted as the result of psychopathology.) He was unable to understand the meaning of the event, but felt that it was of great personal significance. Soon afterwards the following powerful dream occurred:

> An enormous blue UFO hovered a short distance above my head, stretching as far as I could see in all directions. From its base brilliant beams of light, as if from many high-powered search lights, shone down onto me. Looking up, I saw that the light emanated from a series of eyes on the underside of the craft which were peering at me.

These two experiences are linked together by the common theme of being seen by something or someone from out of his ordinary world. We might say that they present to him an otherness from beyond ego consciousness, to which he must relate as a Thou. In his vision, the subject is presented with many of the criteria (discussed further on pp. 11–13), which define contact with the numinosum. He feels a special type of fear that is the result of encounter with the uncanny. This has a different quality than the fear of something known. In both experiences he is awed; he realizes that he has encountered something that is at the same time amazing, mysterious, beyond understanding, in relation to which he is very small indeed, and to which he does not normally have access. Faced with the dream, the depth psychologist takes the position that, although we may not know what the *physical* basis of the UFO phenomenon is, we approach the dream of a UFO with an attitude that is grounded in the reality of the psyche. Jung (CW 10, 307–433) noted that, from this perspective, UFOs are psychologically important. They are part of a living myth; during dark times, there have always been rumours of intervention from the beyond. Jung points out that the UFO is mandala-shaped (see p. 46), that is, it is a symbol of order, containment and wholeness of a kind that tends to appear as a compensation during times of chaos. In other words, the UFO can be seen as a symbol of the transpersonal Self (see p. 39), that core of the personality that is a part of the Totality. In traditional language, the dreamer is seen by the eye of God.

It is typical for the numinosum to present itself in a manner that is directly relevant to the developmental history of the experiencer. In this case, our subject had never felt really seen; when he was a child, his parents were preoccupied with their own view of what they needed him to be, rather than with what he actually was. Therefore, feeling unseen and alone with his feelings was part of a long-standing complex (a neurotic difficulty) for this man, and his contact with the numinosum addresses the heart of this problem. For him, the dream UFO (not an 'actual' UFO) is both a healing symbol and also a personal bridge to the intrapsychic experience of the transpersonal realm. Whether or not UFOs have this meaning for other people need not be of concern to him; the experience is part of an individual revelation that speaks directly to him. Like much mystical experience, both events address an area of vulnerability. But they are at the same time helpful; they enable him to not feel so alone and isolated. These were awakening experiences; if he was in any doubt before, he is now quite certain that he exists in relation to something not of this realm that is conscious of him. The question of whether these events originate from within or from beyond the psyche is unanswerable. In the former case the psyche would be the causal agent of the experience, in the latter the psyche would be a transmitter for religious experience. The depth psychological approach cannot decide between these possibilities. The important point illustrated here is that we locate the numinosum within the deepest subjectivity of the individual, and we connect it with our psychological needs and difficulties. Because of this connection, the result of numinous experience is often a reorganization of the empirical personality. In this particular case, the subject lost his worries about being seen and about being alone with himself.

Many further examples of contact with the numinosum will be provided in the course of this book. Here I want to make the point that they are not confined to the psychotherapist's office and they are not always related to the pathology of the individual. Coles (1990) tells the story of a young African-American girl in North Carolina in 1962, who was trying to enter her newly desegregated school. To do so she had to run the gauntlet of a racist mob screaming at her:

> I was all alone . . . and suddenly I saw God smiling, and I smiled. A woman was standing there [near the school door], and she shouted at me, 'Hey, you little nigger, what you smiling at?' I looked right at her face, and I said, 'At God.' Then she looked up at the sky, and then she looked at me, and she didn't call me any more names.

> (Coles, 1990)

This example serves to illustrate another important area of debate that will later be taken up in detail. This girl was in a terrifying situation, but to see her experience as simply defensive, or psychodynamically motivated, rather than to accept it at face value as a direct perception of the numinosum, is reductive. There is no reason to doubt that, in some interior and personal way, she did see God. There tends to be an almost automatic assumption that such childhood experiences are illusory. But if her experience had not been genuine, I doubt that the girl's hateful accuser would have been so satisfactorily shamed into silence. Apparently this experience was intended for both participants.

To reiterate: numinous experience arises from an autonomous level of the psyche that is either the source of, or the medium for, the transmission of religious experience; empirically, we cannot say which. We cannot know whether religious experience arises 'beyond' the psyche, or from within it. But having such an experience immediately implies the presence of the psyche, without which there would be no experience, or no experiencer. Therefore, for practical purposes we cannot distinguish between numinous products of the transpersonal levels of the psyche and the simultaneous intrapsychic presence of the divine. The religiously oriented depth psychologist takes these experiences at face value and eschews speculation about their possibly trans-psychic origin. The religious approach to the psyche is thus directly in accord with the mystical traditions of all world religions, in that it tries to approach the divine (or transcendent levels of reality) by locating it directly and deeply within ourselves. To this I would only add that, although the experience of the autonomous psyche can be deeply healing, in fragile personalities it can trigger severe disorganization. (The problem of psychosis is discussed on p. 102.)

The intermingling of the transpersonal and the personal levels of the psyche which occurs in the course of religious experience makes it necessary for both to be included within the purview of those psychotherapists who choose to work within this model. Otherwise, as is tragically often the case, the totality of the individual's inner life is subject to a process of splitting, in which either religious elements are excluded from the psychotherapeutic field, or personal material is seen as irrelevant to spiritual development. This attitude has disastrous consequences for unconsciously acting out the shadow, or the dark side of the personality. By contrast, the religious attitude to the psyche sees psychotherapeutic work on the shadow as itself an integrally religious endeavour.

I espouse the view that the production – or the transmission – of numinous experience is an intrinsic function of the psyche, and that the contents of such experience may be quite independent of the individual's cultural conditioning. This is a fact of major importance. As Jung pointed out, mythical, that is to say religious, imagery which is unknown to the conscious personality occurs in psychopathology and in dreams. But despite the fact that it is unknown, such imagery has an uncanny relevance to the life of the dreamer, indicating the continuity of the personal and non-personal levels of the psyche. Depth psychology offers an approach to this religious function of the psyche which follows the lead of the psyche itself. Rather than a major emphasis on notions of the sacred which are imposed from the outside, which is the position of many dogmatic or doctrinal approaches, we also pay attention to sacred imagery as it arises *de novo*, from within the psyche. The psyche's religious function has powerful relevance to depth psychotherapy, enabling such work to be experienced and practised as a spiritual discipline. To indicate briefly some of the ways in which these two are connected in practice, it is noteworthy that, although some transpersonal experiences speak for themselves, others require interpretive work for their meaning to become clear. It may also happen that the numinosum inspires too much terror to be managed without help. And, although sometimes an archetypal event may feel immediately and unequivocally sacred, psychodynamically motivated resistances may prevent this quality from emerging. At such times, psychotherapeutic work may release a sense of the sacredness of an experience which was previously obscure. Sometimes the therapist may only be required to point out that, despite the fact that an event (such as the UFO dream) is not understandable by reference to an established religious system, its numinosity qualifies it as authentic. Sometimes, too, the individual needs help in locating the meaning of such an experience within the total context of his or her life, and this discovery then becomes the major function of the therapist.

It has often been pointed out that psychotherapy consists not only of its standard technical aspects, but, as the etymology of the word suggests, it is also a process of our attendance on, or service to, the soul, especially in its relationship to spirit. It is typical within the depth psychological approach that terms arise such as 'soul' and 'spirit', which have an already existing theological quality and history. However, because of the increasing maturity of depth psychology, several writers have construed these terms in their intrapsychic sense. They do not need to be used to refer to metaphysical entities or to concepts about the nature of absolute or extrapsychic reality.

Unlike the traditional theological approach to religious experience, which applies the experience of a few exceptional people (such as Jesus or Mohammed) to everyone, the depth psychologist takes the position that, by and large, individual religious experience refers mainly to the person concerned. It is not at all clear that its meaning can be generalized to others, unless, when hearing of the event, such emotional resonance occurs that another person is deeply affected by it. But this is not a matter of dogmatic application to others; its relevance is given through the truth of authentic feeling.

It is also important to note at the beginning what is *not* being attempted here. This book is not a psychology of religion, but a religious approach to a certain dimension of individual psychology. This paradigm is not based on existing well-articulated theological considerations, nor is it grounded in the the axioms of any particular religious tradition. It is not intended to be syncretistic, nor is it a psychological comment on the question of the nature of religion. Rather, the basis of this work is Jung's suggestion that the level of the psyche which he terms archetypal, provides that quality of experience which is synonymous with what has always been considered the religious domain. The depth psychological method is not intended to produce yet another theological system, because it is not concerned with arguments about the actual nature of divinity, but only with its personal experience. The psychological attitude is grounded in the belief that the experience of divinity is amenable to depth psychological hermeneutical methods which are totally independent of preconceived doctrinal assumptions. Of course there are other valid platforms from which to discuss the content of religious experience – the sociological, the historical and so on. My intention is not to insist on the primacy of the psychological approach. It is to emphasize the potentially religious value of subjectivity itself and to clarify the relevance of religious experience to the practice of psychotherapy and to the development of a personal spirituality. I hope that the intrapsychic approach will bypass arguments about authority and truth of the kind found among competing established religions, and will enable people not interested in or committed to predetermined systems to validate their own mode of access to the transpersonal. With this goal in mind, I would now like to elaborate on the concept of the numinosum with special reference to its appearances in the psychotherapeutic setting.

2

PERSONAL SPIRITUALITY BASED ON CONTACT WITH THE NUMINOSUM

We have been so conditioned by our western religious heritage to expect the divine to appear in prescribed ways, such as the Judaeo-Christian forms, that we may not recognize novel or highly personal appearances. Within the traditional heritage, the tendency has been to receive the sacred by means of a prescribed text, sacrament or ritual. But in fact the numinosum may take forms that are not necessarily orthodox or traditional. Therefore it is first necessary to discuss the quality of its appearance so that it may be recognized for what it is when it appears in an unexpected manner. Then, in situations where its meaning is not clear, we also need a method of amplification or interpretation that will allow us to appreciate the sacredness of the experience while at the same time linking it to the rest of the subject's psychological life. Our approach must discern the connections between the particular form that the numinosum takes, the developmental history of the person and the future course of the personality. Finally, there must be no reduction of numinous experience by attributing it to some simple intrapsychic mechanism, such as a defence, that belies its transpersonal origin.

THE QUALITY OF THE NUMINOSUM

Jung borrowed the word 'numinous' from Rudolf Otto's (1958) book *The Idea of the Holy*, which had a major influence on Jung's thought (CW 11, 222 and 472). According to Otto, the essence of holiness, or religious experience, is a specific quality which remains inexpressible and 'eludes apprehension in terms of concepts' (Otto, 1958, p. 5). To convey its uniqueness he coined the term 'numinous' from the Latin *numen*, meaning a god, cognate with the verb *nuere*, to nod or beckon, indicating divine approval. Otto (a Kantian) felt that the numinous is *sui generis*, non-rational, irreducible – a primary datum, which cannot be defined, only evoked and experienced (1958, p. 7). For him, the presence of the numinous is the crucial element of religious experience; it is felt to be objective and outside the self (1958, p. 11).

The numinous grips or stirs the soul with a particular affective state, which Otto describes as a feeling of the '*mysterium tremendum*'. Here is his description:

The feeling of it may at times come sweeping like a gentle tide, pervading the mind with a tranquil mood of deepest worship. It may pass over into a more set and lasting attitude of the soul, continuing, as it were, thrillingly vibrant and resonant, until at last it dies away and the soul resumes its 'profane', non-religious mood of everyday experience. It may burst in sudden eruption up from the depths of the soul with spasms and convulsions, or lead to the strangest excitements, to intoxicated frenzy, to transport, and to ecstasy. It has its wild and demonic forms and can sink to an almost grisly horror and shuddering. It has its crude, barbaric antecedents and early manifestations, and again it may be developed into something beautiful and pure and glorious. It may become the hushed, trembling and speechless humility of the creature in the presence of – whom or what? In the presence of that which is a *mystery* inexpressible and above all creatures.

(Otto, 1958, p. 12)

The numinosum produces a kind of holy terror, awe or dread, commonly expressed as the paralysing fear of God, for example: 'I will send my fear before thee' (Exod. 23: 27), or 'let not dread of him terrify me' (Job 9: 34). It has an uncanny quality which, Otto suggests, gives rise to its objectification within myth and folklore as the presence of demons or gods. For Otto, the experience of this dread and the attempt to rationalize the experience of the numinosum underlay the evolution of religion (1958, p. 15). (These factors are also the basis of much resistance to a psychology which includes the idea of an autonomous psyche.) Not only is this experience the hallmark of primitive dread of demons, it can also erupt in modern man as the experience of the uncanny or the supernatural. Such awe may be overwhelming, or gentle, as the still small voice. The uncanny is not a function of intensity but of a specific quality, quite distinct from ordinary fear, found even at the level of the pure worship of God. It produces a shudder within the soul which, 'held speechless, trembles inwardly to the farthest fiber of its being' (1958, p. 17). According to Otto, another element of this experience is its quality of 'absolute overpoweringness' (1958, p. 19), so that the creature in relation to it feels extremely small, or experiences religious humility (but certainly does not become inflated). For instance, Abraham, pleading for the people of Sodom, says: 'I have taken upon myself to speak to the Lord, I who am but dust and ashes (Gen. 18: 27). Otto calls this the 'creature-feeling', overwhelmed by its own insignificance in relation to the divine (1958, p. 10). Otto feels this experience of 'creature-consciousness' in the face of the inexpressible is a feature of all mysticism when the self is momentarily, and to varying degrees, able to identify with transcendent Reality (p. 22). A temporary loss of personal identity then occurs.

So much for the 'tremendum' aspect of the numinosum. The 'mysterium' element, according to Otto, means the feeling that one is in contact with something that is 'wholly other' – beyond the sphere of what is usual, intelligible and familiar, 'filling the mind with blank wonder and astonishment' (p. 26), producing the effect of stupor and wonder because it has no place in our ordinary reality. For Otto, the 'void' of the Buddhists and the 'nothing' of the western mystic are ideograms of the 'wholly other'. A further important quality of the numinosum is its attracting power or fascination. The divine may be dreadful but it is also alluring, and even though the creature is cowed before it, he is also entranced, captivated and transported (p. 31). A longing for it occurs.

The appearance of the numinosum is fairly common during the course of psychotherapy, although its presence is not always recognized. This presence is one of the pillars of any depth psychological approach that recognizes a transpersonal dimension to the psyche. Jung made much of its therapeutic potential.

THE HEALING POWER OF THE NUMINOSUM IN JUNG'S THEORY OF PSYCHOTHERAPY

In a letter written in August, 1945, Jung states that:

> [T]he main interest of my work is not concerned with the treatment of neurosis but rather with the approach to the numinous. But the fact is that the approach to the numinous is the real therapy and inasmuch as you attain to the numinous experiences you are released from the curse of pathology.
>
> (Jung, 1973, p. 377)

Here Jung articulates a theory of psychotherapy which stands in contrast to all personalistic therapies, and which expresses the essence of his thinking. It is perhaps no coincidence that this letter was written following the extraordinary visionary experiences Jung (1965, Chapter 10) had while 'on the edge of death' during his heart attack.

The fact that Jung links the experience of the numinosum with the healing process is a key part of his theoretical system. And like it or not, all psychotherapists have a theory of therapy which guides them. Anything we say carries with it the implication that it will in some way be helpful to the patient to whom it is addressed. Every move we make in therapy therefore implies a personal commitment to a particular theory of what is healing. Every theory of therapy carries with it conscious or unconscious assumptions about the source of healing, about how the patient 'uses' the therapist for his own needs, and about the correct role of the therapist in this process. It is worth being as conscious as possible about one's own ideas here, because each theory of cure implies fundamental notions about human nature, about motivation and about the value and uses of relationships. We should be aware that Jung's theory of the healing power of the numinosum is actually a religious theory, and those of us who adhere to it, rather than practising psychotherapy in a purely secular manner, are returning the care of the psyche to the province of spiritual practice, as was the case in antiquity.

Because the many schools of psychotherapy all proclaim their own value and are all apparently useful in certain hands, it has been difficult to distinguish their helpful common factors. Many suggestions have been made about the nature of the healing or curative elements which operate in therapy. Typically, we read of the value of insight, of making the unconscious conscious, resolving unconscious conflicts, binding intensely painful affects, focusing on infantile destructiveness, improving the sense of mastery, combating demoralization, freeing creativity, reparenting, providing a corrective emotional experience, understanding one's complexes, integrating the shadow, getting to know the anima/-us, facilitating individuation, strengthening the self, and so on *ad infinitum*. Jung's (CW 16, 179) sensible advice about this plethora of approaches is that the therapist should practise the therapeutic method that has helped the therapist personally. Accordingly, those therapists who, from personal experience, agree that the experience of the numinosum is itself a healing factor, or at least is a contributory element in therapy, are most likely to be drawn to the approach described here.

THE NEED TO ARTICULATE MECHANISMS

It is not sufficient simply to give examples of how the numinosum manifests itself. Even though we are ultimately dealing with a mystery, for several reasons it is important to try to explain the *process* by which it is healing. To the extent that we can do so, we will be in a better position to facilitate its emergence and relate it to the totality of the person's psychological life. Although in the last analysis the experience of the numinosum always seems to be an act of grace, I suggest that good working technique is important for it to appear, especially in the area of the relationship between therapist and patient and in the provision of a good therapeutic container. Unless these are attuned to the patient's needs, the therapist does not help the patient to withstand the pressures of archetypal material, much less its direct appearance into consciousness. A sound personalistic base to our archetypally informed work also grounds our practice and stops it from degenerating into vague speculation which cannot be taught. This kind of problem has contributed to the collective image of Jungian therapy as softheaded, and fuels the conflict within that discipline between classically and clinically trained practitioners. Since it is difficult for most of us to be 'in touch with the gods' or to 'speak out of the Self' all the time, it helps to have some working road maps to describe the interactive field, and in practice this usually means some version of personalistic psychoanalytic theory. The fact that profound symbolic experiences are facilitated by good clinical technique renders obsolete the old symbolic–clinical division which has become such an irritation to those Jungian practitioners who see no such contradiction. Anyone who works with a human being is of necessity working clinically within a particular model of the therapeutic relationship; only the artist or philosopher works *purely* symbolically (I am indebted to Dr C. M. Rives for making this point to me). With this necessity in mind, we are now prepared to review some of the details of numinous experience as they manifest themselves within the therapeutic relationship, and consider the ways in which they may be helpful.

VARIETIES OF THE NUMINOSUM

Jung (CW 11, 6) defines religion as the 'careful and scrupulous observation of the numinosum'. But the variety of forms in which the numinosum can appear is not always recognized; some of them are completely neglected in the psychological literature. A partial list, examples of some of which can be found in this book, includes:

1 As a numinous dream.
2 As a waking vision.
3 As an experience in the body.
4 Within a relationship including the transference/countertransference aspects of psychotherapy.
5 In the wilderness.
6 By aesthetic or creative means.
7 As a synchronistic event.

All of these modes are important for a personal spirituality or for psychotherapy oriented towards its appearance. In order not to appear pollyanna-ish it is crucial to note that all of them may take a positive or a negative form. The psychotherapist also has to remember that, in the community at large, the nature of this kind of experience opens the subject to the risk of being described as either inflated, hysterical or frankly psychotic, so that it feels risky to talk about such events. These criticisms are often the result of ignorance, but are occasionally due to fear or envy. In order to avoid repeating the damage that these attitudes produce, the psychotherapist must have a grasp of the differences between healthy mystical experience and psychosis, and must also be aware of how contact with the numinosum actually removes any tendency to grandiosity, sometimes to the point that it takes years for some people to gain the courage to tell of their experience.

Numinous experience is synonymous with religious experience. Translated into psychological parlance, this means the relatively direct experience of those deep intrapsychic structures known as archetypes. (This term is described in detail on p. 57). The archetype is a fundamental organizing principle which originates from the objective psyche, beyond the level of the empirical personality. In the religious literature, what the depth psychologist calls an archetype would be referred to as spirit; operationally they are synonymous. But crucially for the depth psychologist, the archetypes are not only numinous manifestations of the divine, they also play a part in the organization of the personality.

Our experience of the transpersonal Self, which is considered to be the totality of the psyche, may also be mediated by means of the effects of one of its constituent archetypes. The Self cannot be thought of as a unitary phenomenon, but rather as the source of all the archetypes, so that any archetypal experience is an experience of some aspect of the Self. These principles of intrapsychic organization do not only produce exotic dream images; as discussed later, they affect development, structure relationships and produce archetypal transferences.

(Kohut's (1971) mirroring and idealizing transferences (see p. 26) are just two examples of instances in which elements of the Self unfold and require a human response.)

What is characteristic of all archetypal or numinous experience is its *affective* intensity, both developmentally and psychotherapeutically. The characteristic affects produced by the archetype provide a clue to its presence, and so will be considered first.

AFFECT: THE NUMINOSUM AS SPIRIT IN THE BODY

The numinosum announces its presence by its affective intensity, or what Jung (1975, p. 59) calls its 'gripping emotionality'. The direct experience of spirit, or archetype, is always accompanied by such affect, for instance, as part of a complex, or simply in the form of interest or emotional investment (Stewart, 1987). In practice this means that the presence of intense affect always indicates the presence of the archetype. This observation is an important counterbalance to those psychologists who insist on the primacy of image. The degree of affect indicates the degree of embodiment of the archetype, since affect is felt in the body. Unless embodiment occurs in this way, the experience usually has little meaning. For many modern personalistic psychoanalysts (e.g. Basch, 1976), affect theory has superseded drive theory as an explanation for the source of human motivation. This is an important development; since archetypal theory is Jung's theory of motivation, and affect is the effect of the archetype, psychoanalysis and analytical psychology have in this way unconsciously closed their differences somewhat. Jung's original objection to Freud's exclusive drive theory has now penetrated psychoanalysis, which, however, true to form is again focusing only on the somatic and personal level of this archetypal manifestation. However, it is important to recognize the transpersonal origin of affect. This is not only Jung's insight; we see the same idea expressed in Tibetan Buddhism, where raw emotions and thoughts are understood to represent the spontaneous radiance of primordial Mind. And affect is essential for communication, both between self and Self and between selves. In this way affect forges links between the individual and the larger consciousness of which we are a part.

Speaking psychologically, when spirit or archetype embodies, it takes on a personally meaningful quality which we call soul, so that soul is synonymous with that level of spirit which is experienced as 'something happening to me'. Soul is also the link with, or organ of receptivity to, spirit; because their natures are the same, soul is able to receive the transpersonal and allow consciousness to grasp it within the realm of the personal, for example, as an intrapsychic image or as an embodied affect. Thus, numinous experience results from the interaction of soul and spirit, and, if successful, allows more of the Self to embody as soul. The experience of spirit surprises us because it does not originate from personal levels of the psyche, and it behaves objectively, or independently of our control. As Jung

16

(CW 11, 6) puts it, 'it seizes and controls the human subject, who is always rather its victim than its creator'.

THE NUMINOSUM MAY TAKE NOVEL FORMS

It is important to reiterate that the numinosum does not necessarily manifest itself as religious experience in one of its traditional forms. The spectrum varies from famous accounts of collective significance, such as the story of the annunciation (Luke 1: 26–38), to transpersonal or archetypal experiences which are mainly relevant to the experiencer. These are not confined to people in Jungian analysis, although they are expected in this field: 'It is not in the least astonishing that numinous experiences should occur in the course of psychological treatment and that they may even be expected with some regularity' (CW 14, 780). Nevertheless, the appearance of the numinosum within personalistic therapy is often the subject of bewilderment or fear, so that such appearance is either defended against by reduction or is ignored, medicated, denied or disavowed in some manner, since the numinous cannot be encompassed by such theoretical paradigms, and it would require a radical re-evaluation of the practitioner's belief system to take the event at face value. Among fundamentalist adherents to mainline Western traditions, numinous experience is often only regarded as authentic if it fits within particular dogmatic frameworks. If it is unique in its form, it is often mistrusted, misunderstood or separated from the person's 'official' spirituality.

The healing potential of the numinosum is not only evident from the experience of the psychotherapist. Here are some examples of healing contact with the numinosum taken from the religious literature, the first from someone who suffered severe depression, until:

> at the age of thirty-three I felt I must be going mad. I felt shut up in a cocoon in complete isolation and could not get in touch with anyone . . . things came to such a pass and I was so tired of fighting that I said one day 'I can do no more. Let nature, or whatever is behind the universe, look after me now.' Within a few days I passed from a hell to a heaven. It was as if the cocoon had burst and my eyes were open and I saw. The world was infinitely beautiful, full of light as if from an inner radiance. Everything was alive and God was present in all things; in fact, the earth, all plants and animals and people seemed to be made of God. All things were one, and I was one with creation and held safe within a deep love. I was filled with peace and joy and deep humility, and could only bow down in the holiness of the presence of God . . . if anyone had brought news that any member of my family had died, I should have laughed and said: 'There is no death.' It was as if scales had fallen from my eyes and I saw the world as it truly was.
>
> (Cohen and Phipps, 1979, p. 27)

It would of course be dangerously easy to dismiss this as the result of a swing from depression to mania, although to the experienced clinician the phenomenology does not really fit that diagnosis; few sufferers from mania are filled with peace and deep humility. But more of the problem of reduction below. The following occurred after a devastating air raid on Plymouth in 1941:

> When the all clear went at about mid-night some of us went up to the top of the house, which was set on a high hill above the city, and looked down at the terrible scene – buildings that were mere shells, with flames raging inside them .... I looked down at it all and in my mind registered that this meant that probably hundreds of people had been killed, thousands maimed for life, many homes lost. It seemed to me my heart should have been torn with pity and compassion and yet all I felt was the deepest peace I have ever known – a peace that had nothing whatever to do with my mind or faculties .... It flashed through me that those who had so suddenly been flung into eternity that night were rejoicing utterly and were trying to convey to us who were left behind something of what they had found .... The veil between this world and the next then seemed to be very thin indeed.
>
> (Ibid., p. 162)

Again, I want to acknowledge the possibility of this account being motivated by disavowal of the emotional significance of the event, only to reject that interpretation. There is too much affective resonance in us as we hear this story for us to dismiss it as a schizoid phenomenon. When affect is split off, the listener feels a sense of something missing; by contrast, this story fills us with a sense of painful but profound fullness and gratitude.

THE PROBLEM OF REDUCTION

I want to stress the importance of taking numinous experience at face value, just for what it is, without trying to reduce it to something else. To talk about religious experience from a psychological perspective is in no way to try to explain it away in terms of simpler or more fundamental psychological components, a process which both diminishes its reality and usually also requires denial of its actual phenomenology. Such attempts include, for example, the attempt to reduce the experience of the *unio mystica*, or the union of the soul with God, to an infantile wish to merge with mother in oceanic bliss. Or it might be suggested that an experience of the divine is simply the result of a defensive operation derived from the personal unconscious because of a need to soothe unbearable terror or loss. A partial list of other well-known reductions of religious beliefs and experiences includes the following: the projection of parental imagos, infantile wishes for parental protection, failure of sublimation of libidinal ties to the father, a special type of transitional object, failures of object love which lead to the creation of a libidinal relationship with an internal object, the concretization of the idea of perfection or an intense need for an unfailing selfobject. (This list briefly summarizes the relevant theories of Freud, Winnicott, Adler, object relations theory and Kohut as they might be (mis)applied to this question.) Although such ideas can often be useful in understanding how our relation to the transpersonal is personally *coloured*, they do not account for the reality of such experience. Contrary to a popular psychoanalytic belief, religious experience is not regressive; rather, it represents a *progressive* level of psychological development.

A variety of transpersonal experiences commonly happens to psychologically healthy people, although they will rarely talk about them for fear of being thought to be insane. As the old saying has it, the difference between the mystic and the schizophrenic is that the mystic knows who not to talk to. (His judgement and personal boundaries are not impaired.) Especially is this reluctance to talk about the experience of the numinosum true in psychotherapy, in situations when, consciously or unconsciously, the therapist is not perceived as open enough to this level. One must remember that when our patients were children their precious experience of the numinosum was often envied, ridiculed, attacked or stolen, and they are understandably reluctant to re-expose themselves to such wounding. Sometimes this type of experience is the only thing that keeps an abused child alive.

THE NUMINOSUM AS REVELATION, RECEIVED OR REJECTED: MYTHICAL AND PERSONAL EXAMPLES

Various mythical examples illustrate the power of the numinosum both to change established psychological structures, and also to produce resistance to accepting it. In the Old Testament, Moses experiences the numinosum as a burning bush which is not consumed by the fire. However, Moses initially needs a great deal of reassurance before he is willing to accept the dangerous commission offered to him. Here the Bible illustrates how resistance to new revelation can be overcome by the intensity of the experience. We see this kind of experience of the numinosum in Job 38, when God appears out of a whirlwind, and Job is overwhelmed by the absolutely inconceivable experience of the divine; his attitude of thinking he understood God is then forever changed. In the New Testament, Saul's experience on the road to Damascus, or the descent of the Holy Spirit at Pentecost as a wind and tongues of fire (Acts 2), are examples of such forceful instances. The radical effect on Saul is to totally reverse his conscious attitude. He had defended against his deep need for belief by persecuting Jesus, but now his resistance is demolished. When the Apostles began to speak 'in other tongues', people were so amazed that 3,000 were baptized.

All such experiences of the transpersonal are examples of revelation in the sense that something is made known which was previously unconscious; some new aspect of the divine shows itself. As well as these collective examples, individuals experience progressive revelation as they gradually experience the Self in a personal manner. This notion is unacceptable to those who believe we cannot know God naturally, and that revelation is only manifest via the Scriptures or through particular saviours. But dogma and defences aside, numinous experience is always felt as personal revelation; importantly, its significance may be accepted or rejected to varying degrees. For example, the following dream of a colleague answered a personal question about the relation between evil and love. This could be gratefully accepted without resistance as a gift of grace:

> I am in a large room filled with people. Before we can get on with the rest of our lives, we each have to walk down a hallway and come face to face with the devil. It is my turn and I am terrified. I walk down the hall and come upon the devil. I am frightened to make eye contact, but I know that that is what I must do in order to go on with my life. I slowly look up and our eyes meet. His eyes are pale blue and look empty. All of a sudden I feel a tremendous rush of love enter me from above and behind me. It flows through my heart, up to behind my eyes, then out through my eyes into his eyes. His face twists with anguish and he crumples to the floor in pain. The love was more powerful than he.

A numinous dream such as this makes an obviously helpful statement without producing resistance. The following dream of a dying woman was helpful because it allowed her to realize that she was not alone, and that death was not the end for her. The psychological background to the dream is discussed in more detail on p. 177. Here the dream raises the question of when the therapist should amplify numinous imagery. 'I am outdoors on a vast plain. Above me is a rich, velvet black sky, embedded in all directions with millions of vivid, multicoloured stars of every possible hue.' This kind of material always suggests amplification, which in this case might have included the Egyptian mythologem that after death the soul becomes a star. But fortunately the temptation to show off was resisted by the therapist, because the patient had obviously grasped the meaning of the dream. To have insisted on further amplification would have been an attempt to arrogate to the therapist a piece of the experience, for the sake of his own narcissistic need to be seen. The therapist's envy might also induce him to try reduce the power of the event. However, amplification *is* necessary on occasions when the patient is totally baffled by a dream of this kind, so that it cannot have its full effect until the therapist amplifies it in order to release its importance for the sake of the patient.

Numinous experience is not always so easy to assimilate. To illustrate this we move from the dream to another category of experience, which was felt in the body and in the waking state, that was partially defended against and partially accepted. We can use this event to compare numinous or mystical experience with psychosis, and also to see how the numinosum works to dissolve narcissistic structures such as grandiosity.

> A 35-year-old man was running through a park on a pleasant summer's day. As if in response to a question, he suddenly felt seized and pushed from behind as if a giant hand was forcing him forward. Quickly he noticed that he was running faster than he had ever run before. To his horror he then realized that he was unable to slow down at all. He was pushed faster and faster, until his legs could barely keep up with the pressure. He felt completely out of control, running, or being run, at a pace that seemed

dangerously fast. At a point of great alarm, just prior to actual panic, when it seemed that he was about to be pushed beyond his capacity, the pressure suddenly evaporated and he was able to stop, exhausted but awed by the event.

The question here is how this experience was of help to the personality – how is it healing? In the evaluation of such an event, it is first important to distinguish it from the passivity experiences of schizophrenia, in which the individual feels 'made' to carry out some action because of remote 'influences' on him over which he has no control, and for which he usually develops a delusional explanation. This is the result of control from archetypal levels of the unconscious, or of an autonomous complex overwhelming consciousness. But the runner had an intact personality, with no disorder of thought process or affect and with no perceptual distortion. The episode was discretely defined in time, with a clear ending. It made sense retrospectively and prospectively in the overall context of his life, and left only positive results. It was an affectively intense experience of temporary control or 'gripping' by the numinosum which could be integrated within his existing self structures, and in the process it built further intrapsychic structure. Unlike a schizophrenic experience, there was no enduring dissolution of the self or progression to increasingly delusional explanations of the event. Neither was there a confusion of personal identity with the source of the experience, which was clearly felt to be 'Other'. The event was structure-altering because reflection on the episode helped to destroy the illusion of autonomy or separation from the archetypal realm which the individual had harboured almost without realizing it. His lack of adequate connection with this level existed partly because of an unrecognized inflation, for which the event compensated. It is as if the Self were saying: 'You think you are running things, but you are being moved by a force other than your own will. However, even when it seems to be too much for you, you will not be pushed beyond your capacity.' This was most helpful in reducing certain narcissistic structures having to do with grandiosity and control. Here we see an example of Jung's comment (1973, p. 377) that 'the milestones of psychological development are certain symbolic events characterized by a strong emotional tone'. Merely by remembering the event, now some years ago, the subject is able to calm down when the events of his life seem out of control. Had the experience not been so emotionally powerful, it would not have been able to improve the runner's capacity to contain or structure his anxiety.

It is important to note that the message would have been the same if the event had occurred as a dream image. Instead, it was experienced in the waking state as a numinous experience in the body, with temporary suspension of the autonomy of the ego, which was present as a participant–observer. The runner has an introverted intuitive temperament, and so finds the body particularly remote and unconscious. It is not unusual for religious experience to occur at the point of deepest unconsciousness. An experienced mystic, who was able to keep his wits about him, might have been able to surrender to the involuntary movement without such fear, which was the factor which prevented letting go fully. Events then may have deepened, because the ego would not have interfered by constantly worrying about what was happening and trying to regain control. Further emergence of the numinosum would then have been possible. But typically, in reasonably well-structured personalities, archetypal experiences and the anxiety they produce are relatively well contained, so that ego controls are eventually able to reassert themselves. In a way, therefore, the runner's psychological health prevented further revelation at the same time as it safely allowed the revelation which did occur. In other words, when the ego–Self system works, it seems to be mutually self-regulatory. The more cohesive and firmly established the self, the more it can safely experience the Self by reordering itself rather than by fragmenting. What is common to all of these types of experience is the fact that the individual's psychopathology becomes the entry point for the numinosum. This leads me to a further discussion of why and how the numinous heals.

THE EFFECTS OF THE NUMINOSUM ON INTRAPSYCHIC STRUCTURE

I have already alluded to the idea of intrapsychic structure, and to the fact that numinous experience is above all structure-building or structure-altering. By 'structure' I mean the traditional notion of an enduring organizational pattern or configuration in the mind, but not as in Freud's tripartite drive model of id, ego and superego. Rather, I mean complexes in the Jungian sense, or the structures of a personal self as they have developed around one's archetypal endowment. My thesis is that archetypal experiences go to the heart of the complex they are concerned with, or they are constellated by that complex to begin with. Hence they are always precisely related either to the individual's pathology or to the individuation needs of the moment, and they alter or rebuild the relevant complex. Their efficacy in doing so is the result of their tremendous affective intensity, which alone is able to dislodge entrenched patterns with such speed. Such affect is mutative; in alchemical terms a *calcinatio* is produced. Of course the complex which is addressed is already associated with its own affective valence, but it is as if the intensity of the affect associated with the new experience disrupts and dissipates existing structures and defences and replaces them with something new. From an ego perspective this fighting of a fire with a larger fire may produce terror or chaos in the process, but eventually a supraordinate, new order is superimposed on the old. The affective component of the experience is also the major vehicle for the cognitive level of the experience to be driven home. Contact with the archetypal realm therefore has the potential for reordering by induction. The archetype superimposes its own pattern of order, sometimes through a soothing or calming effect and sometimes through the production of apparent chaos until reintegration occurs and the new pattern is recognized.

It must be admitted that major, rapid personality change of this kind is not often attributable to a single discrete episode in which the numinosum erupts into consciousness. Usually we see gradual pressure from the unconscious in the form of dreams or symptoms. This restraint seems purposeful, since what is happening is the attempt to initiate the person into a higher state of consciousness, but the risk incurred by too powerful an experience is the production of excessive, unmanageable anxiety, or even psychosis when the structures of the personality are fragile or not firm enough to cope with the affective intensity of the experience. As Jung (1975, p. 120) put it, sometimes the divine asks too much.

THE PROBLEM OF INFLATION AND THE RADICAL RELATIVIZING OF THE PERSONAL SELF

In order to address the question of inflation in relation to the experience of the numinosum, the following numinous dream has been chosen because it is easy to see how the dream is healing but not so easy to see why it treats rather than exacerbates inflation. This dream occurred during one of those periods of doubt which is familiar to all psychotherapists, during which the dreamer was wondering if he had chosen the right career, if he really was doing any good to anyone he saw in therapy, if he really had the authority to do what he was doing, and so on.

> The dream opens as I leave my body; all around me are people in the process of dying, and their souls are leaving their bodies. Some of the souls are having difficulty because they are afraid, and my job is to help and reassure them, while others are eager to leave the body but are confused and simply need direction. I have to guide the souls to a doorway which is at the beginning of a long dark tunnel down which the soul must proceed.

How is this helpful, and why does it not produce an enormous inflation? Let us look at the dream in the light of the idea of changing intrapsychic structure. The dream addresses a structure or complex which concerns an area of self-doubt, and lack of confidence in the dreamer's ability, perhaps related to feelings of inferiority. That was the conscious situation. After this dream, from which the dreamer awoke awestruck, this structure was simply gone as if it had evaporated. Each component issue had been addressed. He no longer had any doubt about the validity of what he was doing, and was able to practise with a hitherto unknown degree of confidence. He literally felt more initiated and empowered after that dream than after all his formal academic training. This was an example of initiation by the Self, which as it were authorizes the dreamer to work as a guide of souls.

My experience is that the numinosum always produces humility, as Otto says, because the ego is so awed that it is radically relativized. Suddenly we realize that we are not who we thought we were; our childhood conditioning is loosened a little. We are also thrust into a relationship with the totality of Mind instead of being trapped within an internal solipsism. This does not feed grandiose pathology, it eradicates it by making one feel very small. In the presence of normal reality testing and reasonably firm self-structures, the numinosum provides the empirical personality with what is missing; it does not produce an experience that will further alienate one from the Self. The exception to the rule that the numinosum does not produce inflation is found when the self structures are too fragile to contain the experience, and psychosis results because of an indentification with the experience as a way of managing terror. Grandiosity as a defensive manoeuvre then serves to protect an enfeebled self. But in healthier personalities the numinosum shores up the self in a way that makes grandiosity impossible, because we realize that we are in contact with an unfathomably superior consciousness. We also feel enormous gratitude. Hence this dream led to internal changes but not in the direction of inflation.

OTHER CATEGORIES OF THE NUMINOSUM

The numinosum acts in ways other than those I have indicated. For instance, it may indicate that psychological healing has occurred and allow termination of therapy. After two years of psychotherapeutic work following a mastectomy, as a woman and her therapist were considering ending, the patient dreamed that her missing breast had regrown, and was more beautiful than it had ever been. There was no need for more therapy. Another woman, dying of colon cancer, had spent most of her time in therapy working on her childhood, which had been made difficult because of very strained relations with her parents and also between her parents themselves. A good deal of routine work was done without the appearance of anything unusual. Then one day, just before she died, she woke up (this was clearly not a dream) with a strong sense of the presence of her parents by her bed. She then saw in front of her a vision of a small golden bowl, shooting off golden rays of light. The bowl contained oil. She felt her parents communicate to her the message: 'You are to use this to bless others.' The vision then vanished, leaving her with a sense of peace and reconciliation with her parents.

THE NUMINOSUM IN THE
TRANSFERENCE/COUNTERTRANSFERENCE

For many dynamically oriented therapists, the relationship between the two participants in psychotherapy is the linchpin of the work. Usually this process is understood purely at the personal level, since the transference/countertransference so much reflects childhood material. However, as is the case with any important life situation, there is also a transpersonal or archetypal level of the relationship. This is the dimension that Jung chose to emphasize. The archetypal level provides the spiritual underpinning of, and adds numinosity to, relationships in general.

The central image in Jung's discussion of the transference is that of the *coniunctio*, or joining together. This process is partly intrapsychic but also occurs in the interactive field between the two participants, so that what occurs intrapsychically reflects what happens in the therapeutic relationship. Jung (CW 16) used the alchemical term *coniunctio* to describe the archetypal basis of the transference,[1] as a way of distinguishing this level from more personal material such as the selfobject transference (see p. 26). The *coniunctio* includes within itself

24

the selfobject relationship. The Latin word is used to indicate that the two personal selves are joined together or immersed within the more global psychological field that is constituted by the transpersonal Self. The unfolding and analysis of the relationship, influenced by the Self, allows the conscious integration of previously unmanageable material and the consolidation of poorly formed structures within the personality. The therapeutic container also acts as a vessel that allows a relationship to develop between the personal self and the transpersonal Self. For many people, relationships are the major source of contact with the numinosum, and sometimes the first conscious intimation 'of this contact begins in the psychotherapeutic setting.

The experience of the Self within the therapeutic relationship accounts for the latter's extraordinary power. This form of numinosity has been relatively neglected in the Jungian literature. It occurs as archetypal strands of the Self unfold between both participants, linking them in a shared psychological process that is called transference/countertransference at the personal level. The Self is of course unitary; unlike the personal self it has no boundaries, so that therapist and patient are immersed in the intersubjective psychic field which it produces. This is a particularly important Jungian concept; other theories of psychotherapy describe a shared, intersubjective field determined by the interaction of both participants, but do not recognize that the psychotherapeutic field which dominates certain aspects of the therapy has transpersonal as well as personal components. These are autonomous – they influence both therapist and patient. In other words, it is insufficient to attribute the nature of the field that dominates the therapeutic relationship solely to the developmental histories of the two participants; as well, a supraordinate archetypal constellation affects both of them. Because the Self always tends towards wholeness, the particular archetypal material which is constellated in any intense therapeutic relationship is synchronistically relevant to the personal psychology of both people concerned, even though the patient's material has to take centre stage.

A modification is needed here in relation to Jung's original conception of the *coniunctio* as an opportunity for the union of opposites within the personality. Many post-Jungian writers have questioned the notion that the psyche is necessarily structured oppositionally. This pattern was a feature of Jung's personal psychology (the 'two personalities' of his childhood are well described in his autobiography), but it does not necessarily apply to everyone. For example, Samuels (1985) has pointed out that the perception of psychic functioning as an interplay of opposites ignores the concurrent mutual support, complementarity, incremental gradations of change and subtle transitions found within the psyche. Hence my suggestion is that the 'chymical marriage' or the supreme act of union which the alchemists depicted as the consummation of their work (CW 14, 104), does not so much represent the union of opposites but the union with whatever is missing from oneself that is needed in order to feel whole. This may be more of some quality that we already possess, such as masculinity or femininity, or it may be a function such as mothering or fathering. In terms of modern psychoanalytic self psychology, the missing quality or function of the Self that is needed to restore the integrity of the self is termed a 'selfobject' need (see the following section), and this can often be provided by a relationship with either a man or a woman. Therefore the lacunae that we feel within us are not necessarily due to the lack of an *opposite* quality, even though the alchemists from whom Jung borrowed the term *coniunctio* represented the healing union as one which occurs between masculine and feminine.

THE NUMINOSITY OF SELFOBJECT NEEDS

In psychoanalytic self psychology the term 'selfobject'[2] is used to refer to the subjective or intrapsychic experience of another person (strictly speaking not the person herself) who is felt to be necessary for the maintenance of the cohesion, vitality or integrity of the self. A selfobject is anyone who keeps us feeling glued together and enhances our sense of wellbeing (Kohut, 1971; 1977; 1984). I believe that the unfolding of such needs within a relationship represents the activation of elements of the Self which act like scaffolding for the developing personality. The child's selfobjects must respond adequately for these needs to be integrated into the structures of a personal self. When selfobject needs are responded to, the Self is able to incarnate into a self. Selfobject needs are numinous because they are aspects of the Self which are intended to bring about what is depicted archetypally as the *coniunctio*. Consistent with Jung's idea that the Self is the archetypal basis of the personality, and is always unfolding into incarnation as individuation proceeds, Kohut believed that the need for selfobject relationships begins in infancy and remains throughout life. This need matures but never leaves us. Kohut objected to Mahler's postulate of separation as the final goal of development. His work leads to a very different value system than the autonomy–independence emphasis of classical psychoanalysis. Selfobject theory is consistent with the notion of the underlying unity of all consciousness. We are linked to each other by means of our relationships, which act as a kind of 'glue' binding us together. The Self is the ultimate source of this glue, and is the matrix of the selfobject field. The experience of the Self is a selfobject experience for the self.

Our selfobject needs are thought to be:

1 Mirror needs. These include such needs as those for affirmation and confirmation of our value, for emotional attunement and resonance, to be the gleam in somebody's eye, to be approved of, seen, wanted, appreciated and accepted. Here the developmental necessity is to transform healthy infantile grandiosity and exhibitionism into mature adult self-esteem, normal levels of ambition, pride in performance and an inner sense of one's own worth.
2 Idealization needs. These include the need for an alliance with, or to be psychologically a part of, a figure who carries high status and importance, who is respected, admired, wise, protective and strong. This figure can be a source of soothing when this is needed; he or she is both calming and inspiring. The

intrapsychic experience of merger with the idealized selfobject lends us the strength to maintain ourselves when we are afraid or gives us direction when we are in search of meaning and goals.[3] The developmental thrust here is both towards the capacity to be self-soothing and also to have an inner sense of direction based on one's own ideals and goals.

3 Twinship, kinship or alter ego needs. These involve the need for sameness with others, and the sense of being understood by someone 'like me'. To be in a community of people of shared beliefs and attitudes in which one belongs, or to have the sustaining presence of even one such person, is supporting and enhancing to the self.

4 The selfobject of creativity. During periods of taxing creative activity there may be a need for transient merger with another person.

5 The adversarial selfobject (Wolf, 1988). There is sometimes a need for a benign adversary acting as an opposing force who allows active opposition. This confirms one's autonomy at the same time as that person continues to be supportive and responsive.

6 Efficacy needs allow us to feel that we can have an effect on the other person and that we are able to evoke what we need from him. 'If I can elicit a response I must be somebody.'

(The archetypal bases of the more important selfobject needs are described on pp. 149–51.)

All of this emphasis on our ineradicable connection to others moves psychotherapy out of what Stolorow and Atwood (1992) call 'the myth of the isolated mind'. We are always selves embedded in a matrix of selfobjects who are responsive to our needs to varying degrees, in ways that sustain us or bind us together. We are never selves in a psychological vacuum. Intrapsychically the self, like the Self, does not end at the skin. It includes those who are affectively important to us. Selfobject experiences are subjective; intrapsychically and often unconsciously the other is acting as a part of the self, carrying out functions that the self cannot provide for itself and in this way acting as a psychological extension of the self. Thus, selfobject needs are like cement for the developing personality. In infancy, qualities of the child's self, such as its structural integrity and vitality, are determined by the qualities of his selfobject relationships, since they are used as the building blocks of the child's own sense of self. To the extent that the selfobject milieu is helpful, the self develops with cohesion and resilience; to the extent that the milieu is unresponsive to the child's unfolding selfobject needs, the self develops varying degrees of structural deficit and proneness to fragmentation. When the child's selfobject needs are unmet, they remain active but immature; there is then a lifelong need to find someone to supply them. The mirror-hungry or idealization-hungry personality lacks the internal glue which would make him or her feel put together, and so constantly searches for cohesion externally by means of a relationship or situation which will provide what is missing.[4] In the therapeutic situation the original childhood needs resurface. If they are then responded to adequately, the deficit within the self can be healed, because the selfobject experience is internalized in the context of the relationship with the therapist. When this is established the patient feels alive and integrated; when it is disrupted, for example, because of a separation or because of the therapist's traumatic behaviour, the patient feels fragmented and devitalized. Kohut (1971) described a series of transference phenomena based on hitherto unmet selfobject needs, which indicate where the patient's self structures are lacking and how these lacunae are attempting to be healed. In the presence of a transference which expresses these early selfobject needs, it takes both participants to allow the patient to experience a whole sense of self. The felt sense for the patient is that he or she is only whole in the context of the relationship with the therapist.(An archetypal image of this process is described in the Appendix, by means of the alchemical Rosarium Philosophorum woodcuts used by Jung in his essay on the transference.) What is not appreciated if selfobject transferences are only understood at the personal level is the fact that they represent the re-emergence in the therapeutic situation of numinous aspects of the Self which were not responded to in childhood, and consequently could not embody but constantly attempt to do so. To the extent that the Self cannot embody because of lack of environmental responsiveness, the child is not fully ensouled. When psycho-therapy is practised with a spiritual sensibility, the therapist who meets the patient's selfobject needs feels that he or she is responding to the attempt of the Self to incarnate.

Within the therapeutic relationship, numinous experiences of the Self are by no means confined to experiences of the transference. They may take many forms, such as that triggered by the following dream of a young woman after a prolonged, severe depression during which she had felt dead.

> I am walking in a mountain meadow which is a blaze of colour; mountain peaks and yellow and purple flowers are in the background. I come upon a large chest with a rounded top, which I open. Suddenly I am filled with golden light and love which pours out of the chest. Christ appears from the chest, surrounded by the light, and smiles at me. I am engulfed by the light and love, which is so powerful that I become love and light. Christ, the light and the love slowly fade away, and I am once again myself, but now I am filled with light and love that I know will never leave me.

When she told the therapist this dream, there was an immediate experience of the *coniunctio,* because the original affect of the experience was evoked in its telling. Enormous emotional intensity filled the therapist's body, which felt as if it were filled to bursting with the sensation of a huge ball in the chest, ringing in his ears and trembling. The feeling was of a profound experience of union.

This kind of experience teaches us that the Self includes within itself both participants in therapy, and reminds us that the Self affects both people in the room. It is the same Self, or totality of consciousness, which experiences all that is happening. For this reason, within an established selfobject relationship the sense of total, boundaried separateness falls away for both people. The transference and countertransference are actually motivated by the Self in a very specific manner, moving both people towards wholeness, although still experienced through the empirical personalities involved. To some extent, this awareness frees the therapist from understanding the whole of the interaction at the personal level. In its turn, this freedom has the eventual effect of allowing the patient to sense the reality of the Self without the necessity of the therapist's presence.

It should not be imagined that the experience of the numinosum is always a straightforward matter of interpretation or assimilation. In various ways, the experience can either engender or encourage defensive operations.

DEFENSIVE USE OF THE EXPERIENCE OF THE NUMINOSUM

It is possible to use the experience of the numinosum defensively, as a way of avoiding problems of the personal self. By focusing entirely on striking images from dreams and fantasy, some people ignore the fact that their everyday life is a disaster. An overemphasis on intrapsychic imagery (sometimes fostered by a therapist who is mainly interested in this material) may allow disavowal of the need for psychotherapeutic work on a relationship or a work situation. It is not unusual for this kind of individual to present him/herself for psychotherapy loaded with volumes of spectacular dreams, while his marriage and children are in dire straits. And indeed there was a tendency among some classical Jungian analysts to assume that dream work alone would solve the person's outer-world difficulties. In fact, such a focus runs the risk of strengthening splitting defences. Borderline individuals in particular may request Jungian work because they are drawn to the idea of working with archetypal material, of which they may have an abundance, but they are actually too fragile to be able to deal with it. Many borderline people experience mandala imagery in their dreams, which may arrest a tendency to ongoing fragmentation, but such internal experiences of the Self are of much less value in the eventual healing of their severe childhood trauma than is a good therapeutic relationship. (The pre-symbolic personality is discussed on p. 96.)

The significance of numinous experiences may be disavowed when they involve affect that is too intense to be tolerated, especially when they force the subject to face material that belongs to the shadow side of the personality. In such cases, the numinosum may appear in a terrifying manner.

NARCISSISTIC DEFENCE AGAINST NUMINOUS EXPERIENCE: THE PROBLEM OF THE DARK SIDE OF THE NUMINOSUM

In the examples given so far I have stressed the positive or healing aspects of numinous experience. I now wish to deal with its more terrifying effects which are much harder to assimilate, and which accordingly tend to be warded off.

29

Important differences exist between the effects of numinous experience which is allowed to penetrate and work within the individual, compared with situations in which the significance of the experience is defended against. When defensive operations inhibit the effect of the numinosum, it does not produce the structural change demanded by the telos of the personality.

The testimony of successful mystics and that of the consulting room suggests that contact with the numinosum may have an integrating effect which improves the overall cohesion of the self and consolidates and deepens one's sense of identity. But the problem with such contact is that it often challenges the very ideas about ourselves and the world which we have used to ward off anxiety and enhance self-esteem. Hence, numinous experience may generate fear, which in the presence of a fragile self can be massive enough to require defensive manoeuvres or precipitate psychosis. This is so because numinous experience is precisely relevant to our pathology, our selfobject needs and our areas of woundedness. These are just the places that the archetype tries to enter the personality for the purposes of restructuring and healing. For example, a man who prides himself on his charity and altruism within the community, which pride maintains his sense of personal worth, has a nightmare in which he sees a figure abusing, starving and imprisoning his children. He is thereby forced to look at an image which at the same time expresses his unacknowledged shadow side and also the deprivation of his inner child. The anxiety this process generates may feel overwhelming, and it is easy to forget such a dream. The man in question had been using his social activism to defend against his personal difficulties; by means of the defence known as turning passive into active, he had succeeded in dealing with some of the pain of his own childhood deprivation. But, in his zeal to improve social conditions, he had tended to neglect his own family and himself, and he was able to look at this fact, presented to him in the dream, only with great reluctance. The dream that represents his personal shadow is also an experience of what has been called the 'dark side' of the Self; as well as its personal referents, it also refers to the larger social problem of the suffering of children.

Shadow elements within the personality such as primitive rage, sadism, destructiveness, envy, hatred and terror are not normally thought of as having primary religious significance, but in fact they must be so considered if we wish to avoid an overly pollyanna-ish attitude to the numinosum. These and similarly painful affects are the effects of negative complexes, and they, too, have their archetypal, or spiritual, cores. To attend to them is no less a spiritual practice than to attend to the positive aspects of the numinosum. The problems of evil and suffering are discussed in more detail elsewhere. Here, I wish to comment on a related problem, namely resistance to the experience of the numinosum that is required when the numinosum is felt as too painful, or even too threatening to the very existence of the self.

Contact with the numinosum may be so intolerable that defences become necessary which allow the subject to not feel the impact of the experience. The experience is then initially rejected, until the pressure of the transpersonal psyche becomes absolutely overwhelming to the individual's defensive structures. The following is a literary example, which I call the 'Scrooge defence' against the spirit. In Charles Dickens's story *A Christmas Carol*, Scrooge is a miserable miser who rejects the spirit of Christmas and all that it stands for. He is mean, hard, sharp, cold and bitter, on the edge of life, rejecting all attempts to contact him emotionally. He is morose, distant, melancholy, isolated and totally lacking in empathy and caring for others. In short, he has typical narcissistic pathology.

On Christmas Eve Scrooge is visited by the ghost of his dead partner, Marley, a shadow figure who in life was just like Scrooge. Initially Scrooge denies that he is really seeing Marley with the comment: 'You are just an undigested piece of mutton.' This is a defensive attempt to dismiss the experience, but the metaphor holds true; he cannot digest what Marley stands for within himself. Marley points out the reality of Scrooge's behaviour, which we learn was the result of painful childhood experiences which made him cynical about human values. Such an attitude of indifference to others is often a narcissistic defence against a deeply felt wound of rejection, depression and bitter disappointment, erected to protect the vulnerable childhood self from further hurt. Scrooge cannot risk being open to love, which he refuses because although he needs it so intensely he is terrified to risk another experience of failing to receive it. He is typical of people who cannot accept what is offered because he is ashamed of his need. Thus, the revelation personified by Marley initially finds him impenetrable, full of narcissistically motivated resistance to spiritual understanding.

At this point, following the failure of a human form, the problem takes on more archetypal dimensions. The spirit of Christmas past now appears to Scrooge and takes him back in time to show him the intense pathos of his childhood deprivations. He is finally able to grieve over the sight of himself as a boy ignored by his family, sobbing and alone. In the presence of the spirit of love, he sees himself as he really is. This experience provides what is in effect a brief reconstructive analysis. The memories of his childhood which emerge soften his heart, and allow him to cry again. As he does so he develops the capacity for empathy for the suffering of others – a most important effect of such experience. He is made to witness a conversation from his young adulthood with a loving woman, who leaves him because she realizes how afraid and empty he is, and how his greed for money is related to his fear of the world. He loses her because of his obsession with gain, an attempt to clutch and hold materially what was lacking emotionally, perhaps to provide the illusion of safety or fullness. A further spectral visitation from the spirit of Christmas to come makes him realize that a lonely death is the only alternative to change. These powerful experiences break through his defences, put him in touch with the inner wound, and force consciousness upon him.

Here the question naturally arises as to why Scrooge is so initially resistant to the experience of the numinosum. This is partly the case because individuals with his type of character pathology find it difficult to rely on the inner life, because in their development it was always devalued and discounted. In order to maintain some kind of tie to their childhood selfobjects they were forced to sequester their

31

own feelings and needs, often to the extent that they lose touch with how they really feel. They need constant outer sources of enhancement, or selfobjects such as money or success, to bolster their fragile sense of self. Their inner world is populated by pathogenic introjects, or negatively toned complexes, which only cause pain and offer no soothing. In its repetition compulsion the fragile self anticipates hurtful relationships and unconsciously either seeks them out, projects or re-creates them. In such circumstances, archetypal experience, if it is not defended against, may prove to be healing, but often it is too terrifying. The case of Scrooge illustrates how, by challenging the individual's defensive image of reality, the numinosum tries to force the underlying pain to be faced. Because their childhood contact with the Self was envied, ridiculed, appropriated or attacked, some people are afraid to rely on numinous experience because it is associated with traumatogenic responses from their selfobject milieu. Finally, archetypal experience is also difficult to assimilate simply because of the raw intensity of the affect it generates; affect integration, the main role of the selfobject, is often impaired in the presence of serious narcissistic difficulty.

DEFENCE AGAINST THE NUMINOSUM IN THE FRAGILE SELF

Narcissistic difficulties, or a vulnerable self, require defensive operations to prevent overwhelming anxiety when confronted with the numinosum. To clarify this situation, it is first necessary to briefly review the notion of defence in dynamic psychology. In classical psychoanalysis, defence was thought to be necessary in order to prevent an unconscious impulse from emerging into consciousness, thus preventing the person from feeling the anxiety or guilt that the unrestrained action would produce. In the more useful self-psychological paradigm, defence is seen as a manoeuvre which the person uses in order to protect and maintain whatever is left of his nuclear self despite the inadequacies of his childhood selfobject milieu (Kohut, 1984, p. 184). Defences are therefore necessary for self-preservation, to maintain the integrity of the self and to prevent further weakening by unbearable anxiety or shame. Accordingly, defences operate when the self feels threatened with fragmentation because of desperate need, rage, envy, or any affect which cannot be integrated. Defence is also needed when feelings, wishes or fantasies arise which are so very different from the way in which the person needs to perceive him/herself that a sense of threat arises which the self needs to ward off.

The more narcissistically vulnerable we are, or the more easily we fragment, the more rigidly we must maintain a particular set of attitudes and views about ourselves in order to hold ourselves together. Thus, we struggle to maintain a defensive self-image through power, status, money or whatever we need to protect or shore up an enfeebled self. The more the self feels endangered, the more defence predominates, and the more likely we are to exhibit narcissistic rage, erotization, projection or other characterological mechanisms. Rigid defence is needed by more fragile personalities, but the problem is that the numinosum may not respect this need. If the affect generated by the experience is too intense, collapse of the self, or psychosis, may result.

FEAR OF THE NUMINOSUM AS A CORE ANXIETY

Within classical psychoanalysis, the core anxieties which afflict the individual were thought to be castration anxiety, loss of the object or loss of the love of the object. Within self-psychology (Kohut 1971, pp. 152–153) the core anxieties are thought to be the fear of fragmentation, fear of the loss of the sense of the reality of the self, for instance, because of the need for merger, fear of isolation due to grandiosity or shame due to exhibitionism. These all relate to the awareness of the vulnerability of the self, the threat of loss of self-esteem or the danger of the intrusion of early needs that are experienced as painful. As we have seen, these fragile areas of the personality are precisely those to which the numinosum will address itself, because they are where healing is most needed and where the barrier to the unconscious is most tenuous, so that pressure from the unconscious is felt most keenly. (This is also why selfobject needs are so numinous.) Because the archetype attempts to provide what is necessary to restore what is missing for the individuation of the self, true religious experience is potentially frightening, and may be related to areas of great difficulty. Thus, within analytical psychology, and especially for the religiously oriented therapist, the fear of the numinosum can be considered a core anxiety. Because the child may not be able to contain or bind the level of anxiety the numinosum engenders, adult help is needed. Hence the need for defence; even for the adult, the experience may be just too big. The numinosum does not necessarily respect our view of the world, but rather tends to present us with the need for radical re-evaluation of our beliefs.

The disconcerting unpredictability of numinous experience is one reason that Jung's psychology is unpopular in academic departments of psychology which seek to measure psychological phenomena and which prefer the search for certainty to the anxiety of not knowing. The numinosum does not allow certainty and respects no neat theories of how things should happen; inductive methodology is not fully reliable in this area of study. When the spirit presses for change in a direction contrary to the ego's established norms, grandiose defences, such as pressure for academic success, are threatened. If they cannot withstand the pressure of the numinosum, they collapse, producing depression or anxiety; the spirit is resisted in order to prevent such dysphoria.

NARCISSISTIC DEFENCE AGAINST THE NUMINOSUM WITHIN TRADITIONAL RELIGIOUS SYSTEMS: ITS CONTRIBUTION TO FUNDAMENTALISM

Narcissistic concerns in relation to the numinosum are also relevant to some of the problems of established religious systems. Narcissistic difficulties contribute to fundamentalist attitudes when dogma about eternal verities is used to buttress areas of personal fragility, either because it would be intolerable to face the experience of the numinosum, even modified by ritual or symbol, or because dogma is used to defend against problems within the personality. For instance, pathological grandiosity which is needed to maintain a fragile self structure may make one depreciate the religious values of other people for the sake of self-enhancement. When self-esteem is low, this devaluation may also occur because of envy, for instance, between 'siblings' in relation to God as Father. In order to bind specific anxieties, such as sexuality, inferiority or a fear of women, it may be necessary to cling to a particular interpretive tradition or a literal, inerrant understanding of a sacred text. For example, it is possible to use the antisexual or mysogynistic bias of some of aspects of Christian dogma to avoid dealing with one's own sexual inhibitions. Further, an intense need for twinship, or the need to feel the same as other people for the sake of self-enhancement, may lead to religious tribalism and exclusiveness (we are saved, they are not). Religious practice, the relationship with God, the guru, the community or the church, may enhance personality integration and reduce anxiety in the face of precarious personality integration because these are powerful selfobjects. But the price of this kind of salvation may be dogmatism, intolerance and a lack of freedom to experience the divine in a uniquely personal way.

For the fragile self, fixed dogmatic assertions help to maintain a degree of narcissistic equilibrium by reducing uncertainty. But then the individual's spiritual life is often brittle or rigid because it is used in the service of binding core anxieties. New symbolic experience is then frightening; if dogmatic ideas are used to hold the self together, the only symbol which feels safe is one which is frozen into literalism and hence rendered manageable. Otherwise, the affective power of the symbol is too much. Ideally, the symbol or ritual bridges between the human and the divine – it is a safe way to contact the numinosum. But for the fragile personality, this contact is intolerable. The experience of the numinosum is then only considered authentic if it takes a form that has been rendered safe, or not too affectively charged, by virtue of its familiarity. Other manifestations are considered 'demonic'.

Narcissistic characters may use religious practice to bolster grandiose defences. Instead of being relativized by spiritual practice, the self may become inflated as a result of a degree of identification with the Self, leading to the arrogant religious leader. This outcome may be related to a lack of differentiation of the self accompanied by fixation on infantile levels of grandiosity because of childhood selfobject failure. Or, the experience of being idealized by followers is used to feed a hunger for affirmation. Such leaders gather around themselves people with complementary selfobject needs who are eager to idealize and be led. This dynamic is seen among those charismatic gurus whose personal need for idealization eventually leads them to untempered inflation, which permits corruption. Because these leaders offer no opportunity for such idealization to be resolved, their followers are stuck in an addictive, transference-like relationship based on infantile needs. This situation exploits the hunger of the true believer for authentic religious experience.

DISAVOWAL OF THE MEANING OF THE NUMINOSUM

In some forms of narcissism we see the meaning of the numinosum depotentiated and its emotional significance disavowed. This latter defence allows one to repudiate the meaning of an event which does not fit into a safe category. Here it is useful to think of 'meaning' as the dispositional power of an event, or what it will cause us to think or do. Disavowal allows the affect that should be attached to an experience not to be felt, without blocking perception itself (Basch, 1983, p. 146), so that the action that would naturally follow can be ignored. We then treat the event as if it did not matter. In this way dreams are reduced to meaningless cerebral 'circuit clearing', and other numinous experiences are dismissed as hallucinatory, regressive, wish-fulfilling or primary process, in order to make them manageable. Many therapists, not only psychologists but even clergy people, play a role in colluding with this disavowal when they rationalize numinous experience with scientific explanations needed to maintain their own defence against it. This kind of defence against the numinosum also has consequences for certain traditional avenues of spiritual development.

NARCISSISTIC DEFENCES AND THE
PROBLEM OF 'LETTING GO'

To illustrate the power of the psychological approach to the development of a personally relevant spirituality, it is useful to examine the way in which it illumines some traditional spiritual problems. The example I have chosen is the injunction to 'let go', especially as it is articulated within Meister Eckhart's twenty-eighth sermon (Blackney, 1941) about spiritual poverty. This sermon is Eckhart's amplification of Jesus' comment: 'Blessed are the poor in spirit.' Eckhart suggests that: 'He alone has true spiritual poverty who wills nothing, knows nothing, desires nothing.' This statement refers to the problem of narcissistic self-absorption in relation to the divine. Eckhart points out that some people remain self-centred while appearing outwardly pious. But for him, spiritual poverty means letting go of one's own will in favour of the will of God, as well as letting go of one's own knowing, so that God is free to accomplish whatever God wills within us. He argues that if I preserve some internal place where I insist on being 'me', then I preserve a distinction between myself and God. In contrast, Eckhart prefers a radically non-dual position, like that of Advaita Vedanta, which is that I and God are actually one. (This is consonant with the classical Jungian idea that the Self is the archetypal basis of the ego.)

From the psychological point of view, the problem that Eckhart deals with here is our self-centredness, our attempts to hold onto a discreet identity that is not continuous with its transpersonal roots. He suggests that thinking, willing, knowing and wanting, inasmuch as they derive from the ego, prevent the Self from living its own life within us. We could look at the rigid maintenance of these ego functions in the face of pressure from the Self as defences against the sense that the self is dissolving. Even when the Self prompts us to change an ego position, as in the Scrooge story, perhaps by producing symptoms of emotional distress, the ego holds onto its original contents because it is so heavily conditioned by personal psychodynamic or narcissistic factors. These are our grandiosity, our need to protect ourselves from feeling inadequate, or simply a need to hold ourselves together to prevent the anxiety of fragmentation. Our knowing, wanting and thinking are inevitably predicated on limited information which is further distorted by developmental factors. We have learned to categorize information in particular ways – that is the meaning of 'ego'. Our narcissistic needs force us to maintain those categories that will allow us to feel valued, wanted, important and safe. The more we are fragile, the more rigidly will we hold to these categories. They constitute attachments in the Buddhist sense. In other words, the ego is a relatively fixed set of developmentally achieved structures – beliefs, attitudes, affects – which prevent us from letting go in the face of the transpersonal because of omnipotence and fear. To point out how difficult letting go really is, Eckhart defines wisdom as full attention to what is immediately at hand, taking delight in it, and doing it wholeheartedly without the assumption that we really should be doing something 'more important'.

Why is it that traditional advice of this type is so difficult to follow? Our disavowal, rage, depression, fear or inflation occur not only because of complexes but also because of our sense of finitude, our separation anxiety, our fear of dissolution, and for purposes of narcissistic enhancement. The problem of letting go actually involves letting go of our defences against such fears, which usually develop because of experiences with our parents that failed to make us feel safe unless we held on with our own efforts. To let go means that we need to struggle with and finally release these painful complexes, which represent the problematic side of the archetype intrapsychically. Within myth, this process is like Jacob struggling with the angel (Gen. 32: 24–32), who looks human outwardly but is actually a messenger of the divine. After this, Jacob is given a new identity. At the personal level, we tend to unconsciously project the contents of our parental complexes onto our image of the divine, which becomes a strict Father or stern Judge with which we wrestle. As the parental complex is digested, we become more open to new experiences of the transpersonal which may redeem early wounds. But until then the archetype is by no means always experienced as benevolent or safe. We cannot easily let go of a self that is poorly established, or of the defences of such a self, with the assumption that a new self will be then present; there does not seem to be a safety net. The psychotherapist interested in a religious approach to the psyche is therefore often walking a fine line between strengthening the self in order that it will eventually be able to experience the Self in a new way, while simultaneously trying to prevent the pain of the negative manifestations of the Self from overwhelming the patient.

To paraphrase Eckhart, we could say that wanting, willing and knowing, judgements, opinions and preferences, can all be used defensively to shore up enfeebled aspects of the self. But the price we pay for this is a relative estrangement from the archetypal realm, while our symptoms, such as anxiety or depression, are the result of the Self trying to incarnate against this – understandable – resistance to pain. Areas of fragility within the personality are essential aspects of religious experience, and can be the beginning of the development of our spirituality. The complex has an archetypal centre, and in Jung's words the archetype is an 'organ of God' within the psyche. Therefore the divine manifests itself intrapsychically as much through our pathology as in any other way. Careful attention to such material results in the ego's experience of a centre other than itself. Then our knowing and wanting, instead of being egocentric, can be authentic expressions of an ego–Self axis or of the Self itself. The self becomes more and more relativized, and is not so dependent on illusory sources of self-enhancement. The Self becomes the ultimate selfobject, the source of the vitality and cohesion of the self.

THE PROBLEM OF INTERPRETATION

All of the examples of contact with the numinosum given here raise questions of interpretation. Should they be looked at from the perspective of established religious traditions or by means of the language and interpretive method of depth psychology? What if the experience in question is not orthodox? Dispute about whether experiences or accounts of the sacred should be described from within a religious or psychological framework may be an exercise in semantics or may be a political problem. Two sources of disagreement are obvious. For the psychologist, the attempt to separate the two realms of discourse could be motivated by an attempt to restrict psychological descriptions of experience to those phenomena which can be understood in terms of a known theory, so that he or she can say something intelligible about them. This leads to the problem of reduction, which needs no further comment. Or the argument might be simply territorial. For example, Hostie (1957, p. 203), a theologian, objects to Jung's attempt to explain the dogma of the trinity psychologically because in Hostie's opinion dogma 'is entirely concerned with God's being, as a thing revealed', and Jung avoids questions of the ontological status of Self images. Rather than applying a psychological method, Hostie wishes to preserve the 'absolute transcendence of the mystery', which he feels is revealed in dogma. But this criticism misunderstands the psychological approach, which does not even try to enter this arena. It only tries to make the experience of the numinosum, and even the experience of dogma, more usable by revealing its psychological ramifications. In the last analysis, psychology, too, stands speechless before the mystery involved. And every dogma has itself both a history and a psychology; it is a product of human thought and intuition as well as inspiration. Wherever dogma originates, even if divinely inspired, it inescapably passes through human levels of the psyche. Dogma has similarities to myth, especially when the same themes are found in different traditions. For example, within Christianity the archetypal idea of the divine as a trinity began as early as the second century, and evolved gradually through a series of church councils. It is also found in other, older, traditions such as the Hindu. As is to be expected with any archetypal form, the content is different; instead of Father, Son and Holy Ghost we see Brahma, Vishnu and Shiva. But there is no particular reason for the psychologist to restrict him/herself to only one of these archetypal notions about the structure of the divine. Hostie's criticism, therefore, could be seen as a purely political attempt to restrict the content of revealed truth about the trinitarian nature or experience of the divine to the dogmatic accounts of one particular tradition by ignoring the fact that the Self has manifested this aspect of itself in other ways. Other, perhaps totally novel, aspects of the Self are not less true than the Christian or Hindu, and the depth psychotherapist is in a good position to witness their emergence.

In summary: for the psychologist, doctrinal notions of God are usually anthropomorphisms coloured by both personal psychology and commitments to a traditional view. Hence, whether we adopt the method of theology or that of psychology, the study of 'God' as an experience inextricably includes the study of psychology. Since we are predisposed to project our own unconscious material onto the unknown, concepts of God are a fruitful source of information about the psyche of man, but not about that, beyond the psyche, which cannot be known. Any religious thesis can be spoken about psychologically, and any experience can have a religious significance if it is approached in the correct spirit. This attitude is facilitated by attention to the religious function of the psyche as it presents itself to us through experiences of the Self, or its archetypal constituents. To further clarify their place in the psychotherapeutic setting, it will be useful to enlarge on the meaning of these ideas within the religious approach to the psyche.

3

THE TRANSPERSONAL SELF
A psychological approach to the divine

The psychological approach to spirituality stresses that personal experience of the divine is more important than any abstractly derived or doctrinal idea of God. In fact, it is psychologically correct to say with the Sufis that there is no God except the experience of God. The depth psychologist is not concerned with the nature of divinity in some absolute sense, and cannot know to what extent 'God' is a human construct or whether God exists outside of ourselves. Our concern is with the meaning of the experience of God to the individual, with how the individual may best approach the spiritual search and with how such experience affects the personality. For the religiously oriented psychologist it is therefore essential to have a way of talking about the intrapsychic manifestations of the divine and a way of integrating them into the total psychology of the individual. Jung was a major proponent of this attitude,[1] and for these purposes his concept of a transpersonal Self and its symbolic effects provides a useful language and framework. However, for this to be an effective method it is also essential that we discard all preconceived ideas of God that we have unconsciously imbibed from classical theism, and not unwittingly transfer or project them onto the Self concept (Asher, 1993). This is easier said than done; as we will see, Jung himself occasionally is guilty of this attribution. Instead, we must remain within our actual experience. To avoid preconceived ideas about the Self, I suggest that the therapist's attitude has to be that of the 'don't know mind' of Zen, or Lao Tzu's 'do not know that you know'.

JUNG'S CONCEPT OF THE SELF:
ITS INTERFACE WITH THEOLOGY

For Jung, since the idea of God is ubiquitous (CW 7, 110), proof of the existence of an extrapsychic or metaphysical divinity is a superfluous problem to the psychologist. 'God' is a psychological fact, and the psyche is real (CW 11, 751). This attitude is an echo of William James's (1902/1958) remark that God is real since he produces real effects. Jung's idea that there exists an a priori intrapsychic image of God, which he calls the Self, reflects an old intuition that something transcendent and eternal, an essence which is distinct from the everyday personality, exists at the core of the person. What is distinct about Jung's contribution to this notion is that he brings the Self into the province of applied psychology, by clarifying its dynamics in both normal development and psychopathology. Within this paradigm, the Self is also thought of as the unknowable totality of consciousness itself, which at times represents aspects of itself as one of an infinite number of possible images, none of which is the Self itself. We thereby preserve the old distinction between the essence of the divine and the divine as it is revealed.

Jung's concept of a transpersonal Self is therefore essentially different from theories of a personal self, such as that of Kohut, which sees the self as derived by a process of the internalized accretion of experience. The fact that the same word is used for two entirely different concepts confuses comparison (Corbett and Kugler, 1989); for the sake of clarity I follow the practice of distinguishing them with an upper- or lower-case letter 's'. We do not know the origin of Jung's Self, and we can say nothing about its essential nature; we only know it by means of its manifestations. The Self gradually unfolds into spatiotemporal reality by a process of incarnation or embodiment. That is, it moves from potential or spirit into body and behaviour lived out in the world. In this way, the Self acts as a template or blueprint for the development of the subjective experience of being, or possessing, a personal self. This is so partly because the embodiment of the Self occurs by means of affective experience, and the manner in which the developing child's human milieu responds to his affective states has a determining influence on the coherence and cohesiveness of the resulting personal self.

The personal self is a complex intrapsychic image which is relatively enduring in time and is a function of memory and learning, held within a body which represents its material aspects. The self concept is based on a series of affectively important experiences and events which are felt to be joined together into the sense of 'I'. Apparently, events happen to the growing self according to a ground plan. It is as though the outer events of the life of the self correspond to an inner predisposition determined by the Self. Hence, it is a mistake to think of the Self as only within the person; it actually determines significant aspects of the field within which the self lives. Or, simply stated, the Self is the archetypal underpinning of the self. Jung (1973, p. 409) refers to the Self as the 'principle by which man is shaped'.

It is axiomatic in Jungian psychology that these two distinct centres of consciousness are in dynamic relation to each other.[2] Jung (CW 7, 405) points out that the individuated ego gradually experiences itself as the object of a supraordinate subject – we realize that something is experiencing us. This happens as a result of experiences of the Self that are focused on our own psychology – the dream of being seen by the bright lights of the UFO (p. 6) is typical. Continuous exposure to such events supplies our personal consciousness with what it needs for its development, and has the potential to reduce suffering and enhance the firmness of self structures. Contact with the Self always leads to an experience of meaning, which reduces anxiety and allows us to feel part of a greater totality, reducing any sense of alienation or aloneness. One could say that the experience of the Self eventually provides a good internal object, or a reliable selfobject. These factors probably account for descriptions of encounters with the divine as acts of grace, which they are, but their helpful effects are traceable to distinct psychological mechanisms, because the Self acts via the particular needs of the individual psyche.

It is important to note that, although the Self encloses or contains the individual psyche, the self feels limited and not part of a totality. This may be because of the way in which the brain's perceptual mechanisms operate; our sense organs inherently produce boundaries because they give the brain finite information. Hence, the self does not experience its continuity with the Self. But in fact, if the Self is the totality of consciousness then it is also the field within which all experience occurs. We are then always experiencing by means of the Self, which is only felt to be an *object* of experience under special circumstances that we describe as contact with the numinosum. The Self is the medium or matrix of awareness, the larger field which encloses the smaller. Translated into traditional religious terminology we could say that the act of self-consciousness occurs within, and by means of, the divine ground. Or, the Self contains all selves; the oneness often described in the religious literature is actually the continuity of consciousness.

THE MYTHIC UNDERPINNINGS OF THE SELF THEORY: AN AMPLIFICATION

To me, Jung's theory is best understood as a psychological restatement of the ancient Vedantic notion of the Atman, an element of the divine within the individual which is identical with the universal, absolute consciousness of Brahman. The relationship between the personal self and the transpersonal Self can be conceptualized psychologically in many ways, all of which can also be found within Hindu thought. In that tradition, theistic schools believe that the task of the self is to regain its lost connection to the Self, and that the relationship is invariably one of devoted servant to master. These are the equivalent of the psychological idea of the 'ego–Self axis', or dialogue. Non-dual schools believe that there is no real difference between self and Self, and the apparent separation is the result of the ego's intense conditioning. The problem then is for us to realize our identity with the divine. This non-dual notion of the Self expresses in psychological language the mystical understanding that, in Eckhart's words, 'my me is God', or, as the Upanishads put it, 'thou art That'. This is an idea not without its opponents; if the self is actually part of the Self, as the mystics testify, then the drop of water is lost in the glass of wine. But for believers in a personal, essentially separate, God of relationship like that of traditional Christianity or Judaism, the objection to this sameness idea has always been that no worship or prayer is then possible, and what need is there of grace? The strict Hindu monists (such as Shankhara) addressed this problem by postulating a higher and a lower religion,

41

but of course the theist objects to the idea that worship of a personal God is lower. The depth psychologist will point out that the experience of the Self is always one of Otherness, not sameness, so that the non-dual viewpoint may seem harder to attain. But this does not mean it is less true. The problem which haunts the dualistic position, including the notion of an ego–Self axis, is that it is very hard to relate to something as apparently amorphous as consciousness, which is not an entity or being in the usual sense, without either slipping into hopelessly inaccurate anthropomorphisms or concretizing a particular image of the Self as if it were a fixed thing. In fact, an image is only needed to temporarily support an experience of the Self, whose reality is otherwise beyond our grasp. Any image is intrinsically dualistic, or a statement of 'this and not that'. Ideally the image only hints at the esssence to which it points, and is a means to this end, after which it can be discarded. It is only the autonomy of Self images, from the standpoint of consciousness, which makes them appear to arise from outside our selves. By contrast, the non-dual idea of ego–Self identity means that, instead of developing a 'relationship' with the totality, the ego has to realize its radical, seamless continuity with all of consciousness. This can only be attained by constant expansion of the boundaries of the self to encompass more and more of the larger field of consciousness of which it is a part. In other words, there is no need to try to get rid of the self or ego if instead we constantly try to discover its true nature, by knowing it as fully as possible. As the Zen teacher Dogen noted, to study the self is to forget the self. The personal self in such a system can be conceived of as a fixed set of learned concerns which keep us so self-absorbed that we are prevented from experiencing Reality as it really is – undivided.

The dichotomy between dual and non-dual attitudes in relation to the self and the Self may be a reflection of different personal psychologies. This may have to do with varying degrees of comfort with the idea of a loss of self in a merger. Or, an intense need for an object of relationship or devotion may require a dualistic attitude. It might also be argued that to see the person as only a fragment of the totality reduces our individuality to an unacceptable degree. Perhaps both the dual and non-dual attitudes are correct to some extent, depending on the level of observation. So far, Jungian depth psychologists have largely been dualistic in this regard, presumably reflecting the unconscious bias of their Judaeo-Christian heritage. Within the dualistic attitudes to the self and the Self, a variety of models are discernible. Some analytical psychologists cast the traditional ego–Self axis in terms of a battle of wills between ego and Self, while others view it as an interactive, mutual field in which both elements influence each other (for example, Asher, 1993). Jung himself (1965, p. 40) talks about fulfilling the will of God, and that he collides with this superior will (1975, p. 526). He also implies this position when he talks about the experience of the Self as an inevitable defeat for the ego (CW 14, 778). But all of this emphasis on will is a hangover from theistic religious systems which stress that the will of God and the will of the ego must at times conflict. Such a battle-of-the-wills psychology is redolent of the ubiquitous parent–child projection onto the divine. The situation may actually be one of different perspective, not will. Bruteau (1974) points out that this problem arises because of the ego's tendency to classify reality in fixed ways, then to reify and set its categories in absolute opposition to one another. Non-dual religious philosophy notes that Reality simply does not operate according to our conceptual categories, which have an extremely limited perspective. Our narcissistic concerns, or the structures of the self, are threatened when events do not correspond to our wishes, and out of long habit we immediately translate the situation into a parent–child struggle.

In clinical practice, the psychotherapist has to discern the position of the patient on the issue of duality or non-duality. For some people, the idea of an ego–Self *unity* is too inflated; for others it is too threatening, too close to a disastrous loss of self. For others, however, the idea of an ego–Self *relationship* itself makes no sense, since if the Self is the totality of consciousness it can only be the Self which is relating to itself. This debate is perhaps left to personal preference. But in any case, because the development of personal selfhood initially involves a sense of separateness, it takes some time and experience for either the experience of unity or that of a dynamic relationship with the Self to become a living reality. For either of these purposes, it is important for the religiously oriented psychotherapist to be sensitive to all the many possible manifestations of the Self.

The need for such recognition highlights the importance of Jung's (CW 5, 612; CW 18, 1624) description of symbolic representations of the Self as God images within the psyche. Jung is quite clear that the existence of such archetypal imagery cannot prove the existence of something beyond the psyche, but believes that the psychological reality of these experiences cannot be ignored (CW 11, 102). He insists that to speak of such an image is simply to speak psychologically, which does not demand a hypostatization (a literal concretization) of the image, and carries no theological implications (CW 8, 528). Furthermore: 'The God-image is not something *invented*, it is an *experience* that comes upon man spontaneously' (CW 9, ii, 303). Inevitably, God images tend to become anthropomorphized (CW 9, ii, 99) and laden with dogma and doctrine. Whatever is of the highest importance within the psyche of the individual tends to become imbued with the numinosity of the Self, so that Christ or any other objectivized figure may become such a symbol (CW 9, ii, 122), but in principle the idea or the experience of the Self could be carried by other means. It is no exaggeration to say that for some people politics, social movements, money, status, artistic pursuits or even psychological theories carry the valence of the Self. Like the experience of the Self, these factors act as supraordinate selfobjects which enhance the cohesion of the self.

TYPICAL SELF SYMBOLS AND MANIFESTATIONS

Before describing some typical manifestations of the Self, certain caveats are necessary. It is important to remember that when Jung talks about the Self, he is trying to do the impossible, since if it means anything at all the Self is beyond language and beyond specific or logical categories. This assertion is the only way to explain the impressive fact that the experience of the mystics of very different traditions is often in agreement. This is because mysticism in any form involves relatively direct contact with the Self. Unless we accept the testimony of the mystics, despite the fact that they represent a relatively small number of people, we are forced to make essentially non-psychological, or theoretical, assumptions about the nature of the Self, or deny its existence altogether. Based on such experiences, some traditions assert a view of the Self as pure awareness, without qualities, while some attribute more formal aspects to it, coloured by traditional ideas of divinity. This latter practice is exemplified by religions such as Christianity, or by those Hindu traditions which personify the Self in a particular figure such as Shiva. Those who adhere to a 'pure mind' view of the Self would simply argue that individual deities reflect certain aspects of the totality of Mind but should not be taken to be the totality itself. The Rig Veda teaches that beyond the Self as image lies a pure essence, and that the Self takes the form in which it is worshipped. Either view of the Self may be psychologically true for the individual whose experience leads in that direction, or for whom a particular belief or figure resonates deeply. In psychotherapeutic work, it is always true that images of the Self which occur at the personal level act as intermediaries between the ego and the totality of consciousness.

If we define the Self as the totality of consciousness, it cannot logically be known as a separate object by another, smaller consciousness, since that would mean the Self was no longer the totality. We must bear in mind, therefore, that what we call the Self remains an intrapsychic representation, which we realize is never the Self itself. This is Jung's theoretical position. He is clear that the Self, or any archetype, is not the same as its intrapsychic image, which points to an otherwise inexpressible 'something' beyond the image itself. This is a major source of misunderstanding; whatever the Self is, it is not reducible to an image: 'The theological parallel is the idea of likeness to God. There is only one *imago Dei*, which belongs to the existential ground of all men. I cannot speak of "my" *imago Dei* but only of "the" *imago Dei*' (Jung, 1973, p. 409). Because the Self is essentially impossible to imagine or define except in limited and specific instances, it is pointless to criticize Jung for logical inconsistencies, such as his statement (CW 12, 44) that the Self is both the totality and also the centre of the personality, which is a straight attribution onto the Self of a concept of God found within Hermetic philosophy (Jung, 1973, p. 412). Paradox comes with this territory. These kinds of descriptions are only pointers or verbal signs, not intended to be taken as if they refer to some kind of entity that can be known. To borrow Polanyi's phrase, we are only able to know the Self tacitly, as the experience of a contextual, interpretive framework, which acts as a presupposition. In Polanyi's (1983) sense, tacit knowing allows us to sense the unity or essence of something implicitly, from an understanding of some of its individual qualities. Certain symbolic experiences allow us to view processes which we refer to as the effects of the Self; they are the Self's own way of depicting itself to our consciousness. Because of the numinosity of these events, they invariably give the impression that they originate in a larger, more all-embracing consciousness. Perhaps they occur as symbols or images because our consciousness most easily receives transcendent Mind in such a form; the simplest way in which the Totality makes itself known to the ego is by means of an image. As the history of exoteric and especially fundamentalist religion clearly demonstrates, there is a great danger of trying to fix these images as if they were unchanging truths, or identifying them with some hypothetical entity to which we then become attached. In fact, they may be only the manner in which the transpersonal attracts our attention, with no permanent meaning in the sense that all Self symbols are temporary and conditional. They evolve according to the needs of the individual and the culture, and to fix them dogmatically may prevent further understanding and individuation both culturally and intrapsychically.

Here, we may need to make a personal choice between Buddhism's assertion that there is no self in the sense of an entity (*anatman*), and the Judaeo-Christian and psychological assumption that such an entity exists. Jung's concept can act as a psychological bridge to either attitude, depending on how it is developed within the individual. The Buddhists may simply mean that what we are trying to talk about is beyond language and beyond any of our categories. For them, the experience of being a self is not the effect of a concrete reality, but is due to the felt unity of experience as the individual frames of a film seem to be connected if they are projected quickly enough. There is thus no self as a separate entity distinct from the totality of consciousness.[3] The psychologically oriented spiritual seeker thus has various possibilities which are analogous to existing spiritual paths. He can take the position that 'to seek' is itself problematic, because it means to separate subject and object, or seeker and sought, which perpetuates the illusion of separateness of ego and Self, based on one of the ego's categories. The dog is then chasing its own tail. Such an individual then has to accept each experience of the Self as merely a temporary expedient or stepping stone, which must be allowed to fall away as a stage towards realizing the illusory nature of ego–Self separation. Or, if one prefers the idea of relationship, one may chose to savour each numinous experience as a way of deepening the ego's relationship to our true centre and identity.

Even if this centre, the true Self, or the Void in the mystical sense, is beyond image, this is not inconsistent with the fact that Self images do occur within the psyche. If the Self is pure awareness, or pure witness consciousness, its movement into image is a movement that puts it within the grasp of a personal self, which consists of a collage of images. Any Self image then serves the purpose of expanding the self's field of awareness. Perhaps a theological distinction serves us best in this area; the Godhead is whatever lies beyond image and experience, and nothing can be said about it, while God is what is revealed, personalized and made manifest as Self images. About these much can be said. We recognize them by their numinosity, which is why they have always been felt to be of transpersonal rather than developmental origin. These experiences are the true motivators of religious devotion. It is also no exaggeration to say that the Self is the real subject of all mythology – it merely changes its clothing according to local conditions. From a psychological point of view, different religious systems project the Self onto different personalities, and document different experiences of the Self. Their doctrines indicate the vicissitudes of the subsequent elaboration of these experiences. Psychologically speaking, any authentic, traditional *or* novel image of the Self is valid, whether it is experienced as positive or negative, the only criterion being its numinosity. Jung recognized that this approach allows true universality: 'I actually prefer the term "Self" because I am talking to Hindus as well as Christians, and I do not want to divide but to unite' (CW 18, 1669). His idea of an autonomous psyche, in which each personal self partakes, indicates our essential psychic unity at the deepest levels of being, and even allows a utopian future vision of some truly non-divisive spirituality. There has been a debate in the depth psychological literature between those who prefer a 'monotheistic' approach to the Self, which implies a single centre, and those who point out its essentially 'polytheistic' or multifocal nature. In such a case, each fragment of the Self has to be given its due (Hillman, 1981). There is no reason to assume that these are incompatible positions, since an underlying unity of consciousness may present itself in any number of ways. Certainly world religions as well as individuals have produced a wide range of different Self images, and we do not know the connection of all these images with their transcendental object (CW 11, 558). Jung (1975, p. 261) believes that statements about transcendent reality are invariably anthropomorphisms; the idea or image must be distinguished from the inexpressible reality: 'I see many God-images of various kinds; I find myself compelled to make mythological statements, but I know that none of them expresses or captures the immeasurable Other.'

SELF IMAGES IN PSYCHOTHERAPY

Given these limitations of our understanding about the nature of the Self, it remains important for the depth psychologist to examine experiences of the Self and its symbols as they occur to the individual, since they are highly relevant at the time they occur. Intrapsychic images of the Self assume various forms, which vary across a spectrum from the abstract to the animal or human depending on which aspect of the person's psychology is being highlighted. Corbett and Kugler (1989, p. 196) noted that most intrapsychic Self symbols fall into one of the following four categories.

1 Mandala imagery. Mandalas are geometric figures which portray symmetry, wholeness and completion. They are usually combinations of circles or squares, in dreams taking the form of cities, wheels, temples, gardens, spirals, flowers or other natural forms. Often these figures are quartered, and the number four has traditionally been thought to express completion. Jung noticed that this kind of material tends to emerge in the dreams and fantasies of people in crisis. He felt that the appearance of mandalas is the result of the psyche's tendency to

try to restore homeostasis by producing images of order and harmony; they remind us that we have a centre and a protected enclosure. Jung provided many examples of such imagery in his essay 'The Symbolism of the Mandala' (CW 12, 95–223). Experience in practice confirms his view that their occurrence is soothing in fairly healthy people, especially those who are able to externalize them as paintings, dance or sculptures. But in borderline people in a state of disintegration they do little to prevent or heal the fragmentation of the personal self. Mandalas also appear prominently in the productions of psychotic people, and Perry (1985) has suggested that this imagery seems to represent an attempt by the Self at reintegrating the disrupted personality. (However, such numinous experiences of the Self are also common precursors of psychosis, reminding us that the Self may be an agent of fragmentation as well as integration.)

2 Transcendent figures. These may be Christ, Tara or other deities, a Guru, the Buddha, royalty or anyone sufficiently idealized to be able to carry such intense projections. Interestingly, when such figures appear in dreams, the dreamer may or may not belong to the religious tradition of the particular figure involved. In this way we may discover that our personal myth is located in a tradition that was not necessarily that of our family of origin. For example, an individual of Jewish ancestry often dreamed of Jesus, because his personal pathology and spirituality were best carried by this mythology. He is therefore also Christian psychologically. Another person dreamed of the Egyptian dog-headed god, Anubis, even though he had no conscious knowledge of the Egyptian pantheon. These kinds of figures appear as authorities in dreams, typically carrying messages, help or gifts to the personal self. One beautiful visionary example is provided by von der Heydt (1976, p. 52). Her (Catholic) patient, disturbed by material she had to deal with in her analysis, was sitting in church when a figure she thought was a priest approached her with the Host; she saw that it was in fact Christ Himself. 'She took it; then He offered her the Chalice, she drew back, but it was offered to her again, and she knew that she had to drink. She said; it was bitter, bitter, bitter – and yet, He was there and it had to be.' Clearly the Self says that she has to deal with her situation, in a clear mythical reference to the garden of Gethsemane. It is not uncommon for such figures to appear as waking visions. A woman fell into a reverie while embroidering a cross on a church banner; to her amazement a Jesus-like figure appeared, pushed aside what she was making and gave her another, personal symbol for her own use. The Self does not always respect convention.

3 United opposites. According to Jung (CW 9, ii, 355), elements within the personality that are felt to be in opposition to each other are reconciled and transcended within the Self. The larger psyche harmoniously contains elements that seem conflictual to the individual self. Consequently, in situations in which we suffer from being pulled in apparently irreconcilable directions, the compensatory effect of the Self is to produce dream imagery of opposites united, such as marriage pairs, hermaphrodites, an old person and a child, a winged snake, and so on. These indicate the transcendence of polarity, and prevent

consciousness from over-identifying with one side of a conflict. In psychotherapeutic practice this is sometimes an over-optimistic view; we may have to wait an intolerably long time for such material, and it may not appear at all. Resolution then has to occur by means of some other channel, which is usually the therapeutic relationship.

4 The Self may also symbolize itself as awe-inspiring natural phenomena such as wild animals or fish, trees, mountains and oceans. Here the instinctual or organic life of the Self is being stressed. This imagery tends to occur when the individual needs to re-establish contact with this level of being. For modern people, it is hard to imagine a God-image taking such a form, but among pre-technological people such was often the case. (An example from the dream of a modern woman is given on p. 118.)

To these examples I would add the fact that the Self is also powerfully constellated by relationships (see p. 26). The Self also manifests itself as the occurrence of synchronistic events. Synchronicity is Jung's term for the fact that events may occur at the same time not because one causes the other but because they are connected by a common underlying, often unconscious, meaning. This happens most noticeably when the Self or one of its constituent archetypes is strongly activated within a person or situation. Events which belong together then cluster within the same time frame under the rubric of the archetype concerned, which enters space–time in this way. Synchronicities are felt as powerful coincidences, which may be positive (choosing the winning lottery ticket) or negative (stepping into the path of a car). In fact, all the formative outer events of our lives are actually synchronistic; the Self in its 'blueprint' function acts like a magnet which draws the inner and the outer together. Aziz (1990) has pointed out that Jung's emphasis on synchronicity moves his theory out of the realm of the purely intrapsychic into the outer world; in Aziz's words (p. 216), within this model 'nature as a whole has become the sacred retort of the world'. In the therapeutic situation, important outer life events, which often occur synchronistically, can be seen to have religious significance when their archetypal basis is taken into consideration. This also requires that we look at them prospectively, that is, in terms of their meaning for the future of the personality. As well as dealing with significant life events concretely, it is also a useful therapeutic exercise to imagine them as if they were a dream in order to glean their symbolic significance.

CRITICISMS OF THE SELF CONCEPT

The psychotherapist who adopts this paradigm should know that several theologians have taken issue with Jung's ideas about the Self. One of Victor White's (1960, p. 51) major criticisms is that Jung does not sufficiently distinguish between Self images and the reality of God. White writes that the Christian 'cannot allow for a moment that any psychic experience . . . can possibly be God. To do so would for us be idolatry.' He seems to mean that an experience of God is different from God, or that we should not confuse the experience, the intrapsychic manifestation, with the metaphysical entity. White believes that, in his capacity as a psychologist, Jung is not competent to decide on the reality of whatever it is that God images may refer to. This criticism is actually a straw man; Jung himself repeatedly made the same point. For example, Jung states clearly that Self images are not God as such, and that: 'This "Self" never takes the place of God, although it may perhaps be a vehicle for divine grace' (CW 10, 874).

An analogy clarifies the distinction between the metaphysical God and intrapsychic experiences of the Self. We must acknowledge that the taste of a bowl of soup is not the same as the soup itself, since the taste comes to us mediated through our perceptual apparatus and not directly. But we can enjoy and benefit from eating soup without even knowing the recipe, much less the real nature of the soup. The exact relationship, and the ontological gap, between the soup and its taste is a problem for philosophers. As psychologists we can appreciate the effects of the experience of the divine as mediated through the psyche without needing to know anything about its absolute nature. The theologian is still able to claim hegemony over this latter territory. The psychologist can only be concerned with the direct experience of the numinosum and does not wish to generalize the result of that experience into a system of thought that can be applied to others. It is obvious that the unknown cannot be defined in terms of the known; Self symbols only point to this Reality as it impinges on the life of the experiencing subject. Although we do not know the nature of what these symbols refer to, their enormous intrapsychic valence is undeniable. For the psychologist to believe that beyond the psyche there is a transcendent reality which is unknowable is as much an act of faith as it would be for the theologian.

The question of a God who utterly transcends the world simply does not belong in the psychological purview, but failure to recognize this fact has led to various misunderstandings and criticisms of the Self concept. For example, Buber (1952) protested that Jung's failure to differentiate between psychology and theology leads him to an insufficient distinction between a God outside of himself and the intrapsychic Self. Buber seems to accuse Jung's religious psychology of an excessive immanence, as if there were not enough distance between the ego and Self, so that the subject and object of religious experience cannot be clearly distinguished. This blurring would cause no problem for the non-dual Hindu theologian, or for any of us who eschew a rigid dualism. We would suggest that the ego is simply that aspect of the Self which has become circumscribed in a body and consequently experiences itself as disconnected from the Totality. The inner–outer distinction is then imposed on reality by human perception. But Buber believes that Jung's concept of the Self would prevent the experience of a relationship with God *understood in the Judaeo-Christian sense*. It is axiomatic within the religious approach to the psyche that the relationship between ego and Self may take other forms. It is also tragically clear that the mainstream of the Judaeo-Christian tradition in its collective form suffers from a God that can sometimes be excessively transcendent and lacking in immediacy. This is in part the result of an emphasis on scriptural authority rather than on personal experience, and partly because of a concept of divinity as a remote sky-God, external to the person rather than known as inner. Obviously this is not true of the mystical traditions, with which our stress on the experience of the Self is in harmony. But the collective idea of a God who is approached only indirectly (through scripture or through revelation that occurs to others) is the kind of deficiency that is corrected by Jung's concept of the Self.

There is an interesting and painful irony here, which indicates the problem of talking about the same process using different vocabularies. Using theological language, Buber (1958) emphasizes the importance of the direct encounter of man and God. He believes that this sanctifies daily life and redeems evil. But in spite of Buber's antipathy to a psychological approach to the divine, both of his important ideas are actually clarified, and their implementation facilitated, by a psychological approach. First, the stress on relationship is found in the Jungian idea of an ego–Self dialogue; the ego regards the Self, or the objective psyche, as a Thou. The Otherness of the Self in its numinous presentation to the ego demands relationship, not only because of its attracting power, but because it obviously does not arise from within the personal sphere. Even though they overlap, the Self can never be be fully assimilated into the ego. Then, with regard to the problem of evil, the personal shadow can be understood as that element of the dark side of the Self that is incarnate in human form and which requires consciousness and if possible integration. Thus, the importance of conscious work on the personal shadow carries a transpersonal significance which illustrates the mutual interpenetration of the human and the divine as it is understood psychologically. Sometimes the dark side of the Self is felt as personal suffering, sometimes as evil or suffering inflicted on others; in either case work on the shadow is the bread and butter of psychotherapy. This gives us a psychological mechanism to implement Buber's idea of the 'redemption of evil'.

Elsewhere in Buber's writing we see another example of the way in which the psychological concept of the Self clarifies a theological proposition. Buber (1947, p. 4) writes: 'The world in which you live affords you that association with God, which will redeem you and whatever aspects of the divine you have been entrusted with.' Here the psychologist points out that the the psyche is not separate from the 'world in which you live'. The Self manifests itself intrapsychically as well as in the outer world; the two are only separated by the body ego. Our own experience of the Self, or our personal archetypal endowment, is precisely that aspect of the divine with which we are entrusted. For example, we are entrusted with our complexes, which contain an archetypal core. Here Buber is apparently so wedded to traditional ideas of divinity that he exemplifies a common failure to appreciate manifestations of the divine which do not conform to familiar expectations. Many theologians are similarly resistant to the idea that intrapsychic God images do not restrict themselves to traditional Judaeo-Christian forms. In fact the variety of presentations of the Self is necessary – the demands of the Self thereby become highly individual, so that one can develop a relationship with personally relevant manifestations of divinity.

For the psychotherapist, this proposition involves the startling fact, which is discussed in detail later, that *our emotional suffering always contains an element of the divine.* The archetype at the centre of the complex, no matter how painful, is this element, so there is no escape from the numinosum at the core of our difficulty. This is why the Self images which appear to us always contain elements of our deepest needs and fears. If the divine is never further away than our suffering, then our suffering becomes the beginning of our spirituality. Any attempt to develop spiritual techniques that do not penetrate and understand suffering, run the risk of avoiding the sacred itself.

The history of religion suggests that some of the established religious institutions may not relish such a focus on personal relationship with aspects of the Self, rather than with a collective Self image such as Christ. If the experience of the Self is actually a manifestation of the divine, then the kingdom of heaven is readily available, without the need for a hierarchical and political structure. We should not underestimate the level of anxiety or rage that the possibility of a non-collective religion of the Self could arouse in those who need fixed religious structures for a variety of personal reasons. Thus we find a modern criticism of Jung's view of Christ as a symbol of the Self given by de Gruchy (1986, p. 106): 'The Christ symbol is reduced to an unbiblical gnostic myth the moment it is separated from Jesus the Jew of Nazareth and his proclamation of the Kingdom of God, and is no longer recognizably Christian.' This attitude freezes the manifestations of the Self to one particular historical, doctrinal or mythical example. But it would seem that images of God are continuously evolving. In Jung's words:

A psychological reading of the dominant archetypal images reveals a continuous series of psychological transformations, depicting the autonomous life of archetypes behind the scenes of consciousness. This hypothesis has been worked out to clarify and make comprehensible our religious history.

(CW 18, 1686)

The study of new Self images is essential to natural theology (CW 11, 102); the psyche is a part of nature, and such images provide us with new information about the nature of divinity, which is as interesting to some of us as new discoveries about the nature of matter. Theological systems which are tied to one form of Self expression, such as a rigid Christology which sees the church's view of Christianity as the final or ultimate expression of divinity, or orthodox Judaism's insistence on the unchangeability of revealed law, cannot do justice to the ongoing revelations manifested via the psyche. In fact one of the dangers of adherence to any orthodoxy is the suppression of individual symbol formation. Jung (CW 8, 92) suggests that, as traditional Christianity fades in intensity, the large number of new Christian sects which are emerging represent a recrudescence of the symbolic faculty – everyone is trying to get at the necessary experience in their own way. He points out that different cultural and personal situations require different symbolic solutions. When a symbol has outlived its usefulness but it is still perpetuated it becomes an idol, which increases unconsciousness (Jung, 1973, p. 60). To avoid this, the religiously oriented therapist is alert for new Self images as they manifest themselves in dream and vision. The resurgence of the Goddess in modern rather than traditional forms exemplifies this tendency (Corbett, 1990). The appearance of such personal symbols when collective symbols no longer have any effect allows the development of a religion of an individual character, and provides an experience which is more usable than any dogma. The validity of such emphasis on personal religious experience is partly dependent on Jung's insistence on the reality of the psyche.

THE REALITY OF THE PSYCHE: JUNG'S VIEW OF THE PRIMACY OF RELIGIOUS EXPERIENCE

Jung was criticized not only for an excessive psychologizing which does not concern itself sufficiently with the question of absolute truth, but also for 'elevating the unconscious to a religious phenomenon' (Fromm, 1950, p. 20). Apart from the obvious fact that the unconscious actually does produce or mediate religious phenomena, this genre of critique betrays a misunderstanding of the psychological method, which is not concerned with proving truth in any absolute sense – since that is a problem for the philosopher – but is concerned with the problem of the individual's ability to find personal meaning in the manifestations of his own and the objective psyche. As Jung (CW 18, 1683) put it: 'The trouble I have with my academic reader is that he cannot see a psychic structure as a relatively autonomous entity, because he is under the illusion that he is dealing with a concept. But in reality it is a living thing.' Jung is here referring to the importance of the living reality of the psyche, which reveals his own philosophical commitment. What is real is what has the force of reality for the person, without regard for questions about an external, objective reality. His example is the fact that the fear of ghosts and the fear of fire may affect a person the same way emotionally, regardless of the different status of ghosts and fire in the outer world. Psychic reality is especially alive during the experience of the numinosum, which is always a symbolic experience arising from transpersonal levels of the unconscious.

It is clear that in arriving at this notion of the primacy of subjective experience, Jung (1965, p. 43) was profoundly affected by the religious problem of his (minister) father, whose faith and teaching seemed to have no basis in personal experience, so that when he preached about grace it sounded 'stale and hollow'. Because of its lack of emphasis on experience, Jung found the teaching of his father's Swiss Reformed Church empty and lacking in numinosity. Consistent with his emphasis on psychic reality, Jung believed that personal experience is the best arbiter of the validity of religious beliefs (1975, p. 257). He felt that the reality of religious experience is absolute and cannot be disputed by one who has not had it (CW 11, 167). Belief is no substitute for the inner knowledge provided by experience, without which faith may not persist (CW 10, 521). He even went so far as to say that faith and outward form without religious experience 'in our own souls' are unimportant (CW 12, 13); faith cannot be produced by learning theology, but is a gift of grace requiring the discovery of the life of the spirit (CW 4, 780). It is central to the thesis of this book that grace is manifest by means of the psyche as an experience of the Self, while theoretical theological disputes, although indicative of individual psychological predisposition, do not assume a central place in most people's lives unless they are narcissistically important. Even someone's belief in the literal truth of sacred history is less important than the power of a single authentic experience which vouchsafes immediate knowledge of the divine. Numinous experience is one of the essences of religious experience; once it has occurred, our consciousness is affected permanently, and this leads to a religious attitude, unless its significance is disavowed.

The particular experience of the Self which occurs is always what is needed by the individual in the service of his or her own completion; it may or may not correspond to the assertions of a particular tradition. As we have seen, the experience of the Self may be a powerful synchronicity, a vision or a dream image. But here the psychological attitude to the numinosum is different from the traditional Christian mistrust of 'extraordinary' experiences. The desert Fathers, for instance, thought that unusual experiences – we would say the numinosum in a non-orthodox form – were delusions of the Devil. St John of the Cross suggested that at the sign of approaching ecstasy one should distract oneself. Ignatius Loyola believed that visionary experiences should be shunned and looked on with suspicion. Because of such mistrust, mystics have often kept silent about their experiences, and set less store by them than by simple, everyday piety (Heiler, 1985). The same attitude is still found; Clark (1986) warns that the disciplined mystic 'will regard special emotional states, beatific visions and raptures, as merely providential aids, no more "like" God than are the occasions of despair and dereliction when God seems far away'. This caveat seems to be directed to altered states of consciousness, which our culture is terrified of because of a lack of ritual containment for them, and because the ego itself is so highly valued. But such warning could also apply to any direct experiences of the Self if it were to be taken too literally. However, from the therapeutic perspective these experiences are considered to be of psychological value, and are therefore welcomed by the psychotherapist. The Christian mistrust of ecstatic or visionary states was also based on the idea that objective, or transcendent, Reality must not be confused with the projection of personal material, but the psychological approach does not make this radical distinction, for two reasons. First, we believe that the personal and transpersonal are inextricably connected within the human psyche, and also because it is a mistake to talk about the experience of the divine as a projection. This term implies a concrete distinction between inner and outer reality, whereas the divine is as much within the psyche as without, in the world; the two are actually inseparable, except as a function of human sensory systems.

We can, however, learn from the traditional teaching that devotion and trust in God are required despite the *absence* of any experiences of 'infused contemplation', or direct experiential knowledge of the Self. For the psychotherapist this absence corresponds to long periods of routine psychotherapeutic or personal work, without any obvious manifestations of the Self. However, it is not necessary to focus on exceptional experiences; if we understand the dynamics of the Self within the therapeutic setting, its subtle manifestations can always be perceived, so that the presence of the Self eventually becomes a continuous experience, a constant current of awareness in the room.

Jung's emphasis on religious experience rather than dogma is the same as that of William James, who (1902/1958, p. 329) stressed the primacy of feelings (rather than concepts) when describing what is most important about religious experience. Like Jung, he downplayed the importance of cognitive approaches such as systematic and moral theology. He believed that feelings lead to change in the person, thereby presaging both modern psychoanalytic ideas of affect as a motivational source and also Jung's idea that affect is the effect of the archetype. James's point is also the basis for my contention that affect is the essential structure-changing and, hence, healing factor in religious experience.

PROBLEMS WITH AN EMPHASIS ON THE PRIMACY OF EXPERIENCE

The insistence of Jung and James on the primacy of experience, which is epistemologically related to empirical theology, is of course debatable (Davies, 1982). For example, should numinous experience only be interpreted in terms of a theological tradition, or can experience itself be the origin of the individual's theology? The psychotherapist who makes use of the latter approach should be aware of some of the theological objections to it, and the psychological reply to these critiques. To begin with, it is not easy to know how to define 'religious experience'. This phrase has been taken to mean anything from direct contact with the numinosum, which takes myriad forms, to experiences of unity with the divine accompanied by loss of personal identity, to intuitive knowledge about the nature of the divine, to the sense that one is related to a personal God. Religious experience must also include the experience of the 'void' of the Buddhists, and of other Eastern traditions which do not describe it in theistic terms, for whom the idea of relationship with the divine reveals an unacceptable dualism. Does one give the same weight to all of these modalities? If not, how do we decide which are more important than others? For the practitioner, the problem of establishing the validity of different experiences all claiming to be religious is actually only a difficult one if we imagine that there is only one correct form, rather than accepting the validity of differing intrapsychic religious mechanisms within different personalities.

Personal experience has also been stigmatized as too subjective to act as a reliable guide or standard of behaviour without an external set of standards. It is feared that an emphasis on personal experience will lead to the abandonment of commonly agreed-upon articles of faith, and the development of multiple, solipsistic theologies. The psychological stance here is that the Self manifests itself through our subjectivity, and external standards only allow adaptation, not individuation. Adaptation is a political and social, not a psychological or religious goal. It may also be asked whether personal experience takes such precedence that we should sever our connections to our history and painfully accumulated store of traditional wisdom. Can experience really substitute for dogma and doctrine? Surely, the traditionalist will argue, during periods of life crisis, when personal experience of the divine is most needed, no new intrapsychic revelation may be forthcoming, so that we may need to fall back on established norms. Our response here is that these very norms are sometimes of little value during a crisis, and the usual problem is not that the psyche says nothing but that we are not using the correct means of listening. Apprehension also arises that an emphasis on personal revelation means that we may consider ourselves independent of earlier revelation, which is then somehow less binding. It will not assuage the theologian's anxiety to hear that the answer to this question is in the affirmative when material from the objective psyche so indicates.

The philosopher or psychiatrist will also point out that experience which is considered to be religious can be deceptive or frankly psychotic, and is consequently always potentially suspect. Here my approach relies on the coherence of numinous experience with the rest of the personality, and on the structure-building effects of the experience. There is no method by which one can verify that a claim about the origin of any particular experience is valid. For example, the individual may describe an ecstatic religious state which the neurologist dismissively attributes to his temporal lobe epilepsy. But it may be countered that, like a psychedelic drug effect, such a seizure merely opens a window, or allows an experience of transcendent reality which is normally obscured. Another problem is that different people have very different experiences which they claim to be those of divinity, and their content is often heavily dependent on preconceived teachings. In fact, mystical experience is often so coloured by expectation and tradition that accusations of suggestion, psychosis or hysteria are never far away. The first criticism is irrelevant if the experience is truly numinous – the experience cannot be disqualified on the basis of content. As to the second, the fact that the Self takes an expectable form is testimony to the validity of that particular form for that person. There may simply be no need for the individual to experience the Self in a new way. In any case, to accuse the experiencer of being sick or weak is often only a way of avoiding scrutiny of the experience itself; the numinosum does not confine its appearances to the psychologically robust.

But it is also true that the claim that religious experience is primary and more important than dogmatic assertions rests on various assumptions. One is that the spirit can present something new and personal which cannot be found in existing teachings, but which nevertheless is needed by the individual. This is a form of ongoing revelation, so we must also assume that revelation has not ceased. Even the sceptical theologian will admit that claims based on experience must be sometimes true, if only as witnessed by the testimony of the originators and mystics of his own tradition. My claim here is that there is no good reason to assume that my personal experience is less valid for me than was theirs to them. They were not selected by their fellow believers to have particular experiences of the divine; it happened to them as it happens to me, as an unbidden gift.

I also believe that it is fair to judge claims about the validity of religious experience by reasonable criteria, such as the traditional notion that the fruits of the experience are important. The theologian must concede that correct interpretation of these events must be possible in principle, since the corpus of dogma in all the traditions is an elaboration of such experience. Some psychologists would apply evaluative criteria only in the absence of any mental or physical illness that would indicate that the event is not to be taken at face value. But it is also arguable that the presence of mental or physical illness does not preclude, and may even increase the likelihood of, an authentic religious experience; indeed, if the barrier between consciousness and the unconscious is more tenuous than normal, they may be more than usually likely to occur. There is no reason that a psychotic should not experience the divine. The problem is that he is less likely to be taken seriously because of his disorganization, and the harsh reality is that his situation is likely to be made worse by the experience. In the end, refutation or proof of any argument for the authenticity or validity of religious experience is often impossible, so that the psychological case again returns to the quality of the experience and its effects within the person.

I would now like to turn to a further consideration of the proximate origin of such experience, namely the objective psyche and its constituent archetypes.

4

THE ARCHETYPE AS
SYNTHETIC PRINCIPLE
Making psychology and
spirituality synonymous

THE ARCHETYPE AS INFORMATION SOURCE

It is not my intention here to review or make use of all of Jung's ideas about the archetype, since this has been attempted on numerous occasions (e.g. Samuels, 1985). Rather, I have deliberately selected, and occasionally elaborated upon, those elements within his use of the term which are most relevant to a religious approach to the psyche. Jung's critics make the archetypes sound like very mysterious entities, but in fact as concepts they merely represent the operation of natural law as it expresses itself in the psyche, exactly analogous to the laws of matter. Just as the physicist is not concerned with the origin of the laws of thermodynamics, but is able to observe and understand matter because of them, so, too, the psychologist in our approach to the psyche can discern a set of laws whose origin is unknown. Archetypes operate as deep psychological structures which govern the organization of experience. At the most rudimentary level, in infancy, the baby organizes its perceptual and affective life according to these innate tendencies, needs or categories. Around the archetypal potential for organizing experiences of a particular quality, such as the selfobject needs described earlier, actual childhood events cluster to fulfil these potentials. The memories and images of innumerable similar events, such as interaction with parents, and the affect associated with these experiences, gradually adhere to form relatively stable intrapsychic stuctures known as complexes. These act as templates for patterns of relationship and for the development of a self concept. Eventually complexes become determinants of perception, because they lead to patterns of expectation which govern behaviour in situations with particular thematic associations to childhood.

The idea of invariant principles in the psyche which are common to all of humanity is not confined to Jung. It is implicit or explicit in the work of Piaget with regard to cognitive development, in Chomsky's linguistics and in Lévi-Strauss's structural anthropology. In ethology the archetype is known as an innate release mechanism. Even Freud (1918, p. 119) invoked the notion of inborn schemata, which 'place' the impressions derived from actual experience and are so powerful that they often triumph over the reality of this experience. But it is an error to try to locate the archetypes as if they were a product of the genes or the neurones. This form of biological reductionism is no more logical than to locate the law of gravity in the brain, and merely begs the question of how the genes themselves became organized. Although archetypes may require an intact, functional brain for their full expression, just as a television set must be intact to receive and transform a signal into an understandable image, it is logical to suggest that they are independent of brain in terms of their own organization, and indeed that they are responsible for the organization of the brain. Unless we are materialists, we cannot fully locate the archetypes within the brain nor reduce them to the emergent properties of the brain any more than the laws of chemistry could be understood to be a function of the brain. Neither, to avoid an unnecessary dualistic approach, is it necessary to postulate that the archetypes interact with the brain as if they were separate. Instead, Jung's (CW 8, 414) metaphor to describe the whole of the archetype is that of the light spectrum; 'blue' at the spirit or intrapsychic end and 'red' at the somatic end, but not divisible except arbitrarily. Since the archetype itself is unknowable, only metaphor is of use in this area, in which discussion rapidly deteriorates into a most unpsychological form of speculative metaphysics. With this caveat in mind we still need to account for the fact that the archetype may become manifest both intrapsychically as image or pattern, and also synchronistically as a body state such as an affect or drive. For these heuristic purposes the archetype can be thought of as a supraordinate information source, imagined as a strand of Big Mind, which informs the structure and function of both psyche and body, thought of not as separate but as an indivisible continuum. This continuum is everywhere permeated and organized by consciousness, but only a segment of it (the 'ego') is self-reflexive and thus conscious of being separate from the totality. Consciousness itself is ordered rather than random; the archetype is then a particular configuration or pattern of consciousness. Metaphorically, during development the archetype informs the nature of the growing plant, acting as the implicit intention to become a plant of a particular species.

If we avoid thinking in terms of a body–psyche dualism, which seems to be only a perceptual artifact, there is no need to worry about how some non-physical source is linked to the body. Here the psychologist can take advantage of the explanatory paradigms of the new physics, by considering body to be information organized at a different density than psyche. To do so requires a mind shift away from the Western scientific materialism of the nineteenth century, which insisted that everything is composed of physical qualities that exist in time and space. Matter is now thought to be composed of vibrating quanta whose exact nature or quality is unknown. It is then at least plausible that matter may be composed of pure consciousness; matter is then that form of consciousness that we perceive through our senses. The archetypes are the laws of consciousness that give order and form to the universe as we know it. But, to reiterate, it is not possible to determine the origin of these laws. Jung himself confuses this issue because of a circularity in his writing; he suggests that the archetypes are collective patterns that grow out of the deposit of innumerable human experiences, but also that they structure experience. Both these propositions could be true if the archetype is evolving, but not otherwise. By assuming the axiomatic primacy of the archetype as an a priori pattern maker, we avoid this chicken–egg problem. It is essential to argue in this way for the sake of consistency; it would make no sense to assume that the laws of thermodynamics arose because matter kept behaving in a certain way.

Aware of the problem of the nature of the archetype, Jung (CW 8, 417) makes a distinction between the unknowable archetype itself and its intrapsychic image. This distinction has been rejected by some post-Jungian psychologists such as James Hillman on the grounds that if the archetype is unknowable there is nothing to say about it, and we should focus on the image itself[1] (the practical consequences of this issue are discussed further on p. 97 et seq). However, many people feel that the distinction is heuristically valuable, because it acknowledges that we only experience the result or effect of the archetype and that any image of it is only an expedient expression of the inexpressible. The image is temporary; it can be discarded when its usefulness is over. An exclusive focus on images ignores their relativity, and maintains a rather conceptual and dualistic approach to the Self. There is a long religious tradition that suggests that beyond any image of the divine lies some unknowable, transcendent essence, which is only inferred or hinted at in its image. It is true (Hillman, 1981) that the psyche is intrinsically polytheistic or polycentric, in the sense that there are many archetypes with many possible centres of interest, any of which may dominate consciousness at a given moment. But ultimately the Self is beyond image.

The narrow range of human sensory systems acts as a filter or reducing valve, so that we remain permanently unclear about the nature of archetypal reality. The archetype allows the potential for a particular experience, and it is important not to confuse the resulting content with the archetype itself. The archetype can be thought of as an empty envelope of a specific shape; many different contents could fill it as long as they belong within this specific category of experience. For example, to clarify a common misconception, it is archetypally true that gender differences exist in the universe, but particular concepts of masculinity or femininity are entirely local and only represent variable contents of the archetype, never the archetype itself. Thus, there is no such thing as *the* archetypal masculine or feminine – only the potential for difference is archetypal. This concept of archetype as pure potential alludes etymologically to the power of the archetype, which exists in latent form until it is given personal content by the events or people who cluster within its orbit. For example, the experience of mother is archetypal, but not the actual human being who fills that potential for the individual, and none of the innumerable archetypal images of Mother found in world mythology can be said to be *the* mother archetype.

ARCHETYPE AS BOTH SPIRIT AND INTRAPSYCHIC ORGANIZING PRINCIPLE

One of the pillars of my thesis is Jung's (1975, p. 130) idea that the archetype, at the same time as it is important morphogenetically within the psyche, is also an 'organ of God'. In other words it is a spiritual principle within the psyche. The child's personal mother represents to him an individual example of what has always been known mythically, in many outward forms, as the Great Mother or the Goddess. In other words, behind the details of the personal mother lies the archetypal power of the divine Mother known to all religions. The personal mother thus has to mediate or humanize a partially transpersonal experience for her child, and the result may be felt as positive or negative.

At the level of psychology, the unknown archetypal ground of the psyche is thought to be the source of those fundamental organizational levels which determine the structure of the personality. These principles act as fields of information which are usually unconscious themselves, but become conscious to varying degrees as they form complexes. This process involves the accretion of personal experience around an organizational core – the personal father around the archetypal potential to experience 'Father'. When an archetype is felt relatively directly within the psyche, its effect is numinous and it is felt as Other. Phenomenologically there is no difference between these experiences and those described as the experience of spirit in the religious literature. This overlap means that archetypal processes are not only of developmental but also of religious significance. Therefore within the logic of the religious approach to the psyche, the personality is organized by means of spirit. Spirit as archetype forms the core of complexes which determine the structure of personality; these complexes are at the same time spirit in human dress. Because the terminologies of psychology and theology differ when they describe archetypal experiences, a pervasive but erroneous sense has arisen that religious and psychological approaches to the person are describing factors that are different in kind. This split has been fostered by the fact that our culture has partitioned off religious experience as if it had nothing to do with normal human development. We are not used to the idea that *elements of the divine are important in forming the very structure of the mind.*

As I have indicated, the origin of the psyche's numinous bedrock is impenetrable to our introspective or analytic efforts. This origin cannot be located within material reality because, on the contrary, spiritual reality actually contains and organizes what we describe as material reality (Corbin, 1972, p. 5). That is, spirit is not found in a 'where' because the 'where' is in it. Spiritual reality provides the underlying organizational principle, or ground, of what we experience within sensory space; the limitations of our perceptual apparatus force this apparent dualism upon us. The archetypal level of the psyche, which we identify phenomenologically according to its numinous effects on us, is thus the limit of psychological theory. It is a 'god-term', used to describe the inexplicable. But it is irrelevant to the psychotherapist that we have no idea what the archetype is in any absolute sense – that is a problem for speculative metaphysics. This fact frees us from some of the nettlesome questions that pervade traditional religions. For example, there are no psychological grounds for speculating on the relationship between a creator and the archetypes, about the extent to which archetypal manifestations are culturally determined or about how absolute or relative they are. These issues cannot be determined by the methods of depth psychology. It is also impossible to settle the question of whether this form of psychological polytheism (Hillman, 1975, p. 170) excludes an underlying monotheism, which would claim that all archetypes are manifestations of the One. These are theological, or at best metapsychological but not experiential, preoccupations. However, there is practical psychotherapeutic relevance to an awareness of the existence of the objective psyche. The practitioner who is used to its manifestations gradually learns to have faith – there is no other word for it – in its apparently superior wisdom. Obviously this faith has a religious quality which is constantly reinforced in daily practice as we observe its imagery and its processes within the personality. Just as we cannot observe the unconscious directly, the therapist can only recognize the effects of these factors by a distinct – to me affective – quality. We can also become aware of them by means of an introspective effort which allows the experience of a sense of 'something in me' which is yet 'not me'. Apart from direct experiences of the numinosum, archetypal processes themselves remain unconscious, so that it is as if personal consciousness were like a small boat trying to navigate a river while deep currents radically affect the craft's course and speed. These currents, usually in the form of complexes, are the spiritual or archetypal forces within the personality. Sometimes, their direction sets the individual against collective standards, so that therapy directed towards individuation (which I regard as a religious goal) is not simply a matter of adaptation. This kind of work can never predict outcome, nor can it ever superimpose any kind of pre-existing theoretical template such as a cognitive paradigm. Unless the therapist is open to the polymorphic appearances of the archetype, we do violence to the individual's soul. Notions of 'management' or 'treatment plans' are meaningless in this area, and tend to repeat the traumas of childhood.

Since the archetypes manifest themselves intrapsychically as complexes which are structurally important within the personality, and are also numinous when experienced directly, it is artificial to separate their spiritual from their psychological aspects. Because these unconscious currents affect humanity in general and are clearly not simply derivatives of personal history, they may legitimately be termed transpersonal. This appellation has been challenged on the grounds that the archetypes are collective but not really transpersonal because they are form determinants, whereas true mystical experience is that of formless awareness (Wilbur, 1991). This criticism confuses Jung's careful distinction between the unknowable *ding an sich* (the archetype itself) with the soul's image of the experience. The latter is experienced as an intrapsychic content, a symbol or a representation (such as a mythical image) that is understood to be at best an approximation. It is true that only the unknowable essence of the archetype is properly termed transpersonal. But we know from its phenomenology that the symbolic experience of the numinosum is the effect of an underlying archetype, and it is difficult to deny that the numinosum produces transpersonal experiences. Further, it is inescapably true that as well as formless varieties of mystical experience, the divine occasionally does take *apparent* form, and it seems unreasonable to restrict the definition of 'mystical' to that of the contentless Void. If we did so, we would need another category for many Judaeo-Christian mystics. I assume that St Theresa of Avila was experiencing transpersonal levels of the psyche even though her experiences of joining with the numinosum in the form of Jesus had a collective form. She was experiencing the archetypal level of the psyche in one of its mythical personifications; there are many others. As discussed in Chapters 2 and 3, the fact that the numinosum is experienced as an infinity of archetypally based images, rather than indicating a *via positiva*, inexorably leads the depth psychologist to the conclusion that none of them, or an infinity of them, is the archetype itself. This leads to the necessity of an apophatic theology, or a *via negativa*.

The approach suggested here traces the archetypes from their unknowable source into personal manifestation within the life of the individual, with all their possible vicissitudes. Some of these manifestations the clinician calls pathology, but these can also be seen simply as the life of the archetype in the time–space world. Therefore the religious approach to the psyche belongs to the long tradition of mediation between, or linking of, the human and the transpersonal realms. Instead of the bridge being made by means of revealed law, as in Judaism, or by means of Jesus, it is here made by means of the relation between personal and transpersonal levels of the psyche. Therefore, we rarely try to 'go beyond' or encourage 'disidentification' with the pathological manifestations of the archetype within the individual's life (in the form of complexes) until these have been either as fully understood or healed as is possible. (The question of transcendence is further discussed on p. 171.) This is partly because the personal and transpersonal levels of the psyche are inextricably mixed, and partly because a purely transpersonal approach can be used defensively. For example, one intention of meditation practice is to develop equanimity in the face of affect, but if affect tolerance is seriously impaired to begin with, it is possible to use meditation to split off affect so that it becomes defensively sequestered rather than integrated. This perpetuates the individual's proneness to fragmentation of the self. Such an attitude also ignores the crucially important incarnational aspects of individuation and psychotherapy (see pp. 128 et seq.).

THE PERSONAL SELF AND SPIRITUAL PRACTICE

The dangers of ignoring the incompleteness and shadow of the personal self are well illustrated by those spiritual teachers who are troubled by difficulties such as alcoholism, sexual acting out and the misuse of power in spite of their access to transcendent wisdom. Typically this occurs because narcissistic difficulties, which are synonymous with a personal self, have been ignored or suppressed in the service of a spiritual goal. Unfortunately, attempts to bypass the demands of the spirit as manifested at the personal level by the archetype at the core of the complex are often not enough to cope with its affective intensity. 'Disidentification' is then impossible without significant defence formation, which usually takes the form of further mind–body splitting. For some people the task of disidentifying with their selfobject needs would be no less difficult than the task of disidentifying with the need for food. It is often believed that the problem of the small self is manageable by adherence to particular techniqes, such as meditation, which are said to purify the psyche. But clinical experience with individuals who have been meditating for years suggests that this may be an optimistic view of things. The demands of the brittle personal self are ignored at one's peril. In such cases it is much easier to integrate painful affect and have one's selfobject needs met in the presence of a therapist who understands these needs than to attempt to deal with them in meditation, trying not to react to them, in a way that is too similar to the way in which they had to be disavowed in childhood. In the process of structuralizing the self in psychotherapy, the very craving, aversion and ignorance which meditation attempts to address are ameliorated to the point that meditation can eventually be effective. Since the Self provides the archetypal ground plan of the self, one is actually following the prompting of the spirit in the attempt to restore the self. As this process continues and the self becomes stronger and more cohesive, it can more easily be relinquished, relativized or expanded, in response to the demands of the Self. What happens in psychotherapeutic practice is that, because of these demands, the self gradually realizes that it is not who it thought it was, and increasingly experiences its continuity with Mind. In the process, childhood conditioning is released and identity is deepened. But to try prematurely to let go of a fragile self as part of spiritual practice is to court emotional disaster. Instead, what is required is a form of spirituality that *includes* work on the self. The rationale for this work to be defined as religious, rather than purely psychological, practice can be further clarified by discussing the meaning of the word religious within the psychological approach to the numinosum.

ARCHETYPAL EXPERIENCE: SHOULD IT BE CALLED 'RELIGIOUS'?

To clarify the sense in which psychotherapy that deals with personal as well as transpersonal levels of the psyche can be considered a religious practice requires some discussion of the meaning of particular words as they are understood within the religious approach to the psyche. Here they are not always synonymous with their colloquial usage. The need for verbal clarity arises partly because of the degree to which existing religious orthodoxies are suspect in the minds of many people. A tendency has accordingly arisen to substitute the word 'spiritual' for 'religious' when trying to describe archetypal experience that we do not wish to associate with dogmatic creeds. Especially is this true when whatever is numinous for an individual does not fit within the norms of the religion he has been taught, so that the word 'religious' feels inaccurate. And even the word 'spiritual' is now beginning to sound hackneyed and suspect by virtue of its association with the shallow and the ungrounded. It seems that a certain degradation of our vocabulary occurs in this area when the authenticity of an experience, or of its reporter, is suspect. Therefore, granted the ontological reality and primacy of archetypal experience one may ask whether it should be termed religious, in view of the historical baggage associated with that word and its modern disconnection from psychotherapy.

The problem we face here is that none of the traditional words escape some criticism. The word 'spiritual' is meaningful in a global sense, but sounds very elevated, and so tends to ignore soulful experience, with which it is not quite synonymous. 'Transpersonal' is not sufficiently experience-near. Therefore, rather than constantly needing new words to express ourselves in this area I suggest that we rehabilitate the word 'religious' by using it in a specific technical sense. We can restore the original dignity and meaning of the term, at least within our own practice, by using it carefully with a restricted psychological meaning which corresponds to the etymology of the word. One such meaning, from the Latin *religens* (which is the opposite of *negligens)* indicates the careful consideration of archetypal experience (CW 16, 395). Another, from the verb *ligare*, meaning to yoke or bind, describes the particular way in which the individual is connected to the divine. The word 'religious' can also be used in the general sense of asking questions of ultimate meaning or purpose in order to express a particular relationship to the infinite. The first two usages are not necessarily synonymous with the usual meanings of the word, where it implies adherence to a particular creed, but it seems reasonable to return to the original senses that the word carried, since these fit psychologically.

THE MEANING OF RELIGION WITHIN PSYCHOTHERAPY

When the word 'religious' implies some kind of religion in the sense of an established tradition, we find that there are too many of them to allow a single definition that will meet all possible intrapsychic or experiential categories. However, the psychotherapist does not need to be troubled by technical problems in the definition of religion of the kind that concern theologians. Our psychotherapeutic attitude to the question of the nature of religion is to concentrate on whatever is numinous for the individual, be it an experience, a question, an illness, a neurosis or a goal in life. Because we have no single commitment to the form in which the Self may manifest, we can afford to ignore any external norms or pre-existing systems except those which correspond to, or are important within, the individual's psychology. Neither do we make demons out of the old gods by suggesting that they are wrong; we simply stay within the psychic field of the individual concerned. Instead of defining religion in terms of hypothetical ultimates, which themselves are indefinable from within psychology, the psychotherapist simply views religion operationally, in terms of a specific attitude or mental set, or as the workings of those psychological processes which lead to experiences of a numinous quality. Within this paradigm our understanding of religion also leads to a concern for everyday psychological problems when these are experienced not only as personal but also in relation to a transpersonal background. This archetypal background is potentially immanent, recognizable by its numinosity, and it provides the major existential questions, problems and responses for the person. We also recognize it by its patterning effect on our lives. It is our recognition of this archetypal context as it manifests itself intrapsychically (not as a metaphysical construct) that defines the religious quality of our practice. This context may reveal itself in any of the ways that the archetype is known to manifest itself – as dreams, symptoms, complexes, synchronicities, relationships, and as 'things that repeatedly happen to me'. The special expertise of the psychotherapist is in the recognition and articulation of this archetypal background regardless of the form it takes, since otherwise it may not be recognized for what it is. Some people tell me that they do not seem to have any religious experiences, and they have no idea of what is spiritually important to them. However, they readily admit that certain situations can be numinous, filling the person with awe and wonder, irresistibly attractive, allowing them effortlessly to lose all track of time, providing joy, or removing all sense of self in a felt oneness with the world. These experiences may occur in innumerable ways – listening to music, dancing, painting, weaving, watching children play, being in the wilderness, writing or cooking are only a few of them. When these experiences are numinous, I have no hesitation in pointing out that they are legitimate channels for spiritual experience, and regular participation in such an activity can be considered devotional or meditative. The problem is only that Western religious culture has not allowed them to be so classified, so that often they are not carried out with conscious reverence. In the case of unexpected archetypal experiences, as well as affirming the authentic religious nature of what otherwise may be dismissed, the therapist is helpful when he or she can discern their relevance to the psychological distress or the individuation process of the person concerned.

THE ARCHETYPE AS DETERMINANT OF PERSONAL RELIGIOUS PROBLEMS

Jung (1965, p. 318) noted that: 'the meaning of my existence is that life has addressed a question to me . . . or, conversely, I myself am a question . . .'. The particular questions that most influence or even organize our lives become clear to us with time and introspection. They are determined by the confluence of archetypal forces within the personality. These patterns are not always obvious, because their forms express themselves at many levels of the person, both in the body and in the psyche, with an almost infinite variety of socio-cultural colouring or content. But they are the real source both of our deepest sense of meaning and purpose and also of our most poignant difficulties. In fact, the religious questions which result from archetypal dynamics may be so important that they develop an autonomous quality within the personality, as if they were independently seeking their own resolution within that person. In such cases, they seem unconsciously to direct much of what happens, as if that life were dedicated to the outcome of a particular issue. Witness, for example, the importance of Freud's preoccupation with sexuality. The Hindu practice of non-violence (*ahimsa*) in the life of Gandhi is a similar dominant. Sometimes a particular scientific problem dominates the life of a researcher, or the need to master a childhood problem makes us repeatedly marry a spouse who embodies that particular difficulty. Such everyday experience indicates that certain people are apparently predisposed to explore particular areas of suffering or attainment.

When this inner pressure is lived out in a way which is manifestly pathological, it is referred to as the repetition compulsion; this clinical term describes the magnetic effects of the archetype which unconsciously influences choices that are made by means of the complex it has determined. The archetype seems to insist on some kind of recognition, either as behaviour, as symptoms, or through becoming conscious. One way this recognition is forced upon us is via the repeated re-creation of similar life situations, which as Jung notes are felt as fate because their origins are unconscious. At the same time as these situations produce psychological difficulties they also become spiritual problems for the individual. For instance, a baby is separated from its mother because of mother's illness. Later in her childhood she is again repeatedly left with caretakers. While her mother is away, the child is poorly cared for and things go badly at home. Mother is often depressed when she returns, so she is withdrawn and unresponsive to the child. Needless to say, as an adult this woman is sensitive to abandonment. What is uncanny and is not explained by a purely psychodynamic approach is that whenever her therapist is away, major problems occur in the patient's home, such as broken pipes or appliances, or her mother or her own children become ill. Obviously these are not events she can consciously control, and they never seem to happen when she is well connected to her therapist. Of course it is possible that she is less cohesive when her therapist is away, so that she ignores early warnings of trouble and allows minor problems to deteriorate. But the impression is of recurrent negative synchronicities – the outer and the inner situation correspond to each other. The abandonment by the therapist, who re-creates the mother problem within the transference, coincides temporally with failure of the normally holding, maternal environment and her own mothering functions. When the negative mother archetype manifests in this way as an apparent 'enchantment' which causes things to go wrong, as if caused by a fairy-tale wicked witch, it seems to operate as the apparently magical effects of unconscious forces which appear to come from outside the person. At such moments we realize the futility of a distinction between inside and outside when discussing archetypal reality. The search for a framework to understand this kind of synchronistic material, without simply dismissing it as a series of coincidences without meaning, requires a religious perspective. In such cases the archetype involved and the empirical personality seem to be at odds with each other, and this tension gives rise to many of the religious questions met with by the psychotherapist, such as 'Why does this always happen to me?' The answer is that: 'This *is* you, or this partly constitutes who you are, but you have never realized it consciously.' The perception of the archetype as an element of the dark side of the Self, incarnate within the self *and* its enviroment, adds the religious dimension to what would otherwise be seen as a purely clinical problem, and makes the patient's suffering a spiritual as well as a psychological issue.

From the point of view of the religious approach to the psyche, not only the experience of the numinosum but also any experience which touches on questions of meaning, value or purpose is potentially religious, depending on whether we contextualize it archetypally or as a purely psychological issue. Any question or experience can become a religious one if we are influenced in our attitude to it by direct contact with the archetypal realm. Any process which explores such questions with a transpersonal perspective becomes a religious process, including psychotherapy. Here, a religious attitude to the psyche is important in the practitioner, especially when we are exposed to questions about the meaning and purpose of suffering, and we try to help the individual to discern this meaning by recourse to the objective psyche without benefit of doctrine or dogma. Related problems such as the nature of the divine and its processes ('Why is God doing this?') are also much to the fore in the minds of some of our patients, stimulated by personal crises of the kind that lead people into psychotherapy. My experience is that many people would like to talk about such religious concerns in psychotherapy, but because of their preconceived ideas about the nature of this work it does not occur to them that the therapist could be interested or useful in this area.

But whether or not they have articulated them, all therapists are committed to particular attitudes to the issues raised by life crises. The questions of meaning and purpose raised by such situations are not necessarily resolvable in intellectual terms, which is for most people the wrong approach to them. But the therapist is unlikely to be able to avoid discussing these questions with some patients unless he or she is closed to such discussion. In such cases, the patient consciously or unconsciously perceives this attitude and avoids the topic, with results that may impoverish the therapy if these concerns are of deep importance to him.

RESISTANCE TO RELIGIOUS ISSUES WITHIN PSYCHOTHERAPY

It is not sufficient for the psychotherapist to ignore or evade religious questions – the demands of the archetype within the personality – when these are important intrapsychic issues. When the patient struggles with such questions, it is certainly possible for the therapist to refuse to participate on the grounds that they are a defence against the 'real' problem, that they are pragmatically insoluble or that they belong to a different discipline. Therapists often prefer that the patient avoid what they fear may be only speculation, and ask that he focus on the search for practical, discoverable personal knowledge so as to better understand his life situation. But such an attitude of avoidance is problematic for various reasons, not the least of which is that it may grossly ignore the patient's deepest concerns and thus represent an empathic failure. The therapist is also ignoring the fact that an answer or response to the patient's question may arise from the autonomous psyche; the transference is not the only medium of psychotherapeutic help.

The actual origin of a dismissive attitude towards the patient's religious inquiry may be that these questions make the therapist uncomfortable, so that her own doubts or anxieties must be defended against. This factor may make the therapist quickly rationalize the patient's search as the result of adolescent or sophomoric immaturity. A more benign reason is that in our training we are led to believe that psychotherapy is simply a technical procedure to do with the alleviation of emotional distress. We are not prepared technically or emotionally for philosophical or religious discussion, which is typically seen as defensive, in the service of avoiding the unconscious. Attempts on the part of the patient to discuss religious questions are either interpreted or simply tolerated, while the therapist waits for 'deeper' material to emerge. What is not acknowledged is the therapist's narcissistic difficulty (leading to a counterresistance) in the face of questions he feels inadequate to address. This may lead to a devaluing of certain aspects of the patient's subjective reality.

Every therapist works within a particular paradigm that dictates what is helpful. All such paradigms are based on fundamental philosophical positions about the nature of reality, whether or not this is articulated. Therefore we may as well be as conscious as possible about our assumptions about the meaning and purpose of our lives, about the place of suffering, and about our theory of psychotherapy, so that we do not inflict them on an unwilling patient for whom they are unsuitable. This is important because our own attitude to religious questions may unconsciously structure our therapeutic behaviour. For instance, if prayer is important to the patient but subtly devalued by the therapist when it is mentioned in sessions, then if the patient needs to maintain his or her tie to the therapist, he or she may feel ashamed of, or even abandon, a valuable personal asset.

The belief that there is a transpersonal background to human life and suffering alters one's attitude and therapeutic stance. With a purely personalistic base, unless he or she is consciously trained in humanistic or depth psychology, the therapist may unknowingly work out of a positivistic or deterministic theory of therapy. From the religious perspective this stance is both inflated and naïve. It means that all healing has to come from the technique of the therapist, the result of the correct management of the relationship of the two participants, or the correct application of a method, ignoring the contribution of the objective psyche. By contrast, it is a radical shift in orientation to realize that hitherto unknown, irreducible archetypal elements may influence the therapy, and that these factors possess a wisdom and purpose of their own. Of course, for the positivistic critic such assertions are merely unprovable verbal tranquillizers based on magical, primary process thinking or wish-fulfilling fantasy. They are either designed to paper over our ignorance of the real mechanism of cure in psychotherapy, or to reduce our anxiety in the face of unbearable suffering.

To these and similar criticisms, the religiously oriented therapist may reply that either one has experienced the archetypal realm or it is merely a theoretical notion of no practical or affective significance. And we must remember that the denial of this level may itself be defensive. To accept the existence of an autonomous psyche is too great a narcissistic wound for some people. Just as it was too much for some of Freud's contemporaries to accept that they were not master in their own psychological houses because of the existence of the personal unconscious, so it has been difficult for Jung's idea to be accepted that there is a level of the psyche independent even of personal experience. To do so would appear to grant even less autonomy to the individual than Freud's theory. One can therefore understand the resistance to the idea, and why Jung's psychology has never been popular in academic circles which value principles such as prediction and control. In particular it may be remembered that, when Freud and Jung wrote, it was not respectable within academic circles to openly discuss matters that sounded non-rational (witness Freud's fear of the 'black tide of occultism'), or to be anything other than a strict determinist. Much of this prejudice was probably motivated by a fear of the autonomous psyche. Such defences against it are still alive and well, and have contributed to the maintenance of our cultural split between psychology and religion.

THE APPARENT SPLIT BETWEEN RELIGIOUS STUDIES AND PSYCHOLOGY: THE ADVANTAGES OF A SYNTHETIC MODEL

The perspective so far articulated is obviously diametrically opposed to the historical manner in which religion and depth psychology have been treated. I would now like to consider some of the difficulties which arise when these areas of study are viewed as separate, which the religious approach to the psyche prevents or bypasses.

Because they have been viewed as distinct fields of inquiry, a relationship has been assumed between religious studies and depth psychology which has not been fully comfortable or easy to define. Such difficulty is inevitable; since the instruments, methodology and purpose of the two fields differ, different results are obtained even when studying the same phenomena. Scholars on both sides have attempted uneasy marriages. But as long as religion and psychology are seen as different in essence, as separate disciplines rather than different approaches to the *same* material, the theoretical mélange resulting from their attempted combination will always have an immiscible quality. For example, from the side of religious studies, depth psychology has been seen simply as a way of providing material for religious reflection, because there are theological solutions to psychological distress (e.g. Tillich, 1959). Religionists have sometimes argued that the proper province of psychotherapy is to prepare the person to be able to deal with religious issues in his or her life, which are of a higher order than his or her merely emotional troubles. When these are dealt with the psychotherapist should depart from the scene in favour of the minister. Traditionally, instead of employing psychotherapy, emotional or existential distress was, and to some extent still is, treated as if it only requires official church exoneration, such as absolution, for its solution. In such a case ready-made theological solutions such as prayer, penance, spiritual direction or the invocation of God's mercy are advised for emotional distress. These attitudes make the psychotherapist suspicious that the minister is naïve about what it takes to relieve emotional distress. All of them are external attempts to find a predetermined religious solution to a problem, without realizing that, from the perspective of the religious approach to the psyche, an intrapsychic resolution can itself provide a religious outcome. This is so because original religious perspectives, or answers to personal questions about problems such as suffering and evil, may arise out of the objective psyche. These may or may not take a traditional form, but they usually satisfy the subject. The problem can then be addressed from within a completely psychological framework without recourse to dogma. The dream about evil on p. 20, and those about suffering on p. 182, are examples of individualized answers to these problems.

From the vantage point of dynamic psychology, the split leads to different mistakes. Problems apparently brought about by adherence to particular religious beliefs, such as excessive guilt, scrupulosity or the neurotic conviction of sinfulness, have always been seen to be psychodynamically understandable. This has led to their treatment by certain psychoanalysts as if metapsychological explanations denied their simultaneous spiritual significance. This attitude tends to confirm the worst fears of the religionist that psychotherapy will undermine faith; it is as if his religious beliefs will be 'analysed away'. In fact, seen from within the religious approach to the psyche, the psychopathology *is* the spiritual problem, because it is archetypally determined, and the archetype is synonymous with spirit. It can be dealt with as such psychotherapeutically. It is possible to attempt to deal with a neurotic problem solely from the perspective of a traditional teaching, but this risks offering a quasi-solution which maintains an unecessary split in the mind of the sufferer and the practitioner alike. Such a split is symptomatic of a culturally compartmentalized view of human subjectivity and sacred experience.

It is my suggestion that some of the mutual mistrust and misunderstanding traditionally found at the interface of dynamic psychology and religion was based on this artificial dichotomy. Historically, the split began when healing lost its ancient association with religion. As psychology and theology became separate disciplines, so linguistic, methodologic and political differences separated them more and more. However, instead of compartmentalizing these areas, I see no distinction between them, because when we approach the psyche from the point of view of its archetypal underpinnings and their numinosity, it becomes a subject of religious concern. And, since all religious experience is integrally connected with of the psyche and is rooted in the psychology of the individual, we inevitably turn to psychology when we describe the connection of particular religious experience to the rest of the subject's life. There is no reason for the psychologist not to do so in our own language with our own methods. The real problem then is not to define a relationship between psychology and religion, or to talk about an interface – here the words make them sound separate – but to directly appreciate the sacrality of the psyche. This involves an approach to the psyche that does not separate experience into sacred and profane, and which does not require that we translate intrapsychic material such as the experience of the numinosum into the language of a discipline other than psychology. Words are powerful categorizing devices, and have enshrined the split I am trying to overcome. Hence, the importance of a shared language to articulate religious experience. Wittgenstein suggested that the limits of my language are the limits of my world, and that what I cannot speak about must be passed over in silence. By opening up religious experience to the language of psychology, we open up possibilities of description, integration and interpretation hitherto closed to us. The language of depth psychology is well equipped to link archetypal, developmental and psychopathological aspects of the person under one roof, without splitting them artificially. There is no need for a distinct pastoral language that is set against that of psychotherapy, or a psychological language that is antithetical to spiritual direction.

I suggest that the alternative, which is to perpetuate the traditional distinction between religion and psychology, allows for impossible inconsistencies. For instance, dynamic psychologists have sometimes viewed religious experience purely in terms of pathology, as if this automatically denied its transpersonal origins. Because of what might be termed 'paradigm blinkering', they have ignored the fact that an event might be pathological from a clinical point of view but simultaneously numinous and meaningful spiritually. This is so because – as described in Chapter 2 – the spirit commonly addresses us where we are most wounded. This is also the place that depth psychology addresses, so an overlap of interest is inevitable, and is evidence that the two approaches deal with the same material. Neither approach is sufficient in itself. Many mystical experiences take the form of visions, voices or other manifestations of the archetypal unconscious that traditional psychiatry only knows of as pathological. Consequently, the biased or careless practitioner is too ready to dismiss these phenomena as invariably due to mental illness, even though careful examination of the individual case may reveal no such confirmatory evidence. In other words, it is possible to have a vision of Christ, the Virgin Mary or a dead relative without necessarily being schizophrenic or hysterical.

The dismissive attitude I refer to is not only true of descriptive or biological psychiatry. There was also a tendency to try to negate religious experience in the early days of psychoanalytic theorizing about religion, by understanding it purely as regressive. But when classical psychoanalysis proposes an explanation of religious experience exclusively in terms of childhood – a 'backward'-looking approach – such a formulation ignores the purpose of the experience for the continuing development of the personality. It also ignores the emotionally integrative effects of religious experience. The assumption of the psychoanalyst who understood a religous experience psychodynamically, perhaps in terms of infantile needs, was that he or she had thereby demonstrated either its falsity or its lack of transpersonal origin. This conclusion is a logical *non sequitur*. The fact that a mystic loses his or her mother at an early age, and later has visions of the Virgin Mary, does nothing to prove that the vision was not at the same time genuine and *also* related to the psychological effects of the loss – a manifestation of the healing effects of contact with the numinosum. The childhood problem is at the same time psychologically and spiritually relevant, and so evokes a religious experience of a particular quality. There is no need to assume that authentic religious experience is not psychodynamically mediated; in fact the precise thesis of my approach is that it emerges from the deeper levels of the unconscious. But to explain the process by which an experience occurs does not mean that the event was not real. It is a gross misunderstanding of some psychoanalysts to dismiss authentic mystical experiences as a regressive analogue of infantile experiences. These are pseudo-explanations; mystical experience can also be a developmentally advanced or progressive form of experience. Reduction to infancy is simply a defensive avoidance of the psyche's religious capacity. The technical difficulties which arise when we try to understand and describe religious experience are more problematic when it is assumed that depth psychology and the study of religious experience are somehow antithetical to each other, or that psychodynamic and religious approaches are not equally valid lenses through which to view humanity. There are many ways to develop a knowledge of the psyche; as Kaufman (1978) points out, it does not seem unreasonable to suggest that a study of religion might tell us more about humanity than a study of rats.

From their side of the divide, in the literature on sin and salvation, traditional theologians focused only on conscious behaviour. They ignored both early developmental vicissitudes and the contribution of the unconscious as a source of both pathology and healing. For example, sin was regarded as a transgression of divine law, or as an innate inclination to evil, as in the case of inordinate sexual desire or pride. But for the depth psychologist these difficulties are not simply a problem of morality, faith or freedom alone; they are not always conscious choices, and to ignore the contribution of the unconscious is to ignore half the picture. Psychopathology which is totally out of the control of the individual can easily be regarded as sinful. But from the point of view of the religious approach to the psyche, this kind of attitude makes the mistake of separating the divine from such pathology, without realizing that spirituality cannot be divorced from pathology. Spiritual problems arise out of the psyche, and emotional distress is archetypally, that is to say spiritually, determined. Here the unifying concept is Jung's idea of the complex, which because of its archetypal core allows us to link the developmental and spiritual history of the individual. Because complexes are often painful or negative, the psychological approach avoids the pitfall of naïvely equating the spirit only with happiness and light. The spirit both produces and alleviates developmental difficulties and their attendant suffering. Hence the content of mystical experience, or contact with the numinosum, may often have a pathological flavour but can also be healing.

THE RELIGION–PSYCHOLOGY SPLIT IN ITS TRANSFERENCE–COUNTERTRANSFERENCE MANIFESTATIONS

The traditional split between religious studies and depth psychology has led to significant consequences for the practice of psychotherapy. Therapists with no personal interest in religion may not associate this word with meaningful individual experience, but only with some kind of organized church or synagogue. They then probably feel that religion is only of importance in therapy when it matters to the patient – otherwise it can be ignored. Sometimes, the tenets of establishment religions are actually a hindrance for the therapist working with orthodox believers, who are notoriously difficult to treat because of several factors which act as resistances (Peteet, 1981). For instance, difficulty can be caused by pressure from co-members of the religious group who distrust therapy, fearing that it will lead the believer astray, or by collective beliefs that certain problems are to be handled spiritually rather than psychologically. Dogmatic assertions can also be used to buttress defences; celibacy avoids the need to look at sexual difficulties, or beliefs about the importance of self-denial may mask a masochistic character structure. A member of a religious order that stresses relationship to God alone may thereby avoid his or her personal relational issues. A compliant, dependent person who needs his or her religious community to meet his or her selfobject needs may have difficulty disagreeing with peers or religious superiors when sensing the stirring of his or her independence or individuality as a result of therapy. This work may also stir up latent conflict within the individual about specific doctrinal attitudes, such as a view of women as of lesser religious importance than men, or other notions of religious élitism.

Countertransference difficulties may also enter the picture when the patient mentions religion, and their origin is not far to seek. In the minds of many psychotherapists, religion only means its institutionalized form. For some practitioners this is synonymous at least with superstition, if not with bigotry, tribalism or racism, not to mention war and murder in the name of God. For these therapists, the word religion has accordingly developed an air of opprobrium or mistrust about it. It is also common for us to hear our patients' childhood memories at the hands of the religious establishment, for instance at religious schools, and these memories can be painful or enraging. For example, there may have been violent and abusive attempts to suppress the child's normal interest in the body and sexuality. Or the child may have been exposed to naïve and unrealistic teaching about how he or she is not supposed to become angry, but always forgiving. These attitudes foster guilt, shame and difficulty in expressing rage and sexuality. These stories may reverberate with the therapist's own early traumatic selfobject failures. Or, when both patient and therapist are members of the same religious group, a potential for countertransference distortion arises from shared religious values which can be used to rationalize or collude with the neurotic aspects of both participants (Spero, 1981).

When the therapist's attitude towards religion is negative because of an early personal struggle with oppressive, rigidly orthodox parents, or from repressive early instruction, the therapist's ability to appreciate fully the importance of the patient's positive and personal numinous experience may be affected. Such negative factors in therapists' lives may be reinforced by their training, for example, in classical psychoanalysis, which has a pejorative view of religion. Socio-cultural factors also intrude. The media are always delighted with the bizarre pronouncements and unconscious behaviour of religious leaders, such as death threats in the name of God. The shadow of the minister is always fascinating when it leaks out, as it is eventually wont to do, because it uncannily reveals what he has been trying to split off, repress or project onto others by his preaching. Religious wars also act as a cover or excuse for political manipulation or frank sociopathy. Working with people who try to stay within a church, the therapist is also witness to the suffering produced by the fossilization of dogma and doctrine, which often seem to have more to do with the pathology of their originators than with personal spiritual needs. These can rarely be addressed by recourse to blanket forms of dogmatic authority. Instead, help is needed that is specifically tailored to the individual.

INDIVIDUALIZED SPIRITUAL HELP: THE DEPTH PSYCHOLOGICAL APPROACH

It is no accident that more and more ministers of religion are turning to depth psychological methods, as pastoral counsellors or analytic therapists, in an attempt to make their ministry more personally relevant. This is a *de facto* admission that religious teachings alone are sometimes inedquate in the face of crisis.

Using approaches such as those of Jung, psychologically sophisticated ministers are able to psychologize the heritage of their tradition. They can relate forms of prayer and spirituality to individual typology, which often makes the tradition relevant to people whose psychodynamics resonate with its particular mythology. But this process does not help people whose psyche is structured in such a way that they need a different mythology altogether. Practitioners such as pastoral counsellors, who work within a particular religious tradition, tend to use that specific belief system as the transpersonal background of their psychotherapy. When these teachings correspond to their patient's psychology, this mixture is very valuable. The danger of using a specific doctrinal system arises when a (possibly unconscious) theological base or bias is used to address issues such as sexuality in a manner unsuited to the individual concerned. For instance, of what use is a doctrine of chastity to a person for whom Aphrodite is an intrapsychic dominant? Or a male sky god if Demeter rules? And what if the same sex is most numinous, but homosexuality is forbidden? Here, it is important to realize that a therapist may reject a relevant psychological concept if it does not fit with his or her commitment to a particular theology. A patient who needs to come to terms with the dark side of the spirit cannot be helped by constant emphasis on the divine as only good. And what if the numinosum is only experienced as pathology or madness? Adherence to dogmatic assertions that deny the patient's reality, or which prevent the therapist from seeing the actual form of the numinosum in the patient's psyche, may lead to a split between the practitioner's concept of divinity and the patient's suffering. This suffering is often the actual psychological field which contains the numinosum, and the therapist interested in the religious dimension does no good if he or she refuses to see how this is actually manifesting itself. In such a case, if the patient is bound to a therapist by an important selfobject tie, then to maintain this vital connection the experience of the divine and this selfobject tie have to be split within the patient's psyche – often a repeat of childhood, and exactly the opposite of what is needed.

A variety of other dangers may interfere with therapy in situations where unconscious, dogmatic assumptions hold sway. For example, mutually unconscious, primitive notions in the minds of both participants may equate suffering with divine punishment. Such unconscious bias may prevent the therapist helping the patient, because of an unspoken sense that he or she deserves the problem. In this way, the therapist may collude with or identify with and act out the patient's harsh introjects. Other traditional ideas may unconsciously operate, such as a prejudice against the body, instead of recognizing it as a sacred container of spirit. Or, there may be a mutual concept of the divine as consisting of purely father, or masculine, characteristics, which may seriously interfere with the perception of the feminine aspects of the divine as they actually manifest themselves in the patient's life.

All of this is to indicate the crucial need to personalize religious feeling and meaning, and to search for the individual's experience of the divine without being bound by assumptions or preconceived ideas. It is often necessary to fall back on faith during times of adversity, but faith in doctrine may be quickly undermined by intolerable, apparently senseless suffering. Faith is still necessary, however. At least the therapist must, as a result of his or her own experience of suffering, be convinced that meaning can be found, and that suffering is mediated transpersonally and is not random. At such times radical re-evaluation of one's beliefs may be needed, and even a new experience of the divine, Job-like, leading to a major breakthrough in spiritual growth. The practitioner who knows this from the inside is an invaluable guide, and is often able to maintain the patient during difficult times, but it is potentially fatal to interfere with this process by insisting on dogmatic assertions, as did Job's comforters. Therapists who can remember their own experience of the numinosum can use a psychological approach without recourse to doctrinal assumptions. Realizing that the therapist's own experience is different in content but not in its quality, such a therapist can be of help to a desperate patient by using the therapist's own experience as a source of faith and belief in the intelligence of the patient's process. Such therapists have sufficient personal resources to contain the patient's anxiety. They know the kind of things to look for within the patient's material, and they are able to help with its integration. I will now indicate some further examples of the value and use of numinous events in the psychotherapeutic context, to indicate the way in which they are relevant to personal psychological distress.

RELIGIOUS EXPERIENCE IN THE PSYCHOTHERAPEUTIC CONTEXT

As we saw in Chapter 2, archetypal experience may take a traditional or a novel form, apparently depending on what is assimilable by the experiencer. In either case, such experience is of considerable developmental and emotional importance to the individual concerned. It is always precisely relevant to his or her current psychological state; the archetype appears in a manner that is meaningfully connected to the rest of the subject's life. Often it provides a context to his or her suffering where none was visible, and this is partly how it is helpful. The advantage of including religious experience in the psychotherapeutic setting, rather than relegating it elsewhere, is that by doing so we can do full justice to the continuity and integrity of the patient's life. The therapist does not need to divide up the patient's subjectivity into those issues which can be addressed in therapy and those which he or she must take to a minister. Here I wish to sketch some of the ways in which archetypal material may unexpectedly present itself, and be utilized, within the psychotherapeutic session.

A middle-aged man, in treatment for a refractory, chronic depression, recalled the following childhood memory. While playing alone in a remote area of a large house, his mother burned to death in the basement, out of his earshot. Not only was his father indifferent to his distress, but the distraught child was blamed for not helping his mother. That night, at the foot of his bed, he saw a radiant vision of the Virgin Mary, which comforted him. He felt that this experience kept him alive. In this type of situation, the therapist is faced with a decision. The 'medical materialist' (William James's phrase) is able to dismiss this kind of event as a regressive wish-fulfilling hallucination, perhaps hysterical or psychotic, evoked by the horror of the situation. The experience could be reduced to the stimulation of a primitive, biologically based brain mechanism, of the kind which has evolutionary survival value. Such a dismissive attitude would be typical of the inability of traditional psychiatry to include any kind of archetypal experience within its canon of normality. By contrast, the perspective of the religious approach to the psyche is to evaluate the event in its total setting, accepting the possibility that this was an authentic archetypal manifestation. As far as I could reconstruct, the child had no evidence of psychosis at any time. The episode was isolated and brief, with no subsequent abnormality of thought process or perception. Rather than being disintegrative, the vision was reintegrative to a degree, with only helpful sequellae in terms of the subsequent development of the personality. It was so numinous that he was able to hold onto it for the rest of his life as a source of support – a typical example of healing contact with the numinosum. There was thus no need to pathologize or dismiss the situation; if the vision had been the harbinger of psychosis, the outcome would have been entirely different. In any case, the phenomenology of the event and the boy's subsequent history make this an implausible diagnosis. These experiences and their differentiation are discussed further in Chapter 2; the important point here is that because this was obviously a *normal* archetypal experience, the therapist was able to respond to it affirmatively and with respect and awe, thereby strengthening its structurally important role within the patient's psyche. To have dismissed it would have been traumatic and hurtful, repeating his early selfobject failures.

Even though this experience had occurred many years before, characteristically its numinosity affected us both as soon as the story was told, and the presence of the Mother archetype was palpable in the room. This constellating power of the archetype, felt as a particular affective state, is evident to therapists who are sensitive to its manifestations. Therefter, simply allowing its reality affected the course of the therapy – a prime example of how the Self may affect the therapeutic field. It is important that the overtly traditional form of the archetype does not mean that it must be understood only in terms of doctrinal Christianity. For it to be of use to this child, the archetype had to appear in a familiar form. But we may also seek its further, personal, psychological meaning in the life of the subject. In this case, the therapy focused on the fact that his life had revolved around problematic relations with women who carried maternal projections. The numinosity of such women was related to the numinosity of his mother and her loss. The blaming reaction of the patient's father illustrates the emotional atmosphere at home, and helps to explain his proclivity to depression. Had the vision not appeared, it is likely that he would have been unable to survive without much worse emotional difficulty. As it was, the vision acted as a selfobject that was able to sustain the self in the absence of adequate human support.

With no plausible, clinically based grounds to suggest that this was a pathological event, it is no more credible to dismiss its objective reality than to take it at face value – in psychological parlance, as the appearance of the Mother archetype in a form that the child could understand because of his background. To tell a patient who is unsure of the validity of an authentic numinous experience that such an event is reducible to a hallucination produced by a brain abnormality or to a psychogenic defensive operation has serious consequences. To do so at one stroke denies the reality of the objective psyche, may prevent its healing effect, calls into question the reliability of the patient, inhibits the likelihood of his or her reporting other such experiences, and sacrifices the patient's trust in his or her own perception. And all of this in the service of a particular commitment of the therapist that happens to be at odds with that of the patient. At present, all we can say about the actual ontological status of such appearances – whether they are real in some external sense or whether they are invariably hallucinatory, hysterical or only subjectively real – is that this question cannot be resolved from within psychology. But what is clear is that the unbiased, experienced clinician has little difficulty distinguishing these phenomena as they occur among psychologically reasonably normal people from their occurrence in the setting of organic and functional psychoses. Even in these latter cases, one often has the impression that the mental illness, like a psychedelic drug trip, has opened a window, which is normally kept closed, into the realm of the objective psyche. Or, contents of the psyche that are normally imperceptible have become enormously magnified. The psychotic is thereby flooded with more than he or she can handle of these contents, but the normal person with an otherwise structurally sound self is able to benefit from the moderate amount of archetypal material he or she is exposed to in the visionary experience.

The opening of such windows into the larger Mind is not uncommon among the general population, it is only uncommonly reported, for obvious reasons. A few illustrations will indicate some of the infinitely varied ways in which experiences of the archetypal realm may erupt into the lives of healthy people in the form of an outer vision rather than the more common inner vision. A woman reported that in church she saw a huge serpent pinned to the cross in place of the Christ figure, with light radiating from it. A man in the midst of a desperate life crisis was lying in tears on the floor of his apartment when he suddenly saw, in the middle of his living room, a group of fifteenth-century monks, praying for him. Both of these instances occurred to people who were very stressed but not in the least psychotic. Should this kind of event be brought into psychotherapy, the therapist has to help in elucidating its meaning when the individual has difficulty understanding it spontaneously. In the first case, various amplifications offer themselves, and these can be explored until one rings true in the subject's mind. The subject is asked to pay attention to the chthonic, elemental, perhaps feminine aspects of Christ (the serpent was an ancient symbol of the Goddess), as well as his traditional attributes. This would add an important dimension to her relationship to him. Among the alchemists, the serpent often represented the 'Spirit Mercurius', or the autonomous spirit of the objective psyche, which is hard to pin down. The crucified serpent is therefore an alchemical allegory for the need to experience the Self concretely, with all the limitations of the material world (see Edinger, 1973, p. 281 for a fuller understanding of this imagery.) In the second case, the sufferer is simply but effectively granted a vision of companionship and help with his feeling of isolation. All that is required is for the therapist to affirm this meaning, reassuring the subject that he is not psychotic and that the experience can be taken at face value.

It is not unusual for the meaning of such a vision to be given with its content, requiring no special amplification. Guy Corneau (1992; translated here by Dr A.-L. Cohen) reports an experience while at the edge of death, in which a figure appeared behind him, seemingly dressed as a monk of the Middle Ages, which reassured and soothed him:

His presence was an infinite softness and at the same time a calming firmness. A phrase ran through my entire being as if it were being engraved in me. I saw it and heard it at the same time: 'Let yourself go! All will be well!' I then realized that the monk's hands were not really hands but long, emaciated skeletal fingers which in fact were electric filaments, just like his arms inside his cassock. I turned my head more bravely with the intent of seeing my benefactor's face, and I saw a black mask all striped like a zebra with geometric lines. I let go. And it was then that I 'fell into God'. At least that is the expression that spontaneously came to my mind.

I had the impression that all my life I had been pushed against a wall, and that the wall all of a sudden gave in. From the little room I was in I had suddenly been catapulted into an immense room, all lit up. It was a feeling of incredible relief, expansion and surprise. At the end of the room were God's smile and his gaze.

(Corneau, 1992)

Corneau describes this experience as 'the first step on the path of internal enlightenments which were to come'. Later in the course of the same illness, another equally astonishing, transcendent figure told Corneau that he was 'repressing [his] angelic nature'. He realized that all his life he had been ignoring his true feelings, and his heart opened. He found that in the following weeks he was plunged into a 'nameless beatitude', and that 'a fire of immense love burned inside' him, to which he had constant access. Corneau realized that 'love was the very fabric of this universe, the common identity of each being and of each thing'. The experience radically transformed his view of life and relationships. His physical and emotional health improved dramatically thereafter. The need addressed by this book is illustrated by the fact that, in spite of the extraordinary healing quality of this experience, and its intense spiritual significance, when Corneau (personal communication, 1992) presented his experience at a public conference a clinician in the audience insisted that it was psychotic. In fact, it is an act of hubris and stultification to assume that we can dismiss as pathological what cannot be explained with our existing clinical paradigms. Religious experiences are normal, and these paradigms need to be expanded to include them. In this case, even if the experience were psychotic – which it was not – that fact alone would not detract from its transpersonal significance.

It is useful to ask why such an event sometimes takes the form of a waking vision rather than the more usual dream. Visionary experience is even more powerful than dreams, because its sensory quality feels closer to everyday reality, and its strangeness makes an impression which is harder to forget or deny than the ephemeral dream. As I have stressed, in such an experience the archetype may appear in familiar or unfamiliar form. For example, a child's mother died unexpectedly when the child was 8 years old. The child was initially inconsolable, until two days later she dreamed that her mother visited her, dressed in her usual travel clothes and carrying a suitcase. The child was comforted, and her grief somewhat attenuated, to the amazement of her family, because in the dream her mother had clearly said that she was well but that she had to say goodbye. Another instance is that of a woman who had always had a troubled relationship with her abusive, alcoholic father. After he died, she dreamed that he came to her and apologised for his behaviour, saying that he had been unable to stop himself drinking. A loving reunion took place in the dream, and on waking she felt that her feelings about her father were radically healed. Here the therapist has the choice of reducing these appearances to creative but essentially wish-fulfilling products of the unconscious, or of taking them seriously as 'visits', or of explaining them as manifestations of the archetype in personal form, presumably (a human assumption) for the purpose of healing. The position which is actually taken is a matter of the patient's and therapist's judgement and belief systems. It is the intention of the religiously oriented paradigm to at least take into account the possibility of the latter two alternatives being valid, so that when these kinds of experiences are brought into therapy, they are not automatically reduced, but are treated as psychologically important events with ramifications for the total economy of the personality. They cannot be understood in isolation, but only in the context of the past and future of the personality, including its unconscious aspects. When the experience is embedded within the setting of a psychosis, there is usually other evidence to that effect, such as thought-process disorder and other perceptual or affective abnormalities which indicate loss of reality testing. In such a case the therapist has a much more difficult task. But in the absence of such pointers to severe fragmentation of the self, the experience can be taken as a circumscribed experience of the autonomous psyche. The fact that we decide that the experience belongs to a non-ordinary type in no way diminishes its significance – we simply give it the weight it deserves in its own right, without pathologizing it. Otherwise the patient's inner life is perforce artificially split between material that has come to be labelled as either psychological or spiritual.

The therapist is especially important in this regard when it is impossible for the patient to discuss his or her experience of direct contact with archetypal reality with a minister of an established church. This occurs because some clergy, while believing themselves to be enlightened and psychologically sophisticated, will not commit themselves about the nature of such non-ordinary occurrences, and are not able to link them to the rest of the psychological life of the experiencer. At the extreme, fundamentalist clergy may even take the position that such transpersonal experience is demonic, unless it is strictly orthodox in its form, because authentic experience of this type is confined to certain approved Biblical personages. In this view, revelation has stopped, which is exactly the opposite of the position espoused in this book. The depth psychological context is a safe container for such events to be discussed at their own level, in terms of what they bring to the experiencer, which is personal contact with an aspect of the numinosum given for his or her individual needs, not to prove a point of dogma. For the therapist to fail to pay attention to such phenomena, or to ignore their importance to the patient's reality, betrays the patient and ignores a crucial area of human experience. Instead, it is my contention that it is possible to study the 'great natural mysteries' from the perspective and methodology of an internally consistent psychological discipline. We do not need to restrict ourselves to the perspective of any particular religious tradition, some of which do not recognize the validity of certain types of numinous experience. In this effort, we psychotherapists are religious in our attitude; we recognize and pay careful attention to the sacred.

As Eliade (1958) points out, the sacred is irreducible – its meaning cannot be grasped by reduction to any other discipline. Using psychological methodology, we can not only preserve but we may also enhance the quality of sacredness of an archetypal experience. This is because although no amount of discussion, unless it be destructively reductive or defensive, can remove the numinosity from a numinous dream, the sacred can be banalized if it is not recognized. The therapist who is open to any form of presentation of the numinosum is able to recognize its uncommon manifestations. Occasionally, during the discussion of a dream that sounds routine, hitherto unrealized numinosity emerges, and with it an inevitable sense of profound mystery. More and more one is led to this mystery, until prolonged psychotherapeutic exposure to these manifestations of the unconscious leads us to realize, with William James, that an unseen order exists. In this awareness we are little different from our tribal ancestors, who, although scientifically primitive, were often our superiors in terms of the technology of the sacred – for example in the use of ritual, which we have largely lost,[2] or in the understanding of the use of altered states of consciousness as a means of contact with the archetypal realm. Our commonality with earlier cultures in the face of the sacred is that it unites us in the common experience of awe. However, in our culture as a whole we lack an adequate method for the evocation and containment of the sacred, except in traditions such as Roman Catholicism or orthodox Judaism, where, however, archetypal moments are prescribed and not necessarily spontaneous. When the manifestations of the sacred are unexpected and un-orthodox, especially if they cause emotional distress, they cry out for containment and understanding, and this is a place in which psychotherapy may be helpful. Just as religious ritual has always allowed safe contact with the numinosum in its traditional sense, so modern psychotherapy allows the numinosum to be valued in its new forms and to be safely integrated into the individual personality and eventually into the culture at large.

For pre-industrial peoples, the presence of the archetype was much more an 'out there' phenomenon, as *mana* or power in nature or in charismatic individuals, than it was intrapsychic. In our civilization, the price we have paid for the development of a consciousness which is not merged with the natural world has been a concomitant separation from the latter's sacrality. In the process, we have relegated the sacred to church and synagogue services; as it occurs spontaneously, the sacred has been split off from everyday life. This split was fostered by the Judaeo-Christian alienation of humanity from nature (by 'subduing' and 'having dominion' over it (Gen. 1: 28)). It is also enhanced by that tradition's emphasis on the divine as transcendent, a remote sky god who is only approachable in prescribed ways or forms. (This is of course only true of the exoteric, not the mystical, strands of this tradition.) We are no longer in the position of the people around Mount Sinai who were forbidden on pain of death to touch the mountain, while the law was handed down from on high. Our concern today is with the healing of that split, including the discovery of the sacred in the psyche, which is itself a part of the natural world. This healing requires the discovery of the correct approach to transpersonal experience as a part of normal and abnormal psychology rather than as a branch of theology. In so doing, using the language and procedures of depth psychology we can discuss our experience of the sacred, whether inner or outer, without a sense of insuperable separation from it, and without radically divorcing it from our personal psychology. We access the sacred individually as it becomes immanent intrapsychically, while in the collective the numinosity of the natural world is making itself felt as an ecological sensitivity. It is this increasing sense of nature as numinosum that adds to the outrage of environmental groups at the desecration of the wilderness, which feels sacrilegious. To treat the psyche as purely profane is equally problematic to those of us for whom the psyche manifests the sacred.

THE SACRED IN PSYCHOTHERAPY: IS THERE A SCIENTIFIC APPROACH? THE IMPORTANCE OF THE METHOD

A loss of connection to the sacred has occurred within fields such as the physical sciences and some branches of psychology because the archetypal or mythical nature of their subject matter has been ignored or not felt.[3] This mistake sometimes arises because of the insistence on a 'scientific' approach to psychology, where 'science' is defined only in terms of logico-mathematical paradigms. It is worth a short digression to clarify this issue for depth psychologists who are uneasy about the methodology of depth psychology as it is applied to the experience of the sacred, compared with the more positivistic methodology they have trained with in the current academic setting. This kind of anxiety occurs when questions arise about the validity of our approach to the numinous psychic contents with which we deal.

Instead of taking into account the intertwining of their experimental data with their own psychology and its presuppositions, some psychological and psychiatric researchers still insist, albeit with less and less conviction, that they are developing factual models of an objective reality. But it is important for the depth psychologist to realize that there is no justification for insisting that the psyche must be studied in one particular manner. There is no generally agreed-upon scientific method which will apply to all disciplines. The extreme position (stated, I believe, by Lord Rutherford) is that there are only two kinds of science – physics and stamp collecting. Hence the notion that a 'scientific' psychology requires quantification dies hard, even though this is manifestly untrue. Newtonian physics is not the best model for a study of human nature, and to insist on a quantitative model for psychology is actually a betrayal of that nature. Quantum physics promises to offer a better model, but our discipline cannot be a function of *any* other endeavour, since the psyche is a universe in its own right. The psyche cannot be studied in the classical manner in which matter was studied, which was by dividing it into its constituent parts and investigating the interaction of these parts, leading to cause and effect statements that can be validated or disproved. In Hillman's words, (1976, p. 169) it is 'impossible for a psychology based on the psyche to imagine itself as a science' – meaning science defined as objectivity and measurement. Hillman further points out that we can apply the methodology of archetypal psychology to science itself, in order to discover its 'root metaphors and operational myths'. This suggestion means that, rather than feeling inferior to the physicists, we can reveal the archetypal motifs at the root of the scientific imagination. Both physics and psychology can then be viewed as products of the human imagination, and their concepts, since they will eventually be seen through and replaced, as mythological structures. In any field, what is called science is the agreed-upon consensus of a group of workers about the best way of studying particular phenomena. Depth psychology is still developing its own working models, but meanwhile there is no need to fall back on currently institutionalized notions of what is scientific. For instance, Jungian psychology applies a combination of psychodynamic, phenomenological, imaginal, symbolic and mythical approaches to the psyche, which is agreed upon by the community of workers in the field to be useful. This methodology also fits well with a study of religious phenomena. We are phenomenologists in the sense that we are interested in the introspective study and description of numinous phenomena which appear within the inner life of the person, without pretending that we understand their origins and real nature.

I would now like to turn in more detail to the mythical dimension of this work, especially as it reveals some of the dynamics of the objective psyche.

5

MYTHICAL, SYMBOLIC AND IMAGINAL ASPECTS OF THE PSYCHE'S RELIGIOUS FUNCTION

A mythical sensibility is integral to the depth psychological approach to the psyche's religious function. The dynamics of the archetypal level of the psyche, at which therapists work when they deal with both infantile material and religious experience, are sometimes closer to the imagery of myth than to any of the sciences based on logic and numbers. Jung (CW 9, i, 259) pointed out the existence of 'myth forming', deep structural elements in the unconscious, so that mythologems reflect the dynamics of the psyche. When the myth in which we live is unconscious, we are like a fish in water; the myth creates the atmosphere in which we live and is taken for granted. Our fundamental attitudes are then derived from it. Because the content of myth is derived from the psyche at the same level as that which gives rise to dreams and visions, similar methods are useful in understanding all of them. In Campbell's words: 'mythology is psychology misreau as cosmology, history and biography' (Campbell, 1969, p. 33). Myth seems to be so universal and essential that, according to Jung (CW 5, 30): 'one could almost say that if all the world's traditions were cut off at a single blow, the whole of mythology and the whole history of religion would start all over again'. The religious approach to the psyche is itself part of a mythical tradition whose roots are found in antiquity, but which is emerging in refreshed form. This re-emergence seems to be driven partly by the cultural need for a new understanding of divinity and partly by the evolution of consciousness. To assume a distinct form, it has had to wait for advances to be made in the technical aspects of psychotherapy.

Earlier I described science itself as a mythology, rather than as a myth, advisedly, in order to note Moore's (1983) distinction between 'mythology', which refers to fixed stories which promise truth, such as orthodox religious traditions or psychological theories, and myth itself, which is a particular way of imagining events. This distinction avoids canonizing and freezing myth, which is always fluid, fresh, self-contradictory and ephemeral, revealing the changing geography of the psyche. Moore (p. 26) points out that it is difficult for us to glimpse our personal myth 'behind the rigid orthodoxy of [our] childhood religious convictions', and that our literal life stories feel so true, leading to such a crystallized sense of identity, that we have trouble discerning our life's actual myth. In clinical practice, in the dreams and life stories of our patients, we usually see individual mythologems or mythical images rather than fully formed myths. The importance of an ability to detect these themes is that they reveal the movement of the objective psyche within the life of the individual, linking one life to the whole of life. 'Not as my sorrow, but as the sorrow of the world; not a personal isolating pain, but a pain without bitterness that unites all humanity. The healing effect of this needs no proof' (CW 8, 316).

MYTH: THE MOVEMENT OF THE OBJECTIVE PSYCHE

It is no accident that in antiquity the butterfly used to symbolize the soul, or that 'psyche' originally meant 'breath' – both of these evoke a sense of alive movement. Nowhere is the movement or the sense of the life of the psyche seen more clearly than in story, which moves images and affects towards a satisfying end that resonates within us. Sacred story, or myth, is distinguished from history or mere folk tale because to the believer it conveys truth or critically important knowledge about creation, life and death. Religion is inseparable from myth; most religions describe or are based on mythical events, transmitted as stories which are integral to the tradition. Myth has been beautifully defined as: 'that haunting awareness of transcendental forces peering through the cracks of the visible universe' (Wheelwright, 1959, p. 360). Depth psychotherapists often seem to take liberties with myths when we use them to amplify particular psychodynamics, because in so doing we tear the stories out of their original context, which is a whole cosmology or world-view, and apply them to individuals in another time and place. One can only say in defence of this practice that the psyche at its depths may still show the same structural forms and dynamics as it did at the time of the origin of the myth. Hence, the value to psychology of what might seem like an ahistorical or unscholarly use of myth. Another, more serious, difficulty is that the canon of western mythology that we typically turn to, such as Greek mythology, is a heavily patriarchal one. This is seen, for instance, in its attitude towards women and in its overvaluing of warfare. Mythologems that are gaining ground today, such as feminism or the environmental movement, are not well represented in the classical stories. Finally, as I will illustrate below, our understanding of myth is a function of the particular psychoanalytic theory that we bring to bear on it, and so is subject to change.

But given these limitations, the psyche's myth- or story-making capacity is of importance to the religiously oriented therapist for several reasons, not the least of which is the fact that classical mythical elements frequently occur in the psychic life of modern individuals. In such a case, an understanding of the appropriate myth contextualizes and amplifies the individual's psychology. For example, a man of Jewish extraction dreamed that he had to bury the body of Jesus after the crucifixion. This dream clearly referred to the need to deal with a complex which demanded a 'suffering servant' attitude to others, with an attendant, until then unrecognized, rather grandiose 'saviour' dynamic.

It is not unusual for the form taken by individual psychopathology to bear this kind of uncanny resemblance to, or correspondence with, mythical imagery. This similarity suggests the possibility that they both arise from the same levels or processes of the psyche; a particular archetypal pattern can then be seen in both its cultural or its individual manifestation. Obvious examples are the myths of Oedipus and Narcissus. Today we tend to regard myth so exclusively in its psychological dimension that we forget that myth deals with what were once felt to be manifestations of the divine. To our ears, the behaviour of the mythical gods seems terrible; Uranus refused to let his children be born, pushing them back into their mother, until he was castrated by Chronos, who in turn abused his own children by swallowing them, until he was finally deposed by his son Zeus. Here it is easy to see parallels with the severe father problems often seen in psychotherapy, reminding us that to a small child the rage of his father carries a 'wrath of God' level of severity. Within such a boy, the divine manifests itself archetypally as depicted by the terrible Father of such mythology. It is common for this ancient imagery to be projected onto contemporary ideas about the divine, leading to adherence to theologies of punishment and unforgivingness. The psychopathology of such a person then has this mythical underpinning, which also determines his lifelong spiritual and psychological problem – how to gain access to qualities of the father which he needs personally, and how to be a good father himself. There are many possible solutions; the hero of the Grimm's fairy tale 'The Three Languages' solves his severe father problem by becoming the Pope, or the ultimate spiritual father. It is not unusual for a man with a severe personal father problem to deal with it by becoming a mentor, or teacher, to younger men. The mentor archetype is itself a mythical one. Mentor was the name of a young Ithacan nobleman, in whose form the Goddess Athena used to appear to Telemachus, the son of Odysseus, when Telemachus was searching for his father.

It is often possible to use the dynamics of myth in these ways to clarify individual psychodynamics, illustrating the intimate connection between spirituality and psychology. But inevitably, attempts to interpret myth are subject to the vagaries of psychodynamic fashion, and so should be understood cautiously and not in any fixed sense. Sometimes the full theoretical articulation of a mythical theme has had to await developments in dynamic psychology. The familiar story of Saul on the road to Damascus, taken from Christian mythology (Acts 9: 1), can be used to illustrate the deepening of our understanding of a myth as a result of advances in psychodynamic theory. The vision and subsequent blinding of Saul was an experience of the numinosum which changed his rabid antagonism to Jesus into devoted service. Before discussing this mythologem psychologically, various caveats are important, which distinguish the methodology of the religious approach to the psyche from classical psychoanalytic approaches to myth. First, the story is seen as an example of the way in which the numinosum can radically changed entrenched, intrapsychic structure (see p. 22); the psychological approach to religious experience does not reduce the event purely to the workings of the personal unconscious. As well, we must remember that, in understanding the mythologem from the viewpoint of outside observers, we are analysing a text; we do not pretend to be analysing Saul himself, which would not be possible in this exterospective manner.

The theme of the story is that Saul saw the intense light of the divine, and this led to a radical revision of his attitude. At the same time, he heard the voice of Jesus asking 'Why do you persecute me?' Apparently Saul had been trying to suppress or persecute his own intense need for everything that Jesus stood for. On p. 162 I suggest that Saul's initial antipathy to Jesus, so severe that he wished to kill Jesus' followers, may have been the result of a defence against his need for an idealized selfobject. This defence was entirely removed by his experience. To illustrate how changing fashions in psychoanalytic theory affect our understanding of myth, it is useful to point out that, using a different, earlier psychodynamic theory, Boisen (1936, pp. 76–78) arrived at a different conclusion. He pointed out how Saul's initial attempt to savagely repress Jesus' followers may have been motivated by intense inner conflict about his own problems with 'the flesh', or his sexual and aggressive drives, which he was attempting to deal with by means of Pharisaic repression. These two understandings of the myth are not mutually exclusive. Saul's intense need for an idealizable selfobject may have been accompanied by a failure to structuralize his drives within a cohesive sense of self, so that he constantly suffered from the discomfort produced by his inability to contain their internal pressure. Such a self disorder would also be consonant with Paul's initial dislike of early Christian leanings towards relaxation of the strict letter of the law in favour of love and forgiveness, illustrating the connection between attraction to particular doctrinal belief and personal material. Boisen does not use his classical psychodynamic explanation of Saul's experience in order to dismiss its significance, but rather to point out how one's psychopathology can be meaningfully rearranged and healed by religious experience. Overtly mythical or archetypal material, as it arises in dreams and fantasy, also seems to have this intention. But in our present state of knowledge we are not always able to correlate its phenomenology with existing personalistic psychodynamic theory.

It is important to contrast this approach, which sees myth as the depiction of the workings of the irreducible archetypal level of the psyche, with the reductive attitude to myth found in some of the classical psychoanalytic literature. Here myth is banalized or despiritualized, reduced to the workings of purely personal psychodynamics. For instance, we find the suggestion that the function of myth is to communicate, in a way sanctioned by the community, particular fears, wishes and beliefs which must be depotentiated because of the guilt or anxiety they produce. The myth is then only a collective symptom, which mediates between an impulse or fantasy and its collective expression. For these writers myth, or its enactment in ritual, is useful for the purpose of instinctual gratification, defence and the maintenance of group solidarity, by presenting an ego-ideal with which the individual can identify (Arlow, 1961; Schneiderman, 1981). Unfortunately, Freud began this clear tendency in the psychoanalytic literature to use individual mythical themes reductively, not as manifestation of the sacred but as though they had fixed meanings. He used myth in order to substantiate preconceived theoretical notions, disregarding more careful scholarship which takes into account many versions of the same events, several of which taken together are needed to reveal the dynamics of the archetypal patterns depicted in the story. There are in fact no uniformly accepted single versions of many mythical events, so that we must look to each version as a variant of a larger story which reveals one possibility within the objective psyche. Any individual version comments on, or corresponds to, some aspect of a particular archetypal pattern as it is manifest within conscious life. This principle is well illustrated by the Oedipal myth, which Freud used as the underpinning of his theoretical system.

THE MYTHIC DIMENSION IN FREUD'S THEORY: THE PROBLEM OF MULTIPLE INTERPRETATIONS

If one remembers the numinosity and magnetism involved in archetypal experience for an adult, one can imagine how compelling must be the fantasy, desire or image the archetype produces in the child's mind – only mythical or fairy-tale imagery could convey its magical quality. I believe that this is the reason that Freud instinctively and correctly turned to myth to try to convey the intensity of the child's feelings. In fact he referred to instinct theory as 'our mythology'. Here began the problems associated with the use of myth as a method of describing psychodynamics. In particular, scholars have always struggled with the degree of correspondence of Freud's theory to the actual myth he used to delineate it. Such was the personal power of one aspect of the Oedipal myth for him that he used a single archetypal strand of a complex story to buttress his entire theory of motivation. Steele (1982) points out how Freud's interpretation of myth in general, also seen in Freud's *Totem and Taboo*, was based purely on his understanding of the Oedipal story and the tenets of his system. In a circular way he used each of these to prove the other correct. He understood several myths from the viewpoint of one theme of one myth. Steele feels that Freud's work on mythology is flawed by the fact that he only finds what he sets out to prove, using Western anthropological accounts of totemic cultures and not the myths themselves.

Jung objected to a purely sexual interpretation of the stories Freud used. In 1912, as part of his disagreement with Freud, Jung pointed out the complexity of the Oedipal myth, arguing that Freud had not examined the text thoroughly enough, especially in relation to the symbol of the sphinx, a representation of the mythical Great Mother (CW 5, 265). Jung's reading highlights the prime importance of the mother in the story, and suggests that the origin of the incest prohibition is to strengthen her position in the family, in contrast to Freud's stress on the father (Hogenson 1982). Jung felt that the Oedipal story was so powerful for Freud in the particular way he used it because that was *his* personal myth. This is a key observation. The structure of myth reflects the deep structures of the unconscious, so that mythology reflects psychological truths, or the dynamics of the Self in relation to the self. Mythic characters personify intrapsychic processes, but there are many characters and plots in any story on which attention can be focused, and only certain of them pertain to the individual self, while they can all be found within the larger Self. This helps to explain why different observers select different themes on which to focus; we are drawn to aspects of the story that resonate personally.

The differences which lie between Freud and Jung in the interpretation of the Oedipal myth are understandable in view of the different childhood backgrounds of the two men. Freud's father was most powerful to him, while for Jung, mother filled this role. This change of emphasis illustrates how the same story contains many intertwined archetypal themes, and in fact has no single, fixed meaning except to the fundamentalist. Many other interpretations of the Oedipal myth have been offered. Stein (1984) pointed out that the story is one of an unconscious neurotic with disturbed parents, and not that of a normal child. Later Kohut (1982, p. 405) also pointed out that Oedipus was a rejected child, and used the myth of Odysseus' bond to his son Telemachus to demonstrate his own thesis that at a deeper level than intergenerational conflict lies intergenerational love, support and bonding, which is the 'true and nuclear essence of humanness'. A family therapist might use the Oedipal theme to illustrate the problem of being a child in the family of the anxious, hitherto childless Jocasta and Laius. The Adlerian would surely note that because of his swollen feet, Oedipus probably had organ inferiority. Kaufmann (1979) noted that the incest motif is only incidental to the main theme of the story; Oedipus does not really desire incest, nor does he intend to kill his father, so that the meaning of the story is that it is impossible to escape one's fate. (Other amplifications are possible; see Mullahy, 1948.)

In his critique of Freud's use of the Oedipal myth, Altschule (1965, p. 179) notes that it is common in many mythologies to see father–son conflict in situations in which the two do not know each other's identity, but that no Greek myth mentions castration of a son by a father (p. 184), as Freud's theory requires. Altschule points out that the usual meaning ascribed to Oedipus by classical scholars is that he represents the solver of riddles. He notes that Freud rejected the idea of an Electra complex (Electra was her mother's rival for the love of her father) and repressed the idea of an Orestes complex (Orestes, with the help of his sister Electra, murdered his mother). However, according to Altschule (p. 185) there is one mythical situation that actually resembles the Freudian concept. The Egyptian god Set, the personification of evil, in the form of a hippopotamus, murdered his father and raped his mother. Therefore Altschule sarcastically suggests that the real name of what Freud described should be the 'hippopotamus complex'. Altschule makes this suggestion in order to ridicule Freud's procedure. But in so doing he confuses the method with the result. Rather than totally discrediting the value of mythical amplification, Altschule simply provides us with an archetypal image of certain complex psychodynamics as they are depicted within a particular myth. And if we try to follow his suggestion of a 'hippopotamus complex', it becomes at least as ambiguous as that of Freud. The use of the mythologem of the hippopotamus illustrates the ambivalent and polysemous nature of the archetype. Set appeared as a hippopotamus, but this animal also represented Tauret, or Ta-Urt (Budge, 1969, vol. ii, p. 285), the usually benevolent Goddess or Great Mother of Egyptian mythology, who according to some Egyptian accounts could appear as the female counterpart of Set (Budge, vol. ii, p.359). The hippopotamus Goddess was generally beneficent, but as the story suggests also had a destructive aspect. To further complicate this theme, the chief opponent of Set was the hippopotamus Goddess Neret, a form of Isis, whose duty was to restrain Set's evil influence (Budge, vol. ii, p. 249). These unexpected twists and turns of the story perfectly illustrate how difficult it is to assign a fixed meaning to any mythical image – as soon as one goes into it in any depth, the story opens out into a new vista. Or, the Self contains more possibilities than we realize.

MYTHIC ELEMENTS IN THE INDIVIDUAL PSYCHE

The psychoanalytic attitude to myth can usefully be contrasted with that of the religious approach to the psyche, which sees myth, in Jung's (1965, p. 340) words, as 'the revelation of a divine life in man'. I understand this remark of Jung to refer to myth as a mirror of the workings of the objective psyche, living within us at an unconscious substratum of the personality. This mythical level becomes visible in the presence of a sufficient degree of either suspension or fragmentation of the usual structures of the self, as in dreams or psychosis. An important corollary is that conscious beliefs, such as those of psychological theory, science, politics or religious dogma often carry out a mythical or religious function for the believer, and are connected to deep structural needs within the personality.

It has long been axiomatic in Jungian circles that the occurrence of myth-like or fairy-tale-like imagery in a dream or fantasy provides a valuable tool in the armamentarium of the therapist. This imagery allows us to locate the individual's experience within a collective story, and to locate collective stories within the psyche of the individual. This procedure may or may not be helpful in dealing with individual sorrow, but at least allows us to see that others have had similar experiences, and that our life is part of a larger life. My experience suggests that we usually only see pieces of a myth within the individual psyche, but knowing the whole story provides us with clues to the unconscious underpinnings of a situation, and its transpersonal contents, as well as suggesting possible outcomes.

When mythical imagery enters consciousness directly, it is typically in rather raw form; it usually does so during states of severe emotional distress, at which times the therapist's ability to enter into this level of the patient's experience is very helpful. Two examples from the literature will illustrate the use of mythical sensibility to help maintain a selfobject tie during states of fragmentation. Von Franz's (1972, p. 12) report of a woman on the edge of psychosis, about to be committed to a hospital, demonstrates how understanding the patient's archetypal productions in their mythical context can help calm the patient, although not for the reason von Franz suggests. The woman in question was almost beyond contact, and unable to understand anything the therapist said. But she was able to talk about a dream in which: 'I saw an egg, and a voice said "the mother and the daughter".' At this the hitherto stymied therapist became 'as happy as could be', because she was then able to talk about creation myths which depict the rebirth of the world from the world egg, about the Eleusinian Mysteries (the Demeter–Persephone story), and how all of this indicated that all would be well. The patient thereupon became quiet, and emotional contact was made even though later she told the therapist that she had understood nothing. The helpful factor was thus not that the mythical amplification was useful in its own right – the patient was far too confused and pre-symbolic (see p. 96) to be able to use it – but the fact that the therapist was able to understand what was happening because of her grasp of the archetypal dynamics involved enabled her to calm *herself* down. By her words and demeanour, she was then able genuinely to reassure the patient that all would be well, that what was happening to her had happened before; it was not unknown, inhuman chaos, it was even part of the therapist's world. Evidently this dynamic allowed the patient to merge with the therapist's now calm psychological organization, which was enough to contain the patient's terror. In other words, an archaic idealizing transference occurred. To be complete, one might say that Demeter had found a lost and terrified Persephone and brought her home.

The second case is one reported by Jung (1965, pp. 128–130). An 18-year-old sexually abused woman, chronically hospitalized with schizophrenia, was catatonic and mute. Gradually she was able to tell Jung about a complex delusional system, in which a vampire who killed women and children lived on the moon. She planned to kill this vampire. Eventually, over the course of the therapy, at Jung's insistence she was increasingly unable to return to the moon, where she believed that life was much better than on earth. She finally grudgingly agreed that life on earth was inevitable, and apparently recovered from the psychosis. Jung felt that the humiliation of her incest had led to a compensatory delusional elevation into the mythical realm, where incest is traditionally the prerogative of divinities and royalty. (Uranus married his mother, Oceanus his sister Tethys, Chronos his sister Rhea, Zeus his sister Hera, and so on. The kings of the Nile valley were considered to be the incarnation of gods, and they were required to marry their mothers or sisters. But, in Greek mythology, mortals were punished severely by the gods for committing incest. It is not clear if the patient knew all this mythology.) After projecting the moon-demon onto Jung while working out her transference to him, she was able to reattach to everyday reality. Jung was able to empathically enter her world by means of his understanding of myth. Again we see how the therapist's grasp of the mythical level of the patient's material, combined with his appreciation for the reality of the psyche, were able to help him contain her, even though to our ears his explanation seems incomplete. He ignores the other mythologem involved, that of the vampire. The patient's delusional system reflects the fact that she had been abused by a vampire-like parent, who drained her ability to live. Her rage at this figure makes her murderous, but it is difficult to kill a vampire, who only lives in the nocturnal, lunar realm. Such amplifications would not have had much direct meaning to her while she was psychotic, and it is arguable that such states of fragmentation do not need to be cast in terms other than those resulting from the pathogenicity of the individual's childhood. But the remarkable frequency with which psychosis reveals mythical themes (see also Perry, 1974) suggests that the disintegration of the self uncovers deeper structural elements which have long been depicted by the objective psyche in mythical forms. Overall, it seems that an appreciation for mythical dynamics allows the therapist to tolerate or grasp the material produced by such patients because it gives a sense of an intelligible process at work, which provides some guide to the otherwise unintelligible.

To the psychotherapist, then, myths represent the dynamics of unconscious forces, or the way in which the psyche represents its own fundamental processes. Myth represents varying perspectives on the psyche's archetypal organizing principles at different stages and states of development. Some of these stories correspond to the dynamics of modern individuals. The story then 'means' something, or is true for that person, because his or her concerns and situation are the same as those of the story. In fact, other than dreams or psychosis, myth is often our only access to the intensity of the sheer horror, terror and, at the same time, stark truth of the archetypal levels of the psyche. The essence of ego consciousness is isolation and limitation (CW 10, 304), and because myth is so magically unlike the way 'I' think, it gives us a glimpse into a world of other-than-me which helps define my own self as separate from the unconscious. But at the same time I must relate to this deeper level of being, which gives me an idea of how the infinity of Mind lives within me. Because it gives a view of order amid chaos, in the therapeutic situation the process of identifying mythical imagery in dream and fantasy may have a centring and calming effect, which may be helpful as a set of coordinates. This process can either help us locate ourselves within the larger experience of humanity, adding depth and perspective, or it can be used to avoid or rationalize personal material. In clinical practice the work of amplification using mythical imagery is not of much help until sufficient development of the self has been done to allow it to be grounded. Premature discussion of myth in therapy is about as much use as any other premature interpretation; it cannot be used by the patient, and has the potential for causing harm. But given this caveat, it is also true that the power of story and metaphor (like art, dance or music) can bypass defensive operations and move the soul much more directly than the same idea expressed as an abstract concept or interpretation. Story resonates with those elements in the listener's unconscious to which it corresponds; it acts as a symbol which conveys the otherwise inexpressible. Hence its fascination – story carries us to the point of the situation, maintaining interest without arousing too much anxiety or mobilizing resistances.

THE EVOLUTION OF MYTH

To orthodox religious believers, the myths of their tradition represent the word of God; if they are fundamentalists, the story is taken literally. But there is evidence that myths are evolving concurrently with the evolution of consciousness. Today we find that new myths may be relevant to certain people, such as that articulated by the women's movement; the archetypal movement within the individual and the culture then correspond to each other. In such a case the evolution of the myth is not finished. This kind of development is inevitable given our need to evolve a new mythology of gender equality. Creative workers in all fields are often the channels or vehicles for the emergence of new myths. Speculatively, such individuals are being prompted by archetypal forces, which as they evolve emerge through creative people into collective consciousness. This process may be no different now than were the artistic representations and refinements of primitive stories through the psyches of Homer and Hesiod. In our field, visionary psychologists are performing this function, for example, as they try to elucidate the real meaning of masculinity and femininity, distinct from the patriarchal fiats which have been imposed on us thus far. Jung's religious writings are seen by some as the harbinger of a new religious myth, which Edinger (1984) calls the new psychological dispensation, different from those of the Old and New Testaments in its stress on the direct experience of the divine. This is the mythical model which is followed throughout this book.

THE USE OF MYTHICAL THEMES IN PSYCHOTHERAPY: AN ILLUSTRATION

The emergence of dream imagery which demonstrates the activity of the mythopoetic level of the psyche is especially seen at periods of major life transition and emotional turmoil. In order to illustrate the usefulness of a mythical sensibility in psychotherapy, I have chosen the following dream of a young professional woman. It occurred during a period of depression, during one of the busiest and most exhausting periods of her life. Even though the major themes of the dream are those of creation, at the conscious level this was a time which felt anything but creative. Such compensatory imagery is often seen during times of major rearrangement of the structures of the self. Apparently the dream is trying to compensate for the dreamer's conscious attitude of pessimism and futility about the future, as if nothing good or new would ever appear again. In spite of its obviously archetypal motifs, the dream presents an essentially personal myth, since it does not correspond exactly to any traditional creation story. Rather, the elements common to many such myths are combined or rearranged in a way which is meaningful to the dreamer. The dream incidentally demonstrates Neumann's point (1973) that creation mythology reveals a projection of psychic material in cosmogonic form, in this case the reordering of the self out of a situation of disorder. This is a dream of a new form of consciousness for the dreamer.

I am in a huge underground cavern, where there is a whole world under the surface of the earth. A sea in this underground cavern is filled with life forms at all stages of development, from amoebae to mammals that are just about to become amphibious. The sea is as thick as soup with these creatures. I am on a horse that is swimming through the sea, so that my body is somewhat submerged in the water. I feel the creatures against my legs, and I am frightened by the contact with such primitive life forms, especially the water snakes. I see ahead a small island, bathed in a golden-pink light. A naked man stands there. He is very beautiful, and I know that I am supposed to make love with him, and that he and I will bring a child into this underground world.

(1973, p. 5)

This dream conveys the sense of a 'cosmos inside a human being' (Olson, 1970, p.53). The dream demands that we try to understand what is happening in the dreamer's unconscious, trying to speak through her in a kind of 'soul speech'. In this situation, we have the choice of allowing the power of the story to speak for itself, as a just-so poem, or to become scholarly, and transfer the imagery to the language of everyday consciousness by means of the technique of amplification. I choose this latter option, a rather pedagogical approach, in order to indicate, by the very contrast it produces to the original, the extraordinary density and beauty of the primary poetry of this level of the unconscious. At the same time we will be able to see how the mythical level of the psyche is relevant to and connected with everyday reality.

Several features of the dream remind us of creation mythology. The underground cavern with its deep water suggests the womb of the Great Mother that is typical of many creation myths. In Sumerian mythology for instance, there is a space below the earth called the 'great below', where dwell the chthonic deities (Kramer, 1972, p. 41). Life seems to emerge out of this matrix, reminiscent of early mythical understanding of creation without a masculine principle. In the dream, progression occurs from this entirely feminine space towards a conscious, creative act requiring both genders. It is common for water to be represented as the source of all existence. There are many water cosmogonies (Eliade, 1958), such as the Babylonian creation myth telling of an ocean of water on which the earth later floated. Many creation stories begin with an original Mother sea, out of which land or light appear, images of the emergence of consciousness out of the unconscious. Temu, in the Egyptian pantheon, was the maternal deep or uterine abyss which gave birth to the universe (Budge, 1969). For the Sumerians too there was a primeval sea, the goddess Nammu, who produced heaven and earth (Kramer, 1972). The Babylonian creation myth starts with primal waters where Father Apsu and Mother Tiamat are initially united, suggesting a primal watery parent that contains within itself both masculine and feminine principles. Psychologically, the water creatures represent contents of the primal unconscious at different stages of development.

94

The source of the dream's golden light is unclear; it is as if the light, the land and the man belong together as a goal. Unlike the situation in Genesis, where light appears early, in the dream much has been created in the dark. This suggests that work had occurred in the dreamer's unconscious before she became aware of the creative processes within her. She is carried by her dream horse, perhaps meaning her instinctual life, acting as a psychopomp carrying her from one stage to another. The image of an island of consciousness in the sea of the unconscious is a common mythical theme (CW 8, 755). On this island she is led to a *coniunctio*, a form of creation that requires union with another, which requires emergence out of containment in the maternal depths. This is a common archetypal theme of many creation stories. Within the kind of difficult situation with which the dreamer was struggling, the psyche typically produces mythical themes which indicate the possibility of renewal. Not long after this dream, life did take on a fresh quality and the dreamer felt reborn.

In contrast to Freud's view, mythical elements in dreams do not only depict pathology, they depict the larger perspective in which we live. This perspective is also alluded to by dream symbols and images that do not necessarily form part of a collective story, but which convey a sense of depth to the individual experiencer. In the popular psychological culture, the idea of a personal myth has gained some favor. But in practice this notion can be used in a rather rigid manner, sometimes defensively. For most people, no single myth captures their entire psychology. Rather, we must look to many mythologems, or the sum of the individual's symbolic experiences, to form his or her personal myth, or his or her personal experience of participation in the life of the Self.

SYMBOL AND IMAGE

One of the main manifestations of the religious function of the psyche is the production of symbols and images, especially within myth, dreams and visions. Their full appreciation is of paramount importance to a psychological approach to religious experience. In common with all aspects of the inner life, religious feeling and experience are often best communicated symbolically and imagistic-ally or via metaphor and story. Indeed there is often no other way to think about or convey the effect of such experience – words may fail, or be misleading, and the significance or quality of the event may remain indescribable. In such a case, the image or symbol may at least locate the experience and point or allude to its meaning. Thus, the religious approach to the psyche regards symbols as inter-mediate between the Big Mind of the Self and personal consciousness. Symbols are seen as one of the ways in which the Self communicates, presumably so that the self can relate to or participate within the consciousness of the Self. Therefore we rely heavily (although not exclusively) on the elucidation of intrapsychic images and symbolic material. However, in practice there are various styles of approach to the symbol which are worth articulating since they lead to different outcomes.

First, it is important to distinguish traditional psychoanalytic uses of the term 'symbol' from those of Jungian psychology. For the personalistic psychoanalyst, 'symbol' is used in a way that refers to a 'sign' in Jungian thought – a representation of something that can be fully known. The early Freudian analysts believed that symbols resulted from unconscious, primary process activity which disguised repressed or objectionable material. In this way the symbol reduced anxiety and so is essentially defensive. In the Kleinian literature, symbol formation is related to loss and the capacity to mourn; loss stimulates a creative process which leads to the substitution of a symbolic, internal representation for what has been lost. For modern psychoanalysts, to whom the symbol also means the use of ideas or language, the capacity to symbolize represents the development of differentiated subjectivity, because it requires that there exists a subject who is able to separate him/herself from the symbol and who can distinguish the symbol from what is being symbolized (Ogden, 1990 p. 217). In other words, there is someone who experiences him/herself as aware that he or she is having particular thoughts and feelings, a subject for whom events and things can stand for each other without concretely *being* each other. Where there is inadequate self development, this level of differentiated subjectivity cannot exist. As Ogden (p. 61) describes this situation, since there is no developed self to mediate between them, at the affective level the symbol and the symbolized are indistinguishable, so that perception and interpretation are synonymous. Events then just occur, without the attribution of many layers of meaning produced by different aspects of a situation. Ogden describes this developmental difficulty using an object-relations perspective, but it is also of major relevance to Jungian work. People who have difficulty with this level of development (they are at a 'pre-symbolic' stage) cannot benefit from traditional Jungian psychotherapeutic approaches to the symbol. Their religious life tends towards concrete understanding of sacred stories, and is likely to be of a fundamentalist cast.

Not only is Jung's use of the term symbol quite distinct from psychoanalytic usage, his use in turn should be distinguished from Hillman's work on image. These approaches represent different philosophical commitments, and the therapist's approach to an individual's religious material is affected by the attitude to the symbol which he or she adopts.

For Jung (CW 9, 524), the symbol arises from the unconscious and therefore acts as a bridge between the unconscious and consciousness. Because of this bridging function, the symbol is important at the personal psychodynamic level, and also because of its ability to bring new sources of sacred imagery from the unconscious into consciousness. The individual's relationship with such material is the basis of much of his or her personal religion, regardless of which outer religion he or she adheres to. Experiences of the psyche's symbolic function have an unmistakably numinous character; at the least they stir up profound feelings, indicating the presence of the archetype to which they allude. Because it allows the experience of the sacred to enter the personal sphere, the symbol is partly accessible to knowledge and partly ineffable; it is the only way to approach something which cannot really be described (CW 11, 307) because it points to meaning beyond the level of intellectual understanding (CW 13, 397). What is revealed is beyond concepts and categories. The symbol is given, not chosen like a sign; it does not merely indicate, but allows an experience. The symbol is a kind of condensation product, which can be understood to be the place or process of contact between the human and the divine. Symbolism is a 'search for the particular points where different worlds meet and where the relation between entities belonging to different orders of things become apparent' (Daniélou, 1964, p. 3). When a theological doctrine really conveys an experience of the divine, that doctrine itself is a true symbol. For those awakened to it, and at the level of their awakening, the symbol is one of the commonest forms of hierophany. It partakes of an aspect of the divine which it renders capable of being grasped by human consciousness, and allows a relationship with the sacred dimension. The symbol awakens and directs our attention to the divine in a specifically usable way. Because the symbol also contains personally relevant psychodynamic contents, such 'downward movement' from Self to self also has the healing effect of filling in something of what is needed by the self, showing the simultaneity of the religious and the psychological.

Instead of Jung's emphasis on the symbol itself, Hillman (1977, p. 62) prefers to stress the overall context in which the symbol appears, namely the image. He draws a clear distinction between symbol and image, suggesting that symbols become images when they are precisely qualified. He believes that symbols 'tend towards universality'; that is, they are conventional and general, compared to the contextual specificity of images. Symbols are always located within a specific mood or scene, always as part of a larger image; they do not appear alone. This may be a hair-splitting distinction; the image as defined by Hillman is a specific type of symbolic manifestation. Jung himself wrote that we are conscious by means of the image, which is how the psyche depicts its own processes (CW 8, 616). In fact he suggests that 'image is psyche' (CW 13, 75).[1] Here Jung does not mean 'image' merely in the sense of a copy or representation of external reality, but more the product of the interaction of archetypal processes with sensory reality. He is in fact championing the primacy of the imagination as the fundamental reality-creator. Hillman (1983, p. 6) takes up this emphasis, suggesting that images are not *what* we see, but, following Casey (1974), are the 'means by which we see'. Hillman has eloquently elaborated the position that the image is the primary and irreducible psychological datum. (This view is not compatible with modern affect theory; the appearance of affect in babies is incontestable, but the status of image at that stage is in dispute.) This point of view holds that the image is the point of contact between inner and outer; appearance and reality are therefore identical intrapsychically. Within the imagination, the realms of imagery, subjectivity and objectivity interpenetrate (Avens, 1984). This approach suggests that, rather than the imagination being in the mind, the mind is in the imagination. That is, mind is a product of soul which is the maker of images.

William Blake was referring to this larger level of the psyche when he described the imagination as 'the body of God in man'.

Hillman's work as articulated up to this point is an amplification of Jung's adherence to the idea that the only reality we know is psychic reality (CW 8, 748; CW 13, 378). But an important difference underlies other attitudes of Jung and Hillman. Following Plato, Jung believes that the image points beyond itself, to an unknowable reality, while Hillman (1983, p. 6) suggests that the image 'has no referents beyond itself'. (For a detailed philosophical analysis of these two positions, see DeVoogd, 1977 and Avens, 1982). Hillman's view seems to minimize religious traditions which have tried to use the symbol to allude to an unknowable reality, to a larger truth expressed in humanly recognizable form. The practical difference is that Hillman rejects Jung's hermeneutical method of amplification, which requires that any given image be examined by reference to other symbol systems, just as one tries to discover the meaning of a word by studying its usage in other contexts. Hillman (1977, p. 74) feels that the clear articulation of the image itself removes this need; the image amplifies itself by restatement, or by being looked at from many points of view, which allows its deeper significance to resonate. His approach has the virtue of remaining within the field of the dream itself, and not detracting from it or making it something else. But it may prevent one from linking the individual dream with the rest of the archetypal experience of humanity, and often makes it hard to place the symbol in its overall cultural context. Because the symbol connects the experiencer with the larger experience of humanity, it crosses geographical and historical boundaries. It seems a mistake to deprive the dreamer of this vista, to which he has become entitled by the occurrence of the particular symbol within his dream.

It is crucial here to realize the broader theoretical matrix in which Hillman has embedded his ideas. He takes issue with the usual Jungian idea of the unconscious as an infinite reservoir of symbolic wisdom. He believes that the unconscious has become excessively reified. He argues that because the imaginal is always present, fantasy is always present; the dream is continuous, and part of the soul is 'continuously remembering in mythopoetic speech, continuously seeing, feeling, and hearing *sub specie aeternitas*' (Hillman, 1972, pp. 173–177). What we call the unconscious is simply our lack of awareness of the constant operation of the imaginal in our lives. But since 'lack of awareness' is a fair synonym for unconsciousness, Hillman does not seem to have made a heuristic advance, especially since an emphasis on the imaginal tends to sequester affect as a primary aspect of the soul's experience. The idea of the 'imaginal' replaces only a part of what is contained within the idea of the unconscious. Both mean realms of the psyche beyond the sphere of the known. But the imaginal and the unconscious cannot be simply equated; the term 'unconscious' also implies the memories of personal experiences which have been affectively unmanageable, and so are repressed or split off. The great danger of a focus on image alone is to produce an overintellectualized, disembodied state of mind that supports schizoid defences. If we include the importance of affect in our concept of the unconscious, we need a broader term than 'the imaginal'; it is impossible to include problems such as unconscious shame, guilt or rage within its purview.

In practice, when working with dream imagery, my personal preference is to pay as much faithful and detailed attention to the image itself as possible, but since this approach may peter out, to then continue to amplify the image in the traditional manner. However, it should be noted that both approaches are useless in the treatment of severely psychologically ill people, where only a sustaining relationship to the therapist makes a difference. When the patient is functioning presymbolically, therapy which is focused around dream images alone leads either to the patient's rage or withdrawal. The patient feels as if he or she is being ignored, or that his or her productions are of more interest than he or she is, which usually repeats the trauma of childhood. When working with a patient with a fragile or incompletely established self, the therapist's problem is to find a way, while trying to restore the self, bring it also to into a manageable relationship with the transpersonal. A human relationship may serve as a bridge to this realm, since within the transference the therapist carries, often without knowing it, transpersonal (archetypal) projections, sometimes of a very negative cast. If he or she can tolerate this situation the therapist is able to help the patient deal with the affective intensity of the manifestations of the archetype within the relationship. The patient's inability to contain intense affect is the result of selfobject failure in childhood, so that a working selfobject relationship with the therapist allows safe contact with the archetypal level of the psyche. *The therapeutic relationship thereby serves the function that the symbol serves intrapsychically.* Approaches to very fragile people based purely on the analysis of symbolic material are doomed. In the absence of a firm self the symbol is not usable. The patient cannot appreciate the symbol because he or she cannot attain any distance between him/herself, the symbol and what is symbolized; the patient experiences the symbol with no 'as if' capacity. But in the presence of firmly established, self-reflexive subjectivity, with good capacity to contain intense affect, attention to the symbol is a a gnosis-releasing factor. And *accurate* amplification of a personal dream symbol in terms of other symbol systems such as mythology does not really depart from the specificity of the image or reduce it to a concept, but makes it more usable.

Part of the success of Jung's approach to symbolic material hinges on the applicability of his comment that 'image and meaning are identical, and as the first takes shape so the latter becomes clear' (CW 8, 402). Certainly, attention to the image is the first stage of the elucidation of this meaning. But in practice the meaning may be anything but evident. The dream image or symbol usually makes no sense at all until it is worked on hermeneutically. In spite of suggestions that it is sufficient to immerse oneself in the image alone, amplification often releases affectively important content which is otherwise unavailable. Then the image may be felt as a gift, an act of grace, or it may be terrifying. The task is to render it assimilable by finding its connections to one's conscious life, or, more rarely, to discover how to assimilate one's whole life to the image, which is an experience of religious conversion.

PERSONAL AND COLLECTIVE SYMBOLS

Some symbolic experiences are only relevant to the experiencing individual. In such a case an everyday object which appears in a dream may take on an extraordinary numinosity which is shared by nobody beside the dreamer. For example, a young woman who had difficulty with her body and sexuality because of a repressive religious upbringing dreamed that she was given a communion wafer containing raisins. This dream tells her that the Dionysian element has been preserved and is also sacred. For her the raisin has true symbolic meaning, linking her with an element of Christ that she had ignored. Christ says that he is the 'true vine' (John 15: 1–5). The grape is sacrificed to make wine; that is, it represents the saving substance, or spirit. This personal symbol links spirit and body for her instead of keeping them in opposition. The capacity to link is always an important function of the symbol. For the believing Christian, the cross, which is a collective symbol with meaning to many people, has the capacity to unite such apparent opposites as God and man, death and resurrection, heaven and earth, time and eternity. For the believer, the symbol stimulates feeling, allowing personal participation in the mystery of the Christian myth. The precise meaning and impact of a symbol to each person will be a function of his or her level of spiritual attainment, but will always include elements which cannot be fully verbalized. This is because the symbol is not a simple category, but is an expression of the ineffability of the archetype. It is not the archetype itself, but a window into it.

Hall (1979) noted three categories of dreams which contain religious symbols.

1 Dreams in which collective religious imagery appears but which are contextualized individually. For example, the appearance of the Virgin Mary or other goddess figure may appear as a reparative dream to a person who had significant maternal deprivation.
2 Dreams in which religious symbols are seen which do not belong to the dreamer's own tradition. For example, a man who knew nothing of Egyptian mythology dreamed that he was being threatened by a dangerous Nazi, and was saved by the appearance of the Egyptian god Anubis.
3 Numinous imagery which is totally idiosyncratic.

THE PROBLEM OF REIFICATION

One of Hillman's (1977, p. 68) useful warnings about symbols is that they have become 'stand-ins for concepts'. This means that although Jung (CW 6, 815) stressed the ultimate unknowability of the symbol and the danger of reducing it to a sign, symbols may no longer be so mysterious; we know what they mean. This warning is important and points out the common problem of missing the experience of mystery when we reduce commonly seen symbols to dogmatic, fixed or dictionary meanings. For example, the ocean in a dream is almost always seen as an image of the objective psyche. But in practice, we also see much new, rich symbolic material which does not lend itself to instant reduction as if it were a sign for what is known. Awe and mystery may still surround the individual symbol or the total image acting symbolically. Hillman's warning is not to reify the archetype into finitude lest we become psychological fundamentalists. If we do try to freeze the symbol into a static entity, we do so because of the anxiety it inspires. Literalizing the image is a narcissistic defence against its numinosity.

THE THERAPIST'S ATTITUDE TO THE SYMBOL

In spite of our interest in the evocative power of the image or symbol, the therapist must remember that he or she can never fully understand them. Ultimately the therapist is only able respectfully to witness them, carefully help the patient to appreciate them if he or she does not realize their significance, and assist in their integration into daily life. Often this includes pointing out that a particular image has religious significance for the individual, who may not realize the importance of personal symbols. To be truly open to the symbol we must not prejudge it by knowing too much, although we cannot help having preconceived ideas about imagery such as the squared circle, whose meaning is relatively well understood (CW 12, 167).[2] Like the symbol of the cross, this too may eventually become a collective symbol because of its antiquity and frequency. In order to avoid the fixity of meanings that preconceptions may produce, close adherence to the specificity of the image, its context and its relationship to the rest of the psychological life of the subject is important. The image is sacred and work on its elucidation is sacramental; the image is a sign of grace. Another problem of which we must be conscious occurs when we try to force the image into the confines of a psychodynamic theory. For example, when mythical imagery is explained as the representation of drives which have been either perverted or spiritualized, symbols such as the lion or bull simply depict the tendency towards domination, while the goat or pig represent sexual perversion (Diel, 1980, p. 80). We cannot understand or explain religious imagery or experience in any such absolute sense; these symbols contain much more profound meaning. Rather than reduce them in this way, the therapist must help awaken or nurture the patient's own symbolic faculty and his or her appreciation of the reality of the psyche.

Certain therapeutic attitudes help in the appreciation of symbolic material. The belief that meaning can be found in the patient's material, in Jung's words, requires a 'definite view of the world which assigns meaning to events, whether great or small, and attaches to this meaning a greater value than bare facts' (CW 8, 817–819). This approach is opposed to a view which places major emphasis on facts alone and subordinates meaning to these facts. Another important attitude eschews an excessively rational approach, since the 'extension and intensification of rational consciousness . . . leads us further away from the sources of the symbols and, by its ascendency, prevents us from understanding them' (CW 11, 293). To be too analytical leads to a process of despiritualization, which has happened within psychology as well as within some theologies. Our therapeutic approach attempts to undo this historical process by circling back in order to recapture the importance of the symbol.

Our endeavour to give religious value to the individual's personal symbolic life helps him with various difficulties. For instance, the traditional Judaeo-Christian images may no longer perform a true symbolic function. The hermeneutical techniques of analytical psychology are particularly valuable for the understanding of personal symbols, which flow as a constant source of sacred imagery. This is of great importance to those who are not 'the happy possessors of faith', as Jung (CW 11, 148) describes them; they are people for whom 'the light has gone out, the mystery has faded and is dead'. Jung (CW 9, i, 28) felt that the loss of the capacity of religious institutions to mediate meaning and the loss of the power of traditional symbols are responsible for much of our spiritual poverty. But new sources of spiritually important experience are available because of the capacity of the unconscious to generate religious imagery. If this imagery is numinous, it may 'seize consciousness' (CW 9, i, 49), but if it is not, the recognition of its importance may be lost. Here a sensitivity to archetypal forms is an invaluable therapeutic skill. Because much of the new imagery we see does not assume Judaeo-Christian forms, it can only be understood by recourse to much wider symbol systems, such as other mythologies or alchemy. The entire Jungian corpus on the amplification of symbols speaks to this task. If the unconscious makes powerful demands whose religious nature is not understood, the result may be 'politico-social delusional systems' (CW 9, i, 49), or psychological systems to which people adhere with religious fervour.

THE NEED FOR INTERPRETATION AND THE PROBLEM OF PSYCHOSIS

Here arises the often asked question: how important is it for the symbol (or the dream) to be interpreted and understood? According to Jung, although conscious understanding is important (CW 10, 732), the experience of the symbol alone may be valuable enough (CW 7, 324). A related, more serious problem is the attribution or projection of *unjustified* meaning onto the event. This is particularly evident in psychotic reactions to numinous imagery, or when the therapist interprets a dream exclusively in terms of a theoretical commitment which actually obscures its meaning. The significance we derive from symbolic experience may be truly given or it may be delusional, and we do not wish to use the symbol in ways that further remove people from the world. The psychotic in particular may be unable to distinguish fully the events of the dream from daytime awareness; for him or her, the dream may aquire an intensity that makes it feel more real than a dream.

Numinous dreams may presage psychosis, and indeed the content of the dream may then become incorporated into the psychosis. In such a case, the therapeutic task is to help the individual differentiate himself from the dream world. To distinguish psychotic from non-psychotic interpretations of numinous imagery, we need traditional diagnostic skills, clear study of the setting and mode of the event and an evaluation of the condition of the experiencer, his or her mental state, thought processes and clarity of perception.

Our dilemma here is that either the events of our lives are meaningless, which is the antithesis of the religious attitude, or the accuracy of our hermeneutical skills is critical. It is my opinion that it is important to decipher symbolic events as correctly as possible. The correct interpretation of a symbol allows us to see a direction in life that is not otherwise visible, and opens up new vistas of understanding. This problem of interpretation is another critical aspect of the Jung–Hillman debate. The 'pure' archetypal psychologist might object to any attempt to find meaning hermeneutically, by the technique of amplification, preferring an aesthetic approach to the symbol. Hillman (1979, p. 143) believes that: 'significance is given directly with reality; all things as images make sense'. But in practice this is an unrealistic attitude; not many people are likely to be helped by the abandonment of interpretation, especially those whose reality is so intolerable that perceptual distortion is needed for them to survive psychologically. The problem of how to use intrapsychic imagery for the benefit of people with severe psychopathology highlights the issue of interpretation and the question of the relative value of therapy which focuses on relationship versus the classical Jungian emphasis on dreams. For such patients, merely to savour the image is to remain entrapped in their illness. Severely psychologically ill people often find that the images of their illness make no sense at all, and attention to them without good therapeutic containment by means of a relationship may produce further pain, hopelessness and despair, for instance, when their dreams depict unmanageable horror. To confine the focus of therapy in such cases to an excursion into the poetic basis of mind would be an affront to such a patient. One patient who had such an experience with an archetypally oriented therapist said to me: 'Please don't talk to me about images, I'm just trying to hold myself together.' For such a person, healing may emerge in the context of a solid therapeutic relationship in which attention is also paid to the imaginal. But it is hard to 'stick to the image' without such a relationship, which can become more important than the most exotic intrapsychic images. This is not to say that the dreams are of no use in such cases; they tell us what is going on, in an overview. But they cannot be the sole focus of the therapy. Problems of the transference have a very different feeling quality than the aesthetics of dream metaphor, and it is easy for the therapist to use an exclusively imaginal approach to avoid the difficult interpersonal issues raised when dealing with troubled people. Hillman's approach requires the patient to be able to take for granted that he or she exists and will not fall apart at any moment. Images do not supply the necessary glue in such cases, but holding connections to people may do so. Even though the borderline person may constantly dream of magnificent mandala imagery, this material, though understandable as the result of the psyche's compensatory function, is not powerful enough to prevent constant fragmentation anxiety. In sum, the approaches of both Hillman and Jung can be helpful in the presence of a cohesive self, but not in the presence of serious self-state pathology.

6

A PSYCHOLOGICAL VIEW
OF SOME TRADITIONAL
RELIGIOUS IDEAS

From the psychological perspective, any religious tradition reveals a particular image of the Self, and there are many such images. Religious traditions are also based on particular experiences of the objective psyche, which have become clothed in particular images and concepts in order that the personal psyche may relate to them. In his writing on religion, Jung's approach is to expose the archetypal themes which underlie the teaching of particular traditions. We tend to associate many traditional notions, such as those of redemption and salvation, with the long-formalized structures of established religions. But these ideas are universal in their applicability and importance when removed of any particular bias and seen simply as important intrapsychic motifs. Themes such as those of redemption and salvation have persisted precisely because they are of archetypal significance; they make a structural difference within the psychology of the individual. If their mediation to the individual is not restricted to any prescribed format, many people will be seen to participate in archetypal experiences that would otherwise be the proprietary claim of one church. For example, the concept of the sacrament is that of a sign, or channel, allowing an inner experience of the sacred, or of divine grace, clearly something of great importance. But for many people the traditional Christian sacraments, such as the eucharist, no longer perform their historical role in mediating the experience of the sacred. Some people experience the divine in different ways, and for them different sacraments are needed. For example, now that we recognize that the incarnation of the divine is a phenomenon that is more widespread than was formerly thought, any form of such incarnation, such as the human body or the body of the earth, may become sacramental.

Similarly, new human problems, or a new understanding of old problems, require new modes of redemption. In its traditional sense, redemption implied sin defined as the contravention of a list of authoritative rules. But today we require redemption from more fundamental causes of human suffering, such as our narcissism. It is increasingly evident that this is often what prevents us from real caring for others, and it is often the root cause of social evils such as war. A new attitude to such problems, based on a new psychodynamic understanding of them, leads to new forms of their redemption.

Earlier I discussed the rationale for the idea that the manifestations of any archetype, and hence of the intrapsychic sacred, include our psychopathology or our complexes. We must include these problems in any psychologically oriented discussion of religious themes; our need for redemption and salvation is intimately linked with our pathology. Some traditional ideas about these archetypal needs reveal attempts to bypass psychopathology, for example, by suggesting that forgiveness is sufficient. But the religious approach to the psyche sees psychopathology itself as a container of the seeds of redemption and salvation. Because psychopathology can lead to the experience of the Self, it is one medium which allows us to become aware of the sacredness of the psyche.

THE SACRAMENTAL NATURE OF THE PSYCHE

Dourley (1981, p. 31) defines a sacrament as: 'that reality through which the holy makes its presence felt'. Since the divine affects us in the depths of the psyche, from where the numinosum emerges, the psyche has sacramental aspects. Any intrapsychic image or symbol capable of expressing the experience of the numinosum is sacramental. The need for communion with the divine seems to be essential; much yearning for substances, material things, or relationships is actually a disguised form of the wish for this contact. Whether an officially sanctioned church ritual, a healing relationship or a spontaneous image from the unconscious, the sacrament is whatever fosters the needed self–Self connection. But for our consciousness to appreciate a symbol which is new to us, we must have a symbolic attitude, an appreciation that the symbol allows a connection with our human level of reality and that of the objective psyche. No sacrament will work unless it is emotionally significant; defence or resistance prevent the symbol from having its effects.

This attempt to view the psyche as sacramental is best seen in the context of an attempt to view the whole of the natural world as sacramental; in this view psyche and nature are not separate entities. The relationship between them can be imagined in various ways. Psyche may be the conscious experience of nature, or may be nature conscious of itself, or the two may be poles of an undivided supraordinate unity. The important point is that to assert the unity of psyche and nature is to repair a split which has bedevilled our culture. Unlike pre-technological societies which viewed the earth as sacred, in our culture an apparent gap has emerged between the spiritual and the material realms.[1] By contrast, Jung's model of the psyche, because of its stress on the numinosum, allows a sacramental understanding of the psyche as coextensive with nature, in which the divine is felt to be immanent by virtue of experiences of the Self. When we experience the numinosum in the wilderness, we are not 'projecting' onto nature something that is actually inside our selves; we are experiencing the reality of the continuity of the Self across the barrier of the skin. The structure of the self, which includes both our psychology and physiology, is determined by the same archetypal or spiritual dynamics as those which obtain in nature at large.

PSYCHOLOGICAL FORMS OF SALVATION

Central to my methodology in this section is the idea that standard religious terms such as salvation and sacrament can be examined psychologically by means of a psychodynamic study of their various traditional theological usages or their original mythical contexts. This procedure elucidates the psychologically important commonalities of these terms, free from dogmatic overlay. A depth psychological approach offers the possibility of a unified understanding of those fundamental psychological needs which have hitherto been provided by established religions in the guise of dogma.

The idea of salvation is so ubiquitous as to be archetypal. Most religious traditions have some concept of a supreme good which is offered on condition that certain conditions are fulfilled. Sometimes salvation requires faith, sometimes works. Within Christianity, salvation involves being freed from evil or sin and allowed closeness to God through belief in the saving power of Christ. Judaism stresses the critical importance of adherence to divine law and that the Messianic era promises final redemption from suffering. Islam requires submission to God in the carrying out of obligations; the Buddhist seeks the attainment of Nirvana or Buddhahood; the Hindu seeks release through knowledge of the reality of Atman-Brahman and its identity with the self. William James (1902/1958, p. 383) has captured the reason that salvation is such a widespread human need. He suggests that it is required because of a feeling of uneasiness, produced by the sense that there is 'something wrong about us as we naturally stand'. Thus we have a need to be saved from this wrongness by 'proper connection with the higher powers'. The individual also feels that there is a 'better part of him, even though it may be but a helpless germ'. Salvation for James implies that the individual is able to identify his real being with the 'germinal higher part of himself'. This occurs as we become conscious that this higher part is 'coterminous and continuous with More of the same quality, which is operative in the universe outside of him, and which he can keep in working touch with'. James points out that all theologies agree that the 'More' exists, although they disagree as to its nature. All of this is an early way of recognizing that, in Kohut's formulation, our tragedy is that the self often forms incompletely. Within our incompleteness lies our psychopathology and the place in which we need healing or saving. Consonant with the etymology of the word (from the Latin *salveo*, meaning to be well) Jung (CW 12, 35) equates salvation with the process of healing. This is a particularly psychological understanding of the meaning of salvation, which is the only tenable one for the psychotherapist. It is quite different from religious ideas about salvation which refer to being saved from sin or death, or that one is specially chosen by God. These are doctrinal propositions that the psychologist is in no position to affirm or deny from within our own discipline. We cannot know whether they are literally true or whether they simply represent mythical or metaphorical solutions to human needs and fears that cannot be taken literally. But we do know when healing is in progress, using criteria such as the appearance of intrapsychic symbols of a Centre which tend towards the re-establishment of the wholeness of the personality (CW 12, 200–202), or when the Self can be experienced as a living entity without fear, or if the self becomes more cohesive and vital. It is the thesis of the religious approach to the psyche that healing is produced by contact with the Self; this is James's 'higher part' or 'More' with which the self is coterminous.[2] Jung (CW 9, ii, 304) also speaks of salvation in terms of the capacity to unite conflicting intrapsychic opposites via the symbol. This is a compatible approach, since the presence of conflict indicates an area of incompleteness of the self. It is only necessary to remember here that salvation, or healing of our incompleteness, is mediated by relationships as well as by the symbol.

SIN AND REDEMPTION UNDERSTOOD ARCHETYPALLY

The idea of 'redemption' has a particular psychological meaning which can be completely separated from the notion of a previous 'fall' in the Christian dogmatic sense. The archetypal meaning of redemption can be gleaned by exploring the mythical underpinnings of the idea, which point to its original psychological referents before they became overlaid with dogmatic accretions. By also evaluating this dogma itself through a psychological lens, we glimpse the intrapsychic difficulties with which its originators struggled. To discern the intrapsychic structures to which the idea of redemption refers, we may regard the Bible as we would any mythical text, interpreting it as a collective symbol rather than taking it literally. Here it must be remembered that a psychological comment on such a mythical text may illuminate it, but has no particular bearing on its truth or falsity as it is understood theologically. But given certain limitations,[3] the dynamic psychologist has to fall back on the probability that generally accepted texts and their subsequent elaborations refer to important strands of collective psychology, because the stories have been told sufficiently often that what has been preserved has been considered to be true. Bearing this in mind, we can read the myths to see how any constituent archetypal theme is related to psychodynamic factors which operated within the psyche of those who are attracted to the myth. These factors are amplified by a study of the dogma which has gathered around the original story. For example, within classical, dogmatic Christian theology, redemption is tied to the sacrifice of Jesus, and it is held that we can only be in relationship with God by means of this sacrifice.[4] For many people this is a questionable proposition because they deny the *invariable* connection between divinity and blood. These individuals have a different image of the Self, a different way of experiencing it, and so require a different myth.

Related to the theme of sacrifice is another psychologically problematic dogmatic assertion, namely that, as Christ is identified with God, the whole of humanity is identified with Adam, who rejected God, so we are all sinful. The Self image implied here dictates that our relation to God must then be purchased by the suffering of Jesus. This is clearly a very particular model of the relationship between man and God. It represents a perspective which may not do justice either to Jesus himself or to the real profundity of his story. Nevertheless, for many generations, Augustine's (*City of God*) outline of the story held sway: creation, fall, incarnation, passion, crucifixion, atonement, resurrection and last judgement. But when we read the actual story of Jesus in the gospels, we find no compelling evidence that his ministry can be read only in this way. Other constructions about the meaning of his life are possible. Several questions therefore occur to the dynamic psychologist. Why is it that the early Christian tradition used the mythical theme of the fall of man to explain death, toil and pain only in terms of disobedience, leading to our separation from God, as if God were a strict parent or lawyer? How has it happened that all of mankind is somehow included in this rebellion, as if 'Adam' refers to humanity in perpetuity? Why has sin been singled out as such a major determinant of the relationship between man and God? From a depth psychological perspective, the problem seems to arise from the particular Self image of the early Church fathers. Apparently, a complex within the psyches of the formulators of these ideas was projected onto their notion of the divine. Their Self image was persecutory, punitive and promoted depressive anxiety. The turmoil that we see in religious life today reflects what happened to Job: a new Self image is again trying to emerge, part of the long evolution of religious consciousness.

Lest this scenario of the large-scale projection of a neurotic Self image seems too fantastic to be the basis for an entire religious system, consider the attempt to include all of humanity as inevitably sinful. At one stroke, this accounts for all human misery and its alleviation.[5] The clinician is familiar with this kind of thinking in patients with severe depressions, and also in the presence of guilt-driven obsessional ruminations. Fortunately, other models of relationship to God or to Jesus can be conceived of, for example, that of Eckhart, which stresses that Christ came to remind us of our divinity (see Fox, 1981). But Paul had the advantage of proximity to the events, and his point of view has held sway. Even though he also stressed the importance of love (1 Cor. 13–14), which would seem to be an infinitely more important and evolved human attribute, the emphasis for many of his followers seemed to be on the problem of sin. This focus attracted like-minded personalities, and even today attempts to define spirituality in terms of creation instead of fall are considered heretical in some quarters, a process which is destined to be as successful as the suppression of Galileo. Throughout Church history, there has continued an extraordinary readiness to see all mankind from the perspective of sin; humanity is either rebellious, stubborn or excessively proud – typical Old Testament complaints – or is seen as 'missing the mark' with regard to faith (1 Tim. 6: 20–21). In the presence of the enormous amount of emphasis on love found in other areas of the New Testament, it is impossible to avoid interpreting such dogmatic emphasis on sin as the result of individual psycho-dynamic factors. Given such preoccupation with sin, the need for redemption is obvious. In order to discern the dynamic underpinnings of this preoccupation, we are first led to try to understand further the meaning of sin from a psychological perspective. To do so reveals the change in the image of the Self that has been brought about by the depth psychological approach.

Sin: its psychodynamic origins

Since the development of depth psychology, there have been many attempts to analyse the meaning of sin in terms of neurosis. As I have reviewed on pp. 191–194, much behaviour that is traditionally seen as sinful, such as sexual acting out, can be understood in terms of its psychodynamic origins. Of course, the moral theologian may argue that this understanding does not necessarily mean that the behaviour is not also sinful. But to the dynamic psychologist, the traditional emphasis on the pervasive or ubiquitous presence of sin sounds as if it includes the projection of a sense of personal defect or shame onto humanity as a whole. This projection has usually been based on an anthropomorphic, idealized notion of the requirements of the divine for human beings, where the divine represents a super ego or father figure. In other words, the Self image implied by such theology is harsh and paternalistic in the old sense. To the extent that sin *can* be equated with psychopathology, the idea that sin estranges one from the divine cannot possibly be true. The premise of this book, based on clinical practice, is that any emotional difficulty is seen as an attempt of the Self to draw the individual towards greater Self-consciousness. One way to the experience of the Self is by means of our psychopathology, since an archetypal strand of the Self is found within it. The religious approach to the psyche thereby allows a different Self image. The emphasis on estrangement found in the old image probably originates in the fact that, in childhood, loss of connection to an important selfobject leads to a sense of personal badness, which can easily be projected onto the relationship with God; the divine as father (or mother) will withdraw his love from me if I am bad. It is of course argued that sacred texts which forbid particular behaviour that is defined as sinful are inspired by God. From the archetypal point of view this makes sense; they are mythical statements with archetypal underpinnings. Perhaps the most vivid example of such a mythical notion of the Self is the idea of original sin.

Building on the idea of the fall, Christian theology developed the doctrine of original sin so that everyone would require a saving grace (Titus 2: 11), only attainable through Jesus. This requires that Adam's sin be transmitted from generation to generation. To justify this doctrine, Aquinas suggested that, because human nature is continuous with that of Adam, it has been deprived of its original divine endowments because of Adam's behaviour. Adam condemned all men, while Jesus saved all. This particular line of development of the original story is so forced when viewed against the actual life of Jesus that it must be understood in terms of the personal psychopathology of its originators and of those who accepted it. For example, according to Augustine, the necessary transmission of sin occurs by virtue of sexuality, which is inherently sinful. This is an understandable projection in view of the difficulty Augustine is known to have had with sexuality, so it is no surprise that he would seize on Paul's writing in this way. We may infer that 'Paul' (at least the writer to whom Paul's name is attributed) had some similar difficulty, a common affliction among intensely patriarchal men with mother problems.[6] Modern theologians have sought to modify the notion of original sin by suggesting that it simply represents our human heritage, which makes us heir to sin because we are all bound by prevailing cultural problems. But this only transfers the reason for our 'badness' to some other, inevitable and external, cause. It perpetuates the projection of the complex onto society instead of dealing with those aspects of it that represent an intrapsychic problem.

Another change in the prevailing Self image, with regard to the problem of the violence within it, can be detected in the transition from the Old to the New Testament as depicted in the story of the crucifixion. There is a close historical association between religion and human sacrifice; some of the early Goddess religions seem to have been particularly bloody. But a paradox exists in the idea that the God of love of the New Testament still requires a bloody, painful sacrifice. This mythologem has a scapegoat quality, as if Jesus has to bear the burden of our own split-off shadow. But as Girard (1979) notes, God is finally revealed as taking the part of the sacrifice rather than simply demanding it, as was the case in previous traditions. God is said to bear this burden as an act of love towards mankind. This mythical imagery may therefore represent an attempt to unify the tension within the Self image that was evolving at the time of the life of Jesus, since he is a bridge between the old and the new dispensations. Wink (1992) emphasizes that Christ does not just reveal the scapegoat dynamic for what it is, and does not just represent the end of sacrificing, but he is also the *final* sacrifice. The early Self image demanded blood; this violence may depict the assumption that God is as violent as humanity. Jesus bears this divine violence as a substitute for mankind, but, at the same time, since he is the incarnate divine, God himself suffers as he has previously demanded suffering. Today, conscious as we are of our own violence, our Self image is different again. It is difficult for us to continue to imagine that the divine literally requires a blood sacrifice. This mythologem implies that God is angry and requires appeasement, a clear anthropomorphism presumably related to unconscious infantile fantasies of an enraged parent, perpetuated by constant referral to the divine as Mother or Father. We thereby contaminate our idea of the divine with our rage at our personal parents. Shades of Freud emerge here: we do have a parent transference onto the divine. Resolution of this transference allows us to experience the Self in a less prejudiced form. We can now conceive of the relationship of human and divine in other terms. Our conscious awareness of our frailties means that they do not need to be projected onto our Self image. We can carry our own wounds, with the realization that they both derive from the Self and are healed by the Self. Our struggle now is for conscious participation in this process rather than for vicarious sacrifice; each individual must make his or her *own* sacrifice as demanded by the Self.

Thus far I have tried to show that the traditional reasons for the archetype of redemption may not now apply, because the psychology of the culture has changed. But the need for redemption itself has not disappeared, it has merely changed its form. Neither can the religiously oriented psychotherapist altogether dispense with some analogue to the idea of sin; to do so would tend to deny the reality of evil. But, rather than using sin to refer to the breaking of official rules of behaviour, we can use a precise, psychologically sophisticated definition. For example, sin can be understood as behaviour which is not in keeping with the truth of the self as revealed by the Self, or behaviour which arises out of intrapsychic splits which represent infantile selfobject needs. In such a case, the Self reveals itself in psychopathology. A psychological understanding of redemption follows from this argument, namely the healing of such splits within ourselves. Jung (CW 18, 1687) notes that the archetype of the Redeemer is present in all of us, which is why the story of a Messiah is so important. Christianity insists that redemption is only possible by means of belief in Christ, but practical psychotherapeutic experience suggests that the archetype of redemption may manifest in other ways.

Within the psychotherapeutic framework, the need for redemption arises because we have experienced parental archetypes negatively, and this and other experiences of the dark side of the spirit require redemption. The shadow, or unintegrated, split-off parts of the personality, can be redeemed by greater consciousness. For it to be authentic, the form that this redemption takes must be affectively powerful and psychologically true for the individual. Psychologically, redemption can also be understood according to the different meanings of the word. If we stop projecting the archetype onto an external Messiah, we can pay our own 'ransom' by means of the suffering we have carried and the consciousness it has bought. We can re-deem, or re-judge, a situation based on a new evaluation of its unconscious underpinnings, or based on a new experience of archetypal reality, perhaps of the kind allowed by psychotherapy. Although we are not used to thinking of the operations of the divine in psychotherapeutic terms, redemption does occur within the process of therapy. It happens as the experience of the positive side of the spirit, as the numinosum, as the *agape* found within the relationship with the therapist, or in any manifestation of the Self. Shades of the old 'suffering servant' usage also remain; when the transference is negative, and the therapist is painfully exposed to hatred, rage and envy, the therapist pays a part of the price for the redemption of his or her patient by suffering with or sometimes even on behalf of the patient. But this suffering also adds to the Self-consciousness of the therapist, which is a gift that the patient brings.

SPIRIT AND SOUL IN PSYCHOTHERAPEUTIC PRACTICE

A further example of the way in which depth psychology provides its own understanding of traditional religious ideas is provided by a consideration of the meaning of the terms 'spirit' and 'soul' as these elements appear within psychotherapy. These words already have a rich history within analytical psychology, where their usage is often quite different from their traditional meaning within theology and metaphysics. Before pointing out some of the ways these principles operate in psychotherapeutic practice, I want to suggest some operationally useful ways of using these words, given that they cannot be defined rigorously.

Spirit

It is an axiom of depth psychology that the objective psyche is itself ordered and is also the deepest source of order, value, motivation and purpose within the personality. Our perception of meaningful design in the psyche is gained from attention to regularities seen in dreams, complexes and synchronicities. 'Spirit' is our name for the psyche's underlying design principle. Like all of nature, the psyche operates lawfully and not randomly; the concept of the archetype refers to this lawfulness perceived as intrapsychic patterns (CW 8, 841). Any archetype reveals the workings of one particular manifestation of spirit; the term 'Self' implies the totality of all of the manifestations of spirit. Just as any natural law (such as that of gravity) extends beyond the person, such psychological order is transpersonal; the archetype is not simply in the body, it includes the body in its larger field of action. Direct contact with one of these psychological ordering fields is felt as an experience of the numinosum. Spirit implies transcendence of the human, something which comes to us from beyond ego consciousness, which is felt as other than myself. It imposes levels or forms of order that may not be discernible by human consciousness except retrospectively, as we look at our history.

The essential nature of this transpersonal reality is a problem for theology or philosophy, and not for psychology; its nature must remain speculative to the extent that it is not directly experienced. Jung believed that there might be a 'supraindividual' (CW 8, 316) or a 'transpsychic reality immediately underlying the psyche' (CW 8, 600). This seems to be synonymous with his idea of the psychoid realm. This word was borrowed from Eugen Bleuler, who used it to refer to subcortical brain functions concerned with biological adaptation, which express a 'quasi-psychic' unity of both somatic and psychic processes (CW 8, 840). In Jung's own usage, 'psychoid' refers to a postulated level of unity prior to the differentiation of what we experience separately as matter and spirit. The psychoid contains a level of the archetype in its unknowable 'suchness'(CW 8, 840). The concept of the psychoid level is an analogous concept to the theological idea of the unrepresentable Godhead, prior to manifestation, about which nothing can be said. Although totally experience-distant, the concept is useful epistemologically in order to describe the putative origin of the archetype or the Self prior to its movement into body as affect or into psyche as image. But we do not solve the problem of the design principle in the psyche by merely naming it. One of the inevitable weaknesses of the Jungian literature is that the terms 'Self' or 'archetype' are used as if they were an explanation for a variety of phenomena, but to use an unknown entity as an explanatory principle is really not very helpful, except descriptively. Because the nature of the archetype itself is unknowable, we do not know its relationship to what is represented within the mind (CW 8, 417); the archetype itself arises from the psychoid realm and not the psychic.

When the psychoid realm manifests itself, it does so as either matter or spirit, which appear to us as discrete qualities. But, as the psyche's underlying principle of order and structure, the archetype itself must bridge and include both – hence Jung's metaphor of the archetype as a spectrum, one end of which is red and the other blue. The red or somatic end includes the archetypal affects (see below) which are the great organizers, disorganizers and communicators of the psyche. An exclusive emphasis on image alone, which is the blue end of the spectrum, is one-sided. To stress the archetypal or spiritual origin of affect is one way of appreciating the essentially spiritual nature of the body; the psychological approach therefore stands in contrast to the anti-body stance of some theological traditions. To understand the bipolar nature of the archetype is to realize that affect can be understood as an influx of the divine (William Blake's phrase) just as much as a numinous image. Since this affect is often perceived as negative, associated with problematic complexes, we are again led to an understanding of the operation of spirit in our suffering.

Archetypal Affects

Affects are important organizers and motivators of behaviour, so they are ordering principles in the sense in which archetypes are understood within this book. We could say that affect is the way in which the archetype stirs up the body. Affect is felt as a physiological process; it is a genetically encoded, unconsciously mediated, total response of the autonomic nervous system, affecting the viscera, skin, blood vessels, glands, muscles and hormones. Affect therefore represents the red or somatic end of the archetypal spectrum, just as image represents the blue or intrapsychic end of what our metapsychology tells us is actually a unitary phenomenon. In the absence of mind–body splitting, image and affect occur simultaneously. Because affect is felt in the body, it is of importance to a psychological understanding of the mythologem of incarnation; *affect is felt when spirit embodies to become soul*. (The details of this embodiment are discussed on p. 26.) The importance of affect is increasingly being discussed within psycho-analysis as a primary source of motivation, as an alternative to drive theory. This development has narrowed the gap with Jungian thought, since affect is the invariable accompaniment of the complex. For Freud, affect was not primary, it was the conscious manifestation of instinct, equivalent to the subjective ex-perience of the pressure for the discharge of sexuality and aggression. The primacy of affective experience in babies was elucidated by Tomkins (1962), who identified and described the facial expressions characteristic of what he thought were eight basic or irreducible affects. (These are: surprise, interest, enjoyment, distress, disgust, anger, fear and shame.) Basch (1976, pp. 759–777) and Emde (1978) have summarized the evidence for the idea that affects are powerful communicators. They are present at birth, enabling mother and child to influence each other immediately and mutually. At birth these expressions are stereotyped, universal and involuntary, hence, since they are universal constants, they clearly meet the definition of an archetypal process in the baby. Basch[7] (1976, p. 771) reduces affect to purely adaptive behaviour mediated by the autonomic nervous system; for him it is a totally physiological process. But this is an unacceptable reduction of psyche to brain. The Jungian view assumes that the body's response is synchronistically accompanied by an intrapsychic image,[8] and that both are poles of a unitary archetypal process that eventually leads to the formation of complexes. In contrast to Basch's physiological approach, Stewart (1987, pp. 131–162) regards the archetypal affects as noetic, innate faculties which provide an 'apperceptive focus on fundamental domains of the world'.

The eruption of the unconscious is always associated with intense affect (CW 8, 841). The numinous property of the archetype expresses itself by means of its affective quality or intensity. The result of this process depends on the degree of cohesion or structural integrity of the self, or its capacity to bind and modulate intense affect. If the self structures are fragile, as in the case of borderline personalities, or as occurs within healthier people with vulnerable sectors of their personality, the individual can be overwhelmed by uncontrolled affects. Affect also gives rise to the sense of self; it is one way that we know that we exist (Descartes might have said that I feel therefore I am). But unmanageably intense affect causes the threat of fragmentation of the sense of self, or its actual fragmentation, resulting anywhere from anxiety or depression to dissociation or psychosis. The imagery which accompanies such overpowering affects is usually expressed as dreams such as those of tidal waves threatening fragile huts on the beach, or tornadoes demolishing buildings. But, when spirit as affect is able to embody without causing fragmentation, producing manageable complexes, the resulting experience becomes personal, and this is referred to as soul.

Soul

There have been several attempts to discuss soul from the vantage point of depth psychology, which mitigates the poignant warnings of some contemporary philosophers that the barrage of technology in our culture has unconsciously led to the attempt to desubstantialize the soul and reduce the core of the person to a conglomeration of learned accretions (e.g. Barrett, 1986). Soul as applied to people refers to the deepest subjectivity of the individual, that quality in us which produces a sense of fullness, interiority and meaning. Jung also defines soul as the function of relationship to the unconscious, which may be personified in dreams as a particular figure (CW 6, 420). He continues:

> The determining force (God) operating from those depths [of the un-
> conscious] is reflected by the soul, that is, it [the soul] creates symbols and
> images .... By means of these images the soul conveys the forces of the

unconscious to consciousness; it is both receiver and transmitter, an organ for perceiving unconscious contents.

(CW 6, 425)

Here soul is understood as allowing the ability to consciously grasp the experience of spirit. Inasmuch as we experience the divine via our psychic depths, the soul allows this awareness to occur, partly by means of its capacity to symbolize or form an image of the experience. To describe the interaction of soul, body and spirit, the metaphor of the film projector has been used (Corbett and Rives, 1992). Spirit is analogous to a film which carries an archetypal ordering pattern; the projecting, decoding and image-making mechanism is the soul, without which the pattern of spirit could not be discerned. The screen that captures or reflects the soul's image is the body, which includes the brain; the audience is the ego. Heat, or affect, is invariably generated in the process.

Soul can also be imagined as the personal receptacle, or embodiment, of the transpersonal spirit, or archetype. Soul is also the 'organ' by which spirit is experienced, releasing both meaning and psychopathology in the process. Soul is the result of incarnation and is also the pivot of incarnation, the meeting place of, or the bridge between, spirit and body. In Jung's words, soul can be understood as 'the psychic phenomenon that mediates between consciousness and the physiological functions of the body' (CW 12, 397). Because the soul is so important in the process of incarnation of spirit, 'soul making' does not only mean deepening into the patient's experience, as Hillman suggests. Part of the 'soul-making' task of the therapist is to assist in the embodiment of spirit, by helping patients to cope with the intensity and complexity of their affective experiences, so that they are not swamped by the affects stirred up by their complexes. Usually the need for such containment and affective attunement is indicative of a failure of this process in childhood; the need is reactivated within the selfobject demands of psychotherapy. Soul making requires containment of painful affects by means of the therapeutic relationship, which allows the embodiment of aspects of the Self that have hitherto remained either dormant or disembodied. This emphasis on affect in relation to soul making corrects a one-sided attention to image found in much of the literature of archetypal psychology.

Soul and psyche are fairly interchangeable terms within depth psychology, but perhaps not completely so. In his early work, Hillman, one of the most important writers in this area (1972, p. 51) defined soul as a 'functional complex of the psyche, acting as a mediating personality between the whole psyche, which is mainly unconscious, and the usual ego'. Later, he felt that soul could not be defined clearly because it is not a substance but a perspective. It is an unknown human factor 'which makes meaning possible, which turns events into experiences, and which is communicated in love' (1983a, p. 16). For Hillman, soul also allows imagination, speculation, fantasy and the experience of metaphor.

It is important to note that, in spite of the etymological commonality of the words soul and psyche, some theological writers have challenged their identity, suggesting that they are concepts that belong to different disciplines. (Writing in favour of their equivalence, White (1960) has summarized these arguments.) But since the same word can be used to carry different meanings within different fields, it is important for us to be clear about our psychological use of the word. Theological and psychological understandings are not necessarily mutually exclusive, as exemplified by Sherrard's (1987, p. 47) definition of soul as 'that supra-rational faculty or organ or power through which the divine may penetrate into the human'. Description of the soul in terms of the mutual interpenetration of the human and the divine fits with a psychological understanding of the interaction of soul and spirit. Another theologian (Prusak, 1979, p. 3355) suggests that the body is the 'substantial expression of the soul'; this, too, allows psychological amplification in terms of patterns of consciousness which are either expressed as images, as affect or as symptoms in the body. For the psychologist, the soul must include the body within itself, not the other way around. In the words of William Blake (quoted by Frosch, 1974): 'Man has no body distinct from his soul; for that called body is a portion of soul discerned by the five senses . . . .' The psychologist differs from dualistic ideas of soul as an immaterial substance separable from the body (e.g. Heb. 4: 12). Whether these ideas are true metaphysically is unimportant; they give us no psychological leverage.

Although I use the term psyche a good deal, I cannot say anything about its real nature, any more than the theologian can describe the nature of the soul. For me, psyche is also synonymous with mind or consciousness, and their nature is equally unknown. All I can say is that there seems to be a transpersonal level of the psyche, that I have referred to as Big Mind, and a human level. My commitment is to the idea of consciousness as an irreducible ontological reality that is common to all experience. Here the psychologist is in good company. Many years ago, Jeans (1930) suggested that the universe itself would increasingly look like a system of thought processes, and modern physics now has to deal with consciousness as part of its approach to matter.

CONSCIOUSNESS AS THE FACTOR COMMON TO BODY, SOUL AND SPIRIT

The depth psychologist works with consciousness in its many modes. For heuristic purposes it is possible to imagine that consciousness, taking different forms, is the irreducible factor common to body, soul and spirit. This is obviously a theoretical statement; it is difficult to prove that consciousness can legitimately be thought of as if it were a fundamental entity which subsumes all others, as we find, for instance, in the monistic philosophy of Advaita Vedanta. But within the realm of competence of the psychologist, spirit, soul and body can be usefully treated as if they were different aspects of the overall consciousness of the Self. The difference between them is due to the ego's perception of their individual quality. In order that we may be able to apply psychological methodology to all dimensions of experience, spirit, soul and body can be considered to be different aspects of consciousness that are experienced at different intensities and with different degrees of familiarity. The soul is then an aspect of consciousness that extends, or incarnates, into the human being; consciousness as spirit extends far beyond the individual. Much of our therapy carries with it the implicit assumption that, not only does spirit manifest itself within and by means of the human body and psyche, it also seeks its own continuing development therein.

SPIRIT–SOUL INTERACTION: THE NEED FOR A HERMENEUTICAL METHOD

One of the problems and limitations raised by a religious approach to the psyche is the fact that the imagery which the soul produces in response to the experience of spirit is often very puzzling and difficult to understand. If the Self has important things to say to the conscious personality, it is often complained, then why are dreams so difficult to understand? The following dream is a good example of such difficulty.

> I am in a space that feels surreal. I am looking after my two younger brothers, who are as they were when they were children. They are sitting on a bed, covered with a quilt designed with intersecting circles. I feel a liquid, dripping from above, fall on us. It is golden, and at first I think it is urine, but then I realize it is actually honey. Above us, suspended in the air, is a magnificent, handsome lioness. The honey is coming from her, as if she is secreting it.

This is the dream of a young psychiatric resident, soon after she had begun her career. It was her first presentation to a dream group, on only her second visit. She had paid no attention to dreams so far in her life, and she had no experience with or interest in Jungian theory. Her reason for attending the group was partly professional, and partly out of curiosity.

Needless to say, the dreamer could make nothing out of the dream, except to say that it was emotionally very powerful. But one of the important facts about such a 'big' or archetypal dream is that it can be deciphered by individuals with widely disparate cultural backgrounds, so that the dreamer's societal origin is not particularly relevant. As we shall see, the dream is connected to a particular quality of the experience of the mother which is not restricted geographically or historically. By contrast, the personal self is a highly locally conditioned entity, a collection of personal events whose relationship to the deep structures present in the dream are not clear until the dream is amplified. This dream is typical of those to which a dreamer has few personal associations.

The first problem, then, is to explain the origin of such imagery. Could the dreamer have read the Biblical story of the 'swarm of bees and honey' that Sampson came across in the carcass of a lion (Judg. 14: 8)? Did she know that Sampson's subsequent riddle to his wife's family was to guess the meaning of the phrase: 'out of the strong came forth sweetness' (Ibid., 14: 14)? Such readily available imagery juxtaposing honey and lions may have made an impression on her when she read Bible stories as a child, and subsequently it may have been forgotten. In fact, the dreamer insisted that she had never read the Bible as a child, and when I told her the story she was simply puzzled by it. Because of her psychological training, she had heard of the riddle of the Sphinx, which Oedipus had to address, but did not know that this figure is a mythical leonine manifestation of the Great Mother. She also did not know that Demeter, the Great Mother of Greek mythology, was depicted as a bee, representing the feminine, transformative power of nature, and that her priestesses were called Melissae, or the bees. In antiquity, honey mixed with menstrual blood was considered to be the nectar of the goddess. Nor was the dreamer aware that Demeter and Cybele (Goddess of wild beasts) were represented as lionesses (Stone, 1984, pp. 199, 204; Walker, 1983, p. 407). In fact, the lioness was a symbol of fierce maternity in several cultures. It was also associated with virgin warrior goddesses such as Artemis and the Egyptian solar goddess of war and vengeance, Sekmet, who is analogous to Shakti in the Hindu pantheon. Tefnut, the Egyptian goddess of the dew and rain, was also worshipped in the form of a lioness, and since she is the sister of Shu, helps to support the sky. The interlocking circles on the quilt, an ancient Goddess symbol, complete the emphasis on this archetype. Even with such a partial amplification of the dream, it is now hardly necessary to add that, in the family of the dreamer, mother was a very powerful figure, and that at an early age the dreamer may have sometimes experienced her mother's attempts at nurturance and protection as though she were being urinated on. This is the reductive level of understanding, in terms of the dreamer's childhood. Like all manifestations of the objective psyche, the dream also makes an important forward-looking comment about the dreamer.

The dream does not simply say that the dreamer is caring for young, masculine aspects of herself under the aegis of the divine mother, who showers her with her womanly sweetness and sacred nourishment. In order to communicate its message,[9] the archetype of particular importance to this woman produces a beautifully ordered, affectively laden experience. Her soul depicts this in a manner which could potentially be grasped whenever and wherever in the world she had been born. Since she is just beginning her career, it is also relevant that in antiquity honey was used as an initiatory meal (Henderson, 1967 p. 52). It does not matter which mythical name we attach to the honey and the lioness; what is clear is that the goddess is claiming one of her own. Herein lies the importance of the dream for the telos of the personality; this modern woman must practise her craft in the overarching manner of the archetypal feminine, as an authentic woman with strength and sweetness, but above all not within a patriarchal mode. This is how she is ordered, how her psyche is constituted. It is noteworthy that the imagery of the dream only makes a faint, perhaps even coincidental, allusion to the Judaeo-Christian tradition in which she was raised. This is common; at a deep level of the psyche, our identity is more complex than we are aware.

If the dreamer were to take this experience seriously, her difficulty would be to place the dream in the context of the rest of her life. To do so, she must realize that the dream illustrates the traditional idea that we are influenced by little understood powers, which the ancients called gods or spirits and we call archetypes. These powers manifest themselves through our lives whether we realize it or not, and one purpose of a dream is to make us conscious of the particular dominants within our own soul. The dreamer's task is not simply to find the meaning of the dream, but also to allow her life to align with its archetypal message. Here a speculation is possible which is founded on a metapsychological premise. If consciousness is unitary, the dreamer cannot be totally separate from the lioness. They are synchronistically (non-causally) related; the dreamer and the dream image both belong to, or even are different aspects of, the same overarching reality. One of these aspects is the human being who dreams, while the exact ontological status of the other is unknown. But it is only our egocentric position which prevents us from realizing that the lioness may be conscious of the dreamer at the same time as the dreamer dreams the lioness, or that they are both contents of the consciousness of a supraordinate Self. The woman and the lioness correspond to each other within two different but interlocking realms of reality, this world and that of the dream. They are undivided within the implicate order but separate when explicate (these terms are discussed on p. 137).

Perhaps the reader is still doubtful about the need for such obscure imagery as that used by the dream. It might be useful to imagine what might have happened if the dreamer had belonged to a pre-technological, aboriginal culture, especially one in which the value of dreams was recognized. (This thought experiment will help to reduce the effects of the reader's cultural and personal conditioning.) The dreamer's reaction to the dream might then have taken a very particular direction. In tribal cultures, in which the distinction between humans and animals is not quite as sharp as it is in ours, she might have felt herself under the protection or tutelage of the lioness, and might enact this relationship in song, dress, art, ritual or dance. The dreamer might feel the lioness as an ancestor; she would be of her kin. The lioness would be a totem animal, distinguishing the dreamer from people of other clans within a system of classification which clarifies her place in the cosmos and links her to transpersonal or spiritual reality. Stanner (1984, p. 163) quotes a thoughtful Australian aboriginal man who said: 'There are honey people all over the world.' If the dreamer were training to become a shaman in such a society, the lioness might be her 'power animal' or tutelary spirit, enabling her to obtain information within non-ordinary reality.

Unfortunately, in our culture the art of understanding such material has been relegated to those relatively few interested people who pay attention to their dreams. But whether or not the dreamer has ears to listen, the fact remains that this honey-secreting animal depicts a spiritual principle representing certain natural laws important to her. It would be difficult to imagine a more powerful gestalt, or a more culture-free way of telling her this. The dream is thus a personal revelation to the dreamer by a larger consciousness, in which she partakes *as if* she were a separate entity. The particular Self-quality which governs her is 'lioness-like'. Presumably this level of her being has not yet incarnated or even dawned on her ego consciousness; the dream is an attempt of the Self to embody this quality within the person so that she may live it.

THE SHAMANIC ASPECTS OF PSYCHOTHERAPY: SOUL-TO-SOUL CONNECTION AND THE SELFOBJECT EXPERIENCE

Various authors (e.g. Murphy (1964), Haule (1986) and Aziz (1990)) have indicated important similarities between the functions of the shaman and those of the psychotherapist. It is of course not surprising that we would find commonalities between healing practices across cultures, since at an archetypal level the elements of healing may be constant. The shamanic experience is a useful model for depth psychology, because, like the religious approach to the psyche, it acknowledges the reality of the archetypal realm and the reality of the psyche. The shaman works with these facts in a literal manner, in a way that is related to the method of active imagination as used in analytical psychotherapy, where the unconscious is allowed voice and form (see Dallett, 1982, for a fuller discussion of this practice). In like manner, the shaman directly addresses personified intrapsychic entities as they appear within the altered states of consciousness produced by shamanic techniques.

I would like to enlarge upon some of the further similarities between psychotherapy and shamanism by means of an exploration of the differences between a healthy self which experiences soul fully, and a self which has lost some of this connection. It is no coincidence that a self which is depleted, depressed or fragmented suffers in ways which are descriptively the same as the phenomena of 'soul loss' described by the shamans of pre-technological peoples, who attribute even organic disease to this problem (Eliade 1964, p. 327). By contrast, the experience of the self as cohesive and vital is one of soulfulness. Before continuing the comparison, let me clarify some of the psychological meanings of 'soul loss'.

Jung understands 'soul loss' in various ways, which I have listed here followed by my own interpretation of what is meant by his terms.

1 The eruption of the unconscious, producing a psychosis (CW 14, 144n.). Elsewhere (CW 8, 590) he describes this process as the result of archetypal or spirit 'possession'. Here the individual soul has been swamped by the objective psyche to the extent that the personal field of consciousness is more or less lost.

2 A dissociative state (CW 18, 440), in which the soul has lost access to a part of itself, which has been split off because of the formation of a complex which is not in harmony with the totality of the personality.

3 A dissociation between consciousness and the unconscious (CW 11, 688), which leads to a loss of the soul's connection to the deeper wellsprings of its being.

4 The experience of listlessness, depression and lack of energy (CW 9, i, 213), which is a typical state of depletion and retreat of the self following selfobject failure.

Such collapse of the self occurs when the experience of soul is dependent on the preservation of the selfobject tie. As von Franz (1980, p. 30) indicates, an unconscious complex which is heavily affect-laden is often responsible for such states. They correspond to the shamanic notion that the soul has been stolen by a spirit – psychologically, by the archetypal core of the complex.

In all of the above situations, the implication is of a loss of contained and conscious relationship to the depths of the psyche in the presence of a vigorous sense of self. Sometimes this loss occurs because of failure of safe access to material that belongs in consciousness (CW 8, 587), but Jung (CW 8, 590) also refers to the emergence into awareness of material which is not normally conscious because it belongs to transpersonal levels of the psyche. These 'spirit complexes' are felt to be alien and uncanny. Whereas the return of lost 'soul material' to consciousness is healing, 'possession' by spirit complexes (archetypal elements which are totally unhumanized) requires therapeutic help because they are unassimilable. This seems to correspond to states of mind typically found in borderline or psychotic people in which the individual is barraged by affective storms and archetypal images which are uncontainable.

SOUL AND SELFOBJECT

Jung made much of the idea that the soul (or anima) is the factor which relates the person to his or her inner world. Jung attributed gender to this bridging function, suggesting that it is personified as masculine in the unconscious of women and as a feminine figure within the psyche of men. In his day this was a culturally determined truth, because certain behaviours and feelings were heavily determined or proscribed by gender stereotypes. Today we see this bridging function to the Self carried out by figures of either sex within the psyches of both men and women, so that the soul does not need to be given a gender (Corbett and Rives, 1992), although to the extent that gender stereotypes still exist we still see contrasexual dream imagery. Just as the soul image within dreams bridges to the inner world, the selfobject bridges to unconscious needs as they are felt and fulfilled within relationships. The soul image tends towards wholeness by connecting us with the Self, while the person who performs a selfobject function for the person sustains the vitality and intactness of the self by bridging to and helping with an unconscious deficit. The intrapsychic soul image connects one to the Self experienced internally, while the selfobject carries out a soul function by connecting us to the experience of the Self as it is experienced within a relationship. The selfobject is therefore at the same time a 'carrier' of some of the individual's wholeness, or soul qualities. Hence our distress when an important selfobject abandons or hurts us; the soul is wounded, or some of it is lost. The manifestations of this damage vary, even to the extent of producing feelings of unreality, since the selfobject provides the personality with a sense of realness and ground; without our selfobjects we may lose touch with important aspects of ourselves. The process of falling in love is extraordinarily animating because the loved one performs both soul image and selfobject functions at the same time. Connection to the loved one allows access to aspects of the soul that are otherwise unavailable. The beloved thereby activates the unconscious, acting as a muse, releasing creativity that only flows from connection to the Self, while at the same time lost aspects of the self are rehabilitated as selfobject needs are met.

SOUL RETRIEVAL IN SHAMANISM AND PSYCHOTHERAPY

In pre-technological cultures, the shaman 'retrieves' the patient's soul by 'following' it with his own soul and bringing it back to the body from the 'land of the dead' (Eliade, 1964). In modern psychological parlance, the shaman enters non-ordinary reality, or an altered state of consciousness, in which he is able to see, via his capacity for accurate active imagination, the patient's situation as it is depicted within the realm of the *imaginatio* (see below). It is as if he is in a waking dream, in which he is able to merge his psyche with that of the patient by a process of extraordinary empathy. In this state of merger he can track the patient's split-off or unconscious intrapsychic material seen in personified form as a human or animal figure with which he can dialogue. This process corresponds to the way in which a good psychotherapist empathically hears what is not being said, or hears the voice of the unconscious as it rides 'piggy-back' on the patient's verbal productions. Because of his perspicacity, charisma and cultural authority – not to mention the transference leverage produced by the ritual – the shaman is able to explain to the patient what part of him has been lost (we would say via splitting or repression), and needs reintegrating. The process is essentially the same as the therapist sensing the patient's difficulty and interpreting it, bringing back into the centre of attention aspects of the personality which have long been sequestered and ignored. This process occurs when the therapist experiences and verbalizes affect or imagery in his or her own mind and body which comment on the patient's situation. This is the prompting of the soul to listen more deeply than the voice of the ego, so that what has long been alienated may return.

For instance, a therapist announces an unexpected absence and is faced with a female patient who is enraged and threatens to leave therapy. The therapist sees, in his or her mind's eye, a frightened little girl, curled up in a corner, hurt by a rejecting, abandoning mother. This is a 'piece' of the patient's soul which is split off; it has been reactivated by the therapist's behaviour and is 'retrieved', or reconnected with the body, by means of the therapist's understanding and explaining the situation and by helping the patient to deal with her rage and pain. Then her split-off, early, selfobject failure can be repaired by finally attending to that part of her self which still suffers from abandonment depression. Another patient dissociates when the self–selfobject tie is disrupted, leading to severe depersonalization and derealization. It is as if his soul is suddenly not in the room. He looks far away, eyes closed, mutters and moans unintelligibly and seems totally unreachable without the therapist's prolonged effort to reconnect with him. In the therapist's mind appear images of the patient lost in a vast desert, terrified and alone. Later, the patient is able to confirm this impression by spontaneously describing the experience as one of being alone in an empty space, in great danger. What finally brings him back to the room is the therapist's affective attunement to his terrifying internal state of mind, so that he realizes that he is in fact not alone. She voices his fears, makes her presence felt, calls his name, interprets his terror, and perhaps within her own subjective imagery supports him in the desert. Finally something in him realizes that she really wants him back. But until then his soul cannot return; only when the tie to the selfobject is re-established can he rejoin the world.

The linking concept between these ideas is Jung's comment that the soul is the function of relationship (CW 16, 475). To regain the unity and coherence of the self by means of a selfobject relationship is an experience of ensouling through a connection to another. The therapist's capacity to act as a selfobject restores the soul of the patient, because not only is the self thus enhanced but a self–Self connection becomes possible which previously was too terrifying. Subjectively, the selfobject experience is a kind of *participation mystique* (a shared consciousness or merger), with an unconscious diffusion of normal boundaries, in which soul-to-soul communication occurs which is analogous to that of shamanic healing, especially when the therapist can imaginatively 'see' the patient's unconscious situation. Schwartz-Salant (1989) has provided many examples of such inner vision. These phenomena indicate that the psyche does not end at the skin. (The difference from psychosis is partly the fact that cognitively we know that we are separate.)

Other similarities can be found between modern psychotherapy and traditional shamanism. Johnson (1981, p. 314) points out that when cultural changes occur within tribal societies, leading to personal emotional problems, the shaman is able ritually to process these difficulties and give them meaning. The shaman can thereby 'mold mental disorders into socially acceptable syndromes and render them predictable and acceptable to both the victim and the community'. In other words, the shaman can tap into the unconscious of the culture and assist in the transformation of its psychological difficulties. Within our society, the loss of soul suffered by individuals often reflects collective problems such as the devaluation of women, the narcissistic exploitation of children or the emphasis on appearances and money rather than a meaningful inner life. Hence, the modern therapist's interest in narcissistic and borderline disorders, with their severe loss of soul. Like the shaman, the psychotherapist helps in the social integration of people who would otherwise be alienated.

Where Does This Process Occur?

As I indicated, the psychotherapist is able to track the state of the patient's soul partly by means of the process of empathy, which Kohut (1971) describes as a process of vicarious introspection. The shaman of pre-technological cultures has an extraordinary capacity for such empathy, to the point of merger of his psyche and that of his patient. The result of the shaman's journey into the 'other world' – the realm of the unconscious – is described in vivid, dream-like imagery. To our ears, descriptions of these journeys sound like excursions into the *imaginatio*, that realm of the reality of the psyche analogous to Winnicott's transitional space, an area 'intermediate' (it is not amenable to spatial metaphors) between the inner and outer world. This *mundus imaginalis* is 'ontologically as real as the world of the senses and that of the intellect' (Corbin, 1972, p. 7.). This world requires its own faculty, that of imaginative power, which is a perceptual system whose cognitive and noetic function is as real as that of our five senses and intellect. It is not to be confused with the 'imagination' in the sense of the unreal – hence the use of Latin rather than English words to describe it. This is a world of subtle bodies linking pure spirit and the material body. Active imagination, which is a means by which we penetrate to the *mundus imaginalis*, is a faculty of the soul. Corbin, and the shaman, are at pains to point out that such inner vision is real perception of another world, and is not merely allegorical. Jung (CW 12, 219) describes the process of the *imaginatio* as an active evocation, which 'tries to grasp the inner facts and portray them in images true to their nature'. Relating these images to the concept of the subtle body, he suggests that here the physical and the psychic intermingle into an 'indissoluble unity' (CW 12, 394).

The imagery of the shaman's journey is fairly similar in its themes in different parts of the world because the shaman experiences directly those 'categories of the imagination' (CW 9, i, 254) which are archetypal. To reach them, the shaman enters or evokes the necessary state of consciousness through ritual, or by means of the enactment of myth, which allows access to the spirit world (the transpersonal levels of the unconscious). Techniques such as fasting, drumming, dancing or hallucinogens all produce intense affective arousal, expansion of the spectrum of ordinary perception and a submersion or suspension of consensual reality. Such altered consciousness is often necessary for the evocation of archetypal material. In psychotherapy, the mental state of the participants is not so obviously dramatically altered as it is in shamanic practice, but all deeply engaged therapists periodically work in an altered state of consciousness, which they may not be aware of. It is within this state that the constellation of a shared psychic field allows the experience of the *coniunctio*, a mutual experience of the Self in which the patient experiences otherwise unreachable parts of himself by means of the selfobject experience. This reminds us of Christou's (1976, p. 102) view that the psyche is a unitary field which contains us, rather than the usual sense that the psyche is somehow contained within the individual. This view of relationship allows a purely psychological view of empathy, in which two apparently separate psyches are actually joined within a supraordinate totality of consciousness, referred to earlier as Big Mind, producing a temporarily shared self that is the result of soul-to-soul contact. This may sound like a metaphysical statement, but is closer to the felt experience than are attempts to reduce empathy to an organic process (Brothers, 1989, p. 13).

7

A DEPTH PSYCHOLOGICAL APPROACH TO THE PROBLEM OF SUFFERING

COMMONALITIES OF THE PSYCHOLOGICAL AND THEOLOGICAL APPROACHES

Attempts to explain the existence of apparently random suffering are staple fare in the literature of all religious traditions. However, in the secular literature the problem of the suffering of the innocents is typically dealt with by social and political theorists, but not by psychologists (Gerstenberger and Schrage, 1980). But this problem must be addressed by those psychotherapists who choose to work within a religious model, because intense suffering often demands a spiritual solution. The effort to address the problem psychologically is a part of our attempt to clarify the psychological basis of existing religious ideas, and also to address such fundamental questions *ab initio*, from within the psychology of the individual in relation to the objective psyche, rather than by recourse to dogmatic, ready-made answers. Panikkar (1979) has neatly summarized the standard religious approaches to suffering: Buddhism seeks to eliminate it, Hinduism seeks to deny it, Judaism and Islam seek to explain it, while Christianity tries to transfigure it. The depth psychologist must psychologize it, non-reductively. That is, a religious psychology must be able to encompass the problem of suffering in a way that is relevant to individuals by locating its meaning in the context of their entire psychology, both its developmental and teleological aspects. In the last analysis the 'answer' to suffering – that is, a personal way of understanding and managing it – ideally emerges from attention to the larger psyche's comments about the situation. Such an answer may or may not be relevant to others in similar straits. It may be seen to be adapted from the existing spiritual literature, and in such a case it is authentic if it truly corresponds to the soul of the individual.

In a sense the problem of suffering is the most serious challenge to the emerging paradigm here under discussion. Can a religious psychology possibly improve on what has already been learned in this area by millennia of religious attention? What new approaches could emerge now? The problem of suffering can be expected to have a major influence on the form of the new psychologically oriented religious sensibility, just as the effects of this problem are very visible within the history of all established traditions. The apparently random distribution of suffering has always provided a challenge for religions, and its effects on their dogmatic assertions has been profound. For example, in the Judaeo-Christian tradition, the fact that righteousness did not exclude suffering and that the wicked prospered required the development of the idea of justice in the next world or at the time of the Messiah. And not for nothing is suffering considered to be the basis of atheism; there is nothing like adversity to evoke the individual's real religious beliefs, and behind them his or her personal psychology. Marx and Freud thought that religion offers an avoidance of harsh reality, an escape or compensation for the world's unfairness (e.g. Freud, 1933). This position has to be taken seriously, since, as we will see, religious beliefs can be used as a defensive operation which safeguards the cohesion of the personality. But the illogical aspect of these arguments is to assume that this fact means that religious attitudes to suffering can be entirely reduced to defence. As Bowker (1980) points out, generalizations like that of Freud ignore religion's 'rigorously cautious exploration of human capacity', and trivialize the religious approach to suffering, which tries to place it within a larger meaning. This is also the strength of the psychological attitude. Finally, it should be remembered that the religious approach to suffering is a major theme of myth. This storehouse of the religious stories of humanity offers possible outcomes and attitudes towards suffering, not an avoidance of the problem. Myth is about wisdom in the face of suffering, not defence against it.

By contrast with the religious attempt to find transcendent or at least personal meaning in suffering, that is, to spiritualize the experience, traditional psychoanalytic approaches attempt a value-free, deterministic and usually positivistic understanding of the origins and effects of suffering. Psychoanalysis uses a kind of disease model of suffering, in the sense that suffering is considered to be something undesirable which needs to be removed. Psychoanalytic theory and psychiatry in general studiously avoid questions of larger meaning, or the 'why' rather than the 'how' of suffering. These theories tacitly assume that the early history of the person is the cause of his or her suffering, but this may be an unwarranted axiom. It is arguable that a supraordinate (archetypal) order both caused the suffering and organized the childhood environment responsible for it. The religiously oriented psychotherapist working in this area still requires a depth psychological approach, but does not stop there. Our psychodynamic understanding has to lead into a religious approach to the information we thus obtain.

At first it may seem that there is no point of contact between such opposing attitudes to suffering as the psychoanalytic and the religious. However there is a linking concept, which is Jung's idea that individuation, or the developmental process by which we become what we were intended to be, is synonymous with the process of the incarnation of spirit. Or, development proceeds by means of the incarnation of the Self into the self. Jung (CW 11, 223) suggests that the subjective experience of this incarnation includes suffering. This suggestion addresses the 'why' question referred to above, and requires further amplification.

INCARNATION: A LINK BETWEEN RELIGIOUS AND PSYCHOLOGICAL APPOACHES TO SUFFERING

Incarnation understood psychologically simply means that the Self, which exists within the baby as potential or spirit, embodies a part of itself as development proceeds, forming a personal self. It is as if the Self acts as a blueprint (Kohut's 'nuclear program') for the growth of the self. Although psychoanalytic theoreticians do not use the concept of the transpersonal Self, we can view psychodynamic developmental theory as an implicit attempt to explain the processes by which the Self incarnates into a personal self. In other words, developmental psychology can be viewed as a modern incarnation myth. This attitude allows an understanding of suffering which integrates religious and psychological viewpoints.

Until Jung's psychological work on the subject, the notion of incarnation was the exclusive province of religion and mythology. The idea of a divine figure taking human form is of central importance in so many mythologies and religious traditions that it must be of general or archetypal significance within the psyche. A brief survey of these traditions will indicate its pervasive quality. The Pharoahs of Egypt were thought to be incarnations of the sun god Ra, who took the form of the monarch in order to impregnate the queen (Budge, 1969). In the Greek pantheon, Zeus, Apollo and other gods commonly took human form for specific purposes. In Hindu mythology Vishnu incarnates when the world is in great need, to prevent the victory of evil and restore righteousness. In Buddhism, a Bodhisattva incarnates in order to help liberate mankind. Even in Judaism, the Cabbalistic notion of the emanation of a beam of divine will from the unknowable Godhead into the world of matter implies a 'downward' movement of spirit, as if the whole material universe is a kind of embodiment of God. For the Gnostics, the divine spark is unhappily trapped in matter and requires a process of awakening and reunion with the Source, while the alchemists struggled to purify matter so that the spirit could incarnate within it. Finally, of course, the idea of incarnation is central to Christianity, which expresses the unique idea of the death and resurrection of the incarnate God, as a once and for all historical event (Parrinder, 1970). (But whereas accounts of miraculous impregnation by a god are common to many mythologies, the Christian dogmatic emphasis on the mother's perpetual virginity is not so common. It suggests that the founders of that tradition needed to maintain an image of mother free of sexuality.) Pre-technological people also express the archetypal notion that suffering is meaningful and is connected to the behaviour of spirit. Eliade (1974) points out that such peoples never experience suffering as meaningless. For them, suffering corresponds to a supraordinate order; it is not arbitrary, but is the result of the anger of a demon, the breaking of a taboo or the magic of an enemy. It is thus rendered intelligible by being placed in the context of a total spiritual system. We should not too quickly dismiss this kind of pre-technological thinking as primitive superstition; these are simply ways of talking about the influence of the unconscious. The desire for explanation remains: modern man attributes disaster to viruses, genetic aberration or parental deprivation, but this is only the substitution of a more developed mythology. Our technical descriptions only push the problem one stage back; a focus on mechanisms alone ignores both the 'why' of suffering and the fact that the effects of agents such as viruses represent the implementation of archetypal patterns.

Overall, the evidence from all these sources points to a broadly found connection between matter, spirit and suffering. Since so many mythologies imply that incarnation is linked with suffering, it seems that the union of spirit and matter is inevitably seen to cause difficulty. In human development, the lifelong movement of the Self into the self is no exception. Our psychologically based mythology now requires explanations which invoke the unconscious, and other jargon, but not much has fundamentally changed. Suffering still binds us to the cosmos and to our concept of the divine in an inexplicable manner, and also to each other as agents of suffering within relationships. Our quandary remains; why do we suffer, what is there to learn from it and what can be done about it? Why does some suffering leave us crippled and bitter, while at other times we are enriched or even healed by it? Of importance to the psychotherapist trying to help a suffering person is the question of what we might do to tip the balance one way or the other, especially in situations in which the patient's difficulty is not likely ever to resolve. Finally, how would a purely psychological approach which is concurrently religious differ from that of traditional dogmatic theology in its attitudes to suffering? To reiterate: for the religiously oriented psychotherapist the key concepts are that the movement of the Self into a self is a process of incarnation of spirit, and that all psychodynamic theories are attempts to describe the mechanism of this incarnation. It is therefore necessary to amplify this tradition-ally religious idea from a psychological perspective.

INCARNATION UNDERSTOOD PSYCHOLOGICALLY

Psychologically speaking, incarnation means that some aspect or fragment of the Self has manifested itself within an empirical personality which is circumscribed by a body. There are many ways to conceptualize this relationship. Here I suggest that the psyche itself is not a function of the body (the materialist position) but rather that the body manifests the Self in a way that we experience as material because of the limitations of our perceptual systems. Because the body is bounded, and the brain's capacity to perceive the Self is limited, the self feels isolated from other selves and not part of the whole. Elements or strands of the Self embody or ensoul themselves as those archetypes which form the core of complexes. These are produced as human experience accretes around these transpersonal centres. Subjectively experienced, the archetype has an imaginal or intrapsychic aspect, but its fullest embodiment is felt through the affective component of the complexes which form around it, leading to particular behaviour in the world. These complexes may be positively toned or they may cause suffering.

The psychological approach to suffering also hinges on the proposal that the process of incarnation is continuous (CW 11, 658), and, rather than incarnation being confined to a few special, mythical individuals: 'now, every man has to carry God. The descent of spirit into matter is complete' (Jung, 1937, in McGuire and Hull, 1977, p. 97). Edinger (1984) has further amplified the idea of the continuing incarnation to mean that: 'God is now to be carried experientially by the individual.' Thus, we may 'recognize experiences of weakness and failure as manifestations of the suffering God striving for incarnation' (Edinger 1973, p. 153). Two other major attitudes underpin the psychological approach to suffering. First, we do not rely solely on dogmatic solutions, although they may be helpful, but as well we look to the comments of the objective psyche for an individualized attitude towards it. Second, the efforts and the attitude of the self towards the Self's attempt to incarnate are important and affect the process. These efforts are exemplified by the story of Job.

AN INTRAPSYCHIC VIEW OF JOB'S PROBLEM

The book of Job is traditionally said to deal with the fact that, in spite of Yahweh's promises to his people, the Hebrew nation suffered disaster after disaster, and righteous individuals met with misfortune and suffering, apparently in contradiction to the teaching that good behaviour would bring reward. The typical Old Testament image of God with which Job deals is a deity who is rageful, vengeful, jealous, sadistic, ruthless and savage. From a psychological point of view, Job is not only dealing with a personal problem, but he also exemplifies and carries the collective suffering of his time. One important aspect of his problem remains unanswered to this day if we continue to use Job's logic, although it falls away if a different Self concept is applied. Job cannot understand why he suffers because, although he is conscious of no wrongdoing, the image of God in which he has been steeped assumes that suffering is the result of bad behaviour. Various solutions have been offered to Job's problem with his God. The authors' (the book is a composite) own resolution to Job's torment was to suggest that Yahweh must be trusted because his ways cannot be understood by man. From the intrapsychic perspective, Satan, or the dark side of the Self in the story of Job, can be regarded as a severe neurosis which persecutes Job and colours his image of divinity. Job has developed a depression; his superficially righteous behaviour actually belies a serious unconscious problem. His situation exemplifies the idea that, because of the overpowering numinosity of the archetype at the centre of a painful complex, emotional disturbance is an important manifestation of the divine for the sufferer. I believe that this approach helps to amplify Jung's view of Job's problem.

Jung became very passionate about Job's dilemma in his essay *Answer to Job*, which stimulated enormous controversy, because on the surface it seemed that within it Jung had crossed a line into forbidden territory. Although he is clearly not talking about a metaphysical, extrapsychic God, but about people's ideas of God, or the canonical God image, Jung constantly uses the words 'God', 'Christ' or 'Yahweh' without this qualification, so that unless one constantly translates from the theological to the psychological use of these terms it appears that one is reading theology. To understand his approach it is useful to remember that Jung believes that Biblical statements and their dogmatic elaborations express intra-psychic truth. His essay is a comment on the problem of suffering, on the development of the canonical God image and also on traditional Christian dogmatic ideas of the incarnation. Jung attempts to show how the collective God image typical of Job's era is modified by a change in Job's consciousness, and, remarkably, that this in turn seems to affect the Self itself. For us, the answer to Job's problem lies in a new image of the Self. In the following pages, I will present my own understanding of Jung's amplification of the Job story, with special reference to some of his more obscure passages.

Briefly, Jung's attitude to the problem of suffering addressed in the book of Job is as follows. He regards the story as paradigmatic for our modern situation; like Job, we have to deal with the unpleasant, dark side of divinity as evidenced by mass suffering and the threat of nuclear war. In his treatment of Job, Jung notes that Yahweh is depicted as one-sided, despotic and less conscious than Job, who manages to maintain a moral stance in the face of Yahweh's atrociously arbitrary behaviour. Jung's (CW 11, 600) comment on this fact is to suggest that (the intrapsychic) Yahweh is an unconscious being – a phenomenon that cannot be judged in human terms. This idea of an 'unconscious God' (which outraged many people who unfortunately took it literally) has been interpreted in various ways. Edinger (1984, p. 68) suggests that 'Yahweh as a psychic reality is a personi-fication of the collective unconscious' – and the unconscious does behave in a terrible manner from the viewpoint of consciousness. Some analytical psycho-logists take the idea of an unconscious God to mean that human consciousness is essential for the divine to be fully conscious of itself. This idea verges on the metaphysical, unless we attribute 'unconsciousness' to the divine only as it manifests itself intrapsychically. In this case, Jung's 'unconscious God' actually means that the Self may be an unconscious experience or image within the individual psyche. We do not realize how we manifest it. This was exactly Job's situation.

Job's concept of God is incomplete partly because it ignores God's dark side; at the beginning of the story Job is not conscious of the degree to which his image of God is traditional and stereotyped.[1] Within Job's psyche (or that of the collective consciousness he represents) the unconscious, dark side of the Self (personified as Satan) causes inexplicable suffering, like any complex which is autonomous and unintegrated. Of crucial importance, Job maintains his own orientation to his suffering and ignores the collective approaches personified by his 'comforters'. He seeks to understand what has happened, and develops the belief that his misfortunes must have some transpersonal meaning and are not random or necessarily the result of some unacknowleged sin. He is eventually rewarded in this position by a new vision or consciousness of the divine – that is, a new Self image, or a more conscious God. I suggest that this is a model for what happens when we really look into the archetypal basis of our complexes, understood as intrapsychic manifestations of the divine.

Jung (CW 11, 641) notes that because of Job's apparently superior consciousness in relation to the outrageous behaviour of Yahweh, Yahweh suffers a moral defeat, so that Yahweh has to 'catch up and become human himself'. This is a difficult passage, but we are helped by James Frazer's (1923) comment that a god can only be judged by the standards of the age in which he belongs, so that the ethical code of a deity may be inferior to that of his human contemporaries. Perhaps this is because at any given time the collective intrapsychic image of divinity may belong to an earlier era, and so may lag behind contemporary thought. This indeed was Job's situation in relation to Yahweh, and it obtains to some extent today. Job's Self image had to change radically for him to accommodate what had happened; forced to consciousness by his crisis, Job's personal standards of behaviour had to outgrow his unthinkingly primitive concept of Yahweh. But there remained a larger, collective need for a transformation of the current God image, and this happened by means of Jesus. In Jung's words, the purpose of the incarnation in Jesus is the 'differentiation of Yahweh's consciousness' (CW 11, 642). Jung seems to mean that the Self, or the transpersonal psyche, is humanized as it differentiates by becoming conscious within the psyche of the person who carries out this task, as he or she becomes aware of the demands of the Self in a differentiated or conscious manner. As in the case of Job, these demands are mediated through our pathology, or our personal complexes with their archetypal core, each of which is a strand of the Self. Making them conscious facilitates the individuation process, which is psychologically equivalent to the incarnation of the Self. Said differently, as we become more conscious because of our pathology, so the Self becomes conscious within our psyche, and this process is one of individuation or incarnation within the individual. Further incarnation of the Self was *brought about by* the increment in Job's consciousness of the Self, or his individuation, while Jesus became the mythical forerunner of this task at the collective level.

Until the individual has faced the transpersonal forces of the Self they seem to behave in a way which is totally arbitrary, so that the person faced with them is in a Job-like situation, facing the 'unconsciousness' of the Self, or an unconscious Self image. Initially, one is unaware of the form which the numinosum takes within one's own psyche. According to Jung, as we penetrate into the unconscious more and more of our image of God will be transformed within individual awareness (1975, p. 314). When the experience of the Self is thus mediated, man becomes an instrument of God (Ibid., p. 156). The Job story is not unprecedented; Edinger (1984) has shown how the encounter with a conscious man transformed God in other Biblical stories, such as Abraham's (Gen. 18: 23–32) mediation for the people of Sodom and Gomorrah, whom God is threatening to destroy.

Jung also asks why the *tour de force* of the incarnation is necessary, since all the world is God's and God is in all the world from the beginning. What is missing if a second entrance into creation has to be staged (CW 11, 631)? He goes on to imply the presence of an evolutionary process in the development of our Self image, an image which thereby is becoming less and less primitive. In pagan times, God was revealed in nature but now 'wants' to be more specific and become man. Thus, we see stages in the idea of incarnation, which Jung suggests was prefigured in Adam and continued in Egyptian mythology, where God becomes man via a human mother. The process of incarnation thus traced through myth has allowed God to become increasingly conscious – that is, the image of God within the human being, or our concept of the objective psyche, is now a more conscious one than ever before. The New Testament incarnation is forced to occur, according to Jung, because a new Self consciousness develops as a result of Job. In order to further differentiate its consciousness, the Self has to incarnate totally in the form of Jesus. The struggle within Job reflects the dialectic occurring within God (our Self image); in particular, Jung suggests that Job is burdened with God's unconsciousness of God's dark side.[2] That is, there is a split within the Self image, as if the light and dark aspects did not know that they belonged together. The incarnation in Christ humanizes the archetype by Jesus' ability to integrate aspects of the Self that were previously unconscious, an example of the maxim that: 'God becomes conscious in the act of human reflection' (CW 11, 238). By emphasizing qualities such as love rather than only law or justice, Jesus began a radically new consciousness of the Self, which has determined the psychological task of the past two millennia, and is culminating in a depth psychological appreciation of the dynamics of the Self.

THE CONTINUING INCARNATION OF THE SELF

In the Christian myth, according to Jung, the differentiation and transformation of the image of God forced upon human consciousness by the Job story led to the two sides of Yahweh (the split in the Self image) being represented by Christ and Satan. Jung justifies his idea that incarnation is ongoing by suggesting that the incarnation in Christ (whom he feels carries the cultural projections of the Self) was only partially consummated, because of the way in which Jesus was conceived (CW 11, 626). Mary's freedom from ordinary sexuality also sets her apart from the rest of humanity; her femininity is injured in the process of being allowed no 'imperfections'. Christ remains outside of mankind not only because of the manner of his birth, but because according to dogma he only incarnates the light side of God. Full incarnation of the Self would necessitate the inclusion of what is split off in Christianity: the body, the dark side of the Self and the restoration of the feminine principle to its due prominence. The Self is a totality which includes what we perceive as opposites, including good and evil. It is no longer sufficient to use Jesus or any other single figure as the projected carrier of an all-good Self image. We are now aware that the Self strives for consciousness through each individual, using the manifestations of the unconscious, which are often painful, to do so. We facilitate this process by attaining consciousness of the Self. In Edinger's (1984, p. 84) words: 'To the extent that the *individual* becomes aware of . . . the Self, and lives out of that awareness, he can be said to be incarnating the God-image.' (Emphasis added.)

The archetype exists as potential which expresses itself within the personal field; or, the archetype needs man in order to incarnate. From the point of view of conditioned consciousness (the ego), whose nature is to make categories, some of what incarnates is felt as negative. We refer to this as the dark side of the Self. For the empirical personality, wholeness demands the conscious integration of this dark side, which, as it incarnates within us, leads to the experience of evil. We experience the coming to consciousness of the dark side of the Self as suffering, but this, too, is part of the ongoing incarnation. Jung expresses the crucial part played by humanity in a letter:

> Although the divine incarnation is a cosmic and absolute event, it only manifests empirically in those relatively few individuals capable of enough consciousness to make ethical decisions, i.e., to decide for the Good. Therefore God can be called good only inasmuch as He is able to manifest His goodness in individuals. His moral quality depends on individuals. That is why He incarnates.

> (Jung 1975, p. 314)

Here we see Jung's idea that human consciousness is essential to divinity; our consciousness should be 'an instrument of divine will' (CW 14, 133). In several places (e.g. 1975, p. 112) he is concerned with the possible inflation that the incarnation may otherwise produce. Jung (1975, p. 495) is clear that the Self needs the 'reflecting consciousness' of humanity; as Edinger (1984, p. 80) puts it, the experience of the numinosum brings with it an awareness that: 'the ego has a *reason* to exist, that it is needed for the *realization* of the Self'. This attitude is one answer to the 'why' of suffering. In an important, unpublished letter quoted by Adler, Jung expresses his personal attitude to the problem of suffering by noting that 'the problem of crucifixion is the beginning of individuation'. Jung goes on to say that:

> [I] submitted to the divine power of this apparently unsurmountable problem and I consciously and intentionally made my life miserable, because I wanted God to be alive and free from the suffering man has put on him by loving his own reason more than God's secret intentions. . . . Thus I suffered and was miserable, but . . . in the blackest night even . . . by the grace of God, I could see a Great Light.

> (Adler, 1975, p. 12)

He also says that we cannot avoid suffering, but that we may 'avoid the worst – *blind* suffering'. In this letter Jung sounds much more like a theologian than a psychologist; he is clearly expressing a personal rather than a technical opinion. It is interesting to note that the letter was written in 1936, whereas *Answer to Job* did not appear until 1952. In spite of this time interval, in both cases we see that Jung's approach to suffering involves offering himself as a vessel for the transformation of God, by means of the incarnation of the Self within him; he refers to this process as the 'Christification of Many' (CW 11, 758). Apparently this attitude gave meaning to his own life and suffering. But Jung's attitude is not one of religiously toned masochism. He accepts suffering because he believes it has a purpose; the ego suffers in order to make way for the Self's emerging consciousness.

Edinger (1984) has offered some further implications of these ideas. He reasons that we must be open to the unconscious in order to transform it, but that to get to know the Self in this way leads to suffering because humanity then has to help carry the divine burden which results from our increased consciousness of the Self. Job's predicament, too, was to carry the divine burden, and Edinger warns that a sufficient number of conscious individuals will be necessary in order to humanize the darkness of the emerging God; only the making conscious of hitherto unknown aspects of the Self transforms it. Here, the word 'transform' seems to mean to make assimilable and usable by human consciousness, so that the experience of the Self has meaning and is of noetic value. We could say that in this new, emerging mythology of the incarnation, not only does God make man but man makes God, in the sense that human consciousness is critical in determining which aspects of the Self will embody. 'Just as man was once revealed out of God, so, when the circle closes, God may be revealed out of man' (CW 11, 267). Whether we allow more dark than light to incarnate may be a personal decision. Edinger (1984) follows Jung by recommending that the individual offer himself 'as a vessel for the incarnation of deity and thereby promote the ongoing transformation of God by giving him human manifestation'. He believes that Jesus sets an example in this regard by offering himself as a redemptive object for the anger of God. Jesus' acceptance of this suffering transforms Yahweh into a God of love 'through the example of a loving man' (Ibid., p. 94). This seems to mean that the divine is now able to manifest as love because this potential of the Self can finally incarnate within a sufficiently conscious individual.

INCARNATION AS THE DIFFERENTIATION OF THE SELF WITHIN HUMAN AWARENESS: GOD ACTS OUT OF THE PSYCHE: IS GOD A NEUROSIS?

William James (1902/1958, p. 386) noted that the unconscious influences the individual in ways that feel like control by a higher power, and that this realm of the psyche seems to be one of contact between the human and the divine. In this vein, Jung believes that because God acts on the person through the intermediary of the psyche, we cannot determine exactly whence these actions emanate. Because they interpenetrate, we cannot determine to what extent God and the unconscious are separate entities. In fact, Jung notes that:

For the collective unconscious we could use the word God ... this God is no longer ... in an extra mundane sphere ... a concept in a theological textbook or in the Bible; it is an immediate thing, it happens in your dreams at night, it causes you to have pains in the stomach, diarrhoea, constipation, a whole host of neuroses. . . . If you try to formulate it, to think what the unconscious is after all, you wind up by concluding that it is what the prophets were concerned with; it sounds exactly like some things in the Old Testament. Then you come naturally to the dilemma; is that really God? Is God a neurosis? . . . Now that is a shocking problem. And that is the truth.

(Jung, 1976, p. 391)

This point is of extreme importance to the psychotherapist. Within our woundedness, our neurosis, lies the numinosum. Hence our suffering is relevant to our spiritual search, and is often the beginning of it. This is because the complex has an archetypal component, and any archetype is an aspect of the Self. Thus, a clear separation of individual Self images and the rest of the unconscious is impossible, since these images are inextricably bound up with our personal unconscious material and the Self is defined as the totality of the psyche. The implication here is that if the psyche is the medium through which the experience of God must be filtered, then in this sense God acts out of our unconscious, so that the unconscious is not only the source of our neurosis but is also the immediate or proximate source of our religious experience. The problem that this creates for us is that 'Like God, the unconscious has two aspects; one good, favourable, beneficent, the other evil, malevolent, disastrous' (CW 18, 1538). But in the unconscious, these opposites, or opposing tensions within us, are undiscriminated; for Jung, discrimination is equivalent to becoming conscious. Until we become conscious of these opposites, they remain 'uncreated' or unmanifest. In many mythologies, such as the Genesis story, creation and manifestation begin with the separation of opposites such as light and dark, form and chaos. In other words, what was an undivided unity splits into apparent opposites, or at least individual parts, as we become conscious of its elements. Jung notes that this process becomes a fearful problem for humanity, which becomes a 'vessel full of divine conflict' (CW 14, 659), because as the incarnation of the Self continues, leading to the conscious differentiation of parts of the psyche into a personal self, we must find a way to unite or reconcile these parts within us. As the unconscious enters consciousness, all its opposites separate, causing new conflicts within the ego (CW 14, 740). Based on this psychological observation, Jung suggests that: 'That is the task left to man, and that is the reason why man is so important to God that he decided to become a man himself' (CW 18, 1662). Jung here implies that God as totality penetrates man's psyche *in order to differentiate himself*, as if only in this process of incarnation can the divine experience itself as divided instead of whole. When this happens, one side of the divine opposites is experienced by the self as negative, the other as positive. The experience of such fragmentation is healed by the symbol or the selfobject relationship, which tend towards wholeness. The experience of the Self feels healing because it tends to bring together what seemed irreparably separate.

136

TRANSPERSONAL SELF INTO PERSONAL SELF: IMPLICATE TO EXPLICATE ORDER

Jung's idea that the Self enters our consciousness in order to differentiate itself sounds like speculation in an attempt to explain the clinical finding that we are internally divided.[3] What we call 'ego', as if it were a noun, is actually a process of dividing and categorizing the unitary nature of reality. Interesting light is thrown on this problem from the perspective of modern physics. In order to explain certain observations at the subatomic level, Bohm (1980) has found it necessary to postulate a level of reality which he calls the 'implicate order'. The term implicate refers to an undivided wholeness, similar to what Jung calls the *unus mundus*, or unitary world, which implies that all aspects of reality are linked with all other aspects, and are not truly separate. This term was first used during the Middle Ages to denote the metaphysical or transcendental concept of the essential oneness of all existence. This level of reality cannot be directly experienced, but Jung believed that the phenomenon of synchronicity provided empirical evidence for its existence. The existence of synchronicity suggests that psyche and matter belong to the same reality, since events that have a common meaning occur at the same time within the psyche and in the outer material world. This level of order, which clearly corresponds to the unconscious because we are so unaware of it, unfolds into the 'explicate' order, which is the domain of classical physics, in which discreet objects appear isolated in time and space. This latter (egoic) level of reality comprises the conscious, manifest world. The implicate order, according to Bohm, is the common ground of both matter and consciousness. It is an unbroken, subtle background flow which breaks up as we construct conscious experience that is so intense that we focus on what is actually a series of fragments. This focus gives us an illusory experience of the nature of reality. The movement from implicate to explicate, or from the unconscious to consciousness, involves a movement from undifferentiation to apparent plurality. An unbroken totality becomes the fragmented condition of everyday consciousness which divides everything into parts. The reason for this fragmentation seems to lie in the way the brain works. Although I do not believe that the psyche, or consciousness, is a *product* of the brain, it evidently works through the brain, as we see from the fact that brain damage can affect psychological functioning. Because the Self, or 'Big Mind', seems to be mediated by means of the brain, just as the condition of a radio affects the way the signal is processed, so the experience of the larger psyche is affected by the way the brain works. Because the brain has to give priority to some pieces of reality over others, in order to allow a degree of order and coherence to our experience, it processes information in a fragmented manner, privileging some data over others. Hence our experience of reality is piecemeal and not unitary.

The movement of the unconscious into consciousness represents a movement from the noumenal Self, whose essence is not knowable, into a discrete personality which feels separate from that larger consciousness. Unconsciousness means that we are unaware of the links between elements of experience that actually belong together as part of the seamless whole of the implicate order. Becoming conscious involves making some of these connections and discovering some of their coherence with the rest of one's awareness; a pattern is recognized. Unconscious material becomes conscious as it is connected with existing structures of personality via the operation of memory or other associative mechanisms. But conscious structures inevitably remain only fragments of the whole of the psyche, since our capacity for awareness is finite. Material which enters consciousness does not do so randomly, but fits into meaningful contexts, allowing us to maintain the organization of experience, which is ordered archetypally into themes with common affective and ideational significance. These cognitive–affective schemata or complexes represent the extension of elements of the order of the Self into the realm of the self. Within this realm the archetypal centres of the complexes become the personal psyche's morphogenetic principles. In this way the self is formed as an image of the Self.

THE COROLLARY: CONSCIOUSNESS INEVITABLY INVOLVES SUFFERING

Since consciousness requires discrimination, tension between its constituents is inevitable; different sectors of the personality (complexes) are experienced as if they have different goals and attitudes. Suffering is thus an inevitable consequence of consciousness, as is joy when unity is experienced. According to Jung, because of the internal tension of opposing intrapsychic tendencies, we may become suspended between apparently irreconcilable aspects of the Self. Jung is rather too fond of stressing the inevitability of such oppositions, since many aspects of the psyche are complementary and do not oppose each other. But he is correct to point out that great distress occurs when we experience constituent parts of the personality which are not in harmony. He believes that the resultant suffering is depicted mythically as the crucifixion, and is essential to the process of incarnation. Jung suggests that ultimately the ego must sacrifice itself by letting go of its central position and allowing the unconscious the chance it needs. However, he adds that the unconscious not only wishes to become conscious but also wishes to remain unconscious; that is, God wants to become man, but does not quite want this (CW 11, 740). This paradox needs to be explored.

BARRIERS TO INCARNATION

Jung does not elaborate on his suggestion that the Self may have difficulty becoming conscious, but various reasons suggest themselves. Incarnation is not always possible; the repression barrier, or any other defence which maintains unconsciousness, mitigates against incarnation. We could translate this to say that we defend against incarnation because we are too fearful of divine energy, or of the numinosum. In the light of Kohut's work on structural deficit, we have to take into account the fact that the Self cannot incarnate if the personal self is too fragile to contain the affective intensity of the Self. Humanity is sometimes too fragile to become conscious of its divinity. The borderline personality, to give an extreme example, is particularly prone to fragmentation in the face of the numinosum, and the structures of the original personality of the psychotic have been demolished by numinous experience. Someone must be there to incarnate into; for an I–Thou relationship, there must be a solid 'I'. (This is one reason that psychotherapeutic efforts to build or restore a self are so important, and are conducive to spiritual development.) Jung has suggested that the Self may occasionally try to:

> force something on us that our human limitation cannot endure. The question is of course whether such things happen. I think the answer is yes, for if God needs us as regulators of his incarnation and his coming to consciousness, it is because in his boundlessness he exceeds all the bounds that are necessary for becoming conscious. Becoming conscious means continual renunciation.
>
> (Jung, 1975, p. 120)

This alludes to the problem of 'letting go', which is discussed on p. 35.

Finally, it is important to note that, with Jung, we have so far concentrated on the Christian model of suffering and incarnation. There are considerable difficulties with this model, and as Hillman (1983b, p. 76) has pointed out, it is a mistake to relate all of our experiences of suffering to this one mythical image: 'We need many models, beside the Christian one, to locate our psychological experiences.' The psychologist has to remember that all theologies have a different God image, but they all claim to be the only true one. It is therefore reasonable to assume that theologies are only partial truths, and that, like all myths, they represent different aspects of the Self in ways which are relevant only to certain people. Therefore there is no need to restrict ourselve to one mythical form of incarnation. For instance, the Hindu perspective offers an alternative to the Christian model.

INCARNATION IN THE HINDU TRADITION

The Hindu concept of divinity leads to a very different picture of incarnation from that of the Christian, and hence to a different understanding of suffering. The Judaeo-Christian God is personal and moralistic in a way which leads to complex intellectual dilemmas, such as intellectually tortuous attempts to avoid making God personally responsible for evil and suffering. Writing from a Hindu perspective, Bruteau (1974) notes that the questions which have historically plagued Western culture, such as the nature of good and evil, are in fact artifacts of the Western ego's habit of classification, which uses itself as the paradigm of clarity. This ego reifies what it classifies and sets the resulting categories in opposition to each other, thereby losing touch with the underlying unity of reality. Consonant with the perspective of the religious approach to the psyche, she points out that in Hindu thought the impersonal and the unconscious are actually of one piece with personal, deliberative consciousness. Deity is all-inclusive and not separate from evil; its manifestations range from Krishna to Kali. Reality in this system does not operate according to the ego's moral categories. For the Hindu, deity is both transcendent and incarnate, personal and impersonal, infinite and finite, creator, preserver and destroyer. A person is both temporal in his body and eternal in his Selfhood. Expressed psychologically, this mythology inextricably intermingles the archetypal and the personal. The Hindu feels that we are all manifestations of divinity and a part of divine life. In this context, it is meaningless to speak of God as one, since divinity is beyond number. The idea of one God inexorably brings to mind the image of an entity with edges. The concept of the divine as infinite mind overcomes this difficulty. As Daniélou puts it:

> To speak of the manifest forms of a unique God implies a confusion between different orders. God manifest cannot be one, nor can the number one apply to any unmanifest causal aspect. At no stage can unity be taken as the cause of anything, since existence implies a relation and unity would imply existence without relation.

(Daniélou, 1973)

Thus, divinity cannot be said to be one or many. The expression of the Vedantists is that it is 'not two', or, there is a non-dual principle existing beyond all forms of manifestation of which the self is a part. This principle is the transpersonal Self.

The implication of this view for the psychologist is to demonstrate a mythology of incarnation which does not require the intense suffering of the Christian story. This mythologem says that the self and the Self are always the same, and suffering results because we are not conscious of our identity with the Self. This image of incarnation provides an option which might be useful for those who prefer a different self–Self relationship to that of a crucifixion model, perhaps one which does not require vicarious atonement or sacrifice. For the Hindu, Christ is one of many examples of the divine incarnate, although they would be puzzled by the statement attributed to him that he is '*the* way'. Further, there does not seem to be a Hindu equivalent to the resurrection. In the non-dual Hindu view, suffering is largely due to the fact that we have forgotten who we are, so that we feel ourselves to be separate from each other and the world.

As well as these mythical possibilities, psychoanalytic theory also provides an unexpected source of models for the mechanism of the incarnation of the Self into a self.

INCARNATION AS THE ARCHETYPAL BASIS OF DEVELOPMENTAL THEORY

It is my contention that all psychodynamic theories of development which postulate the unfolding of innate endowment are in fact archetypally related to mythologies of incarnation. This is because psychoanalytic explanations of the origin of suffering all involve and attempt to explain the way in which the infant's

140

potentials – those of the Self, which represent the core of the person – find their way into behaviour and the body, and eventually form a personal self. In the process, from the ego's perspective, things go wrong and 'pathology' results, so that incarnation causes suffering.[4]

To explain development, personalistic theories (in contrast to transpersonal theories) typically suggest that biologically encoded engrams interact with people in the child's world. They imply that only genes are involved in the child's endowment. But in Jungian theory the genes represent only the 'red' or somatic end of the archetype, which also has a spiritual pole. However, the unconscious ontological assumption of traditional psychoanalysis, which is reflected in personalistic therapies derived from it, is to ignore or deny any spiritual determinants in the formation of personality – these are considered to be unscientific (the arbitrary nature of this appellation is discussed in Chapter 4). By contrast, in the religious paradigm, the Self is thought to be an element of the divine, so that the person's innate or archetypal determinants are manifestations of the spirit. Jung actually refers to the archetypes as 'organs of God' (1975, p. 130). This metaphor can keep us aware of the divine origin of our suffering, via the complexes which form around the archetypes. These filaments of spirit clothe themselves with personal material in the process of incarnation. At the same time, and this is crucial to my hypothesis, these determinants also describe the principles of intrapsychic structure formation, and represent irreducible psychological bedrock. When these two usages are not split, they indicate a confluence of the human and the divine within the personality. They should *not* be split if we wish to deal with the person as a whole and not as parts.

The archetypal component of the complex therefore represents an incarnate aspect of the divine for that individual, so that the process of the unfolding of the Self in childhood, which is responded to and mediated by people in the child's environment, constantly intermingles personal and transpersonal elements. Or, during development, the human and the divine interpenetrate. Thus, the lifetime spiritual task of the individual expresses itself early on and is not different from the psychological goal of the personality. But to reach a reconciliation with these elements of the divine is difficult, because they involve us in suffering as well as joy.

We can now consider various theories of personality from this point of view. But as a prelude to this comparison, I should note that although I have concentrated on suffering produced by psychopathology, I also include illness in the body within the purview of my thesis. Although physical maladies often seem to be an arbitrary disaster, the ill body can reveal an unconscious archetypal problem in symbolic form which is somatized because it has no other access to expression. The archetype uses whatever environmental means it can to embody itself: bacteria, virus, accident or toxin (Zeigler, 1983). The body thereby becomes a final common path of material that is unable to become conscious; whatever rolls down hill collects in the body. Because individuation occurs in the body as well as intrapsychically (Mindell, 1982), somatic symptoms are often that part of us which cannot find any other way to live. 'Psyche and body are not separate entities but one and the same life' (CW 7, 194). Because mind and body express two aspects of the same entity (CW 8, 618–619), when the body is diseased the archetype is insisting on incarnating itself, albeit in a painful way for the person concerned. Physical illness also expresses the general rule that suffering is the subjective experience of the attempt of the Self to incarnate into a self in whatever way it can.

THE MECHANISMS OF THE INCARNATION OF THE SELF

The problem we now seek to address is to describe mechanisms by which the Self *appears* to emerge from some trans-temporal, trans-spatial dimension into a body and a personal self, into space–time as we experience it. The word 'dimension' here is actually meaningless, since no concept of place or time could apply to the Self in its pre-incarnate state. In fact, the whole question of incarnation and development is probably only an apparent problem, an artifact of our need to explain our experience of growth in terms of our own categories. The budding self is always enclosed within the Self of which it is a part, and it differentiates by the development of a sense of separateness. But from the ordinary sensory perspective, development *seems* to occur as if a process of incarnation is unfolding.

Elucidation of the actual mechanisms of incarnation seems an important task for two reasons. First, if we take the position that the archetypes cannot be reduced to the genes, or as Jung put it they are not simply given with brain structure (1975, p. xli), then some other explanation for their mode of being in the world is necessary. Second, because they offer an experience of divinity via the complex, we would like to locate their effects within everyday psychotherapeutic experience so that they are not simply abstract, experience-distant concepts. This grounding within our practice can be achieved if we remember that the archetype is found both as a recurrent pattern of behaviour and also as a producer of affect. Developmental psychology must be integrated with the teleological approach, since the archetypes do not simply operate as highly spiritualized imagery after personality development has consolidated, as some of the classical Jungian literature implies. They represent themselves as developmental imperatives, powerfully present from conception. When the baby is at the breast, an archetypal event is occurring, whose vicissitudes must be studied as much as we try to understand the Mother archetype as it appears in dream imagery or religions.

The Self begins to express itself as soon as the baby is born. But, with the notable exception of the London school, there is a clear bias in the early Jungian literature against investigating the details of the archetype in the body and in early development. Although Jung (CW 8, 414) eventually described the archetype as lying on a spectrum between a 'red', or somatic, and a 'blue', or spiritual, pole, in his earlier work he focused on the blue end, often implying that development preferably grows from the red to the blue, as occurs, for example, when sexuality becomes 'spiritualized' (CW 8, 43). This was written at a time when he was still differentiating his work from Freud's sexual theories, and also reflects the prevailing anti-body sentiment of his era, which was still suffering from Christian ascetic values. Much later he was to note that:

> the spirit is the life of the body seen from within, and the body the outward manifestation of the life of the spirit – the two being really one – then we can understand why the striving to transcend the present level of consciousness, through acceptance of the unconscious, must give the body its due, and why recognition of the body cannot tolerate a philosophy that denies it in the name of the spirit.
>
> (Jung, CW 10, 195)

Or, simply put, the Self 'has its roots in the body' (CW 13, 242). Such appreciation of the importance of the body is our link to infancy, where psychology and physiology are more indistinguishable than at any time of life. Of this period we have no subjective data except what can be inferred empathically, but it seems safe to say that the archetypes are felt in the baby's body. Therefore from an archetypal viewpoint, psychodynamic theories about the origin and development of the child's consciousness are all attempts to explain mechanisms by which the primal Self of the baby, via its archetypal endowment, incarnates into a personal self.[5]

Thus, a firm grasp of personalistic psychoanalytic theories which deal with the roots of psychopathology in childhood development is essential for the psychotherapist interested in a religious orientation to clinical practice. These theories bridge notions of the archetype as a transcendent, unknowable reality with descriptions of the practical, experience-near effect of the archetype as a dynamic intrapsychic agency. Or, we could say that since the archetype manifests as the complex, and the archetype is a manifestation of the divine, we need to understand the dynamics of the complex in order to understand the mechanics of God in the psyche. In the process of elaborating the mechanism of the complex, these theories also attempt to explain the origin of the suffering which accompanies the process of the incarnation of the Self, and they clarify the way in which the Self tries to manifest itself in the transference. Psychoanalytic theories which confine themselves to single themes, such as the Oedipal or the narcissistic motifs, are not so much wrong as particular examples of the origin of emotional suffering, relevant to people who share certain archetypal backgrounds. Other people require different backdrops in order that their suffering can be placed in its mythical context. The very fact that we find such mythical reflections of psychopathology as that of Oedipus and Narcissus helps to ground psychoanalytic theory within archetypal theory.

If we look at any major psychodynamic approach from the point of view of its archetypal underpinnings, for example, as reflected in myth, it becomes clear that, wherever we look, some archetype has a major role to play in the origin of suffering. In the following sections, I would like to show how different theories of psychopathology emphasize different archetypal manifestations.

SUFFERING AND INCARNATION IN JUNG'S COMPLEX THEORY

Complexes are the cause of emotional suffering in Jung's theory of psychopathology. The complex is also the mechanism by which the archetype as an 'organ of God' enters into manifestation, or incarnates within the individual. Complex theory describes how mental representations, affects, impulses, memories and images cluster around an archetypal core. Complexes behave like relatively autonomous centres within the psyche, often opposing each other's attitudes or the usual conscious attitude of the personality. (Within the self psychological paradigm, they correspond to the contents of vertically split-off material. To different degrees complexes are free of conscious control; in the extreme they act as splinter psyches, or sub-personalities, and, when constellated (stimulated), can appear to 'possess' the individual by overriding the wishes of the majority of the personality. It is then as if each fragment of the divine pulls in different directions; if we were within a myth this would look like different gods or goddesses wanting incompatible ends from the same human being. (Hera and Hestia want me to stay home; Artemis or Aphrodite do not.) But complexes are not all pathological; the sum of all of them form the structure of the personality as a whole.

Because of their affective intensity, complexes influence perception, and when negative produce painful, inexplicable feelings and behaviour (CW 8, 201 and 202). Embodiment of the archetype in this way is synonymous with soul; material which is too affectively painful cannot embody, so that in such cases a piece of the child's soul remains split off or repressed. Jung believed that the tension of intrapsychic opposites, or complexes with opposing goals, is essential to development and is not problematic if the opposites can be reconciled within the larger personality. But neurosis occurs when splitting takes place because of the intensity of the difference between the fragments. Then, the internal harmony of the personality is lost because different aspects of one's being cannot agree.

When the dark side of the archetype predominates – equivalent to the mythical Terrible Mother or Father – the resultant affect states are too difficult for the individual to integrate. It is then as if the person is bowled over by the wrath of God. In this situation one could say that some aspect of the divine is pushing too hard to incarnate. Assistance with this process is the province of psychotherapy and is one of the main rationales for this work to be considered a spiritual practice.

SUFFERING IN FREUD'S THEORY: ITS ARCHETYPAL BASIS

In Freud's theory, the only forms of the numinosum, or the only archetypes considered as pathogenic, are those of sexuality and aggression. (The mythical underpinnings of this theory are discussed on p. 88.) Perhaps the main weakness of Freud's theory is that he ignores other archetypal potentials within the psyche.

His theory of psychopathology is essentially one in which unconscious sexual or aggressive urges, which want release but are forbidden, cause suffering. This theory can easily be cast within Jung's spectrum metaphor for the structure of the archetype. The original biological impulse corresponds to the archetype at the somatic or red end, and the intrapsychic wish or fantasy to which it gives rise corresponds to the blue pole. These are too anxiety-provoking to be allowed into consciousness, so that defences are needed against them. That is, translated into archetypal theory, the presence of these archetypes is overwhelming for the child, either because his or her parents mediate them in a pathological manner or because the parents cannot help the child attenuate the intensity of these archetypes in the particular way that they are present within him or her. If we again remember the numinosity of the archetype, we can imagine how extraordinarily powerful it must feel to the child. The archetypal affect – the attempt of the archetype to embody – associated with the unfulfilled or forbidden wish is impossible for the child to cope with, so that conflict or a complex develops. Freudian theory suggests that the resulting neurotic difficulty contains the original impulse, the anxiety and guilt it produced, and the defences against it, in a disguised or symbolic form. The divine element thereby becomes encased within a matrix of human events and memories, which may painfully obstruct the expression of healthy aggression and sexuality in later life.

Freud saw the way in which, in many religious systems, this pathological structure is projected wholesale onto God images, leading to a neurotic image of the Self. In particular, the super ego, that hypothetical agency of the mind which forbids the expression of the archetypal wish, is often projected as the wishes of a remote, strict father–legislator type of sky God who keeps track of all our misdeeds and has a list of 'thou shalts' and 'thou shalt nots' which have been elucidated by the fathers of the tradition. Most importantly, in most Western religious systems, the forbidden archetypally based urge itself, such as sexuality, is not consciously considered to be a part of the divine. By contrast, the religious approach to the psyche considers it to belong to the numinosum, as it was for Freud himself. Within Christianity and for various types of ascetic practice, the drive aspect of the numinosum is considered to belong to the devil and to be fought. This attitude is one of the ways historically that the needs of the body were demonized. To restore the split in the collective image of the divine which results from a God who is all spirit and all good, we must realize that the archetype, via the complex, is responsible for the patient's suffering. What it seeks is not to be split off but to be made conscious and allowed to incarnate into the rest of the self.

It is ironic, in view of the gravity of the Freud–Jung split for depth psychology as a whole, that there is nothing inherently incompatible in Freud's theory with archetypal theory. They both require a preformed mental organization with structured characteristics which restrict perception to certain preferred modes. Classical analytic theory was simplistic, because it emphasizes only one (the Oedipal) complex, and it suggests that human behaviour is motivated by only two instinctual drives or their derivatives, or by the defences against their expression.

The Jungian model recognizes more complexes, allows many more archetypal possibilities than those of sexuality and aggression, and does not permit an exclusively genetic or brain-based explanation for the origin of these archetypes. It is noteworthy that some modern Freudian psychoanalysts have given up the classical drive theory of motivation, and now consider affect to be the major motivator of human behaviour. This development brings psychoanalytic theory further in line with Jungian theory, since affect is the effect of the archetype in the body. Affect is the sign that incarnation is attempting to occur. But, true to the Freudian tradition, psychoanalytic affect theorists only attend to the somatic pole and ignore the spiritual aspect of the archetype.

A refinement of classical psychoanalytic theory occurred with the development of object relations theory, which evolved in an attempt to explain how the child and its fantasies interact with early caregivers, and how this interaction affects the subsequent development of personality. Object relations theory assumes that people are essentially relationship-seeking creatures, and the need to form relationships is itself a motivational urge. Archetypally, this theory recognizes the importance of the *coniunctio*, and moves away from considering sexuality and aggression as the only manifestations of the numinosum. It is a theory which easily fits with complex theory, since object relations actually refer to intrapsychic structures which are enduring mental representations of self and others that fundamentally affect relationships in the external world. These structures are the residue of interactions with early objects. They correspond to complexes in the sense that they are structurally and dynamically important within the personality. This theory also requires the presence of intrinsic organizing tendencies, based on an innate readiness to perceive and respond to the caregiving environment. This is of course a definition of the archetype, which determines internal psychological structure formation, or complexes which dispose us to perceive and organize ourselves in particular ways. Without using the word archetype, infant researchers of this school agree that the child has an inborn tendency to respond to its objects in a particular way.

It has been suggested that defective parental care, or disturbances of early object relations, distort archetypal development or thwart the intention of the archetype. However, this view implies that the archetype is only intrapsychic, only 'in' the child, and only good. There is another way of looking at this question. Instead of looking at the child's endowment and its fit with its environment as determined by chance, it may be more useful to regard the maturational environment of the child and its archetypal endowment, its inner and outer worlds, as synchronistically belonging together, both an integral part of the child's identity. The archetype seems to have a 'field' effect; the constellating power of the archetype – its 'magnetic' tendency to stimulate and draw to itself events which correspond to it – ensures that inner predispositions and outer events belong together. The structure of our inner life and our outer relationships mirror each other.

This hypothesis requires that beginning in infancy there is an archetypal predisposition to relationships of a particular quality. Our suffering is therefore intrinsically a part of our archetypal endowment, and it is brought about by the archetype via the quality of the relationships it evokes. Later in life, the process of forming relationships is affected by the mutually interacting complexes of the participants and is therefore also archetypally coloured. Complexes activated in this process cause suffering, so that again we invoke the presence of spiritual determinants in the etiology of suffering.

KOHUT'S SELF PSYCHOLOGY: ITS ARCHETYPAL BASIS

In order to ground my own approach to the psyche's religious function within day-to-day psychotherapeutic work, I have emphasized selfobject and intersubjectivity theory, because I believe them to be the best of the current personalistic theories.[6] Many clinical observations of earlier object relations theory are encompassed within these paradigms and are explained in an improved manner, without falling back on discredited drive theory or spatial and mechanical metaphors of the psyche. Selfobject and intersubjectivity theory represent the continuing development of field theory within psychoanalysis that was begun by object relations theorists, but the newer models have less of the Cartesian bias of earlier theories.[7] As well, selfobject theory seems to be the personalistic theory which is closest to Jung's emphasis on the importance of the *coniunctio*. On p. 26 I have examined the ways in which Kohut's self psychology clarifies this alchemical idea as it expresses itself at the personal level. Here I will further suggest how Kohut's ideas can also be fruitfully applied to the problem of the mechanism of the incarnation of the Self into a personal self, and also further clarify the psychological, rather than theological, meaning of the terms 'spirit' and 'soul'.

Kohut uses the term 'self' to mean the whole person, in a way which is similar to Freud's early use of the term 'ego' before this came to designate a set of psychological operations. Kohut's self psychology is both an intrapsychic and an interpersonal theory. It suggests that the child's psychological life is formed by a process of gradual accretion, built up as a result of the interaction of its early caregivers and certain innate determinants of a healthy self. These determinants can be termed 'narcissistic', since in Kohut's view narcissism is not necessarily pathological. These inborn factors, or selfobject needs, are described on pp. 26–27. Briefly, the term selfobject refers to the intrapsychic experience of another person who is necessary for the maintenance of the cohesion, vitality or integrity of the self. During development, myriads of interactions with the child's selfobjects are 'transmutingly internalized', or taken in and used to build a sense of self. Depending on the quality of the relationships between the child and its selfobjects, the self develops with varying degrees of either cohesiveness or tendency to fragmentation. The vitality of the self also varies from being more or less vigorous to states of increasing enfeeblement, and it may be more or less internally harmonious or chaotic. The degree of failure or success in the original selfobject milieu determines the degree of structural deficit or wholeness of the self; in

Jungian terms, the child's selfobjects determine the nature of its complexes. A structurally firm self allows one to tolerate loss, failure, disappointments or triumphs without excessive fluctuations of self-esteem.

For several reasons, psychoanalytic self psychology is not an object relations theory in the traditional sense of the term. It considers other people to be important in the building of self structures and not necessarily as the object of drives. When another person is important, intrapsychically that person becomes part of the self, and so is no longer a separate object. The drives themselves, rather than being seen as primary, are considered to be constituents of the self, so that their appearance in 'raw' form indicates fragmentation of the self. A further major difference from classical theory is that disturbances of the self are not considered to be the result of conflict in relation to parents, but are due to structural deficits in the integrity or soundness of the self which occur when early selfobjects fail to respond to the child. This leads to painful feelings of fragmentation, emptiness, depletion, unreality or hopelessness. Many symptoms, such as addictions or sexual perversions, which were previously thought to be the result of intrapsychic conflict, and in the theological literature to be 'sinful', can now be seen to be attempts to counteract the sense of internal emptiness or chaos produced by a selfobject milieu which was chronically emotionally deficient. Where conflict is found, it is usually secondary to a primary defect in the integrity of the self, or it is the result of the child's need to sacrifice his own needs in order to stay connected to essential caregivers (Stolorow and Brandschaft, 1987).

The patient's selfobject needs are reactivated in the therapy to the extent that they were not met in childhood; the therapist is called upon to perform those functions which the patient is unable to carry out for him/herself because they have never been internalized, but which are necessary for psychological health. Therefore, intrapsychically the therapist is not experienced as separate, but as an extension of the self who provides essential mirroring, idealizing or twinship needs. From the religious point of view, the therapist is thereby assisting in the incarnation of the Self. At the same time (Kohut, 1984), cure is produced by a process in which the patient gradually takes over these functions for him/herself, a process that is facilitated by the analysis and interpretation of manageable disruptions in the self–selfobject tie, which tend to repeat those of childhood. The interaction with the therapist is used to rebuild self structures which need repair. Kohut's view of man is therefore one of incompleteness as a cause of suffering, a view which is found throughout Jung's work.

Elsewhere (Corbett, 1989; Corbett and Kugler, 1989) I have reviewed the major disparities between the entirely different concepts of the self in Jung and Kohut. Jung's Self is a priori, while Kohut's self is built up in development, although Kohut admits to a rudimentary self which consists of the baby's phase-appropriate expectations of parental responses, and the capacity to assert its needs and turn towards its human environment. Kohut's self has nothing of the *imago dei* quality found in Jung's concept, and nothing of the latter's numinosity. Kohut has no explanation for the *origin* of the child's grandiosity and its need for an idealized parent imago, so that his theory requires a hypothetical 'blueprint' within the baby – this is Jung's Self, which provides the potential for the selfobject experiences that are actually experienced by the child. Kohut has therefore identified some of the archetypal aspects or components of the Self as they emerge in development and attempt to incarnate from a state of potential into manifestation. The two theories require each other for a full understanding of the incarnational process and the suffering which it causes, since, the responses of the child's selfobjects to the unfolding of the Self's attempt to incarnate affect the state of the personal self which results. I would also suggest that the contents of the numinous manifestations of the Self described by Jung are strongly influenced by the individual's selfobject relationships. In other words, the classical Jungian emphasis on dream symbols has not paid sufficient attention to the fact that these symbols are in part a reflection of the dreamer's selfobject milieu. In Jung's words (1973, p. 172), 'In the deepest sense we all dream not out of ourselves, but out of what lies between us and the other.'

SOUL, SPIRIT AND SELFOBJECT

Psychologically speaking, as the Self unfolds by the process of reaching out to the human environment in the form of selfobject needs, spirit is attempting to incarnate in the child. Spirit is synonymous with archetype; it is the transpersonal principle that gives pattern, meaning, discrimination, and order to life. When spirit embodies, its effect is affect, often felt as part of a complex. This affective component of the archetype represents its channel into the body. This embodiment is the somatic pole of a process which we call soul, which at the same time produces intrapsychic imagery. In other words, as Hillman (1985) puts it, soul brings spirit into personal experience. The result of this spirit–soul interaction is a process of incarnation.

To further link the two theories of Jung and Kohut, it seems that, reluctantly, there is no choice but to 'adultomorphize' the baby. What Kohut calls infantile grandiosity, or an intense need to be responded to in an attuned manner, seems to correspond to the baby's experience of joy at its inner experience of the Self, and its awareness that it is in touch with, or is a part of, that Totality. To use theological language, it feels its 'child of God' nature; in psychological parlance, this 'grandiosity' is actually a manifestation of what is seen mythically as the divine child. In infancy, this archetypal aspect of the Self reaches out to the world for acknowledgement, so that it can continue to incarnate in the child. This recognition or mirroring of the Self is seen mythically in the story of the Magi bringing gifts to the Christ child. When the Self shining through the child is recognized, it can embody as soul; it is then felt to be a part of the child. The transpersonal is then able to be safely experienced at the personal level.

For the Self to embody in this way, a reflecting (mirroring) consciousness outside the child is necessary, because consciousness arises from reflection (CW 8, 242), and reflection is a function of the soul, which personifies the result as image (Hillman, 1985) and as a manageable affective experience. This recognition and attunement with the child's joy at its sense of the Self is provided by the soul of the parent or the child's other available selfobject. It takes soul to make soul; soul mirrors spirit, which is felt as soul when it embodies. In the adult, soul bridges to the unconscious (CW 13, 62), so that the self is able to experience aspects of the Self. But in childhood this function of safely mediating the Self has to be carried out for the child by the selfobject.

Idealization means the perception of a person or a belief system as a source of order, direction, value and meaning. According to Jung (CW 9, ii, 33), these qualities are carried by spirit; for example, in the production of religious or philosophical ideas. Jung (CW 8, 633) equates spirit with ideals, and suggests (CW 8, 648) that spirit gives meaning to life. Idealized people are seen as the carrier or even source of spirit. Neumann's (1973) idea that the child projects the Self onto the parent is synonymous with Kohut's idealizing parent imago.[8]

The child must idealize the parent, if only because of the overwhelming affective intensity of the raw experience of the archetype, with which he or she requires help. The experience of the archetype, especially in negative form, is potentially overwhelming, so that the child needs soothing and containing by his or her selfobjects in order to structuralize these affects into complexes, which allows the personality to become coherent. In this way, spirit is personalized into character structure via the complex. If the parent is able to carry these idealized projections, the idealized selfobject is gradually internalized, allowing self structures to be built which are an internal source of self-soothing, values and ideals. These allow the individual to integrate and order archetypal experience, the numinosum, without fragmenting. The selfobject function thereby becomes an internal capacity to experience spirit, and this is of major relevance to the religiously oriented therapist.

We have seen that whatever aspect of the child's archetypal potentials are recognized by its selfobjects can be built into a personal self structure. In order to ground the soul of the child in its body, it is critical that the selfobjects are empathically attuned to the complexities of its affective life. Affect is the factor which embodies spirit, and is crucial because of its connection to archetype and complex. Parental attunement mediates and contains the child's affects, so that the effect of the archetype does not overwhelm him or her. The child is then able to receive his or her transpersonal ground and make it available to everyday awareness. Otherwise this aspect of the Self has to split off; it may embody as a part of the 'dark' side of the Self, it may become a source of pathology, or just lead to narcissistic vulnerability. Eventually the child will internalize this ability to reflect, know him/herself and develop his or her own relationship to experiences of the Self.

Mirroring allows the Self to incarnate into a self; but, because parents are not perfect, mirroring is always partial. Thus, depending on the responsiveness of the selfobjects, different aspects of the Self incarnate preferentially into positively or negatively toned complexes. Which aspects are allowed and which are not tolerated is a function of the selfobject's own needs, and their pathology and typology, leading to a particular fit between parents and child. The resulting self is always a partial incarnation of the Self, with dark or unincarnate areas, which become the source of future selfobject needs and psychopathology.

The archetypal basis of Kohut's psychology is clearly seen in myth. The child is in a position which is depicted in the myths of child gods such as the infants Jesus and Krishna. Even though the divine child is helpless at present, he senses his enormous potential, he knows who he is, and people are attracted to the Self which he manifests and which shines through him. The idealized Great Mother is found in many myths; stories of the Mother Goddess and her divine son–lover, Attis, Adonis, Tammuz or Osiris, reflect the need of the child not only to adore his mother but also to differentiate himself from her. In the Jungian literature (Neumann, 1973), any figure who is idealized is said to carry the projection of the Self; such a figure is spiritualized and made larger than life. This mechanism is used when the child needs help with overwhelming affects, especially terrifying ones. Kohut has noticed both the need for the inner experience of the Self to be mirrored and the need for the child's parents to carry projections of the Self, but he has described these needs in personalistic, rather than archetypal, terms.

Kohut's view implies that suffering is caused by the failure of the child's selfobjects to attune to the child's experience of the Self, or by their failure to allow themselves to carry such projections. Often the parents are envious of the child's contact with the numinosum, whose light can be seen in the eyes of any joyful baby. Or, they wish to steal or otherwise usurp it for their own use. In later life, the experience of the numinosum then becomes a source of shame or fear and must be vigorously defended against.

In therapy, the re-emergence of childhood selfobject needs links us to our desire to feel whole. These needs represent the constellation of the Self, again trying to elicit a response which will allow incarnation. The therapist is called upon to mediate the demands of the Self, and must recognize the intense numinosity of the resultant selfobject needs. Therapy with such a consciousness is not a mere technical matter. It has to do with the experience of the divine in the relationship, either trying to manifest itself through the patient's emotional life as a mirror need, or in the form of idealized projections onto the therapist. Just as, in classical Jungian analysis, wholeness is said to be achieved by the experience of the symbol which carries the experience of the numinosum, so wholeness may be achieved by the experience of the selfobject, which allows the Self to provide what is missing in the self. Such constellation of the Self in therapy produces a powerfully felt field with its own dynamics, within which both participants are held and influenced. The selfobject experience is one form of this Self-generated field. The therapist is asked either to see the patient's connection to the Self by mirroring what is affectively important to the patient, or he or she is asked to carry idealized projections which represent the patient's search for the Self. In either case, by casting the situation in terms of the Self and its experience, psychotherapy can be practised as a spiritual discipline.

8

SUFFERING

The search for meaning

DOGMATIC AND PSYCHOTHERAPEUTIC
APPROACHES TO SUFFERING CONTRASTED

In the previous chapter I presented a case for several propositions. These include the idea that suffering and joy are a part of the subjective experience of the attempt of the Self, or its archetypal components, to incarnate into a self. As well, such experiences, via the complexes which contain them, have an intrapsychic aspect (in the form of thought or imagery) and synchronistically an affective or bodily aspect. An image is the soul's portrayal of the experience of the Self, which is synonymous with spirit. Spirit or Self gives rise to soul as it embodies – what was transpersonal becomes relatively personal. What we call 'ego' is that aspect of the soul which is self-reflexively conscious in the body. But this kind of formulation is of course far too removed from experience to be of much use to the suffering individual. The sufferer wants to know why he suffers, and this search for meaning is often the beginning of spiritual or psychological awakening. The eventual achievement of a sense that one's suffering has meaning is an end point of the process of incarnation, and makes suffering more bearable. This goal may be achieved in as many ways as there are ways to gain wisdom, but here I want to focus on two particular types of search for such meaning; that which proceeds by means of adherence to a traditional theological system, and that which is gained in psychotherapy.

It is worth providing a brief overview of these two possibilities. In psychotherapy the painful complex is gradually 'digested', or mollified, by a process of increasing consciousness, so that it loses its grip on the sufferer. The self structures which are necessary to contain the childhood difficulty are built or strengthened, and eventually its archetypal underpinnings are clarified. This result is achieved by means of the relationship with the therapist, which ameliorates the effects of early pathogenic relationships, and also by the elucidation of intrapsychic material such as dreams and fantasy. In people who are open to such possibility, a spiritual perspective gradually develops during the therapy as transpersonal elements such as numinous experience enter the picture. In this way a manageable relationship to the Self develops, as the Self is experienced within the individual's own psyche.

Using the metaphor of the book of Job we might say that one's own new image of God appears out of one's own whirlwind. The sufferer comes face to face with the unpalatable fact that the spirit both causes his or her suffering via the complex and also resolves it by means of direct contact with the numinosum, by the experience of the symbol and by the experience of the Self mediated in the relationship with the therapist. Of course this is an idealized picture and many things can go wrong in the process. But at least in principle this brief overview describes how *individual* reconciliation with the Self occurs, which may or may not be generalizable to others. Here it is important that the therapist not impose any preconceived value system on the patient's suffering. This may happen when the therapist places an excessive emphasis on healing because of some personal need, without recognizing that the purpose of the work and the patient's destiny may not lead in that direction. The fact that the patient does not heal does not necessarily invalidate the work that has been done; as Freud noted, the work is also done for the purpose of discovering our essence. The difficulties with the psychological approach to suffering are that it requires a capacity to tolerate enormous uncertainty for prolonged periods of time, and that the outcome may be ambiguous. But the rewards which it brings are the authenticity of the result, a deeper connection to the Self and enhanced personality integration.

By contrast with the psychotherapeutic approach, recourse to ready-made or traditional dogmatic solutions to suffering offers explanations which are intended to be generally applicable. The sufferer is asked to find his or her answer within an existing systematic explanation of suffering. But, because traditional systems imply that all problems have the same solution, dogmatic answers may not deal with the specifics of the individual situation. This is especially true when they do not resonate with the archetypal constitution of the individual. To balance this statement, it must also be said that a considerable fund of wisdom and experience can be found within the traditions, so dogmatic solutions certainly may be helpful if they correspond to the sufferer's personal psychology. But what of the plight of the individual whose psychology does not fit with the dogma, or whose emotional difficulty is actually worsened by it? For instance, when the individual turns to traditional Christianity for help with inexplicable suffering, he or she is told that Christ's suffering was redemptive and on his or her behalf and that faith in Christ will keep him or her from despair and provide the answer he or she needs. Through baptism in the Church and by remembering the cross the individual can participate in the consolation it brings. If the Christian myth is alive for the sufferer, this approach may bring enormous comfort; one literally partakes in the life of God (the beneficial aspects of this mythologem are further considered on p. 164). But here I wish to focus on individuals who are not helped, for instance because, like Job, they do not feel that their suffering is particularly the result of sin. They may feel that the idea of vicarious atonement via the crucifixion stops them from feeling their own situations fully, which may require a different myth or metaphor to be fully reflected. In such cases individuals are left feeling angry with God, if they still have one. If they suffer from low self-esteem and have been taught that suffering is the result of sin (initially by parents and teachers and now by intrapsychic Job's comforters), they may search their consciences and berate themselves. If such individuals feel worthless, they may imagine that for this reason they have been abandoned or punished by God. Several psalms typify this attitude, which projects a parental reward–punishment psychology onto the divine. (Archetypally, the sufferer has become a divine victim, tormented by the dark side of the Self and out of touch with its benevolent light side.) Notions that suffering is a 'test' are similar anthropomorphic projections onto the divine which may have no basis in reality. They fail to take into account that the relationship between self and Self cannot be directly compared to human relationships; it requires its own unique conceptual and affective framework. But the traditional Judaeo-Christian attitude to this relationship perpetuates the use of parental or legalistic parallels. In situations in which these kinds of projections onto the divine make the sufferer's situation worse, a different approach is needed. In the search for an alternative mythology, the Buddhist attitude is relevant.

Suffering is the crucial beginning of the Buddha's teaching. Pain, or its avoidance, is considered to be one of the prime motivators of behaviour, including the motivation to become enlightened. The sufferer who turns to Buddhism hears that his or her suffering is the result of attachment to the idea of a fixed 'self', with its craving and aversions, whereas in reality there is no such concrete entity. What we experience as a self exists only in a relative sense. In absolute terms the self is impermanent, empty, constituted by the flowing together of transient mental phenomena which are not worth grasping onto as if they were permanent. Essentially, therefore, suffering is the result of craving produced by ignorance of the real nature of things. Ideally this approach results in the attainment of equanimity in the face of suffering, because, with the attainment of a sufficient level of spiritual development, there is no longer judgement about 'good' and 'bad' states of mind, there is no sense of the absolute separateness of oneself and others, nor attachment to pleasure and avoidance of pain. There is simply equanimity in the face of the continuous flow of phenomena, or the ability to rest in absolute Mind. The problem here is that to attain the level of consciousness which knows reality at this level takes long years of meditation practice, for most people longer than the average psychotherapeutic treatment, and the discipline and application required are out of reach of many people without the requisite background. And, paradoxically, it is impossible to utilize meditation in the absence of firm intrapsychic structures because it stirs up too much fragmentation anxiety. Meditation requires good affect tolerance, which means a firm sense of self in the Western psychoanalytic meaning of that word. In a way, the Buddhist perspective is diametrically opposed to that of psychotherapy, because the Buddhist in meditation does not spend time deliberately mulling over the meaning of the contents of his psyche. They are noted briefly and allowed to pass away, whereas the psychological approach involves detailed amplification and interpretation of these contents. The factor common to both methods is attention, but this is used differently in the two approaches. The Buddhist consciously trains attention, or trains consciousness itself by means of the focus of his attention, without much regard for the individual contents of consciousness such as thoughts and feelings. But the psychotherapeutic approach has to be concerned with these contents of the self and cannot afford to ignore them peremptorily. An interesting area of overlap is that, as a result of psychotherapeutic work, many troublesome contents of consciousness seem to slip away of their own accord, apparently because of the effects of attention itself. Some people object to the Buddhist approach on the grounds that it detracts from our essential humanity, and fear that it may lead to the splitting off of important affects. Ideally, it does not result in such splitting, but rather in the capacity to experience intense affects with equanimity and mindfulness. Meditation has powerful behavioural consequences because it disconnects the practitioner from *automatic* affective responses to situations. It allows affect to occur without flooding the individual and without inevitable identification with the affect. (See also the discussion of this question on pp. 225 et seq.) But clearly, this is a method that requires much preparation to be of value during a life crisis; it is not a method that can be applied quickly, as can a psychotherapeutic approach.

Despite the drawbacks to the two traditions of thought which I have noted, it is also clear that they may be of inestimable value to those who are *able* to use them. In practice, one frequently sees people struggling with emotional difficulties who are trying to apply such systems. They illustrate Jung's (CW 18, 370) comment that religions can act psychotherapeutically. Some clinical examples of this principle follow.

RELIGIONS AS PSYCHOTHERAPEUTIC SYSTEMS: AN EXAMPLE

In her childhood, a woman who now belongs to a religious order was always enviously attacked and shamed when she exhibited any form of her considerable creativity, or indeed any of her childhood 'grandiose' self. (As we have seen, this means that her connection to the Self was cut off.) She was constantly devalued and accused of being 'swollen headed'. Now, as part of her spiritual practice, she is careful never to attribute any of her good ideas to herself, but always to God, so that she never claims the credit for her intelligence or ability. This avoids the envy issue, and stops her being flooded with what would be unmanageably intense exhibitionistic feelings. Her childhood difficulty helps explain her attraction to the idea that she is 'only an instrument', or that she must always 'give over my will to God'. But our psychodynamic understanding of her choice of spiritual practice does not necessarily invalidate its value, which in this case helps her contain important anxieties. However, we wonder whether the pressure of her un-recognized, but never validated, healthy grandiosity (the movement of the Self through her, which is made manifest as her considerable creativity) will ever allow her real peace of mind within the spiritual technique she has chosen. As these nagging internal pressures to 'show off' continue, will she always fear that she is failing? Or, could it be that such constant subjugation of herself to God is actually therapeutic for such a problem? She has chosen a path which requires that she recognize everything of value that happens within her as a manifestation of the Self. She is thus made more and more permeable to the Self without inflation, as long as she never believes that what moves through her is 'me'. In this way her original 'neurotic' problem points to a particular line of spiritual development, since the 'me' continues to assert itself. What makes her life difficult is the shame she must grapple with, which results from her childhood belief that her self-valuing is wrong. She constantly compares herself, or is compared, with an external standard of piety.

The psychological approach, instead of trying to suppress an emotional difficulty by fiat or by recourse to saintly example, suggests that the problem itself is caused by an element of the divine (the archetype) operating within the personal field. This element causes suffering by means of the complex it produces. In the case in point, the therapist's attuned attention to the patient's attempts to be seen and heard in her own right led to a gradual acceptance of her abilities and her power, so that she was slowly able to 'own', or embody, her split-off sense that she was somebody important. As the integration of her 'grandiose' self proceeded, she felt less like an impostor, more able to value herself, and was less fearful that exposure of her creativity would lead to envious attacks. Her Self image changed from one that required constant submission to avoid danger to one of relationship to the material that flows through her. Her task became one of finding the best way of incarnating her creative potential by means of her technical knowledge, rather than being fearful of it. The effect of attention to this kind of complex in psychotherapy is to stimulate spiritual awareness by asking questions about its meaning and purpose. In traditional terms, we could say that we examine the way in which the Mind of God operates within our own life and mind. As suggested earlier, it is possible to adopt Jung's position that this work is somehow necessary to divinity for the purpose of its further differentiation. This belief would form one basis for an acceptance and blessing of suffering, for a response to the 'why' it happens. Another, less complicated basis for such affirmation of suffering, which is not based on weighty intellectual considerations, might simply be its acceptance as an act of love for the divine.

The particular spiritual practice which allows increasing relationship to the Self may actually be based on an emotional problem which is itself caused by the Self. In this way the Self, by means of the complex, is urging consciousness of itself. A traditional spiritual practice or belief that corresponds to such personal material may then be useful and authentic. However, spiritual practice can also be used merely to mask or rationalize neurotic difficulties; in such a case the experience of the Self is actually avoided. For example, celibacy may allow problematic sexuality to be avoided, while fear or envy of women based on a mother problem may be dealt with by adherence to a doctrine of women's religious inferiority. Similarly, in the presence of a masochistic character structure, traditional, dogmatically based religious approaches to suffering may lead to a rationalization of ascetic denial or the glorification of pain. Traditional doctrines may also lead to Pollyanna-ish attempts at reassurance or to the suspension of critical consciousness in the presence of a frightening situation. But for all of this, Freud's (1962) insistence that religion defends against suffering by delusionally distorting the real world or by resorting to masochistic submission is an overgeneralization. Traditional religious responses to suffering can be used non-defensively, and it must be remembered that Freudian, biological, or behavioural theories can themselves be defensive when they ignore the religious function of the psyche. This happens when theorists use narcissistic defences to deny the reality of the numinosum, or when they disavow or reductively rationalize the seemingly non-rational, intrinsically religious aspects of human nature. Freudian theory sees humanity as limited in its freedom by the constraints and conflicts caused by competing intrapsychic forces. This theory of the origin of our limitations requires a theology which begins where psychology leaves off, and which specializes in the mediation of grace from outside the person. I believe that it is preferable to begin the spiritual search with the intrapsychic difficulty itself, and to see this as the operation of the divine within the personality. Suffering, when it is used as an opening to new consciousness of the Self, bestows grace. There is then no need to separate religion and psychology. Hence the religious approach to the psyche has two goals. It seeks to understand the meaning of suffering for the telos of the personality, and simultaneously it recognizes that a larger consciousness than that of the self must be consulted for this purpose.

DOCTRINAL AND DEPTH PSYCHOLOGICAL METHODOLOGIES CONTRASTED

In order to seek larger meaning and purpose, and to enhance spiritual development, the psychological approach to spirituality examines the manifestations of the Self within the individual psyche by means of depth psychological methods of amplification and interpretation. For the same purpose, dogmatic approaches often utilize comparison of the individual with a saintly or 'official', well-established, set of standards. This is useful if one needs an idealizable figure, but, because the saints are dead, such an idealization can never be resolved. To the extent that an external standard is idealized, the Self remains a projected experience. And if the behavioural norms of the tradition violate the psychology of the individual, it becomes an act of violence to try to force her psychology into a doctrinal mode. Of course, within traditions such as monastic Christianity, it is argued that an insistence on submission to ecclesiastical authority is itself a spiritual discipline; it helps to decrease the emphasis on selfhood. But the use of authority to impose a spiritual system that is alien to the soul of the aspirant is diametrically opposed to the approach advocated here.

Nowhere can the difference betweeen the two approaches be seen more clearly than in their attitude to the shadow, the less savoury aspects of the personality. The psychological approach uses the shadow as grist for the spiritual mill. By contrast, in some traditional approaches, both eastern and western, the shadow is ignored, split off, or actively suppressed in the guise of 'discipline', 'transcendence', or 'going beyond the personal'. The shadow is then in danger of being projected, in which case it causes havoc in one's community or family. It may be an internal source of shame and guilt, and is then fought with and labelled demonic. For example, a member of a religious order has a problem with easily triggered rage, clearly traceable to the way she was treated as a child. Within her community, the 'official' or doctrinal response to such difficulty is to draw from the image of Christ crucified an example of loving forgiveness, and not to express any anger. However, this is an almost impossible task for this individual, who grew up in a home where enormous demands were made on her, but where nobody was interested in her feelings. She is now in a similar situation in her community, where she is once again required to take care of everyone else while ignoring her own needs. The attempt to change her feelings by means of traditional teachings is a 'top-down' approach, which tries to superimpose different behaviour. In such a case the gap between expectations and possibilities can better be bridged by psychotherapeutic intervention than by attempts at greater piety and forgiveness, which only make her feel like a failure. For this woman the shadow problem of unforgiving rage has to become a spiritual task in its own right, one which is not dealt with by suppression or splitting but by a working-through process. It is important to ask how the rage arises, what it means, and how it has affected her relationships, rather than telling her to stop it. In the therapeutic situation, she feels rage at the therapist under certain specific circumstances (when she feels ignored, depreciated or not heard) and in this way her rage can be understood, explained and tempered. Rather than seeing her rage as sinful, she can see it as a reaction to the repeat of a childhood situation, and as secondary, rather than a primary, aspect of her being. She can see rage as a way of holding herself together when she feels devalued, a way of communicating her pain while trying to stay connected to the (selfobject) therapist, and an attempt to make the latter treat her differently than did her parents. When she becomes enraged with him, and he repeatedly acknowledges all of this, including his part in triggering her rage, without making her feel ashamed of herself, the rage gradually becomes manageable. Over time, she is able to forgive others and forgive herself as she is forgiven, not out of dogma but out of experience. Forgiveness becomes an organic development of her spiritual life, not a forced choice which feels more like a reaction formation than a deep truth of her personality.

PSYCHOLOGICAL HELP FROM TRADITIONAL RELIGIOUS SYSTEMS

Given that traditional exhortations about shadow problems may not be successful, it is also important to note that at times the established religious approaches to human development may produce far-reaching, genuine changes in the personality. As Bowker (1980) points out, spiritual traditions have developed techniques

158

of intensive personal investigation and exploration into human nature. Traditional methods involve teaching stories and maxims, prayer, fasting, meditation, spiritual direction, the charisma of the teacher and other tools designed to trigger a re-evaluation of the conscious perspective. As a result of dealing with suffering from their specific perspectives, the traditions have accumulated a good deal of intuition and practical experience about spirituality which it would be foolish for the depth psychologist to ignore. An outstanding example is the Hindu recognition that different types of people approach the divine in different ways, depending on their temperaments. Hence arose the ideas of different 'yogas', or ways of being united with or bound to God. The main ones are *karma-yoga*, or the approach through selfless work (such as Mother Theresa), *bhakti-yoga* or the path of devotion to God (typified by a monastic life), *raja-yoga*, a path through meditation, *hatha-yoga*, through the body, and *jnana-yoga*, a path through the intellect and enquiry.[1] The idea that we may begin our spiritual practice by understanding the archetypal basis of our pathology is another approach; in effect it is an intrapsychic yoga.

The problem for the psychologist or for the spiritual seeker is to discern which spiritual method is most consistent with the individual's temperament and current needs, without becoming encumbered with concerns about their relative validity or efficacy. Some people need a path that emphasizes the heart, others the mind, still others the body. Unless an approach is used which is consonant with individual temperament and level of openness to the archetype, resistances come into play which can nullify any teaching. Traditionally, the student is then assumed to be not ready for the teaching, but the psychotherapist does not have the luxury of simply sending away someone who comes for help. The reason for a lack of fit between the student and a traditional religious teaching is often that the doctrine originally emerged from the experience of one individual, such as Jesus, and was subsequently added to and incorporated into dogmatic assertions as if it applied to everyone. But even the most sublime wisdom is of no value if it is given at the wrong time, to the wrong person or in the wrong manner. For example, the development of compassion for others, or the capacity to turn the other cheek, require considerable capacity to put aside one's own needs and feelings of the moment. This level of selflessness is usually only possible if the self is well integrated, strong enough to contain painful affect and not in danger of falling apart. It is pointless and harmful to tell a child to suppress its anger in the service of an ideal that he or she is too immature to grasp, and which, if he or she accedes to out of a need to stay connected to his or her selfobjects, will result in the child prematurely sacrificing an important part of him/herself.

Many spiritual teachers, such as Meister Eckhart, have been gifted intuitive psychologists but are misunderstood by people who are not at a level of personality maturation which allows them to use such teaching, especially when the teaching is developmentally premature or produces too much anxiety within the recipient. For instance, Eckhart's 'my me is God', or 'I am the cause that God is God', succinctly express the essence of a religious approach to the psyche (see Fox, 1981). These ideas anticipate Jung's writing on the Self as the archetypal basis of the ego and echo much of the Upanishad's and Jesus' teachings. They are the statements of a religious genius that can only be understood in their mystical sense; understood exoterically they sound inflated and make no sense in terms of everyday logic. The establishment against its envy and anxiety Hence some of Eckhart's teaching was posthumously condemned by a church which was unable to understand him, because he was too far ahead of it developmentally. The establishment defended against its envy and anxiety by accusing him of looking into matters which he should not have.

To avoid such painful mismatch, research is needed to find ways of matching particular temperaments and stages of development with their corresponding spiritualities. This problem links us with the larger one of understanding the relationship between personality and dogmatic assertions.

DOGMA AND PERSONALITY STRUCTURE

Jung (CW 11, 459) points out that dogmas (by which is usually meant fixed beliefs, decrees or edicts said to be authoritative by the established Church) contain archetypal themes which express symbolic truths (CW 11, 294–295). Although the psychologist cannot say whether they are true in the metaphysical sense, like myths, dogmas remain important psychological statements about the structure and dynamics of the psyche. For example, the 1950 dogma of the Assumption of Mary asserted that Mary was taken body and soul into heaven after her life on earth. The timing of the appearance of this dogma corresponds to the cultural resurgence of the importance of the feminine principle as an aspect of divinity. For a long time the importance of this principle had been suppressed by the Church in its official proclamations, but it is consonant with popular Mariological devotion. The dogma of the Assumption of Mary as the Queen of Heaven essentially re-establishes the importance of the Goddess, the Divine Mother, after her devalued appearance as the serpent, an ancient symbol of the Goddess, in the Garden of Eden. At the time of its issuance, the dogma of the Assumption had symbolic meaning that corresponded to an important psychological truth; it was important to women struggling with traditional patriarchal notions of an exclusively masculine God.

Whereas, at one time, dogma was able to function as this kind of bridge to the inner world, unfortunately it no longer necessarily expresses such personal truth. When it is 'merely believed' (CW 9, ii, 276), such belief is often only a 'substitute for the missing empirical reality' (CW 14, 666). For example, the 1950 dogma can be contrasted with the Marian dogma of 1854, which confirmed that Mary was immaculately conceived (without original sin; her perpetual virginity had been established 1,200 years before). Both these teachings about Mary evidently were intended to convey a gradually deepening insight about her place in the history of salvation as it is understood by the Roman Catholic Church. But whereas the 1854 dogma may have found some collective resonance during the Victorian era of repressed sexuality, it affects people now very differently than does the dogma of the Assumption. The ideas of immaculate conception or virgin birth may even offend people today who want to value Mary by seeing her as fully a woman. Thus it is that whatever meaning is originally contained in dogmatic statements may eventually become inaccessible when this meaning ceases to reflect one's personal psychology and the cultural *Zeitgeist*. It then becomes an emotionally inert body of teaching. The traditional emphasis on celibacy in some traditions illustrates another way in which dogma may become disconnected from personal psychology, and may even be used to support a neurosis.

DOGMA AND PSYCHOPATHOLOGY: THE EXAMPLE OF CELIBACY

To suggest that dogma reflects archetypally based, intrapsychic dynamics means that at times it must also reflect psychopathology, because the archetype is much concerned with pathology; it wounds as well as heals. Spiritual systems that emphasize celibacy illustrate this possibility very well. Celibate love is clearly an archetypal structure, found across all cultures and religious traditions, so the depth psychologist must take it seriously as a possibly authentic spiritual form in a given case. Within Roman Catholicism, celibacy for priests is rationalized as the imitation of Christ (although it is impossible to know whether he was celibate), as a sign of exclusive service to Christ who talked (albeit in a different context) about leaving one's wife for his sake (Mark 10: 29) or for the kingdom of God (Luke 18: 29). The calling is said to be a special grace and vocation (Matt. 19: 11–12). Paul (1 Cor. 7: 7) recommended celibacy, but it is difficult to know why he did so; it could have been the unthinking continuation of a cultural bias against women, or it could have been part of a neurosis that caused him to devalue women and sexuality. This latter explanation seems plausible, since as far as we can tell from the text itself, that is, the writing attributed to Paul, the body and sexuality acted as a kind of negative numinosum for him.[2] He was at once terrified and fascinated by it. It therefore makes sense that constant preoccupation with 'the flesh' and its temptations became part of his personal spirituality. Rather than altogether dismiss Paul's teaching on the grounds of its neurotic basis, we could see celibacy as a workable container for his emotional difficulties. Whatever Paul's personal reason, this teaching appealed to Church fathers with similar difficulties, so that the idea was promulgated and gradually gathered historical authority. The problem is that, from a psychological point of view such a path is not generalizable to everyone. (Ranke-Heinemann (1990) has shown, on purely theological and textual grounds, the specious nature of the biblical passages quoted above as a basis for the universal applicability of celibacy for priests.)

However, the archetype of celibacy also has its non-neurotic aspects, and some individuals may be captured by it for these reasons. Dourley (1987) has offered an amplification of celibacy based on the ideal of an inner marriage. In such situations the energy of relationship is restricted to union with the divine as an inner experience, found for instance in the mysticism of Mechtilde of Magdeburg who experienced erotic imagery in which she and Christ were lovers. Jung (CW 14, 761) notes that hers is an example of the *hieros gamos*, a sacred marriage of the soul with God. The literature of mysticism is replete with such experiences. The reductive interpretation of such celibacy as a way of avoiding human sexual relationships is too obvious to need articulation, but without the possibility of personal psychological examination of the love mystics we cannot decide their real motive for the practice. What *can* be said from their writing is that if some of them are avoiding relationships with people on the basis of psychoneurosis, their capacity for relationship with the Self as it manifests to them personally is in no way impaired.

To return to the problem of psychopathology as a determinant of one's spiritual assertions, the dogma that Mary is 'above' the 'sin' of sexuality may only reflect the personal psychology of its originators. These men, perhaps because of their own difficulties in this area, adhere to a long Church tradition of maintaining a particular intrapsychic split, which is the need to keep the image of mother free of any taint of sexuality. The Madonna archetype is a symbol which unites the mother–virgin polarity. Lest there be any doubt of the severity of this split, we need only recall that in the service of its maintenance 'witches' were burned and women were seen as instruments of the devil. The demonizing of women also served the purpose of dealing with men's terror of women and their sexuality. The Inquisition reveals how some men could project both their own neuroses and wickedness onto others, purging them in projection instead of facing their inner difficulties. These are further examples of how religious practice and teaching can be interpreted so as to provide a container or framework for dealing with personal psychopathology. A modern example is provided by those churches which manage to link Christianity with racial prejudice. Or, consider the position of a person who suffers from either infantile terror or untempered infantile grandiosity or omnipotence. If, at the same time, believes that he has a direct grasp of the will of God, he will feel justified in trying to impose his version of that will on others.

In the presence of a neurosis, it should not be assumed that I recommend a solution such as that of Paul's rejection of sexuality, but, under certain circumstances, it may be the best possible solution. In Paul's case (again I mean the Paul of the text), before his conversion experience on the road to Damascus, he was an avid persecutor of Jesus' followers, thereby resisting and externalizing his need to idealize Jesus. The intensity of this reaction formation against what he so desperately needed suggests that he was given to extreme defences. A person who has neurotic difficulty with sexuality may be drawn to a dogmatic belief in the superiority of virginity for this reason. But such a system may actually prevent spiritual development by freezing it; rigid adherence to such dogma cuts off the possibility of healing the difficulty which draws one to it, and prevents access to that aspect of the Self which is creating the neurosis. However, the fundamentalism which results from rigid defences against the Self is not entirely useless from the point of view of individual psychic economy. Some people cannot tolerate new, real religious experience, and a rigid religious system has the value of protecting individuals who need defensive containment to deal with an emotional difficulty. The associated community of believers provides essential selfobject needs of all kinds. Belief in the teaching itself – like belief in a psychological or political theory – can also supply some of the needed coherence and structure to the personality, albeit from the outside. These may be workable solutions to what otherwise might be an unmanageable selfobject deficit, so that in these ways the religion acts as a psychotherapeutic agent.

THE PSYCHOLOGICAL VALUE OF TRADITIONAL APPROACHES TO SUFFERING

It is important here to reiterate that the depth psychologist cannot advocate the wholesale dismissal of traditional teachings, because they often have immeasurable profundity for certain individuals. Granted that they must not be applied in a blanket manner which ignores individual needs, in this section I would like to illustrate how traditional teachings may be of psychological value. For this purpose, the psychologist does not need to remain restricted to traditional interpretations of the sacred stories. By the application of depth psychological hermeneutics to their study, treating them as we would any mythical text, we can discover new depth of meaning within traditional stories. This may allow a reconnection with the numinosity of the original mythical events and with the dogmatic assertions to which they subsequently gave rise. Much of Jung's religious writing, such as his essays on the Mass and the Trinity, is just such an attempt to allow dogma to live again by revealing its often unconscious meaning. Essentially this method involves treating the dogma or story as an imaginal product of the soul, that is to say we treat it symbolically, the way we approach a dream. Using this method, even stories that have long seemed to be inert may become helpful anew as we find elements within them that are alive for us.

This process of remythologizing may be carried out within a format that does no offence to the origin myth of the tradition. For example, in traditional Christianity the answer to the problem of suffering is found by expressing the story of the suffering of Jesus in terms of the love of God for mankind; this love was intense enough for his own son to be sacrificed as an act of reconciliation with the world. This idea is a continuation of the Old Testament notion of vicarious or substitute suffering, found as the song of the suffering servant in Isaiah (53: 4–5): 'Surely he has borne our griefs and carried our sorrows . . . . But he was wounded for our transgressions, he was bruised for our iniquities' and 'he bore the sin of many, and made intercession for the transgressors' (Isa. 53: 12). Jesus' sacrifice is therefore an expiation which mediates between sinful man and God. For certain individuals this seems to be a necessary dynamic, for instance when there is a sense of personal badness which is so severe that it cannot be redeemed directly. Or, a masochistic character structure may require that the individual sacrifice him/herself in order to maintain the essential tie to his or her selfobjects. The suffering individual can then reflect on the experience of Jesus and participate by a process of vicarious identification. Then the sufferer's pain is located within a much larger drama and is not an isolated event. This procedure uses the myth as a way of amplifying and deepening one's own condition; the myth has become a personal myth. When the myth and the individual's psychology coincide in this way, personal pain may be radically relativized. But, the problem with this mythologem as it became incorporated into dogma is that it teaches that vicarious suffering is *necessarily* the way to God; not all traditions agree with this premise, and it is certainly not suited to every psychology. This provides an example of the potentially rigidifying effect of adherence to a single myth.

Here we can invoke a general principle (discussed fully in Chapter 5), that there can be no single interpretation of a myth. Thus, one may reflect on the Christian story and use it in a radically different way than orthodox interpretation would allow, but which allows it to become meaningful to an individual with a different psychology from that of the orthodox believer. Perhaps it does not matter that we then substitute our own projections onto the text for those of the early Church fathers. For instance, the dogmatic idea that the Holy Spirit is the father of Jesus has been traditionally interpreted to indicate his divine rather than human sonship. But this mythologem is open to other interpretations at least as profound. It provides a model for the understanding of a certain type of relationship between the human and the divine (within a dualistic, matter–spirit framework) which comments on the problem of suffering produced by the incarnation of spirit, as described earlier. Again, the dogma of the virginity of Mary may be used to indicate a particular quality of body and soul which is as yet unopened to spirit, or one which is fertile but still undifferentiated in terms of meaning and consciousness. Although it may be self-contained and authentic, it requires penetration by the transpersonal in order to become pregnant with potential, or spiritually pregnant. This process will eventually give rise to a divinely conceived product born in human soil – that is, within the human soul. This occurs because spirit is an ordering, value-endowing and enlivening factor which stimulates differentiation and allows the emergence of a new form of consciousness which partakes of the human and the divine. To allow this to happen requires great courage, and submission by the individual to transpersonal demands, as in: 'Behold I am the handmaiden of the Lord.' Unfortunately, the product of such spirit–soul–body interaction is likely to be so misunderstood and threatening to the establishment that the new consciousness may be crucified by collective ignorance, envy and fear, but it is also redemptive to those who can understand its meaning. One should not underestimate the degree of threat this divine child produces to the establishment, whether this is understood intrapsychically or socially. Jesus was in danger from King Herod, and in Hindu mythology the baby Krishna was threatened with death by King Kamsa. We could see this mythologem as the attempt of the entrenched ego to destroy the new attitude demanded by the birth of the Self, or as a reflection of a pathogenic complex representing the internalization of parents who cannot allow the divine child to be manifest within their offspring.

The mythologem of the crucifixion has other meanings which Jung described in his essay on the Mass (CW 11). An additional two are suggested here. First, it depicts a pinning down of the divine onto matter when it assumes human dimensions. This speaks to the difficulty of maintaining a spiritual discipline, or an awareness of one's divine life, in the midst of the requirements of everyday demands. Perhaps the path of love, exemplified by the life of Jesus, is most likely to suffer in the face of hatred and fear. The world of the body and of matter in general is a severe testing ground for such a path; our capacity to love is limited by this environment at the same time as it provides love's supreme opportunity. As well, the crucifixion reminds us that even in the ideal state of being totally in harmony with the divine ('I and the Father are one'), suffering is still to be expected. The story also points out that suffering is indicative of one's spiritual identity; when the disciples demanded proof of the identity of Jesus, his wound indicated who he was. But it may be noted that the wound was no longer bleeding.

THE PLACE OF METAPHYSICAL ASSERTIONS ABOUT SUFFERING AS THEY ARISE IN PSYCHOTHERAPY

As I will indicate in the next section, the individual may arrive at a totally idiosyncratic solution to his or her suffering, for instance, based on an archetypal dream or on a relationship which clarifies and helps to heal a particular problem. But there is also the possibility that the patient may adapt an existing metaphysical idea for his or her personal needs. For instance, belief in the Buddhist and Hindu idea of *karma*,[3] when not used in the service of denial, avoidance of responsibility, or to support a sado-masochistic character defence, may enable an individual to tolerate a painful situation with increased equanimity. This idea may either provide an authentic, non-neurotic answer to a realistically difficult life situation, or it may be a glib rationalization for indifference or selfishness. It is usually not too difficult to distinguish these two usages clinically. In the latter case the therapist must treat the situation as he or she would any situation of defence, on its own psychodynamic merits.

The doctrine of *karma*, used to deal with the problem of suffering, raises the question of how the therapist might approach this or any other metaphysical belief of the patient. All of metaphysics (I use the term to mean speculation about what lies beyond what may be experienced) may be said to be an attempt to understand and question the universe by means of the imagination, and this endeavour is therefore relevant to the psychotherapist, since the imagination extends well into the realms of pathology. As Kant pointed out, speculative metaphysics goes beyond experience and so cannot be proven. But the fact remains that many people are influenced by speculative ideas, so that the psychologist cannot ignore their presence. In the therapeutic situation we only have to decide whether a metaphysical assertion is adhered to because it is supported by dogma, which may be defensively or delusionally believed, or by intuitive knowledge, as a piece of personal gnosis. Or, and perhaps ideally, an apparently metaphysical assertion may actually arise from experience. For example, a conviction that the soul survives death often arises from a peri-death experience. It is usually obvious to the clinician which mechanism is operating. Some of the patient's metaphysics may coincide with those of the therapist, and in such a case they tend to be taken literally and possibly uncritically. They can then be as useful or as problematic as any shared belief system. But when the patient's religious beliefs stretch the therapist's credulity, rather than hearing them only as speculation or fabrication in the service of defence, they might also be regarded as mythical truth. This kind of truth is the result of those archetypal or imaginative functions of the psyche which indicate its own internal dynamics and are appealing to certain individuals. (Jung's paper on flying saucers is in this category; it postulates that UFO reports are at least cultural concomitants of the intrapsychic experience of the Self, whether or not UFOs literally exist.) Even in the philosophical literature it is commonplace to assume that a particular metaphysical belief reflects the psychology of the believer, or is a fantasy in the psychoanalytic sense. Such an idea, like a religious belief, is adhered to by the individual for reasons which fit his or her overall psychology. The therapist may be able to link a particular belief with the developmental history of the person and thereby understand his or her metaphysics as a symbol.

THE MEANING OF SUFFERING: A PSYCHOLOGICAL PERSPECTIVE

The psychologically derived religious approach to suffering is most relevant to people for whom none of the usual dogmatic or traditional views helpful. It is an approach which seeks to discern the personal meaning of the suffering, both from the reductive point of view of the individual's psychodynamics as well as with a prospective attitude that looks at the meaning of the suffering for the future course of the personality. We may also be able to discern a transpersonal point of view, perhaps even *sub specie aeternitatis*. My emphasis on meaning is predicated on Jung's idea that, while meaningless suffering is unbearable, meaning allows one to withstand what would otherwise be an impossible burden. Meaning here is not used in the cognitive sense of asserting verifiable factual information. It usually refers to the emotional satisfaction which is gained by the sense that one's suffering is purposeful rather than random. According to Jung (CW 7, 224), to achieve meaning requires the deepest possible understanding of a situation and the bringing together of what were previously experienced as separate elements within a situation. In other words we achieve meaning when we see patterns, especially how our suffering is linked with the totality of our lives, both developmentally and teleologically. These links are initially often unconscious, but they are sometimes uncovered in therapy, and their elucidation ideally includes the discovery of the archetypal background to the suffering. The discovery of such a transpersonal backdrop allows the archetype to be viewed as an 'organ of God' element within the suffering. Meaning is also important because it impels us to behaviour, and this is how spirit ultimately embodies.

It is not difficult to justify the necessity for an individualized attitude to suffering. The therapist is often presented with a suffering patient who is not committed to an orthodox tradition but who is asking essentially religious 'why is this happening to me?' questions. The therapist may not feel qualified to address issues of suffering and its meaning from the standpoint of traditional theology or philosophy. But we may rest assured that, even among experts within these fields, there are no final or agreed-upon solutions to many of our patients' concerns about the meaning or purpose of suffering. If there were, or if a dogmatic answer were useful, recourse to therapy might not be necessary. Therefore, in the course of dealing with suffering, it is often reasonable and necessary for the psychotherapist to assist in the discovery of personal meaning, along with the attendant question of how true this meaning might be. We usually feel that the kind of meaning that is arrived at in psychotherapy is never absolute, but is only relatively true for the individual. When we insist on the primacy of such subjective truth we must always be aware of the caveat that the problem with the idea of something which is 'true for me' is that such a solution may only be a means of self-deception. W. Kaufman (1978, p. 108) points out that sometimes personal truth may not mean 'truth' as much as a feeling of subjective certainty. Or this term may simply mean sincere belief, or just whatever makes one happy. Bearing this in mind, it is incumbent on us to develop reliable psychological criteria for deciding what can be considered personal religious truth, and for assessing the validity of our personal answers to our suffering. In Chapter 2 a case was made for the propositions that contact with the numinosum addresses issues of suffering, and that such ex-perience is inherently meaningful. Here I would like to enlarge upon the intrapsychic criteria that the psychotherapist may use when evaluating religious experience from the perspective of its validity for the individual.

It is not easy to define meaning or truth to the satisfaction of the philosopher, because there is more than one way of defining truth. But logical or theoretical proof of a personal religious belief based on transpersonal experience should not be necessary for the psychotherapist. Depth psychology has its own methodology, and there are operationally useful *psychological* standards which can be applied to this question, distinct from theological discussions about the truth of various tenets of faith. The therapist does not need to be concerned about whether the patient's truth corresponds to objective or extrapsychic reality, or even worry about whether there is such a thing, unless he or she is so predisposed by some personal commitment. We are most usefully served by a kind of psychological pragmatism, which allows us to apply particular tests of truth without being able to comment on its absolute nature. In the therapeutic setting, I suggest that an answer to the patient's suffering which is based on numinous experience and is therefore felt to be true, needs to meet at least some of the following criteria for his particular concerns to be authentically contained.

1 His truth is valid at an affective level and is not simply cognitively correct.
2 It has a strengthening effect in terms of the overall cohesion, integration, and vitality of the self.

3 It enhances the self's relationship to the Self.
4 As far as can be discerned, it must not be simply defensive.
5 His truth makes sense when viewed in its developmental context and also points to the future of the personality.

I believe that these criteria will take the truth value of a religious experience beyond the claim that it simply has narrative coherence for the individual.

The psychotherapist who wishes to define the meaning of a religious experience from within the psychology of the individual must do so not only in terms of cognitive criteria. Meaning is automatically attained when an event is emotionally powerful. A meaningful event carries significance because it reverberates with earlier, often even infantile, experiences; it belongs to a pattern or theme which has played an important part in the subject's life. Meaningful events are not emotionally neutral – they either reduce or stimulate important anxieties. When such an event occurs in the life of a patient, because of its emotional reverberations the therapist can empathically grasp the fact that something significant has occurred. It is also fairly easy to adduce evidence that strengthening of the self has resulted from a religious experience. Such strengthening is manifested by factors such as increased self-esteem, the discovery of a new direction in life, increased capacity for self-soothing and increased vitality. By contrast, quasi-solutions to suffering that are evidently delusional, neurotic or defensive are also detectable clinically, as are purely intellectual responses that have little effect on the self structures. This means that a belief or an experience is true for the individual if it builds intrapsychic structure that is not based on the needs of the persona or of the 'false self'. Not only is it then true in the intrapsychic sense but it is also immediately meaningful. Freud (1927) realized (in his *Future of an Illusion*) that to question the meaning of life is a sign of (emotional) illness, but he suggested that to find meaning in religion indicates psychopathology. By contrast, my personal experience indicates that if the above critera are met such discovery usually enhances psychological health. A persistent sense of meaninglessness or *anomie* usually indicates some kind of self disorder. Thus the search for meaning, quintessentially part of the religious life, is not simply defensive but is an essential means of self development, and in this way religious experience is life affirming.

Here a disclaimer is necessary. When a person obtains help with a religious question about the meaning of his or her suffering using a depth psychological approach, the answer obtained is often so personal that no authority can be claimed about the relevance of his or her answer for others. In other words, the individual's personal *rapprochement* with the transpersonal may not be generalizable or verifiable according to positivistic criteria. It is not intended that such personally derived truth will be used for dogmatic or doctrinal purposes. Indeed, it would contravene the psychological attitude to do so, even though it must also be said that sometimes the truth which arises from the psyche does correspond to existing traditional teaching, which is very comforting. The point is that personal truth does not need to withstand logical scrutiny as long as it is of importance within the psychological economy of the experiencer (the problem of delusional truth is discussed on p. 172). Here, I espouse a kind of psychologically based empiricism; what we believe at any one time is open to change and correction in the face of ongoing revelation, so that the conscious personality remains an empirical one.

The meaning and truth to which I refer may be obtained in different ways. It may arise through the relationship with another person such as a therapist, or it may be directly given as an experience of the Self, in what feels like a pure act of grace. Symbolic experience, relationships, authentic mystical experience, artistic and aesthetic experience or synchronicities are all vehicles for its manifestation. All of these have the potential to place personal consciousness in relationship to the numinous Other, thus relativizing and de-centring the self. The truth and meaning of these experiences are discernible by means of the particular quality of feeling that they produce, which produces an enhanced sense of the reality, groundedness and integrity of the self. This quality confirms the sense that one exists in relation to another, larger life. The truth produced by authentic contact with the numinosum is affectively based, felt in the body at a level that produces states such as calm, joy or abject terror. Validation of the affective importance of the experience by means of the affirmation of another person, such as a therapist, is only needed when early selfobject failures have produced a mistrust of one's own subjectivity – otherwise a sense of inner certainty occurs.

If this intrapsychic approach to the truth of religious experience needs justification, it can be pointed out that different religious systems, which are simply different approaches to archetypal reality, all locate truth differently. To argue that one system is better than another is merely a political statement. To insist on it and try to impose it, is religious fascism.

Of course, to allow the validity of a purely personal religious truth as the answer to one's suffering leaves us exposed to the philosophical problem of multiple realities, or whether there can be more than one kind of truth. But since the psychotherapist is not concerned with external verifiability, we can concentrate on the search for that truth and meaning which is necessary to develop the integrity of the personality before us. From this perspective, the therapist soon learns that many attitudes that are logically contradictory when compared between people, nevertheless may each be relatively true within the individual personality. Our metatheory of a Self which is the totality of consciousness and which therefore includes the consciousness of each little self, implies that there is a supraordinate Truth of which we observe personal fragments, each of which feels meaningful to the individual. But this single Reality is not directly observable because it is obscured by thick layers of conditioning, referred to in the Eastern traditions by such metaphors as dust on the mirror or clouds obscuring the sun. Psychologically, what obscures our view of a larger reality is self-absorption, or narcissistic defences against the numinosum.

Finally, the individual may experience an aspect of the Self in a way which helps him with his or her suffering and which is therefore personally true, but

169

whose essence cannot be conveyed. Ordinary categories of language and logic cannot convey the reality of an experience of the divine which is completely true for one person but which is, at exactly the same time, *not* true for another self.

PERSONALLY DERIVED TRUTH: SOURCES FROM THE UNCONSCIOUS

Evidence that it is not necessary to rely on pre-existing dogmatic assertions in order to address religious questions is provided by the fact that new light on a problem emerges if we attend to material from the unconscious. Here I include attention to any way in which the unconscious may reach consciousness, such as dreams, fantasies, somatic states, symptoms, transference manifestations, jokes, slips of the tongue, creative products and so on. The material which emerges is specific to the individual, acting as a personal revelation. It may be obtained laboriously in therapy as a result of a gradual process of uncovering, or it may erupt suddenly as a mystical experience or a numinous dream. A dramatic example of this process is found in the case of demoralized, suicidal people whose lives are radically transformed by mystical experience. In the psychiatric literature these events are typically reduced by dismissing them as 'residual primary narcissism', or they are considered to be transitional phenomena which act as internal soothing devices necessary for maturation (Horton, 1973, pp. 294–296). Such events are indeed soothing, providing order in the midst of chaos. But their origin is the objective psyche, not the personal unconscious, and they are helpful because they are numinous. Testimony to the restructuring power of this level of the psyche is given by the fact that this contact can be integrative even in psychotic people. But paradoxically when the self structures are not firm enough to cope with the experience of the numinosum, it can precipitate a psychosis.

The manner in which the objective psyche mediates personal truth is exemplified by the following dream. It occurred during a time in which the dreamer was feeling disconnected from the transpersonal realm, and was preoccupied with the question of how personal consciousness could possibly contact transcendent levels of being.

> I see a shooting star fall to earth in the distance. It buries itself in the ground, but is unearthed by unknown people, cleaned and given to me. It is actually a huge, shiny silver dish, in perfect condition, exactly like the dish of a radio telescope.

The dream says that the instrument which is needed to listen to signals from far beyond this realm is actually provided by, or comes from, that place. The stress is on receptivity, reflection and listening. This dream settled the question for the dreamer. At the same time, such a commonly seen dish also became for him a personal symbol of contact between the realms.

Often such a dream is entirely personal, offering the comments of the objective psyche on a situation – no different in kind from traditional accounts of the 'voice of God' offering guidance. These kinds of dreams, seen in everyday practice, are analogous to mythical examples, such as those of Joseph, in which he is told that Mary has conceived by the Holy Spirit (Matt. 1: 20), or that he should flee to Egypt to escape Herod (Matt. 2: 13). These latter lay claim to being the most important dreams in religious history from a collective point of view, but they are no different in principle from those given to anyone during a personal crisis.

Here the sceptic may protest that a dream such as that of the radio telescope dish is simply derived from the personal unconscious of the dreamer. It might be claimed that there are more parsimonious explanations to account for it than the postulate of a level of the unconscious which reveals transcendent wisdom, through which, in some metaphorical sense, the divine speaks. But clinical experience with many such dreams suggests that they provide information or contextualize one's situation in ways that are too profound to attribute to the dreamer alone – sometimes they contain material that is beyond the dreamer's fund of information. One of Jung's major discoveries was that mythical themes which are unknown to the dreamer arise in dreams.

THE QUESTION OF TRANSCENDENCE

Authentic personal answers to questions such as the meaning of existence in the face of great suffering do arise from the autonomous levels of the unconscious. But it is more common for the therapist to see (or sometimes even suggest) defensive or persona-restoring solutions, which may masquerade as 'transcendence' of the problem. In this context, unless we are engaged in purely supportive rather than exploratory or reconstructive therapy, it is important not to collude prematurely with potentially defensive metaphysical ideas which purport to 'go beyond' our usual human limitations. The search for transcendence may actually represent a wish for avoidance of the world, or of some aspect of it which is intolerable to that person. Occasionally this attitude must be respected because there is little hope that the problem will be resolved. The search for a transcendent solution may then be a sensible compensatory structure which can be encouraged.

In the approach espoused here, real transcendence has a particular, psychologically defined meaning, which is in accord with the etymology of the word. The Latin verb *transcendere* means to climb across, not to avoid or skip over. Climbing across something entails getting to know it. In order to truly transcend the world – when this is really necessary, 'one must have experienced it, assimilated it, and utterly seen through it' (Bernoulli, 1960, p. 326). We can often only transcend what we have outgrown; who we really are, including our pathology, must be seen, owned, worked on and digested before it can be left behind in a meaningful way. Then, what we discard are usually aspects of the false self that we had to develop to survive childhood, and our defensive persona, or our immature narcissistic concerns which are no longer necessary. As the experience and iconography of enlightenment in all the eastern traditions (such as the Zen ox-herding pictures) teaches, one is then in the world in a different way, with a different consciousness.

My insistence on not avoiding the problems of one's actual life is not the result of an abstract conviction. Many people who enter therapy complain that their lives are meaningless because of intractable emotional difficulties. When these improve, the person is able to relate and belong to the world in ways which make notions of transcending it irrelevant. For them, transcendence means radical change and the growth of a firm sense of self. An intact self which is able to experience normal joy and grief without fragmentation does not transcend in the sense of ascetic withdrawal from other people, or by denial of the body or of pleasure. Such a person is able to transcend by means of a process of radically decentring, or relativizing, the self. That is, he or she no longer needs to see the self as the necessary centre of the universe, requiring all available attention and resources in the service of its own needs. This decentring may be demonstrated as service to others, in an act of compassion, or as altruism not unconsciously motivated by a need for self-enhancement. Or such transcendence may occur as an act of love. This kind of behaviour always requires a conscious sacrifice of the self, which is possible without bitterness or resentment only if the self is strong. We then transcend in the sense of going beyond the limits of strict individuality, realizing our essential unity with others. But this level of attainment – so beloved of Eastern thought – is only possible when true selfhood is achieved, because a fragile self would collapse under the strain. Here is a way in which the fulfilment of the developmental possibilities of the person leads naturally to what has always been thought of as spiritual growth. Of course, as the great meditative traditions indicate, this level of selflessness can be attained in ways other than by attention to one's narcissistic difficulties in psychotherapy, but this is our particular focus.

THE PROBLEM OF PSYCHOSIS

At this point one may ask how the principle of personally derived truth and meaning applies to psychotic people, who may proclaim all kinds of 'truth' which bears no relationship to consensual reality. The distinction between delusion and the discovery of authentic meaning is important. Psychotic beliefs may be so bizarre as to defy understanding until one applies a certain framework of theoretical understanding to them. For example, one such theory suggests that the patient is concretely symbolizing a purely subjective version of reality in his delusions (Stolorow *et al.* 1988, p. 103). The psychotic has been unable to sustain a belief in the validity of his or her subjective reality because of the unreliability and distorting effect of his or her early selfobject milieu, which exposes his or her biological vulnerability to cognitive and perceptual instability. According to this intersubjectivist school of thought, his or her delusions attempt to concretize his or her experience of an intolerable world in order to try to preserve an endangered sense of reality, or what is left of his or her sense of self, from further disintegration. In other words, psychotic meaning and truth attempt to be restitutive; they try to make whatever sense is possible of the world so as to bind the terrifying anxiety of a fragmenting self. To this description of the etiology of psychosis the Jungian would add that the terror is also, in part, the result of exposure to archetypal levels of the psyche whose affective intensity is over-whelming because of the fragility of existing self structures, owing to chronic failure of the individual's selfobjects to help contain such affects. This is an instance of what Jung calls the divine 'asking too much'.

Delusional truth tries to preserve the self, but it differs from the authentic meaning found by an intact self, which is calming, orders the personality and is understandable to others. By contrast, because of the well-known cognitive and affective transformations of psychosis, psychotic beliefs are only quasi-solutions. Even if they are not manifestly absurd from the viewpoint of consensual reality, clinically they always appear to be embedded in a self structure which is frantically trying to steady itself around a delusional solution to an impossible problem. This process always produces a very brittle quality in the person, in which palpable, often thinly veiled terror is partially bound by rigid adherence to a belief that is obviously necessary to hold things together. It feels as if the delusional truth is more important than the person who believes it. Not for nothing is the psychotic desperately trying to find whatever meaning will shore up a sense of self; the experience of meaning and the sense of the self's vitality and cohesiveness are inextricably related. One could even argue that they are synonymous, because 'my' life only has meaning to the extent that there is a 'me'. The more coherent and cohesive is the state of the self, and the less we are subject to states of anxiety, depression and other forms of fragmentation, the more meaning in life we experience. When the self is intact, that is in non-psychotic people, the psychotherapist has to evaluate whether the meaning a person feels is merely attributed to, or projected onto, experience, rather than being real in a deeper sense. The therapist can then only rely on the overall coherence of the individual's subjectivity.

People with significant self-state pathology notoriously complain of meaning-lessness. They must also defend against the experience of spirit, which could potentially allow meaning to occur, because their self structures are too fragile to contain its affective intensity. Therefore they tend to disavow its significance in order to avoid affective flooding, since if this fails they suffer from uncontained archetypal affects such as rage or terror. Because of this difficulty with the process of the embodiment of spirit into soul, they may also suffer from the lack of a felt sense of reality, which often accompanies a sense of meaninglessness. These are therefore the people who most need to struggle with the question of meaning, and who are also most helped by an affectively attuned relationship with the therapist. The therapeutic container for affect, which allows the Self to be felt between the two participants in a safe way, eventually allows the patient to feel alive but not in danger. And the experience of being treated as a meaningful human being by the therapist may be sufficient to kindle a sense of meaning in an otherwise hopeless individual.

MEANING IN NEUROSIS: JUNG'S APPROACH

Earlier I noted Jung's pivotal idea that suffering represents the experience of the attempt of the Self to incarnate into a self, which is equivalent to individuation. As well, the archetype (considered to be one strand of the Self) incarnates via the complex, especially its affective component, since affect is felt in the body. Here I would like to further amplify his view of the meaning of the painful complex, which I loosely equate with neurotic suffering. Jung's writing has the advantage of stressing contact with the objective psyche, but this emphasis does not necessarily lead to a relational theory of psychotherapy, and may ignore the importance of relationships with other people as a source of meaning. He is somewhat of an 'isolated mind' theorist in this area.

Jung (CW 4, 415) considered the symptoms of neurosis to have meaning and purpose for the telos of the personality – they are an attempt at healing. He suggests that neurosis is the attempt of the Self to stimulate the incorporation of the neglected side of the personality into consciousness (CW 7, 438).[4] This forward-looking or purposeful approach is an important contrast with classical psychoanalysis, which only looks to the past for the origin and meaning of symptoms. According to Jung, the issue of meaning is critical; the mere lifting of unconscious contents to consciousness, although of value, may actually produce more suffering if the patient then feels further caught or crucified between opposing aspects of himself (CW 7, 224). Here Jung has recognized that insight alone is often insufficient for cure. He believes that a change of attitude is necessary (CW 8, 684–685), and that only the discovery of meaning liberates us from suffering; science and common sense afford no answer to the problem. Ultimately, he believes that neurosis must be understood as the suffering of a soul which has not discovered its meaning; the soul suffers because of spiritual stagnation, and the therapist has to find the 'meaning that quickens' (CW 11, 497). For Jung, such meaning is to be found in the amplification of the spontaneous products of the unconscious. To find meaning allows objectification, the development of perspective and the beginning of disidentification from suffering. 'Meaninglessness inhibits the fullness of life and is therefore equivalent to illness. Meaning makes a great many things endurable – perhaps everything' (Jung, 1965, p. 340). According to Jaffe (1971), Jung elevates the importance of meaning to mythical status. His myth of meaning is synonymous with a new myth of consciousness; it implies that humanity's metaphysical task, which will make life meaningful, is the continual expansion of our consciousness. Here is Jung's personal explanatory myth for the goal of man in the scheme of creation; man renders to God the service of enabling him to become conscious of his creation, and conscious of certain aspects of himself, by means of a reflecting consciousness. Needless to say, in spite of Jung's disclaimers, this assertion is pure theology or speculative metaphysics and not practical psychology. I include it here to illustrate what may be an emerging myth, relevant to others as well as to Jung himself, because if this idea resonates it will provide some people with an answer to the 'why' of suffering.

Jung's symbolic approach, which was, and for some of his followers remains, the mainstay of their therapeutic method, can be understood as the attempt to discern the meaning of unconscious imagery which is obscure but vitally important to the individual. Perhaps its major weakness as a therapeutic technique lies in its lack of applicability to patients with severe, developmentally early, psychopathology. In practice, much of what Jung wrote about the importance of meaning derived purely from symbolic experience is of most value to more psychologically mature people. People who are developmentally presymbolic do not seem to benefit from the extraction of meaning out of a symbol in the way which Jung implies. They may *understand* the meaning of a numinous dream, but gain no benefit in terms of their intrapsychic structure – it is as if they cannot *use* the meaning. Rather, these people seem to gain most from a correctly managed relationship with the therapist. Jung's stress on the amplification of manifestations of the objective psyche presupposes a reasonably intact self. His strictly intra-psychic, one could almost say solipsistic, approach burdened the work of his early followers. It has to be balanced by an understanding of the dynamics of the Self as it tries to build a self in the context of the relationship to the therapist. But Jung's stress on meaning is always of importance to the therapist, whatever the patient's level of development. The conviction that the patient's suffering is not meaningless, even though its meaning is not yet known, may be enough to sustain the therapist through difficult times in the treatment, and this in turn allows the patient to survive when all seems lost.

An interesting note of Jung is his idea that neurotic suffering may actually be an attempt to conceal more legitimate, underlying suffering which the patient is refusing to carry consciously. For instance, hysterical symptoms allow the patient to avoid experiencing certain more difficult feelings (CW 16, 185). He suggests that this kind of suffering is actually an unconscious fraud, which avoids pain by refusing to deal with the real problem (CW 17, 154). What Jung refers to here is a fact known to all dynamic psychotherapists, which is that the patient's conscious complaints are often not the fundamental problem, but are his or her attempts to deal with an unconscious difficulty. When the fundamental problem is faced, the pain becomes authentic. This attitude of Jung is similar to Freud's wish to convert neurotic suffering into everyday unhappiness. Today we do not see much hysterical illness, but the principle is illustrated in the common example of the eating disorder. A woman with a severe mother problem may suffer from pain about her weight and her body shape, from envy, shame, depression and so on. But a deeper level of difficulty may be accepting the reality of how toxic her mother really was, how she never had the kind of mother she should have had, how her mother will never change and how she was cheated out of her childhood in an irrevocable way. This terrible level of the truth causes the most difficult but also the most authentic suffering. When this stage of her work is reached, the patient is on the way to recovery. This is because she has sufficiently strengthened herself to be able to face the original trauma, with the help of the therapist, without recourse to layers of defensive operations.

Such a situation also provides an example of the value of meaning in allowing one to better carry an emotional burden. The woman suffering from an eating disorder may realize that her personal suffering is not hers alone. The fact that she is in therapy means that she has to carry the burden of making conscious and resolving the pathology of generations of her forebears, which they themselves simply passed on to her and which she is determined not to pass to her own children. In the case of eating disorders, this pathology is also in part the result of millennia of abuse and unhappiness to which women have been exposed, so that in some of them the quality of mothering has been degraded. Such a woman is thus struggling with both a family and a collective problem within herself (CW 7, 16). From the religious point of view, she is also struggling with the negative mother archetype, which is an element of divinity in its dark aspect that she has to transform within herself. The whole issue of mother and nourishment is numinous – will have extraordinary meaning – for her. If such a person is herself a therapist, or is active socially, she will be able to use her hard-won consciousness for the benefit of the collective. If she is a mother herself, she will be sure not to pass on the difficulty to her daughter. Why some people are chosen to carry such collective burdens consciously is a mystery, only solvable by recourse to ideas of reincarnation or just pure bad luck, according to taste. Most of us have some aspect of the total burden to carry, and to give back to others the hard-won benefits of one's own struggle is often helpful when considering the meaning of personal suffering.

THE PSYCHOLOGICAL EFFECTS OF SUFFERING

Suffering may be helpful or damaging to the personality. The beneficial effects of suffering seem to be recognized by many cultures. For example, the polar explorer Rasmussen quotes an Eskimo, Igjugarjuk, as saying:

> All true wisdom is only to be learned far from the dwellings of men, out in the great solitudes, and is only to be attained through suffering. Privation and suffering are the only things that can open the minds of men to those things which are hidden from others.

> (Rasmussen, 1927, p. 18)

This is a clear articulation of the idea that what we might call 'successful' suffering opens one to what otherwise might be unattainable levels of wisdom and understanding, and that those who have not suffered similarly cannot share such wisdom. At the same time, it is also commonplace to see suffering which seems to have failed in its purpose, leaving behind only bitterness. It is important to try to clarify the difference, especially since the psychotherapist may be able to affect the balance in certain instances. I consider suffering to be successful when it results in any of the following outcomes: increased empathy for the suffering of others; improved ability for relationships; the dissolution of narcissistic structures such as arrogance; new experiential knowledge of the Self; increased wisdom;

increased capacity for humour and play; a restructuring of values, and deepened identity or self-knowledge. Perhaps the fact that these results are possible is why Meister Eckhart described suffering as 'the fastest horse which will carry you to perfection'. The psychotherapist's problem when dealing with intractable suffering is to try to facilitate some of these resolutions rather than that of chronic despair. Various factors operate to allow something of value to occur in the midst of suffering.

Sometimes suffering is successful because it provides a setting for the eruption of the numinosum. A brief example is provided by a 68-year-old woman who was dying of disseminated malignancy, in great distress. To my amazement, she announced at the begining of a therapy session that she would not need to see me much more, because of the following dream (which is discussed in another context on p. 20):

> I am standing on a vast plain, at night. Above me is a rich, velvet-black sky, embedded in all directions with millions of vivid, multicoloured stars of every possible hue. I realize that I am actually a part of all of that.

As a result of this dream, her death anxiety, rage and depression radically improved. This kind of experience seems to speed up the sufferer's process of individuation. On awakening, and on reflection, she felt gratitude, awe, peace and a sense of rightness. This woman had suffered considerably, and was at the end of her own emotional resources, so that she was very open to transpersonal experience. The suffering caused by her illness, and the attendant need to rely on others, had finally undermined her lifelong narcissistic defence of extreme independence and self-sufficiency, forced on her by an indifferent childhood milieu. Her attitude had always been one of 'I am alone and I do not need anyone', which had not only made relationships problematic but had also rendered her impervious to experiences of the Self. She was now receptive precisely because her own strength had failed her, but it was not until she was in extreme pain that she became permeable to human relationships and to the numinous. This vignette is typical; sometimes suffering seems to increase as resistance to the experience of the Self increases. As pointed out earlier, it is typical that such numinous experiences directly address our pathology, in this case making the point that the dreamer is not in fact alone. By undermining defences against the experience of the Self, intense suffering seems to predispose to an eruption of the numinosum. The experience of the archetype then imposes a sense of order and meaning on what would otherwise be felt as chaos. 'Where the archetype predominates, completeness is forced upon us' (CW 9, ii, 123). This dream illustrates how archetypal experience has the potential radically to alter personality structures.

An experience of the Self makes it clear that a consciousness other than one's own must be taken into account, and this is exactly what is needed when we suffer. The sense of a larger presence prevents us from feeling that we are at the mercy of a random universe that is merely a 'tale told by an idiot'. When we realize that we are part of a larger whole, it is impossible to maintain an attitude of persistent egocentricity with its attendant sense of isolation. To illustrate the importance of the experience of a centre other than the ego, Jung (CW 11, 415) quotes an apocryphal song of Christ, which he sings as the disciples dance around him just before the crucifixion: 'yours is this human suffering which I will to suffer. . . . If you had understood suffering, you would have non-suffering. Learn to suffer, and you shall understand how not to suffer.' Jung comments that if we realize that we are in a relationship to the One in the centre, we see ourselves as an integral part of the whole. We need the relativization of the ego in relation to the Self in order not to be caught in hopeless, ego-bound subjectivity. We then have an outside, Archimedean point from which to view our suffering (CW 11, 427–428). A philosophical or religious attitude, one informed by an understanding of the purpose of suffering, is necessary for us to 'know how to suffer'. Again, the psychotherapist's task is to assist in the patient's discovery of such understanding, and to try to prevent the suffering from adversely affecting his or her future development.

DERIVATIVES OF SUFFERING

Unsuccessful suffering results in increased hatred, envy, rage, bitterness and intransigence in relation to other people, cynicism about human values and increased self-absorption. Various mechanisms may operate to inhibit the potentially useful effects of suffering and produce these painful effects, which add to the individual's primary difficulty. One such process is to make derivatives of the suffering, by which I mean to add to it, or to convert it into something else, by reacting to it in ways that add layers of additional suffering over the original problem. These layers are those such as excessive self-pity or self-reproach, unreasonable blame of others, the prediction of even more catastrophic consequences and the addition of anger, resentment and judgements about the rightness or fairness of the suffering. Here I am influenced by Krishnamurti's emphasis on the importance of simply paying attention to 'what-is', without giving it any slant or interpretation. He suggests that:

> Understanding comes through being aware of what-is. To know exactly what-is, the real, the actual, without interpreting it, without condemning or justifying it, is surely the beginning of wisdom. It is only when we begin to interpret, to translate according to our conditioning, according to our prejudice, that we miss the truth.
>
> (Krishnamurti, 1971, pp. 20–21)

Krishnamurti believes that unless we remain strictly with what-is, we avoid or escape it, and this prevents us understanding and transforming it. Staying with what-is allows direct perception, which is obscured by our conditioning, which is essentially synonymous with the small self. Direct perception allows freedom and transformation of consciousness. Krishnamurti wants us to stay with what-is without escaping by means of a derivative of the problem, such as a choice or judgement which is actually only a narcissistic defence of the self, or of the conditioned mind, to avoid the reality of what-is because of fear. This is an echo of Jung's idea that inauthentic suffering avoids the real issue.

This position can be amplified as follows. If we cling to the gap between the way things actually are and the way we would like them to be, we add another level of suffering to an already painful situation. For instance, we may have a narcissistically motivated need for success, fame, beauty, money or some other means of buttressing the self, based on what the self has learned is important to its survival. If this support disappears or is not attained, perhaps because of misfortune, we feel not only the misfortune but also the added pain of the loss of the fantasy or image of how we 'ought' to be. The origin of such narcissistic fantasy is always to be found in one's early conditioning about what is desirable and what is to be avoided. The self-image is a highly conditioned entity, which is partly dependent for its continuing existence on a collection of props, such as our achievements and position. It is this conditioning that makes us hold onto suffering by refusing to move as the situation requires; the resulting inertia worsens suffering. Suffering is often necessary to undo childhood conditioning and reveal our true nature; suffering promotes the essential 'who am I' question by forcing us to examine our values and ask ourselves *why* we are so hurt in a particular situation. Our conditioning not only keeps us from being really free agents, but also guarantees suffering if its demands are not met. Such failure to live up to the demands of a narcissistic fantasy adds a derivative, such as an element of bitterness and depression, to the primary problem. We then refuse to carry the primary burden in all its fullness because we are so distressed about its implications for our image of ourselves. The authentic level of suffering is thereby made into a derivative of itself, or added to, by virtue of our refusal to let go of what is often only a defensive fantasy. We can also add layers of additional suffering to a problem by making other people suffer because we ourselves are suffering, for instance by being in a constant rage about the problem so that the atmosphere around us becomes intolerable to others. Or, we can become envious and hateful of those more fortunate. All of these are devices which avoid the full impact of the problem itself. By focusing on the derivative problems, we are distracted from the real issue and the situation is less likely to open us to new levels of awareness. This kind of reaction to suffering takes us in the opposite direction from the quest for its meaning and purpose in one's life; in a sense it is an anti-religious attitude.

Here I must clarify the fact that I am not arguing for a passive or fatalistic resignation to suffering, without trying to deal with it. Rather, I find that consciously accepted suffering without evasion is more likely to lead to correct action, whereas suffering which is added onto with derivatives leads to evasive action. We therefore need the wisdom to be able to distinguish suffering which can and which cannot be changed. But suffering which cannot be changed is not simply accepted with a sense of resignation; rather it is penetrated psychologically, or investigated as fully as possible for its meaning. Luke (1984) notes that the etymology of the verb to suffer implies the carrying of a weight, which is different from being flattened by it, which is more like depression than suffering. In her words:

> the only valid cure for any kind of depression lies in the acceptance of real suffering. To climb out of it in any other way is simply a palliative laying the foundation for the next depression. Nothing whatever has happened to the soul.
>
> (Luke, 1984, p. 90)

She points out that much neurotic misery is the result of the ego's unwillingness to allow any diminution of its demands or its sense of importance. But refusal to pay this price, when it is necessary, inhibits growth and freedom.

Acceptance of suffering about which nothing can be done, or even its affirmation as potentially valuable, requires a particular state of mind. For example, the sufferer may realize that there is no other way for change to occur, or he or she may be able to trust that a transpersonal process is taking place that is beyond personal understanding. One must then allow oneself to be affected by it and not resist; resistance worsens the suffering. But at the same time it is important for the psychotherapist trying to help in such a situation to avoid any repetition of certain theologies of power, masochism and submission (Soelle, 1975, p. 103). These suggest that we must suffer in order to stay well connected to God, and are another example of the projection onto God of parental attitudes, this time sadistic ones. Rather, affirmation of suffering is better served by a sense of the love of God, however that has been experienced, just as one is able to suffer patiently on behalf of any loved one. It is surely this attitude which allowed Job to maintain his equilibrium in the presence of his affliction. In order to give suffering a religious dimension, and to allow the Self the opportunity it needs, we could actively embrace suffering which is insoluble, or we could carry it consciously in order to discover its purpose, rather than trying to preserve some semblance of personal control or image. This might be one meaning of knowing how to suffer. Such an attitude is of course nothing new, in the sense that the traditional Judaeo-Christian advice to sufferers is to trust that God is near to the sufferer, that God is ready to help, especially if the sufferer repents, and so on. The psychological view is similar, except that there is no emphasis on sin as the necessary cause of the suffering. Perhaps the nearest equivalent villain is unconsciousness, but this does not carry the flavour of moral evil chosen deliberately, even though unconsciousness is the cause of enormous evil in the world.

With regard to emotional suffering, a striking feature of the psychological approach is that although the Self is held responsible for the affliction, via its archetypal manifestation at the core of the painful complex, at the same time help is expected from the Self. The major differences between this and the traditional religious model are:

1 The form that the Self's intervention takes may be totally new and is directly connected to the individual's personal psychology.

2 The process of healing involves a transformation of consciousness, which is facilitated by the methods of psychotherapy using a specifically psychological hermeneutical method, not a doctrinal one.

3 Despite the gloomy personal psychology revealed in the ideas of certain theologians, such as the idea that only the elect of God are to be saved, the psychological view recognizes no possible gulf between man and God, since the Self is never further away than our suffering itself. This means that our suffering is a part of the divine life as it is lived within us.

What we hope for in the course of psychotherapy is noted by Jung (CW 11, 531) to be healing which arises from the same depths that the problem comes from; he suggests that at the height of the illness the destructive power of the unconscious is converted into a healing force, as archetypal images emerge which allow contact with the numinosum (CW 11, 534–535). But immediately it must be admitted that for many people such healing images either do not occur, or they do not produce the healing that Jung suggests, perhaps because the patient is too disorganized or fragmented to benefit from them. For these patients, in particular, the relationship with the therapist is crucial, and this is then more likely to be the healing factor.

Accordingly, it is important that the therapist him/herself knows how to suffer. Personal suffering has a kind of hollowing effect; it allows us the internal space to be able to contain the suffering of others, which would otherwise not be possible. Without the prior experience of consciously accepted personal suffering, the therapist must constantly defend against the patient's suffering when it becomes too intense to bear. This defence leads to a counterresistance to work in depth, because this work absolutely requires the ability to bear emotional pain – not masochistically, but in the service of necessary individuation. The alternative is of course to get rid of the suffering as soon as possible with medicines or behaviour therapy, both of which are ways of avoiding the depths of the psyche when these levels become unbearable. But no negative value judgement about these modalities is implied here; sometimes survival to fight another day is more important than self-sacrifice in the service of an ideal.

Jung's position that the self is the product of the incarnation of the Self, and that suffering is a subjective aspect of that process, has certain important implications. It suggests that suffering is essential for the telos of the personality, and that, whether we like it or not, whatever happens to us actually belongs to us, even if we cannot see the point of it at the time. Sometimes the actual cause of suffering is the friction generated by our resistance to what is happening. Usually this friction is produced in relation to events that either do not fit with the image we have of ourselves, or it involves loss of aspects of the self that we thought were important. Acceptance of suffering then requires the conscious renunciation of an image of the self, or of aspects of oneself, which the situation allows us to see are not essential even though they have felt important because of our conditioning. Suffering is then like a sculpture in progress; when material is cut away, what is left is increasingly like the true, underlying form of the self. In other words, suffering clarifies real identity, as the wound of Christ was his means of proving his identity. The therapist who has successfully been through such a process of moulding of the personality knows that it leads somewhere. Usually he or she has experienced the comments of the objective psyche on his or her own situation in a way which is too definitive to argue with. It is worth looking at some of these manifestations.

COMMENTS FROM THE UNCONSCIOUS ON THE PROBLEM OF SUFFERING

At a time when he was struggling with the problem of suffering, and different religious approaches to it, a psychotherapist had the following dream:

> I see before me a very old and bent woman. She is extremely haggard and sad, but her face is remarkable for its expression of intense suffering combined with transcendence. It is a dark-brown Asian face, intensely lined. She is dressed in long robes, of an off-white or grey colour, reminiscent of a shroud but also like Christian nun's habit, although I know she is a Buddhist. They are folded in a fluted design. I realize that as a child she had her legs broken by her parents in order to make her a more appealing beggar for their use. I am horrified by this. She has suffered enormously because of this deliberate crippling, which permanently damaged her legs. But she has truly transcended her suffering, avoiding none of it. Suddenly I am holding the actual instrument which was used to break her legs. It is like a thin, hard, baseball bat; it too has a fluted design along its length, exactly the same design as the fluting on her robes.

Like the perfect symbol she is, this dream figure combines in herself both Buddhist and Christian approaches to suffering, which at first seem radically opposite. For the Buddhist, suffering is simply inherent in the nature of existence. It can be extinguished by freeing the self from craving and from the desire for concrete selfhood, so that one can see the world as it is, in its suchness, without resistance and without experiencing the self and the world as absolutely separate. For the Christian, suffering is more of a consequence of sin than an inevitability (excluding the effects of original sin). Christ as the incarnate God suffers terribly and purposefully, but, rather than being defeated by it, he is the conqueror of suffering and death on behalf of others. In some ways Jesus' path seems antithetical to the spirit of Buddhism, which asks the individual to find his or her own salvation and not to be sidetracked by dependence on a saviour to the exclusion of personal development. But some of Jesus' teachings are identical to those of Buddhism, especially when he emphasizes compassion and non-retaliation to violence, which require non-attachment to oneself. And his willingness to sacrifice himself for the sake of others is directly in accordance with the Bodhisattva ideal. The dream figure wears the habit of a western nun, but is also

182

a Buddhist, emphasizing the many similarities of Jesus' teachings and eastern wisdom ('consider the lilies of the field . . .'). The dream figure has not avoided her suffering, but she does not identify with it; it simply happened. Her parents brutalized her for their own needs, but she is no longer bitter or resentful. She has been through these feelings but no longer needs them. Her legs are deformed, but her spiritual stance is unequivocal, and indeed is forced upon her by the damage to her actual legs. The pattern of the cause of her suffering is imprinted on her garment; it is her habit to allow this pattern to indicate the form of her spiritual practice. And she is very old; this process takes a long time.

This dream acts as a constant reminder to the dreamer that his suffering cannot be avoided, but, properly responded to, also leads to spiritual development based on understanding the archetypal pattern which caused his suffering. During difficult periods, remembering this dream allows him to maintain a correct attitude, one which is specifically given to him by the Self and which would not easily be arrived at from an ego perspective.

Another dream comments on the beneficial effects of suffering on perception:

> I am trying to read the New Testament, but it is written in braille, which I cannot read. Suddenly the text is wet, and I can then read it easily. I realize that the wetness which allows me to understand it actually consists of my tears.

The New Testament is written for that part of the dreamer that is blind, but he cannot understand it until his suffering flows. Some things are best understood by feeling.

A woman dreamed:

> Two women are dancing together in harmony; one is black, the other white. Then I am in bed, sleeping face down. Suddenly I feel a heavy weight pressing me into the bed – it is the spirit of an old black man that wants to take me over. I wake up terrified that I am paralysed.

She associated sleeping face down with a period in childhood of the beginning of reflective self-awareness and the end of unselfconscious play. To black people she associated persecution and its burden of suffering. The old man seemed to her to imply fatigue, disillusionment and poverty, but also the development of forbearance and a distinct philosophy of life which has enabled him to cope. The dreamer (a psychotherapist) realized that she had been afraid that conscious awareness of suffering, both her own and that of others, would depress her and take over her personality, thus paralysing her. Instead the dream notes that there is in her the capacity to 'dance' with her suffering element, that is to be in a creative, rhythmic relationship without being overwhelmed by it.

Finally it has to be noted that certain situations seen by the therapist seem hopeless, and no sense of meaning emerges from suffering. In one such case, the objective psyche suggested a perspective which in the event proved to be unusable.

The following dream is that of a patient whose parents inflicted enormous suffering on her. For years we had struggled together to find a sense of meaning in what had happened to her, with no success.

> I am far out in space. I see the spokes of the wheel of the universe whirling beneath me. I hear the voice of an old man say to me: 'Tell your mother and your doctor that the point is to be like a child, without identifying with the punishment that children receive from adults.'

This dream figure speaks to her from a point which is above and beyond the whole physical universe. Apparently what is needed for this woman is a position which is totally spiritualized and disidentified with her punitive parents. Such a radical, unearthly remedy may have been recommended because the intensity of her suffering was overwhelming. However, the dream suggestion proved unhelpful because of the overall fragility of her personality. This situation reveals the weakness of the religious approach to the psyche; sometimes the comments of the Self are incomprehensible, and sometimes the Self appears to be silent and offers nothing. These are very difficult periods for the therapist who tries to sustain the sufferer. They can best be handled if the therapist has been through his or her own dark night, and has discovered through experience that such periods are meaningful. At such times, if the therapist can remember his or her own experience of the numinosum, this acts as a source of strength. The therapist can then offer a usable relationship to the sufferer, in the role of a companion who tries to understand as best as possible. For many people, to not be abandoned when they are in trouble is enough to help them weather the storm.

9

SIN AND EVIL
A psychological approach

The problem of evil, like the related problem of suffering, is one of the core problems for any religious system of thought. But it is less difficult for the practitioner of a psychological approach to religious questions, which focuses on the individual, than it is for the traditional theologian or moral philosopher who tries to propose an absolute or universally applicable attitude to evil. In this chapter I wish to suggest a psychotherapeutic approach to evil which is distinguishable from the approach of the philosopher, the theologian or the social scientist. To this end I try to understand evil as much as possible from within the psyche of the individual, aside from definitions of morality in terms of generally accepted standards of behaviour which are approved or disapproved of by the community at large or by a certain theological system. The depth psychologist can afford to remain relativistic in this area, and acknowledge that since the human mind is not equipped to perceive or comprehend ultimate or transcendent reality, the problem of evil is not a simple empirical one that can in principle be solved to everyone's satisfaction. I agree with Jung (CW 10, 860) that what we regard as evil is a subjective judgement, and the nature of the fundamental quality of evil is unknown to us. He suggests (CW 10, 866) that the psychotherapist must take an empirical attitude, hoping that we are correct in the individual case, realizing that we cannot always say what is good or bad for the individual. The depth psychologist is not a moral theologian who can suggest eternal standards based on his or her understanding of the will of God. Given that there are incontestable instances of evil, it also seems that what is labelled good or evil is often only the conditioned choice of a limited personality, motivated more by individual psychodynamic or cultural factors than by any other consideration. Attribution of good or evil to particular behaviour may be only a way of making oneself feel self-righteous, or a way of avoiding one's own shadow. Again the 'don't know' mind serves the psychotherapist best; the attempt to impose absolute standards of morality may have more to do with the therapist's capacity for tolerance and understanding than with any other factor.

In spite of this limitation there is no need for the depth psychologist to adopt an attitude of sceptical pessimism towards the problem of evil. Rather, we must be conscious of the relativity of our personal values in relation to evil, and remain within the realm of intrapsychic reality when we struggle with its meaning in the therapeutic setting. The position that I suggest the psychotherapist use to deal with the problem as it affects the individual is to approach it as much as possible from within the individual's frame of reference, inasmuch as this is potentially accessible to empathy and introspection. Kohut (1971) suggests that this stance defines and delimits the psychotherapeutic field, and it is certainly the only tenable position for the therapist to assume when dealing with religious issues. Our central emphasis must be on the individual subjectivity of both the doer of evil and the one who suffers evil. The psychological attitude to evil may give as much weight to the use of feeling and intuitive judgements as it does to the use of the intellect. This emphasis on direct introspection and empathy without moving into doctrine or collective morality allows the psychotherapist to suspend judgement on the thicket of philosophical problems in the area of ethics. Perhaps the crucial requirement for this to be a tenable attitude is that the therapist must be very conscious of his or her own attitudes in this area, and of his or her countertransference to patients with different values.

To define evil in relative terms, we may stay with an everyday approach such as: 'I know it by its effects on the person.' To try to tighten the definition leads us quickly into difficulty. For example, Russel's (1977) working definition of evil: 'The essence of evil remains deliberate violence done to a being that can feel pain' may not include categories of behaviour whose status as evil is hotly debated collectively, such as the destruction of living species, damage to the environment motivated by greed, racial prejudice or the domination or exploitation of other people or of animals. The problem here is that these arguments take us out of the realm of individual psychology into social science. Whether particular behaviours are considered evil within the collective may be a problem of social evolution. The intrapsychic perspective stresses an attempt to understand the motive for evil behaviour, which is often unconscious, as well as the psychological consequences of evil on its recipient. The psychotherapist is concerned with what troubles the individual; we also let the patient define what he means by evil. Since everyone has feelings or impulses to behaviour that are potentially hurtful to others or to themselves, our therapeutic task is one of understanding the nature of the self disorder that gives rise to these difficulties and which does not allow them to be contained without acting out.

In this area, the theologian who adheres to a traditional concept of God suffers from an age-old difficulty. How is he or she to explain the coexistence of an all-good, omnipotent God with the presence of evil? If God cannot prevent evil, he is not omnipotent, and if he allows or creates it, he is not all good. In the history of theology many different models have been advocated to deal with this problem, all of which reflect fundamental assumptions about the nature of divinity or of ultimate reality. To cite only three of many such attitudes: Hindu belief stresses the illusory nature of evil, which is a function of seeing the world and its contents as multiple and separate, instead of seeing everything as a manifestation of the infinite Brahman, whose consciousness is beyond our divisions of reality. Evil and suffering are therefore the result of our low level of consciousness, leading to faulty perception and categorization of reality. Buddhism sees evil as the result of the workings of the inexorable law of cause and effect. Evil behaviour is the result of delusional attachment to the desires of an ephemeral, essentially unreal self. Traditional Christianity stresses moral evil as synonymous with sin, which is interpreted as a turning away from the will of God which requires divine grace for its redemption. The precise nature of God's will is determined by Church doctrine. Another Christian approach is exemplified by that of Hick (1966), who invokes the arguments of Irenaeus (second century). Whereas Augustine believed that the world's evil is attributable to the Fall of Adam, Irenaeus believed that the world's hardships are necessary for the development of sprirtual values and our struggle for the good. This is probably the meaning of Keats' idea that the world is a 'vale of soul making', rather than only a vale of tears. Hick also presents the traditional free-will defence: only if there is freedom to choose the good can there be free will; there must be evil in the world to allow choice. This attitude is similar to that of most contemporary Jewish writers on the subject (Jacobs, 1973). Unfortunately these arguments seem to pale into insignificance in the face of the suffering and evil done to innocent people. They sound like defensive, somewhat strained rationalizations that almost mock the horror we see around us, because even if they are true in some absolute or transcendent sense they are assertions which are not based on average human experience, and they may not help the sufferer very much. Occasionally, however, it must be recognized that the problem of evil *is* helped by recourse to established theological teachings, such as the doctrine of *karma*, when they are emotionally satisfying to the individual. There is then no need for the therapist to interfere.

The psychotherapist's difficulty in this area is lessened by adhering to a firm and clear distinction between the Godhead and 'God'. Here the term 'Godhead' refers to a level of reality which is beyond experience, so that speculation about it is not within the province of psychology. But, for the depth psychologist, 'God' means a psychological experience of the divine which is referred to as the Self. Because this does not imply any doctrinal notion of the divine, its effects can be subjectively acknowledged to be painful, at times even appearing to be evil, the so called 'dark side' of the Self. Since 'God' means the *experience* of God or the Self, the psychologist has no need to justify any particular theory of why the Self appears to cause pain; it simply does so.

Within established religious traditions, there is clearly no universally agreed-upon theodicy, or justification of God in the presence of evil. To the depth psychologist uncommitted to a particular religious tradition, these justifications sound like attempts to remove any responsibility for evil from the divine, in order to assuage the anxiety that such attribution would cause. Or, there is a need to justify a particular dogmatic assertion, such as the idea that God is only good, in the teeth of the evidence to the contrary. At the psychological level, this problem is only approachable with authenticity by the individual who seeks hard to understand his or her own evil, or shadow, and who is able to develop a personally useful attitude to the evil of others. A degree of reconciliation with one's own shadow can be developed by becoming conscious of it, for example, in psychotherapy or through other means of honest self-examination. One can then attempt to integrate or master it as fully as possible so that it hurts others as little as possible. But intention and consciousness alone are not enough; with the best will in the world, shadow impulses cannot be contained in the absence of firm self structures, because they are associated with unbearably intense affects such as rage or envy. Only a psychotherapeutic firming of the self is then of value.

When the self is able to use it, a solution to the problem of evil may also arise by means of a change in our state of consciousness, as a result of a personal experience of the meaning of evil given as an act of grace. It is possible that if we could experience reality from some supraordinate perspective, the problem of evil would not exist as it does to everyday consciousness. We have some evidence, from the testimony of the mystics and from numinous experiences of the archetypal realm, that such a level of reality does exist. It is to this level of the autonomous psyche that we must turn for help with the problem of evil if we are concerned with the psychological approach to religious experience. The dream described on p. 20 about the relationship between evil and love describes one such reconciling image. Another is the following dream of a young woman:

> I am being held hostage by two dark, brutish men, who are going to kill me. I am terrified. I accept death, and decide to do the Buddhist 'Tonglen' meditation. [The meditator imagines the suffering of another person being drawn into the meditator's heart with the breath, where it is transformed and released back to the other as joy and peace.] After 2–3 breaths, the worst 'brute' softens and changes dramatically. He is obviously greatly moved and touched, and now seems to love me. I am amazed the meditation has been so powerful; I feel no fear, only love.

These dreams are the kind of experience which allow us to take an authentic personal position on the question of evil.

For some people the personal necessity to deal with evil, for example, in concentration camps or the political prisons of repressive regimes, forces the problem to be faced. One then hears surprising testimony. A young Danish resistance fighter, regularly tortured by the Gestapo, reports that the experience gave him a new understanding of Jesus, which is: 'the perception that one should live solely according to the dictates of one's soul'. He gained spiritual strength from being tortured, and surprisingly: 'One other strange thing. I felt absolutely no hatred' (Soelle, 1975, p. 82). Such genuine transformative effect of suffering caused by evil is impossible to predict, and it would require a detailed understanding of the man's psychology to explain. We can only speculate that he may not have had a reservoir of infantile hatred to draw upon, that he had an unusual capacity for compassion based on a very secure childhood and that although he was in a situation that would fragment most people he had no need for revenge in order to maintain his self cohesion. Perhaps he could use the ideals of love and forgiveness for this purpose. This example, although inspiring to others, may be only relevant to certain individuals with a similar personal psychology. I mention it to indicate the need for a personal response to evil, in this case one which is authentically drawn from the Christian tradition.

PRIMARY AND SECONDARY EVIL

There remains, then, the problem of understanding the psychology of the torturer. This does not simply mean the mind of Hitler or Stalin, but that of anyone who inflicts brutality on others, ostensibly in the service of the state or because he is so ordered, but who is also acting out a potential within his personality which had remained dormant until given the opportunity. To reiterate, here I suggest that the psychologist is limited in his or her enquiry to whatever can be grasped by means of empathy and introspection. Questions about the ultimate origin of the potential for evil remain imponderable, because we cannot determine the exact ontological status of evil. We do not know the degree to which evil behaviour is determined by factors outside the individual's free choice, or the extent to which the torturer's behaviour is an archetypal capacity which has *inevitably* evolved. To what extent is evil learned, and how much of it is behaviour which would not have developed without certain developmental vicissitudes? Does all evil behaviour arise out of personal pain, or does some arise *sui generis*? In spite of these uncertainties in psychotherapeutic practice, the therapist's struggle to help understand and deal with the patient's shadow amounts to what has traditionally been called the redemption of evil.

The only form of evil which is the legitimate province of depth psychology is that which is developmentally or psychodynamically understandable. This level of the problem, which I refer to as 'secondary' evil, is in principle amenable to psychological enquiry by means of the empathic–introspective method. Whether there is a transpersonal underpinning to the personal shadow, or a level of evil that might be called 'primary' because it is not attributable to developmental factors, remains an inaccessible metaphysical problem. If there were such a principle, it would represent a level of evil that is beyond the realm of psychological discourse. Such a principle is only of theological concern. By secondary evil, I refer to the developmental origin of feelings such as hatred, rage, envy and revenge which cause enormous destruction and pain to others. I do not mean that these feelings are necessarily bad in themselves, only that they may lead to damage when they are so intense that they pervade the personality, when they override the individual's usual judgement, or when they are so intense that only acting out relieves them. Some writers, such as Alice Miller, insist that evil behaviour is invariably the result of an abusive childhood, that cruelty to others is always an act of revenge. And at times the psychotherapist can understand the origin and development of these problems given what happened in childhood. But in other cases people's savagery seems incomprehensible. In the therapeutic situation, we must then either assume that the patient is repressing the real intensity of his or her childhood trauma, or there is some other explanation for his or her behaviour. This dilemma illustrates a weakness of the empathic stance in relation to understanding evil; different practitioners have varying capacity for empathy, and may use theories of therapy that have more explanatory power in some situations than others. However, this latter problem pervades the psychotherapeutic field, and the only alternative is a more theoretical, completely exterospective approach which in this case would lead us back into doctrine, be it religious or psychological. I must therefore admit that what I call primary evil is strictly a function of what cannot be understood by the individual psychotherapist, and is in no sense an absolute term. I suggest its distinction as a separate category in order to be better able to deal with evil as an intrapsychic problem rather than a purely moral issue. The therapist who feels that he or she can understand and work with a patient's shadow tends to look at it in a different light than is the case when the therapist feels the patient is behaving in a reprehensible manner for no apparent reason. The sense that we are dealing with a 'bad seed' rather than a bad childhood makes the average therapist want to give up.

The primary–secondary distinction is not an attempt to excuse evil, or to reduce its reality, or to develop a psychological defence for a *privatio boni* (evil is only the absence of good: see below) approach to it.) Rather, I hope to define evil and sin in a more psychological manner than is possible by defining them only in terms of behaviour which breaks a set of rules. I also wish to derive an attitude to evil that is of practical use for the psychotherapist. For example, even if sin is understood as deviating from the will of God, the depth psychologist is interested in how this 'God' manifests itself to the individual concerned, as the intrapsychic experience of the Self. Our question then becomes: what are the imperatives of the Self for this individual, and is he or she paying attention to them? Certain individuation paths may require that collective norms be breached in order to be true to the Self. In such a case the unconscious or neurotic following of external standards itself constitutes an evil for that person, even though no social norms have been violated. The obvious objection to this suggestion is that it ignores collective standards, or the possibility of a generally applicable morality, and thus seems to open the door to outrageous behaviour. However, at least in psychotherapeutic practice, when following the promptings of the objective psyche as they manifest in dreams, for example, this fear of abandonment to terrorism, licence and unbridled hedony does not materialize. Instead one sees the growth of an authentically individual ethic (Neumann, 1973). It is therefore crucial for us to discern when behaviour that might be labelled as evil by the collective is actually motivated by true connection to the Self. The main point is that one cannot judge behaviour from the outside looking in. When a patient is tormented by his or her shadow, that is reason enough for psychotherapeutic attention, but not for condemnation by the psychotherapist. Often the patient will define something about him/herself as evil that seems fairly benign to the psychotherapist, but we are not there to quibble about definitions. Or, the patient may seem evil to the therapist, but not so to the patient him/herself. Again, the therapist has to try to reserve judgement as much as humanly possible, or else refer the patient. We are not representatives of the legal system, nor are we philosophers or theologians. The psychological need is to understand the internal sources of behaviour that has been labelled as evil in the consulting room. Our major problem when hearing about behaviour such as child abuse is the containment of our countertransference reaction, so to some extent dealing with the patient's evil is a matter of the psychotherapist's tolerance for his or her own intense feelings. To the extent that this is possible, the therapist can regard the patient's behaviour as a psychodynamic issue and not a moral one. Seen psychodynamically, the patient's and the therapist's evaluation of evil behaviour may look entirely different from a view based on purely collective grounds. For the therapist, behaviour cannot be evaluated at face value, or in terms of intention, which is only a conscious level of motivation and is notoriously prone to lead to unintended results. The unconscious sources of motivation are more important in our work, even though this is of no help to the victims of evil.

There are certain behaviours such as rage, sexual difficulties and promiscuity, greed, envy, vanity and so on, which have traditionally been regarded as sinful when looked at from the outside in terms of a particular set of rules. In fact the word sin may have originated in a Latin root meaning guilty. But there is an alternative way to view such behaviour that tries to understand it without such a heavy moral cast, seeing it as a manifestation of psychopathology rather than badness and which acknowledges its tragic aspects. In the light of modern self psychology, the behaviours listed above can often be understood as frantic attempts to bolster or shore up an enfeebled self which is struggling with fragmentation anxiety. For example, a person who is falling apart as a result of being unbearably lonely, anxious and empty, finds that being with someone, or being held by someone, is calming. Driven by the pain produced by a developmental deficit in the structure of the self, let us imagine that he or she eventually becomes sexually promiscuous, as lover after lover is used temporarily to meet this powerful need for soothing. This behaviour is damaging to others, perhaps by spreading disease, but I suggest that such promiscuity is not necessarily the result of a primary wish to do harm. According to one's sensibility or moral sense, it may be construed as due to emotional disorder, to stupidity or to weakness, but the harm which results is a by-product of the behaviour and is not what drives the individual. Such behaviour can easily be condemned without understanding its motivation, and it is easy to project one's own sexual shadow onto such a person. But the traditional, scapegoating approach is of no use; the individual is already burdened with shame, and being told that this behaviour is sinful will not help. I would consider this to be a clear example of secondary evil. Many such examples could be given, and their developmental origins are sometimes complex, requiring sophisticated psychoanalytic theory to unravel. For example, Fairbairn (1954) described a theory of the childhood origin of hateful behaviour in schizoid personalities. Such children do not feel that they are loved in their own right, for who they are, and that their love for their mothers is rejected, making them feel that their love is bad for their mothers. Such persons eventually may decide that loving relationships are intrinsically dangerous to themselves or to others. If love is destructive, the child must neither love or be loved. He or she then gives him/herself to hating, and gets some satisfaction from that; he or she makes an 'evil be thou my good' pact with the devil, because it is better to destroy by hate and risk being depressed than to destroy by love, which he or she feels is his or her fate in life.

But there are situations where both our current level of theory and our empathy fail us, and this method is then difficult to apply. For example, we might feel that behaviour that hurts others is much more wicked when it occurs in an individual who is essentially intact, not suffering from fragmentation anxiety, not in desperate need of shoring up a fragile self, but who *chooses* to behave in a way that hurts others because he or she enjoys it. Evil is simply part of this individual's hedonic repertoire. This situation could be dismissed as a manifestation of archetypal or primary evil that is psychodynamically impenetrable; this would be an 'original sin' or 'bad seed' approach that assumes that some babies are born to cause evil. But we cannot jump to this conclusion; such a person may have a developmental (or neurological) failure at a level that makes him or her indifferent to the pain caused to others in the process of meeting his or her own needs, or quite possibly he or she was treated this way in childhood. It is then arguable that if this sociopathic behaviour could potentially be traced to some type of developmental or constitutional failure, it too is secondary, even though it may be much harder empathically to grasp its origins. This may be because we are too repelled by the perpetrator or because we do not yet have an adequate theory to explain the behaviour. We thus arrive at the unsatisfactory conclusion that different psychotherapists have different levels of tolerance for evil, and varying capacities to understand and work with it, based on their own psychology and the limitations of their theoretical allegiance. I see no alternative to this dilemma if we wish to individualize our work and avoid global generalizations. This option seems to me to be preferable to the application of broad notions of 'sin' cast without regard to the inner world of the individual. Having said all that, it is also true that at least for societal if not philosophical reasons we cannot afford to remove the idea of personal choice altogether. Nor do I wish to propose a developmentally based legal defence, based on irresistible impulses, for any reprehensible behaviour. To do so would go too far beyond my goal of simply understanding evil more clearly in terms of the primacy of the psyche rather than only in terms of social, theological or moral imperatives. The question of accountability or punishment remains a separate one, to be determined by the society we live in.

To distinguish different forms of evil behaviour from the psychological perspective, in order to decide whether psychotherapy may be of help, my suggested criteria are the developmental history of the individual, the level of intactness of the self, the severity of fragmentation anxiety and the degree of internal splitting which are present. There is a point of useful contrast between this psychological view and Tillich's (1948) notion of sin as a state of separation or estrangement from other people, or from oneself, produced by turning away from the divine ground. This descriptive level of the problem can be amplified psychologically. For example, Tillich's 'estrangement from others' is typically the result of very archaic selfobject needs that are so intense that they cannot be met, so that the state of the self precludes healthy relationships. This level of pathology would also not allow a normal ego–Self axis. This is a psychological and not simply a moral difficulty, since such an individual is at the mercy of those sectors of his or her personality which contain vertically split-off, infantile terrors and needs, and it is these which act as the separating agents. Elsewhere, Tillich (1963, p. 55) essentially equates sin with what we would now call pathological narcissism: 'Sin is turning towards ourselves, and making ourselves the centre of the world and of ourselves ... the desire ... to draw as much as possible of the world into ourselves.' Again, the individual so afflicted may be an incomplete and fragile self, trying hard to hold him/herself together, and so preoccupied in the process that he or she is not able to put aside his or her own needs and look to the needs of others. To call this sin in the sense of badness occasioned through deliberate choice is to ignore what we have learned about the developmental origins of human behaviour.

In order to add the question of personal freedom to the equation, it is useful to consider one important further example of secondary evil. This is provided by Kohut's (1977) distinction between narcissistic rage and non-destructive aggression. According to Kohut, when the vulnerable self fragments under stress, it is as if an atom is split – we then see the energy of raw, uncontained aggression or sexuality, which are fragmentation products of the disintegrating self. The rage and wish for revenge seen when the self fragments are actually used to try to restore the cohesion of the self, as well as to communicate to the selfobject that a serious disruption in the relationship has occurred. The kind of vengeful, unforgiving rage which results from narcissistic injury has a totally different quality than the anger of an intact self which is faced with an obstacle to its wishes, and which uses anger in a controlled way to deal with the interference. Such behaviour of an intact self, when used deliberately to hurt others purely for the sake of personal gain or pleasure, would qualify as primary evil to the extent that the self's motivation is not (at least at present) developmentally understandable. Here again we encounter the limitations of our understanding of human motivation. It might be argued that the apparently intact self who deliberately hurts others is actually suffering from a gross lack of the ability to sense empathically the effect of his or her behaviour on others, and that this always happens as a result of developmental difficulty. But the fact is that some evil people are capable of empathy for the suffering of their victims, yet this in no way ameliorates their behaviour – in fact it may enhance their enjoyment of the situation. Empathy itself, or the capacity to experience the internal world of another vicarious, is value neutral (Kohut, 1971), and so can be used for good or ill. Therefore in order to deal with this kind of situation, another variable must be introduced, namely the question of the amount of free choice which is available to the individual. This raises the thorny and unresolved philosophical problem of determinism; to what extent do we have genuinely free choices in our behaviour? (See Glover, 1988 for a discussion of this problem.)

Perhaps the degree of freedom of choice available to the person who commits evil is the central psychological question at issue here. The misuse of rational freedom is what Hick (1966, p. 18) understands as moral evil or sin. My argument is consonant with his idea that there is a distinction between people who possess self-determining freedom and those who do not. It is my suggestion that severe defects in the self structure, leading to severe fragmentation anxiety or painful emptiness, deprive us of such freedom of choice and force us into behaviour that may be hurtful to others. Of course, the weakness of this model is the grey area of cases in the spectrum, in which the unconscious motivation is not clear. Perhaps the truly healthy self never wants to be deliberately evil. But, only by advocating a strict determinism could we understand *any* choice for evil as secondary to deficits in the structures of the self, rather than a primary choice of an intact self. Even if we were to choose this position (which we would have no choice in choosing) we would still be able to understand the origin of evil without excusing it socially or legally, and without denying its reality. In either case, from the point of view of the therapist, to distinguish different types and origins of evil in the context of the state of the self of the perpetrator is more useful than an approach which sees all evil as a manifestation of an innate quality of badness which just happens to be excessive in some people.

In summary, for the psychotherapist the problem of evil is more of a combination of endopsychic, interpersonal and therapeutic issues than a moral or social one. I realize that it will be objected that we have thereby replaced the idea of sin with that of psychopathology. But this is only a matter of necessary working emphasis or focus, or perhaps even of taste. We cannot answer the question of whether there exists objective evil, rather than evil as manifested in intrapsychic processes. In any case, I assume that one can be relatively free of emotional pain but simultaneously evil, and also that being neurotic does not remove one from personal responsibilty.

THE *PRIVATIO BONI* ARGUMENT

The implication that *all* evil behaviour can be traced to some kind of developmental failure might seem to advocate a *privatio boni* approach to evil. This is the argument of some of the Church fathers in whose refutation Jung became polemical. He came across the idea in a patient who excused his reprehensible behaviour by adherence to the idea that, because evil is only the absence (or privation) of good, it is negligible, 'a cloud passing over the sun' (CW 11, 457). Jung (CW 9, ii, 96 and 114) points out that this makes light of the reality of evil and allows the possibility of demonic inflation within the individual. In fact, Jung's logic is askew here; it has been pointed out (Anderson, quoted by Sanford, 1982,

p. 142) that the doctrine does not deny the *reality* of evil so much as state what evil *is*. Similarly, we acknowledge that a fragile self in the act of falling apart may do evil things, which are still perfectly real. Evil might be the result of psychopathology or unconsciousness, but it remains evil.

THE DARK SIDE OF THE SELF

Related to the denial of the reality of evil as an independently existing entity is the Judaeo-Christian idea that God is only good. Evil cannot belong within a totally good God, and so must be not substantive. Then evil must be split off from the divine and lodged in the figure of Satan. Presumably such splitting is an attempt to control the problem. This idea causes much more difficulty for the theologian than it does for the psychotherapist; Jung's other objection to the *privatio boni* doctrine is that it contradicts the facts of practical psychotherapeutic experience. Regardless of the nature of a transcendent extrapsychic divinity, with which we are not concerned as psychologists, empirical psychology provides ample evidence that at least the Self as manifested within the human psyche has a dark as well as a light side. This everyday psychological observation is consonant with the many mythologies of opposing dark and light divinities, such as those of Set and Osiris, Ahriman and Ahura-Mazda or Loki and Baldur. In the therapeutic situation, the dark side of the Self is seen regularly in the problematic effects of complexes which cause enormous suffering. A mythical example of 'possession' by an autonomous complex is seen in the Biblical (1 Sam. 18:10) story of Saul's envious paranoid depression and rage, when he throws a spear at David because 'an evil spirit from God rushed upon Saul'. Psychologically, such an event belongs to the dark side of the Self.

The dark side of the Self is seen in the archetypal core of our complexes which produce destruction and pain. And just as the alchemists projected their intrapsychic processes into matter, so we continue to do so today. Garrison (1982) is correct when he says that 'we must see the handiwork of God in the atom bomb'. In terms of the incarnational model I have proposed, our painful complexes incarnate the dark side of the Self. This is a radical statement from the point of view of those theologies that try to maintain that our emotional difficulties are nothing to do with God. From the psychological perspective they have everything to do with the divine as it is experienced intrapsychically as the archetype at the centre of our difficulty.

THE PROBLEM OF THE SPLIT-OFF SHADOW

The traditional Christian attitude to evil which separates it from the divine provides a very good example of the process of intrapsychic splitting, both in its horizontal (repression) and its vertical (disavowal) aspects.[1] Here dogma uncannily reflects personal psychology. An intrapsychic split which disavows the personal shadow has been projected onto an all-good image of the divine. Because of this defensive operation, it is difficult for certain theologians to be reconciled with the idea that God has a 'dark' side, even given the comments in Isaiah (45: 5–7) that: 'I make peace and create evil', and in Amos (3: 6): 'Does evil befall a city, unless the Lord has done it?' And in Proverbs (16: 4) 'The Lord has made everything for his own purpose, Yea, even the wicked for the day of evil.' It is also noteworthy that the Kabbala, acknowledging the reality of evil, does not see it as totally distinct from God, but sees evil as the result of the splitting of God's judgement or wrath from his mercy (Sholem, 1961 p. 237). Unlike these strands of Hebrew mythology which acknowledge God as the author of evil, Christian theology insists that God, or Christ, is totally light. Accordingly Jung is accused of being a 'latter day Manichean, or a Hindu, but certainly not a Christian' (de Grouchy, 1986). This is because in his discussion of Christ as an image of the Self (which he is at pains to emphasize is a psychological and not a metaphysical statement), Jung discusses the Antichrist as corresponding to the shadow of the Self. According to Jung (CW 9, ii, 76), in Christian dogma the archetype is 'hopelessly split into two irreconcilable halves, leading ultimately to a meta-physical dualism'. Dogmatic Christianity made the figure of Christ too sublimely light, so that the 'coming of the Antichrist is an inexorable psychological law'. Hence all the fundamentalist worry about Satan as if that figure were a concrete external entity – material that has been forced into the unconscious is projected as it presses for recognition. Dogmatic attempts to maintain an image of the divine which is only light may be an attempt to bind the anxiety which results from the terrifying prospect that the divine may have a dark side, or that the 'devil' actually refers to an experiential aspect of the Self, and of course the self. We are logically forced into such a belief because of a dualistic perspective; if we view the Self or spirit as only good, then we tend to see body, matter or nature as the carrier of the bad, which attitude has been a part of the Christian heritage.

THE DEVIL

In the same manner in which we treat all mythical figures, it is possible to discuss the devil psychologically, and not only theologically. Jung (CW 12, 88) describes Mephistopheles as the 'diabolical aspect of every psychic function that has broken loose from the hierarchy of the total psyche and now enjoys independence and absolute power'. Because of their autonomy, and tendency to behave in ways alien to the totality of the personality and its ideals, such splinter aspects of the psyche have always been personified. For example, Rabbinic theology describes an 'evil inclination', an inner force that prompts us to sin, and is synonymous with Satan. In its Hebrew root, this word means to persecute, which fits well with its intrapsychic meaning – something within oneself that causes persecutory anxiety. In terms of self psychology, the devil, or the presence of potentially autonomous evil within the personality, represents the contents of a split-off sector of the self. This sector lives a separate life in the psyche, and its goals and values are at odds with those of the reality ego, or with the totality of the personality. Such split-off sectors of the self, synonymous with complexes, remain infantile and demanding and are often the result of selfobject failure in childhood. When they break loose from their mooring within the totality of the personality, they cause us to behave in ways that shock the reality ego, reminding us of the original meaning of the word 'devil' – a slanderer. It is important to note that the complex, or our archaic selfobject needs, represent the unlived life of the person. Their claims are important; in order to be heard they cause distress. Their rebellion against the established order is for the purpose of making themselves conscious. This dynamic corresponds to the fact that in mythology Satan is so often personified as an accuser, or one who will not let the status quo rest, but who incites rebellion. For example, Luke (22: 3) says that Satan inspired Judas; he was therefore essential to the evolution of the myth. Thanks to Satan, Judas may have been the only one of the disciples who realized what had to happen.

It is also psychologically accurate that in the mythology of Satan his traditional sin was his pride. Untamed grandiosity is typically the result of vertically split-off material, or complexes, which often lead to demonic behaviour. Mythically this pride was represented as an unwillingness to submit to God; psychologically these complexes refuse to blend harmoniously with the totality of the personality. But Jung (CW 11, 290) also notes that the figure of Lucifer is necessary to creation. He is a figure of autonomy, or opposing will, which is essential, or there would be no need for salvation; people would just be clockwork. Within the personality, autonomous complexes cause pain because they act like loose cannons, but the internal tensions they produce are essential to the development of consciousness (Lucifer as carrier of light). The intrapsychic tension produced by such material may also be an important stimulus to individual creativity.

EVIL AND THE CONTINUING INCARNATION

Our 'demonic' complexes are formed around negatively toned, archetypal components of the Self which have not been humanized or integrated but which still press for incarnation. One has only to remember the demonic quality of borderline rage, for instance, to appreciate the importance of the integration of the affect associated with such material. The totality of complexes of this kind constitute the shadow; their archetypal cores are pieces of the transpersonal shadow, or the dark side of the Self. Herein lies the possibility of a psychologically based theodicy, if one is needed. From the perspective of the ego we label these elements of the self as evil, but it is possible to imagine them from the perspective of the Self, as aspects of the Self which continue to strive for incarnation. It is questionable whether this kind of psychologically based theodicy is helpful in the presence of the suffering which results from the dark side of the Self, but the connection between evil and incarnation is important, and contains the the seeds of a new mythology.

Here we find ourselves back at the theme of suffering as the subjective aspect of the attempted incarnation of the Self. Jung suggests that in the Christian story of the incarnation the dark side of God and the feminine principle were 'stripped off' and are missing. Thus, further incarnation is necessary in order for these principles to manifest themselves. Humanity is instrumental in carrying out this incarnation – Jung suggests that we serve a supreme power, and our demonic, destructive nature should show how we are penetrated by God, or how God incarnates his darkness through humanity (CW 18, 1660). This divine darkness, or the archetypal shadow, is felt as negatively toned complexes. In Jung's words, such continuing incarnation of God becomes 'a fearful task for man, who must now find ways and means to unite the divine opposites in himself. Christ will not take care of the problem for us – Christ illustrates how we must face our own destiny.' To load the whole problem on the shoulders of Christ has allowed us to shift our personal responsibility:

> The bill of the Christian era is presented to us: we are living in a world rent in two from top to bottom; we are confronted with the H-bomb and we have to face our own shadows. Obviously God does not want us to remain little children looking out for a parent who will do their job for them. We are cornered by the supreme power of the incarnating Will. God really wants to become man even if he rends him asunder.... If God incarnates in the empirical man, man is confronted with the divine problem.
>
> (CW 18, 1661)

Jung seems to believe that an individual can choose whether to incarnate the dark side of the Self, although this view ignores the fact that for some people the pain produced by their complexes is too great to resist, and causes involuntary acting out. We are then destined to engage with evil; we do not understand why, but our metapsychology (or metaphysics) suggests that this process is a part of the differentiation of the Self, just as is the case when any other aspect of the Self incarnates. This is to reiterate the idea that the Self consists of all possible opposites, such as good and evil, which are initially united in the unconscious and become polarized as they enter individual awareness and behaviour. Hence it is that the problem of evil is less difficult – that is theoretically – for the depth psychologist than for the theologian. The psychological argument finally arrives at the Eastern view that evil is a function of the ego's splitting into categories of what is actually a unitary reality, one that is not necessarily concerned with morality in our terms. But here we must be careful not to confuse different levels of reality; evil is very real, but it belongs in the realm of dualism, time and space in which the ego, or our tendency to categorize experience, operates. The implication of the limitations imposed by this perspective is well stated by Jung:

> Psychology does not know what good and evil are in themselves; it knows them only as judgements about relationships. ... In our field of experience white and black, light and dark, good and bad, are equivalent opposites which always predicate one another.
>
> (CW 9,ii, 97–99)

Jung specifically excludes the possibility of our knowing about good and evil from a metaphysical point of view. Subjectively, some judgements of this kind are learned, and are the result of internalized ideas. Our notions of good and evil may be forced on us as children by threats of punishment, shame, guilt and so on, or they are chosen because of pleasure, talent, interest and temperament. They also arise spontaneously from the unconscious. But in any given case, the ego can never know the larger ramifications or implications of its choices and categories. It lacks the absolute knowledge of the objective psyche, and is at the mercy of pressure from the Self, whose ends may be unclear.

Here arises the legitimate but unanswerable question: why can the Self not differentiate or incarnate itself without the development of such an automatic categorizing mechanism as human consciousness, which cannot experience the unitary nature of reality, and so behaves and suffers terribly? To respond to this question we must step out of direct experience into the realm of metaphysical speculation, or mythology. My reason for including the subject at all is an extraordinary uniformity of views about this 'why' question, found in widely differing mythical structures, which hints at an archetypal solution that may be relevant psychologically because it can give meaning to individual lives. According to the Upanishads, revealed knowledge is intended to maintain our sense of individuality. Daniélou understands this idea as follows:

> Everything in the work of manifestation is intended to create the illusion of multiplicity and to prevent the realization of the basic oneness of all beings, for this would lead to the destruction of the notion of I-ness, which is the power of cohesion that holds together the individual being, the witness that gives reality to the cosmos. Any weakening of the centripetal tendency characteristic of individuality is contrary to the process of the world's creation.
>
> (Daniélou, 1973, p. 33)

The Kabbalists say the same thing; the reason for man's existence is that God wished to behold God. He wished for a mirror of his own existence. We are here to witness the creation, and man is a co-creator. Jung (1965) referred to this idea in his autobiography, as he enlarged on the 'cosmic meaning of consciousness. . . . Man is indispensable for the completion of creation.' In other words, someone must be present to know that this is the world. Neumann (1969) invoked this idea in a letter to Jung, asking: 'What is creation for? The answer, that what shines in itself when unreflected may shine in infinite variety, is ages old, but satisfies me.' In his reply, Jung (1975, p. 459) illustrates the enormous importance he attaches to the development of consciousness. He asks why God would create the world since he already knows

> what he can reflect himself in, and why should he reflect himself at all since he is already conscious of himself? Why should he create . . . a second, inferior consciousness – millions of dreary little mirrors when he knows in advance just what the image they reflect will look like?
>
> (Jung, 1975, p. 459)

Jung uses this argument to maintain that God may have an unconscious aspect, a point he also makes in *Answer to Job* (see p. 131). In a letter he explains that:

> If God's consciousness is clearer than man's, then the creation has no meaning and man no *raison d'etre*. . . . In that case God does not in fact play dice (with the world), as Einstein says, but has invented a machine, which is far worse.
>
> (Jung, 1975, p. 118)

Rather, God needs man to make aspects of himself conscious (Jung, 1965, p. 338). The same idea is found in the work of Jacob Boehme (see Stoudt, 1968), who also suggested that the divine needs to make of itself a duality of subject and object in order for it to become self-conscious. Boehme writes that God is self-generated through oppositions which arise within his own nature; opposition, limitation and reconciliation are necessary for reason, will and love to be manifest.

Hindu thought expresses this idea in a grand fashion. The universe materializes as *maya*, the power of illusory reality or the ego world which is a localized disturbance in the eternal immensity of the otherwise unmoving divine – a thought in the mind of God. According to Daniélou, *maya* is at the same time the

> source of the cosmos and of the consciousness that perceives it . . . . The non-perceived universe has no existence and the non-perceiving consciousness no reality. Manifestations exist only in relation to perception. If none perceived the cosmos, one could not say that it exists. . . . The perceiving consciousness is the necessary corollary of the manifesting power; the living being and the divine being exist only in relation to each other. Hence the necessity of the individual consciousness of the living beings for the creating power, the dependence of the Creator on his creation.
>
> (Daniélou, 1964, p. 30)

According to these mythologies, our sense of separateness, or the ego, is essential for witnessing to occur, and so essential for creation. But at the same time this separateness allows evil behaviour, which would not occur if we realized our essential oneness with each other. But these mythologies also suggest that consciousness itself requires separateness or duality, even for the divine. Assuming that such a mythologem refers to the creation of a self, rather than being taken literally to refer to the cosmos, it stresses the importance of a relationship with a reflecting other for coming-into-being. This is a mythical underpinning of Kohut's notion of the mirroring selfobject.

What, then, is a useful therapeutic position in relation to evil? (Here I can only deal with the problem at the intrapsychic level; for a larger picture, the reader is referred to the anthologies by Woodruff and Wilmer (1988), and Nelson and Eigen (1984).) The usual goal is increased consciousness and mastery of the personal shadow, which reduce the autonomy of split-off sectors of the personality from holding sway. We then are able to suffer the shadow without inflicting it or projecting it onto others. But an important caveat is that such containment is only possible if the self structures are strong enough to withstand the intense affects, such as terror, envy, rage, shame and guilt, which are involved. These should not be underestimated; it is to avoid them that much acting out occurs, and it is unreasonable to expect that some people will be able to contain them without psychotherapeutic help. But this is not the only way; many people deal with their shadow with humour, which is a particularly mature style. Consciousness of the personal shadow allows humility and understanding for others to develop; increasing awareness of the personal shadow actually undermines the ego's existing categories, allowing them to expand or alter to include material that was previously unassimilable. As I realize and admit what I had been disavowing or repressing, the superficial, or purely narrative, nature of who I think I am becomes increasingly apparent. According to Neumann (1973), such awareness of the shadow forms the basis of truly ethical behaviour, not based solely on collective standards. An important result is the transformation of the dark side of the Self, because my personal shadow is an element of the larger, archetypal Shadow.

TRANSFORMATION OF THE DARK SIDE OF THE SELF

Jung speculates on the possibility of the transformation of God (I assume he means the God image) in a letter (1975, p. 314): 'it can be expected that we are going to contact spheres of a not yet transformed God when our consciousness begins to extend into the sphere of the unconscious'. Edinger (1984) has discussed the general meaning of this statement fully; here I want to focus only on the possibility that we can affect the archetypal shadow, meaning problems such as nuclear war or the holocaust, by work on the personal shadow. (The shadow may be positive, but here for obvious reasons I am referring to its negative manifestations.) Jung implies that incarnation transforms the Self, and that our conscious choices affect this process. The shadow takes the form of destructive complexes whose archetypal components are like strands of the divine within the psyche, which interpenetrate a covering of human experiences. As the human level of the material emerges and is understood, within the transference and in other products of the unconscious, the core archetypal issues gradually clarify themselves. What we then hope for, although it is not always seen, is that the transpersonal level may change in tandem, becoming more positive and less toxic. What was initially a negative manifestation of the archetype reveals its positive side. In this way is the archetypal shadow transformed through work on the human level. The work of making the complexes conscious is like Job asking God for help with God; one lesson Job teaches is that of acceptance until real understanding dawns. Llama Govinda (1977) suggests that: '[W]e are transformed by what we accept. We transform what we have accepted by understanding it.' Acceptance here must mean that we no longer deny or project the shadow, but pay attention to it.

Overall, Jung's concept of the evolution of consciousness implies that humanity is an integral component of God, and that our individual consciousness is simply an aspect of a greater Consciousness. Humanity is then God's growing place. But here we have strayed into realms of theological speculation, away from that realm of personal experience which is the province of everyday psychology. My justification for doing so is that for many people the power of this idea is such that we have in fact entered the realm of myth. This new myth, like the old myths, inevitably involves conflict and pathology, as different elements of the spirit seem to vie with each other within the human soul. It is the suffering which this causes that is felt as the dark side of the Self.

PSYCHOPATHOLOGY AS THE DARK SIDE OF THE SELF

If the sacred manifests itself directly via the psyche as the spirit or archetype at the core of the complex, then psychopathology can be conceived of as an experience of the dark side of the spirit. This darkness either causes outright suffering or evil, or it produces chaos, which is often retrospectively recognizable as an attempt to break down pre-existing intrapsychic structures for the purpose of establishing a new level of order. In any case, the ego is forced to submit to the sense of a power felt as other: 'I see in my members another law at war with the law of my mind' (Rom. 7: 23). Just as the mythical gods conflict with each other endlessly, so we must realize that our bodies and souls are sometimes the battleground of incompatible archetypal principles.[2] Hillman (1975, p. 70) has noted that psychopathology is an essential mode by which the psyche reflects upon itself. 'Symptoms' are of central importance to the soul; they are about its depths, especially those depths which make the ego uncomfortable. To call them abnormal is only one perspective; they are aspects of the Self which are independent of conscious will, but which insist on their own life in the psyche. The fact that these aspects of the spirit cause suffering indicates that our suffering is at the same time our soulful path to spirit. The archetype which is dominant is essentially the god to whom we have to answer, by means of the complex it forms as we develop. Our suffering thereby indicates our unique relationship to the divine, and the divine's unique incarnational pathway within us. Different approaches to this suffering are, essentially, different religions. Depth psychology can also provide a religious process if approached with this theoretical basis.

It is instructive to compare such a purely psychological approach to the dark side of the spirit with an orthodox religious attitude. In his commentary on Jung's autobiography, Dunne (1969) commented on Jung's personal experiences of the dark side of the Self. Dunne sees them as a paradigm of our experience of God without mediation, in which: 'there is nothing human between man and God to put man in touch with God or to shield him from God'. Dunne recognizes that the kind of experiences Jung had in his confrontation with the unconscious can bring the individual perilously close to disintegration, and Dunne asks how we can cope with such manifestations. His specifically Christian answer to such suffering requires the presence of Christ as redeemer. Because of his orthodox beliefs,

Dunne is dissatisfied with Jung's personal solution, which was to differentiate, amplify, understand, and eventually integrate his experiences. This is exactly the depth psychological approach; such experiences contain the seeds of their own transformation because they are the *prima materia* of the experience of the Self. Human mediation in the form of a therapist may be necessary, in the sense that he or she must provide a loving and safe space, a selfobject field for the experience of the Self, the necessary hermeneutic skills, and if necessary the ability to carry for the individual the faith that his or her suffering is not meaningless. It is arguable that this role has some priestly aspects to it.

Although psychologically based redemption from suffering and evil requires the co-operation of the objective psyche, it is a human task to the extent that our knowledge and ability permit. However, there is a level of evil that is so apparently irredeemable that our only recourse is containment. Even if it begins as the result of developmental disasters, evil can become intractably consolidated within the personality. This level of evil appears in dreams as figures that cannot be integrated, often in the form of mythical imagery such as the vampire, which has to be destroyed by fire, or as a Medusa-like image that has to be killed. Here the psychotherapist is powerless except to assist in the discovery either of an apotropaic symbol, equivalent to the crucifix in vampire mythology, or one which will act like a stake through the heart of the vampire.

10

PSYCHOTHERAPY AND SPIRITUAL PRACTICE

SHOULD THE THERAPIST DEAL WITH RELIGIOUS QUESTIONS?

The approach of this book has been to deal with numinous experiences in a purely psychological manner – that is, by trying to stay as much as possible within the psyche, however much one is tempted to stray into realms of experience-distant, doctrinal assertions. Ideally, when dealing with problems of meaning and suffering, the technical principle which is applied is to try to discern the comments of the objective psyche on the situation. Now it could be argued that to dabble in these areas is fraught with danger for the psychotherapist. What advantage is to be gained by recommending that the psychotherapist work with such material? Is it not best dealt with by some other specialist, such as the minister of religion? This question allows us to contrast the approach of the transpersonal or archetypal orientation with those of the mainstream attitudes to the psyche. It also allows useful comparison of the psychological approach to religious issues with a purely theological or doctrinal approach.

Jung's intrapsychic approach to religion produced professional difficulties for him, and was a source of misunderstanding with which he constantly struggled, because of the criticism that he had merged what should not be merged. But for many people, his psychology compensates for the sterility of the behavioural psychology which for a long time dominated our teaching institutions at the expense of the deepest subjectivity of student and patient. For much of Jung's lifetime, and to some extent today, 'respectable' academic psychologists were only taught cognitive–behavioural or learning theory, and other quantitatively verifiable subjects, using a model of the person based on nineteenth-century deterministic physics. But none of this preparation adequately qualifies the practitioner to deal with serious existential crises except at a relatively superficial level, because an entire genre of the most important intrapsychic events – contact with the numinosum – is not quantifiable, predictable, repeatable or even measurable. They require a totally different methodology, namely a phenomenology of the human soul. At the same time, until relatively recently, mainstream psychoanalysis was wedded to a simplistic drive-defence model of the psyche which was almost equally numbing, while most of modern psychiatry has increasingly abandoned the psyche in favour of the chemistry of the brain. All of these approaches to the person are useless in the face of profound religious enquiry of the kind raised by serious personal difficulty. Consequently, in such situations, practitioners of these systems of therapy are *required* to turn over their patients' questions of meaning to the minister of religion. For the religiously unaffiliated patient, the practitioner must abandon any pretence at the development of a solution arrived at by other than personalistic means. These approaches deprive the sufferer of usable access to the transpersonal levels of the psyche, and so reduce the possibility of individual revelation from this dimension of being. The area of contact between the personal and transpersonal is exactly that in which Jung's contributions are most helpful.

Further, many people find that traditional religions are increasingly unable to provide psychologically relevant spiritual direction. What is available often sounds to them like platitudes of no direct meaning. Much of the usable spiritual direction now found is distinctly psychologically informed. Looking back on Jung's original debates with the theologians, one can imagine the degree to which they were threatened by Jung's capacity to work directly with numinous experience at a personally relevant level. This probably accounts for some of their polemical attacks on Jung's religious writing; it seemed that he had crossed a line into their province. But in fact in doing so he only followed the lead of the psyche itself, which produces numinous experience the way flowers bloom – without regard for human understanding or categorizing.

From the psychotherapeutic point of view, attempts to deal with spiritual questions by recourse to external authority, to doctrine, or by reference to someone else's experience, run the risk of doing violence to the individual soul. For example, as we have seen, to insist on celibacy for a whole group of people represents the blunt application of a principle that is only authentically applicable to the spiritual life of particular individuals. Such broad application of rules not based on individual spirituality merely allows the defensive avoidance of *truly* important areas in which major spiritual growth could occur, such as relationship. For the psychotherapist interested in an individual rather than a collective approach, the problem is to discover what a particular individual needs for his or her spiritual development, so that we do not ask an Aphrodite to be celibate or an Artemis to have a huge family.

DOES A PSYCHOLOGICAL APPROACH ENCROACH ON THEOLOGY?

The religious approach to the psyche carries with it major implications for the dialogue between depth psychology and traditional theology. Objections can be anticipated from both disciplines. I will first consider the theological objections. Theologians have often warned that psychology must not encroach on theology. For example, Goldbrunner (1964) describes Jung's religious writing as 'psychologism' – meaning that it reduces 'supra-psychological realities to the level of purely psychological reality'. Buber's (1952) criticism is similar. These writers are understandably anxious to preserve the idea of a God who is beyond the psyche. This objection is answered more fully on p. 43; suffice it to reiterate here that, since we only become aware of the world, or of the sacred, through the psyche, the psyche is our *only* means of experiencing this Reality. The psyche necessarily contains whatever seems real to the person, whether or not these contents correspond to some trans-psychic, objective reality. The psychologist makes no claim about what lies beyond psychic reality, but inasmuch as the divine is experienced intrapsychically it is in the province of the psychologist, regardless of its origins or extensions outside the psyche. (The word 'outside' would then cease to have any meaning; Jung [CW 8, 814–815] speculated that the psyche itself shades into dimensions beyond space–time, but this is a metaphysical suggestion of no direct relevance to practice; it has to be invoked to explain the phenomenon of synchronicity.) In summary, no separation can be proved between psyche and world, or between psyche and the divine. No meaningful claims can be made that the entrance of divine reality into the psyche distorts divinity in some *discoverable* way. We also have no idea whether the psyche is itself coextensive with divinity; the important point is that 'the psychic nature of all experience does not mean that the transcendental realities are also psychic' (CW 18, 1538). But where and how else can we deal with them?

The depth psychologist rests his or her case on the following propositions. First, if there is a transcendent, suprapsychic reality, the psychologist is competent to study it when it becomes immanent by entering into personal reality. Not only that, but if the numinosum becomes an important object of relationship in a person's life, the psychologist is duty bound to treat it as such, and to study the unique qualities of such a relationship, rather than leave the whole matter in the hands of the theologian or minister, who may be less qualified to understand the dynamics of such relationship within the individual's overall psychic economy. And if, as Jung suggests, an image or, I prefer to suggest, an element of the divine exists as an a priori or primary intrapsychic object, not present as a simple internalization,[1] then the psychologist is doubly required to study its manifestations, since it must be an important factor in human development. The theologian may then not dismiss the psyche as a purely human phenomenon which excludes divine participation. Jung's argument suggests that the divine partakes of the psyche and gives it order. Where this merger occurs indistinguishably, psychology and spirituality become synonymous.

Thus, there is no question of misapplying psychological methodology to theological categories. Rather, we apply well-established psychological methods to personal psychological experience which happens to be of a religious nature. Should the result have theological implications, of course these may be subject to further theological scrutiny. All religious traditions are based on the ongoing amplification of such individual experience. But here I am not concerned with 'second hand religion' (William James's phrase) but with the primary data.

Conceivably this phenomenon arises where the divine penetrates the psyche, although I dislike the dualism implied here. In any case, such experience may offer theologians evidence for their assertions about the nature of the divine, or it may contradict some existing images. For instance, I (Corbett, 1987) reported a dream which radically changed the dreamer's concept of God, and which has implications of interest to feminist theologians. The dreamer was a 62-year-old woman, brought up in a traditional patriarchal religion, who was afraid of aging and death. In the dream she is presented with an image of an androgynous Godhead; the divine is depicted with both male and female heads. She is also given a mysterious dream *koan*; she is told that the purpose of aging is the 'rejuvenation of God', because 'when we are born God is old, as we grow old God becomes young, and when we die God experiences rebirth'. As well as helping her with her fear of aging and death, the dream stimulated the dreamer's awareness of the feminine aspects of the divine. This dream illustrates Jung's (1975, p. 314) point that as our consciousness extends into the unconscious, we encounter images of God that we then transform. This process is one of continuous revelation.

Such psychologically derived data cannot logically prove or disprove metaphysical theories about extrapsychic realities, since the latter belong to a universe of discourse removed from experience and therefore beyond the scope of psychological procedures. In Jung's (CW 14, 667) words, 'The psychic is a phenomenal world in itself, which can be reduced neither to the brain nor to metaphysics.' But metaphysical statements may express psychological truths, since like mythology they are products of the psyche. And human experience produces data for metaphysical speculation. But from our standpoint, such outcomes are not primary, although they are of corroborative interest.

When the psychologist professes competence to discuss matters traditionally held to be the province of professional theologians, and at the same time checks their traditional assertions against the comments of the psyche, one might expect a certain degree of narcissistic injury to occur. Or at least we can foresee the emergence of issues of professional turf. Among theologians, these factors may contribute to a degree of resistance to the acceptance of a religious psychology which is not simply related to its content. This resistance may be disguised or rationalized. For example, it is easy, and misleading, to argue that the kind of natural religion proposed by the religious approach to the psyche is, for instance, anti-Christian if it leads to attitudes which cannot be encompassed within the traditional dogmatic tenets of Christianity. For example, Christ occasionally appears in a dream as a woman. This criticism ignores the fact that the Christian story itself, as it is told in the Gospels, can be approached psychologically or doctrinally with equal validity unless one feels that the Church fathers had special authority to decide the final meaning of the story. For many people, the intrapsychic approach actually revivifies Christianity. Jesus himself was hardly a model or proponent of orthodoxy, and his story can be appreciated freshly by the psychologist in a manner which bypasses the accretions of dogma. To do so merely requires focus on the meaning of particular events of his life as they apply to the psyche of the individual, and their amplification as mythologems. (As an example of this method, see for instance p. 165 and Edinger, 1987.) This kind of procedure is important for people for whom the religious instinct is not satisfied by simple adherence to doctrinal assertions about Jesus which do not necessarily resonate with what Jesus represents to that person. In the light of depth psychological interpretation, the life of Jesus seen as a particular mythical image is a most important comment on love, suffering and the relationship between man and God. Regardless of its historical truth – and here we most obviously differ in our method from that of the official Christian view – the life of Jesus takes on entirely new archetypal meaning when themes within the story correspond to important aspects of the individual's psychology. For some people this approach is more important than the historical emphasis; as Eliade (1974, p. 43) points out, we do not so much remember particular historical personages as archetypal categories or mythical models. Finally, it is important to point out that the assertion that a relationship to Jesus via church doctrine is the only way to relate to the divine is a political statement, not a psychological truth.

OBJECTIONS FROM WITHIN PSYCHOLOGY

Among psychologists who object to a religious approach to the psyche, several criticisms are voiced. The most superficial and easily dismissed is that this attitude turns psychology into a religion. The inherent oversimplification in this statement actually misses the point; I do not propose that behaviourists should regard the statistical analyses of their rat-maze experiments as sacred texts. I mean that we can approach the psyche's own manifestations of the sacred using psychological techniques, rather than by means of theological presuppositions, while still maintaining a religious attitude. The kind of objection referred to is always made with a horrified exclamation, implying that psychology must not on any account be made into a sacred science. But this is actually already the case, since it deals with a medium of expression of the divine. And here seems to be the reason for the psychologist's protest; the religious function of the psyche produces the experience of the numinosum, which is very anxiety provoking, especially for those psychologists and psychiatrists who adhere to approaches which enable them to ignore the problem of the unconscious.

In the face of the experience of the numinosum, the criticism that the proposed model turns psychology into a religion implies a non-existent dichotomy between the two fields. My proposal is actually more radical than that. I am not concerned with the usual problem of the relationship between psychology and spirituality, or the need to integrate them as if they were separate. My case for the inseparable intermingling of the divine and the human psyche requires a religious psychology, with no arbitrary distinction between the two disciplines. It is my belief that, if we have eyes to see the archetypal dimension, the sacred is always present as a part of human experience. Any major human situation has archetypal under-pinnings, and hence a sacred aspect. To recognize this dimension in therapy not only facilitates the individual's connection to it, but also enables the therapist to remember that the practice of psychotherapy is a spiritual, or sometimes even a pastoral, discipline.

Such an attitude may seem excessive, in that it turns what is culturally defined as a secular pursuit into a religious one. But to do so simply acknowledges the primacy of numinous experience for many therapists, and also our intuition that the psyche is a source of the sacred, instead of our having to ignore or cloak this attitude for the sake of professional acceptance. Surely it would be of value to cast such instinctive religious feeling, combined with technical knowledge, into a cohesive spiritual form and practice, based on the primacy of personal religious experience. I have suggested that doctrinal interpretations of sacred texts may project the interpreter's own pathology onto the story, as we see in the case of the Church fathers' imposition of their personal sexual problems, irrelevant to most people, onto the story of Jesus. This unconsciousness, so disastrous from today's perspective, demonized the body and the feminine. These attitudes became incorporated into dogma but have nothing to do with the life of Christ or his teaching. It seems more useful to stay with the psychology of the individual experiencer when trying to understand religious experience, and to recognize that any generalizations made from one person's experience of the numinosum only apply to other people with very similar psychodynamics.

If this argument has not allayed fears that we are trying to turn psychology into a religion, for the sake of perspective one might usefully contrast this endeavour with the self-evident fact that, for many people, money, power, fame, status and appearance have already become quasi-religious pursuits, because of their unrecognized numinosity, with the blessing of the culture. Therefore it seems not too much to ask that those of us who are interested in more direct manifestations of the numinosum, and who share a particular commitment to the religious dimension of the psyche, consciously articulate this feeling without inhibition.

In this context it is worth recalling that there is actually nothing new about the proposed model. In antiquity (and today within shamanic cultures) illnesses of all kinds, including emotional problems, were the province of religion; the ancient religions themselves have been described as 'cults of the psyche' (Meier, 1967, p. 3). Some modern historians of psychology sigh with relief that this situation is no longer the case, and that psychology is finally becoming scientifically respectable. They might claim that to include psychotherapy within religious practice is culturally regressive. But in fact I believe that the original historical impulse to do so was instinctively correct. After a long detour and period of exile, the approach proposed here returns the care of the psyche to its rightful setting, with the benefit of our modern perspective, our differentiated consciousness and all the advances that have been made in psychotherapeutic understanding in this era. This is not to decry what was known about healing in antiquity. Early theurgic healing cults, such as the Aesculapian religion, contained the archetypal essence of truly healing procedures. They accepted the intention of the divine underlying the illness, and their rites tried to establish a proper attitude to it. Invocation, pilgrimage, purification, incubation and sacrifice were all constituents of their attempts to heal. The temple attendants, or therapists as they were called, helped interpret the divine message as revealed in the incubant's dream. In different dress, we have incorporated much of this ritual behaviour into our own practices.

To the sceptical psychologist we may therefore reply that depth psychology can in fact become a legitimate religious pursuit, especially in its study of the autonomous levels of the psyche. I have shown how this attitude benefits the patient, for example, when the psychotherapist is able to call on his or her own experience of the archetypal dimension during difficult times in the therapy. Perhaps it is redundant to add that this approach would be meaningless to therapists with no personal knowledge of the archetypal psyche. When Jung was accused of offering a substitute religion, he noted that: '*I* did not attribute a religious function to the soul, I merely produced the facts which prove that the soul is *naturaliter religiosa*, i.e., possesses a religious function' (CW 12, 14). His evidence is not based on a particular transcendental or ontological argument, but simply on the encounter with the numinosum as a primary datum or irreducible unit of experience.

Here the still-worried reader may argue that the psychotherapist is not set apart by ordination, or necessarily called by vocation, to the work of assisting people with religious questions and experience. And this is true – it is perfectly possible to do good therapy without this level of reality ever needing to be addressed. But for those who wish to do so, it is reassuring to remember that the necessary initiation can come directly from the Self, and that such initiatory experience gives the therapist the archetypal authority to act as a spiritual director. (The 'guide of souls' dream described on p. 23 is an example of such initiation.) Initiation need not take an obvious form; by definition, initiation includes contact with the sacred, so that any powerful experience of the numinosum may be initiatory. In practice, when such an experience occurs, if it is not defended against, it changes the attitude of the practitioner and opens him or her to working in a religious mode.

A COMBINED PSYCHOLOGICAL AND RELIGIOUS APPROACH TO PSYCHOTHERAPY

The spiritual needs of those disaffected by established religious systems are not met by authoritarian psychological and psychiatric systems which discount the primacy of the subjective world. Consequently there has been a countercurrent of popular and professional interest in depth psychology, which is in keeping with both an unmet thirst and the cultural *Zeitgeist*. The groundswell of fascination with Jungian and other psychologies of meaning testifies to the persistent presence of an intense spiritual search, motivated by the psyche's intrinsic religious function but not bound by traditional church limitations. This work appeals to those psychotherapists who are themselves engaged in such a search, and who are unable to deny the power of numinous experience by defensively reducing it to some infantile equivalent such as a regressive merger with mother, or a return to the oceanic bliss of intrauterine paradise. Religious experience and questions of a religious nature are ubiquitous, not only culturally but especially in the course of any psychotherapeutic work that admits a transpersonal dimension. What needs emphasis is the fact that *original* responses to personal religious questions may arise in the course of contact with the transpersonal levels of the unconscious. The question which always arises here is the validity of such responses, especially as they might be challenged by established theological positions. As mentioned above, one typical criticism of the psychological approach is that it reduces the divine to the status of a 'psychologism', or a purely intrapsychic entity. This charge requires a further look at the problem of reduction.

Jung (CW 12, 13) pointed out that the *mysterium magnum* is 'rooted in the human psyche', so that the religious function of the psyche 'produces itself of its own accord' (Ibid., 14). Jung is here following the tradition that insists on the a priori nature of the numinosum (Otto, 1958). This point is one answer to the accusation of psychologism levelled against him; it means that there is no need to fear that the intrapsychic matrix of religious experience makes it derivative, or reducible to simpler, personally derived, psychological components. The fact that the psyche is the inevitable medium for the expression of the divine does not invalidate the ultimate reality of divinity, as the common 'do you mean it's only psychological' type of protest suggests. Where God and man touch, they must do so within the psyche if there is to be human consciousness of the experience. That said, we in no way reduce or even comment on the original nature of what it is that has been experienced. The therapist can legitimately bypass attempts to comment on the ultimate nature of the divine, in the manner of some theologies, by remaining naturalistic. That is, we simply adhere to the intrapsychic manifestations of the divine, resisting the temptation to work out their implications for a theoretical system. I find that pre-existing traditional notions about the nature of divinity are actually likely to interfere with the reality of direct experience, when the subject cannot accept the reality of an unorthodox manifestation. As this section was being written, a friend who is immersed in and committed to a traditional church dreamed that a voice said to him: 'God dooms us to live a life apart from him.' He was distressed by this dream until we recalled Meister Eckhart's distinction between God and the godhead. In his remark 'God save me from God', Eckhart makes the point that one's concept of the divine can interfere with the experience of the Reality (see Fox, 1981, p. 229). The dream seems to say that, if the dreamer retains his current doctrinally based concept of God, that concept will separate him from the actual experience of God.

Even as we avoid making the mistake of equating the psyche and the divine, it is also true that one cannot define the relationship between them. The nature and the origin of the psyche are themselves as unknowable as any metaphysically postulated, extrapsychic divinity, so that we are dealing with two unknowns. But here there is an interesting overlap found in theologies which equate consciousness with the divine, as in the Hindu concept of the Absolute as *Satchitananda*, or 'being, consciousness and bliss', an appellation which is only intended to stimulate the intuition of the seeker, since traditionally the words are said to bear no relation to ultimate reality. We see this idea used by those Jungian writers who refer to 'psyche' without using the definite article, as if the psyche itself is personified or considered to be a subject in its own right. This position implies that consciousness itself, rather than only its contents, can be both the matrix and also a causal determinant of behaviour. Within this logic, while the Self is the totality of consciousness, intrapsychic images of the Self are merely its temporary, and local, formal contents. Whether or not this is philosophically tenable for the depth psychologist, there is considerable practical justification for such usage, given the autonomy of the objective psyche and the concomitant experience of oneself as the subject of a larger consciousness. (In other words, I realize that Something is experiencing me.) In this way, it is possible to imagine consciousness as a fundamental, irreducible entity in its own right, although a physicist might opt for the enthronement of energy as more fundamental. Here again, the obvious caveat is that to personify consciousness itself in too literal a manner may be merely the modern equivalent of the archaic personification of the divine as a celestial entity. Perhaps the problem here is partly linguistic. Our use of the word 'consciousness' is about as precise as our use of the word 'snow' would be to an Eskimo. In Sanskrit there are about twenty different words for what we subsume as 'consciousness'.

The conclusion from all of this is that to suggest that there is an innate religious function to the psyche is not to explain its nature or origin. Therefore our methodology when dealing with it is best if it remains descriptive, amplificatory and interpretive, always trying to understand the meaning of transpersonal experience within the larger context of the total psychological life of the subject. Such experience is always related directly to this life; in the psychological paradigm there is no need to maintain a rigid supernatural–natural split, as if our humanity could interfere with our spirituality.

At times, because the use of psychological procedures does not necessarily validate traditional assumptions, the use of such methodology to study religious phenomena may seem to ignore, or ride roughshod over, cherished traditional belief systems. However, our purpose is not with the proof or disproof of such systems. We are only concerned with the exact form of religious experience itself and its implications for personal development and psychotherapeutic practice. In fact, within this method, doctrinal assertions themselves are not privileged – they are also considered to be psychological products, often indicating the psychological needs or difficulties of their authors. Traditionally, some scriptural texts are considered to be divinely inspired, but I do not consider the numinous dream of the obscure individual to be any less inspired. To argue otherwise is to favour a dangerous form of religious élitism.

The psychotherapist committed to the possibility of continuous revelation prefers to grant priority to the primary or naturalistic data of observation rather than to any body of dogma. Even given the fact that we can often only see what we already know or believe, it is remarkable that those of us who are interested in the manifestations of the numinosum are so often surprised at the originality of what occurs. Listening to dreams all day in the consulting room, and perusing the literature in this area, one cannot avoid the feeling that something religiously new seems to be emerging from within the depths of the psyche. These new manifestations of the divine need a way to be understood and incorporated into everyday life. This is the importance of the psychological paradigm; the divine as it appears today may not be able to be forced into old conceptual bottles.

I have asserted that no positivistic methodology is remotely capable of capturing the essence of the manifestations of the objective psyche, and that a religious approach to this level of reality based on a depth psychological hermeneutic is optimal. To support this position, I wish to compare such an approach with some other possible paradigms for the study of religious experience. The psycho-therapist interested in a religious approach to the psyche may be interested in the values implicit in this attitude, and how they compare with those of alternative, currently collectively approved, psychological models.

PARADIGMS FOR THE STUDY OF HUMAN SUBJECTIVITY: AN APOLOGIA FOR THE RELIGIOUS APPROACH

A discussion of various paradigms within which to view the psyche and the individual's contact with the numinosum is not merely academic; it has major implications for the work of psychotherapy. Choice of a paradigm may reveal conflicts of values and opinions about fundamental aspects of human nature. It is now understood that any therapeutic method implies an ontology, or an image of reality. For example, it has been suggested that positivistic psychology pre-supposes that people are things, while behavioural psychology treats people purely as organisms. The conscious psychotherapist has to choose which of the many systems of practice to commit to, albeit possibly temporarily. The depth psycho-logist, and especially the religiously oriented therapist, is currently in a minority, and may feel that he or she is swimming against the collective tide. But we can take heart from a historical perspective on psychology and psychiatry, which makes it clear that establishment attitudes often seem trivial a few generations later, and that to be working within currently accepted guidelines says nothing about the correctness of one's attitude. It is also clear from a study of the history of psychiatry that the greatest betrayals have been perpetrated on suffering people in the context of therapies for emotional distress, based on theories which can now be seen to be grounded on faulty and unconscious premises. Sometimes these therapies were carried out by well-intentioned people with only the most sincere desire to help, while sometimes they seem little more than ways of defending against an unconscious terror of mental illness. In this century, many such therapies have been proffered in the name of scientific objectivity. Today it is generally agreed that no such objectivity is possible. What is true in any field of enquiry is particularly true in psychotherapy; the personal psychology of the investigator, his or her theory of cure, the questions asked and ignored and the method of investigation all inextricably influence the nature of the data obtained. This is so especially when the two participants share the common field of consciousness of the psychotherapeutic situation. Sherrard (1987) has pointed out that scientific theories are simply the objectification of consciousness. Therefore, we have to know our own biases; otherwise when we develop general psychological theories we are in an analogous position to that of the alchemists, who projected their own intrapsychic material onto matter, as if what seemed to be happening was 'out there'. To exaggerate only somewhat, in the case of the psychotherapist we project our theories mixed with our own prejudices onto our patients' productions. Obviously the religious approach to the psyche is also burdened in this way, so it is worth examining its axiomatic basis. When this is done, it seems that its assumptions contrast starkly with those of other methods to explore and explain human subjectivity.

For example, it is implicit within the religious approach to the psyche that it is impossible to reduce religious and psychological dimensions of the person to the emergent properties of brain processes. This materialist attitude is held by many psychologists and psychiatrists oriented to the primacy of neurobiology. For these practitioners, only theories with a physiological basis have any credibility – Jung's 'psychology without the psyche' (CW 11, 496). This approach actually abandons psychology and spirituality as distinct fields of enquiry, reducing them to epiphenomena of brain. It ignores the fact that complex fields of enquiry require their own methodology. Adherents to this materialistic belief also often deny the ontological reality of spirit and soul. This attitude is typified by computer models of the brain which explain consciousness itself as a by-product of neuronal information processing. (Some objections to this kind of biological determinism are found in Rose, 1982.) It is not my intention here to summarize the entire mind–brain debate, but only to point out that, because it is still moot, materialist approaches, which dominate current psychiatric education and research journals, are actually ideologies in scientific clothing. The reasons that their adherents cling to these theories are not simply technical, but are also emotionally determined, an article of faith. Of course, economic and social factors, such as an insistence on a quick therapeutic approach, also play a major part. The materialist takes the completely arbitrary position that consciousness or intelligence is a product of matter, or brain, even though there is no possible refutation of the position that brain is a product of intelligence, or spirit. From a purely technical point of view, the materialist has not solved the problems which arise when it is assumed that matter is the causal substrate, or the organizing principle, of psyche. To cite only a few of the difficulties: they ignore the fact that to attribute psyche to brain mechanisms merely shifts the problem onto another system without accounting for its own structure and organization. Here one can perfectly well postulate spirit as the organizing principle which is supraordinate to brain. And, except for some generalities common to all systems, the organizing principles of human psychology, and of the manifestations of spirit within the psyche, seem to be totally different from, and independent of, the organizing principles of matter. (Simplistic examples are that learning theory or the structure of dreams are different from the laws of chemistry.) Nor is it clear how macroscopic psychological regularities (complex behaviour) could emerge out of microscopic electrochemical events, such that the psychological regularities exhibit autonomy and sovereignty.[2] At best, at the present state of our knowledge, one can only take a provisional position in this debate, based on a commitment to a point of view that itself may actually be determined by psychodynamic factors. But in spite of these reservations the materialist viewpoint has achieved the level of unchallenged orthodoxy in many teaching institutions, so that the sceptical depth psychologist begins to feel that such approaches may be unconscious, defensive ways of ignoring the anxiety generated by the mystery of the psyche and its incomprehensible nature. In his turn, the sceptical materialist wonders if his religious interlocutor simply cannot tolerate the idea that all the latter's ideas about spirit and soul are merely the wish-fulfilling or anxiety-reducing products of an electrochemical device (the brain), with nothing transcendent involved. My point here is that the psychotherapist wittingly or unwittingly takes a position on this belief spectrum, and this position will influence the way he or she practises.

To illustrate the difference one's point of view makes in practice, a controversial example is provided by the varying attitudes towards reports of peri-death experiences.[3] The elements of the experience usually consist of being out of the body, movement down a tunnel, encounter with a being of light or other religious figure, conversation with dead relatives and the offer of a choice about whether to return to the body. A reductive explanation is that these phenomena are the result of the acute organic brain syndrome produced by cerebral hypoxia or toxicity. But it seems odd to argue that the acutely impaired brain could elaborate complex, coherent imagery which, unknown to the experiencer, is *identical with* that experienced by many other people, without the subsequent memory loss which is the pathognomonic hallmark of acute brain damage. It would be as if a large group of patients with alcoholic delirium tremens all reported exactly the same, intensely meaningful and helpful content of their perfectly remembered hallucinations. For the psychologist who does not adhere to a theory of brain-produced consciousness, it is more parsimonious to accept the experience of the near-death survivor the way we accept the reality of dreams, as part of the reality of the psyche. The psychologist cannot definitively answer the question of whether consciousness is literally able to move out of the body into another realm of reality. But given that these are all equally unprovable assertions, to insist on a purely organic explanation of these events is to abandon true openness in the face of an unanswerable question. This seems to be the result of a dim awareness that to allow the alternative is to open the door to a religious approach to the person.

Another paradigm or approach to human subjectivity is that of learning theory, which is built upon statistically verifiable observations of external behaviour. This approach tries to solve the problem by ignoring it, by dismissing the qualitative and introspective aspects of personhood, and therefore offers little to our understanding of numinous experience. It has been rightly said that behaviour therapy must pretend that the person is anaesthetized; it ignores consciousness by insisting that it is irrelevant to behaviour. The rejection by behaviourism of the importance of introspection is due to the latter's lack of verifiability. But within the religious paradigm, introspection actually becomes one of the primary roads to meaning, and verification is of a quite different order than is amenable to statistical analysis. From the depth psychological point of view, the rejection of the importance of subjectivity is merely an avoidance of the problems of selfhood, not to mention the defensive function of this rejection against the numinosity of the Self. Seen in this light, the self-protective structures of behaviourism are an elaborate defensive operation in the guise of science, designed to avoid the sacramental nature of the psyche, and an avoidance of the fact that reason alone cannot grasp the numinosum. Conceptual thought such as that based on inductive methodology is an imperfect instrument for the study of the psyche, because the psyche is too prone to produce hitherto unknown and unpredictable elements.

All of this is to make the point that attempts to develop positivistic approaches to the psyche invariably fail to grasp any meaningful understanding of the essence of human nature, especially those transcendent aspects which current scientific paradigms have no capacity to include. The kind of knowledge we seek in the religious approach cannot be confirmed or refuted objectively, but only from within the psychology of the subject. In the attempt to find personally relevant spiritual values which are not simply utilitarian, we look for purpose and meaning rather than mechanisms alone. The depth psychological approach to religious subjectivity relies for outward or cultural clarification on an understanding of the psychology of myth, metaphor, image and symbol. Internally, only qualitative methods of study are useful because each case is unique, so that the best research approach is the heuristic method (Moustakas, 1990), which emphasizes the experiencer's own frame of reference. The subject has to undergo a profound and often prolonged and painful dialogue with his or her own religious questions and experience, until personal meaning emerges. No methodology based on the primacy of statistical validation or quantification could do justice to such material, which is essentially the study of the archetypal ground of the psyche interacting with that segment of itself that we experience as human consciousness.

The religious approach to the psyche assumes not a simple control of psychological life from 'below upwards', by molecular means or by means of earlier conditioning or psychodynamic factors, but equally important control from 'above downwards', via the supraordinate effects of the archetype. This view challenges traditional assumptions, such as the idea that development only proceeds in one direction, from the past to the present, or that what happens at any moment in time is purely the effect of what happened at an earlier stage of development. To accept the existence of the archetype means that complex ordering processes are responsible for smaller-scale behaviour, which in turn requires Jung's idea that the personality has a goal. It is then as if that goal, which has not yet been reached, is somehow causing the present situation. None of this makes sense from a linear viewpoint, within which the future cannot cause the past. But just as the micro-physicist has to contend with the possibility that time reversibility may occur, so there is evidence (from synchronicity and parapsychology) that some levels of the psyche are not contained in linear space–time. Hence macro-concepts of causality do not necessarily apply to archetypal reality.

If such 'downward' control exists, then spirit becomes an important regulatory agent within human personality, and so is grist for the psychotherapeutic mill. Those organizers of behaviour which Jung calls archetypes are here regarded as such spiritual determinants. The archetype must be a self-organizing intrapsychic principle; to say this begs the question of its morphogenesis, but at least keeps the idea of the Self within the realm of discourse of psychology, and attempts to account for the intentionality of the psyche without recourse to extra-psychic structural principles such as brain chemistry.

PSYCHOTHERAPY AS SPIRITUAL PRACTICE

Psychotherapy is the latest arrival to claim a place on the smorgasbord of spiritual practices. As yet, psychotherapy lacks the authority of millennia of tradition, nor can it claim cultural approval as a spiritual pursuit. Indeed, in our culture psychotherapy has become a mercantile commodity, with 'clients' like any other service industry.[4] But several justifications can be advanced for regarding psychotherapy as both a mode of spiritual direction and also a medium for spiritual development in its own right, for both therapist and patient. In fact, the apparently sharp distinction between psychotherapy and spiritual practice begins to blur when one considers the similarities which exist between them. To begin with; the psychodynamic origin of many of the problems which are addressed in the established spiritual traditions, such as attachment, craving, greed, fear, delusion, inflation of the self concept, ignorance, anger and hatred are well understood by depth psychology. In earlier times and simpler cultures, practices such as prayer and meditation were often sufficient to deal with these hindrances to human growth without taking into account the dynamic unconscious. But it is also possible to reduce the hold on the personality that such problems may have, by psychotherapeutic work on their unconscious underpinnings. This in itself facilitates spiritual maturity.

As well, many of the same underlying mechanisms can be seen to operate in both psychotherapy and standard spiritual practice. For example, consider the similarity between psychotherapy and meditation (see also p. 227). In traditional Buddhist practice, undesirable mental states and contents are dealt with by dispassionate observation of their arising and passing away, recognizing that attempts at their suppression or disavowal by willpower only generate counter-reactions. The goal is the attainment of steady, undistracted mindfulness, or clear awareness of the processes of body and mind, without impulsive responses to these contents. In this way, the practitioner gradually experiences their impersonal and transitory nature, weakening his or her conditioned, automatic responses to them, thereby dissolving the unconscious assumption that they belong to an enduring personality which has to have its needs met. However, a good case can be made for the proposition that in our culture the intensity of early childhood abuse and deprivation are such that psychotherapy may sometimes be the preferred method of addressing painful internal states, because they are simply too emotionally intense to be dealt with by meditative observation alone. The psychotherapeutic process can deal with such affect in ways that have important similarities to meditation. As painful affect states arise within the therapy, often in relation to the transference/countertransference, attention is paid to them. Because affective transactions from infancy onwards shape the sense of self, understanding the details of these responses allows us to understand the pain of the self, and why we are constantly pulled back into the sense of self. In psychotherapy this pain is re-experienced, and its roots are explored and exposed, in a setting of containment and acceptance by another person. Over time, as the causes of suffering are understood and responded to, there occurs a process of de-habituation of the usual responses to pain, and the intensity of these affective storms subsides. Gradually the schemata (complexes) within which they arise can be viewed with increasing understanding and dispassion. In the same manner as occurs within formal meditation practice, the result is a loss of automatic, conditioned reactions to painful states of mind. Attention to the ways in which the patient brings to the therapist aspects of the therapist's own self, combined with attention to the selfobject relationship, affirm for both participants the interdependent, purely relative nature of the self. At the same time, transpersonal elements that arise within the therapy allow a sense of contact with the world of spirit, which becomes a living reality as 'deep calls to deep'. Because psychotherapy that pays attention to transpersonal elements fosters relationship with this realm, this work can reasonably be termed spiritual direction.

When the difficulties caused by negatively toned complexes are either removed, ameliorated or integrated by means of psychotherapy, self-absorption is reduced. The old self is partially deconstructed, often revealing a new capacity for values such as altruism, compassion and love, as well as a direct experience of transcendent levels of Mind. These developments are an inexorable consequence of prolonged attention to the manifestations of the Self, which is the mainstay of psychotherapy carried out within a religious framework. Rather than view such psychotherapeutic gains as *preparatory* to spiritual practice of some other kind, the process of their attainment is actually integral to spiritual development; it matters little whether these attributes are attained by means of traditional practices such as prayer or meditation, or by means of psychotherapy. What matters is that these states of mind become felt experiences, known directly, embodied and lived in the world; they are not simply concepts.

Within the religious paradigm of psychotherapeutic practice, attention to the human psyche, with all its problems of relationship, its depressions and anxieties, shades into the discovery of the divine Mind as coterminous with the empirical personality. In this practice, we do not adopt a particular version of God through the force of family or culture. Rather, we discover the numinosum as it manifests psychologically. This work gradually becomes a spiritual rather than a primarily therapeutic practice as we realize what it is that we have found within ourselves. The advantage we have today over those of our forebears who also realized this fact, is that our knowledge of developmental and archetypal psychology and psychopathology allows us to understand the structure and dynamics of the Self within the psyche in a much more detailed manner than was previously possible. The Gnostics realized that ignorance was an impediment to spiritual development; similarly, the religiously oriented psychotherapeutic task is greater Self-knowledge or Self-consciousness. No element of the psyche is excluded; we embrace our psychopathology as a means of understanding certain forms of the divine, while advances in psychotherapeutic technique allow us a method to study these forms, sometimes even allowing us to transform them, which we call 'treatment'. The therapist's attitude is all important in this work. If we are conscious that we are assisting in the incarnation of the Self when we respond to the patient, or that we carry the projection of the Self for him or her, our attitude is different from what would occur if these procedures were regarded only as technical necessities. And work with complexes and their intense affects feels different if we remember that we thereby struggle with strands of the divine within the personality. The numinosity of these experiences means that our religious sensibility cannot be merely considered a form of anthropology, in the sense (of Feuerbach or Freud) that the divine is merely a product of the human mind because we project our highest values onto an imaginary deity. It is the burden and the distinction of the religious perspective on psychotherapy, compared to its secular practice, to insist on the ontological reality of the psyche as the 'Ground' on which we rest. We experience this Ground like an infinitely pleomorphic substance which can endlessly re-imagine itself, but which cannot itself be any of its numberless forms.

The Self-imagery by which the psyche depicts itself is both real and not real. This paradox exactly parallels the Buddhist contrast between form and emptiness, since, for the depth psychologist, form is synonymous with image and emptiness with Mind itself, which is beyond image. Without form, or image, psychological existence is not possible, but form is inherently empty in the sense that its distinct existence is dependent on its relation to other forms. The images that constitute the personal psyche are in constant flux, not permanent, always changing. The personal self exists as that collection of forms or images which is stable enough over time to produce a feeling of continuity. The transpersonal Self also appears as images or experiences, without which it too could not be experienced. But it is obvious that none of these images is the Ground of Mind itself, so that none of them can be assumed to be ultimately real in itself, but only relatively and temporarily so. It is the privilege of the psychotherapist to witness and assist in the evolution of this Ground within the personality.

11

THE RATIONALE FOR A CONTEMPLATIVE PSYCHOLOGY

The practice of depth psychology with a religious sensibility belongs within the contemplative tradition, because it represents an active attempt to experience and understand the ways of the divine as they operate within the human psyche. Here I would like to offer a vision of a possible future development of this idea in a somewhat institutional variety, namely a new form of the contemplative or monastic tradition in the shape of centres dedicated to the experience of the Self.

The religious literature recognizes that spiritual experience may occur in at least two ways. It may be acquired by human effort, or an experience of the divine may be directly instilled into the soul passively, without human effort, as an act of grace. The hard work of everyday attention to, and amplification of, intrapsychic material belongs to the former category, while sudden, unforeseen eruption of the numinosum defines the second form. In both cases we ground our definition of religious experience on the idea that the core, or the archetypal basis, of the personal self is the transpersonal Self. This fact is both the central tenet of analytical psychology and is also the foundational axiom of a religious approach to the psyche. This psychological tenet is identical to the Upanishadic insight: 'thou art that', where 'that' refers to the divine. The idea of self–Self identity or overlap is amenable to a degree of psychological understanding, although it is a mystical statement whose truth can only be grasped experientially. It cannot be taken literally without confusing different levels of the psyche, because the Self is essentially identical with the whole of the objective psyche. However, there is a level of identity or at least overlap between Self and self which can be described conceptually. This identity occurs because the self is a humanized, incarnate aspect of some strands of the Self. It has been suggested that the process of the humanizing of the divine occurs when the Self, which in itself is beyond form or categories of any kind, enters the human psyche and body as fields or filaments of intrapsychic and somatic organization, corresponding to natural laws which we call archetypes. Around these cluster images, affects and memories of related quality. The latter three elements are provided by our human environment, which provides the contents of a transpersonal container. In this way aspects of the Self are able to gradually take on human features which coalesce to become the sense of a personal self. This self is built up of aggregates of relationships with other selves, and is developed in response to the organizing principles of the Self (including selfobject needs) as they unfold within the human milieu. The sense of temporal continuity of the resulting structure of the self is a function of memory, which is partly somatic (cerebral). Thus, unlike the absolute nature of the Self, the self is a relative structure. It is only able to conceive of its identity in relation to schemata which fill the contents of its memory, both conscious and unconscious. Because of this dependence on memory, the self is unaware of its identity with the Self.

GNOSIS

Given a certain level of identity of Self and self, the old injunction to 'know thyself' assumes additional religious significance. Depth psychology has a good deal to offer in this endeavour, since it deals with the personal material which constitutes the self as well as with the manifestions of the Self within the consciousness of the self. But in this area we must bear in mind the warning of another Upanishadic maxim: 'It is not understood by those who understand, it is understood by those who do not understand' (Kena Upanishad, 2, 3. 'It' here refers to the Self). This injunction stands as a warning to the psychotherapist against the overenthusiastic application of theory to the religious dimension of psychotherapeutic practice. By 'religious' I refer to Jung's understanding of the activity of *religio* as the careful observation, and attempted integration, of important intrapsychic (soul-derived) images, including those considered pathological. We observe, we intuit, we feel, we reason, but above all we experience a kind of radiance and power from these experiences, a form of discovery which takes us beyond simple cognitive and affective categories into true gnosis, or experiential knowledge of the divine. Depending on the individual's temperament, and whether one wants to relate to the Self or realize one's identity with it, I believe that to pay attention to personal experiences of the numinosum is either a form of prayer, or a path to enlightenment, or both.

Prolonged immersion in such material transforms ordinary depth psychology into a religious form that might be called 'contemplative psychology'. This practice belongs within the long tradition of the experience of the divine by means of the human faculties, leading to a form of naturally acquired, experiential knowing. And this is the only form of knowing which really matters in the religious realm; it leads to understanding which is obviously not purely humanly based, but which is given from beyond the self. The consciousness brought about by attention to such experiences expands the boundaries of the self, which is gradually brought to realize that its consciousness is not the limited entity previously thought. The intensive study of numinous experiences of the Self has the effect of rendering fluid the structures of the self, allowing its contents to be felt as temporary, always open to radical rearrangement in response to the Self. In a dream for instance, the fact of so many initially unknown elements which on reflection are felt as parts of myself, makes me realize that my consciousness is at the same time much more limited but also enormously larger than I had been aware. These new elements of the dream at first only belong to the Self, but are potentially assimilable into the self. In this way, gradually, the habitual assumptions and organizing principles that constitute the structures of the personal self either dissolve or radically alter their perspective and meaning. Various analogies express the effects of greater awareness of the relationship between self and Self. It is as if the ego, or the conscious aspects of the self, comes to realize that the music of which it is composed is actually part of a larger background melody. Or, to use the metaphor of Ramana Maharishi, the ego is seen to be like the moon shining in the daytime, palely reflecting a larger light. At this level of awareness it is not as though the ego does not exist, but rather it is not felt to exist as a separate entity, and thus the ego realizes that it is not the source of its own consciousness. This realization tends to free us from limited narcissistic concerns, as sufficient immersion in such experiences of the Self induces a kind of permanent awe which makes evident the limitations of the ego. Each dream becomes a *koan*, pointing to a reality that is not grasped by means of thinking, feeling, sensation or intuition but by gnosis, which can be understood as a kind of independent faculty or organ of the soul.

THE LOCUS OF GNOSIS

In antiquity, the divine was experienced in a holy place, such as the Jerusalem Temple. For the psychotherapist engaged in his or her work as a religious practice, the human psyche and body can assume the function of the temple, which is now no longer projected into an outer space. In some ways this truth about the sacred nature of the psyche as a bridge to the divine has always been known; an early pointer in Genesis (28: 12) is Jacob's dream, which depicts a ladder reaching from earth (the embodied self) to heaven (the Self). The numinous dream of any kind has always been such a ladder. We realize that the vision so gained is incomplete; the Self remains essentially unknowable to us, just as Moses was only allowed to see the 'back' of God, as through a veil (Exod. 19: 9; 33: 7). Analogously, contemplative immersion even in the most numinous dreams always falls short of cognitive understanding, because it is an attempt to experience the divine mysteries, seen 'through a glass, darkly'. But I do not mean to overemphasize the more exuberant or ecstatic experiences of the numinosum at the expense of simply living from day to day in a consciously sacred manner. This becomes possible if we cultivate a continuous awareness of the presence of the archetypal basis of everyday events, instead of taking them for granted. Above all, we must remember that what is considered sacramental does not need to take any particular form; the divine dispensation is infinitely variable within the psyche.

Here the religiously oriented psychologist may sense a conflict with the position of the established churches, in a way analogous to the conflict between the Church fathers and the early gnostics about the nature of true gnosis. Perhaps the central disagreement is this. The psychologist agrees with the theological principle of *per sensibilia ad invisibilia*, that is that we sometimes require a perceptible image or experience in order to access the divine reality. But unlike any fixed doctrinal system, we allow the Self to determine its own symbolic presentation, and we do not insist on particular symbols or sacraments; these can be individual, based on whatever is numinous for the person. We also realize that none of these symbols can be the Self itself, and that the symbols that an individual uses now may change during the course of life. In view of this difference of opinion, it will be useful to further clarify the nature of gnosis as it is understood psychologically.

A GNOSTIC PSYCHOLOGY

Jung's enthusiasm for Gnosticism is well known, and has been reviewed by Segal (1992), who also points out certain inaccuracies in both Jung's understanding and that of contemporary Jungian writers. Notwithstanding some misinterpretations, there is an important area of overlap between Gnosticism and depth psychology. The strand of Gnosticism that remains very attractive to depth psychologists is its emphasis on self-knowledge and direct experience.

Contemplative psychology produces a form of gnosis, or inner knowing, which is not primarily dependent on pre-existing doctrine, on reason, on thought, or even on innate intuitive knowledge. Most importantly, the knowledge that we rely on is derived directly from its source, largely unfiltered through another's psyche. In Jung's (CW 9, ii, 350) words, gnosis is 'psychological knowledge whose contents derive from the unconscious'. Sometimes this occurs gradually as unconscious contents are slowly assimilated, whereas at times gnosis seems virtually to force its way into consciousness. To exemplify the latter experience of gnosis, the following event occurred to a woman lawyer who had successfully used a powerful inner masculinity throughout her life. She termed this her 'General MacArthur complex' – by which she meant that, although useful, at times it could make her dictatorial, authoritarian and only concerned with winning at all cost, sometimes at the expense of her femininity. She had changed careers in mid-life by training to be a psychotherapist, partly with the intention of finding a vocation that allowed her to develop this relatively unused part of herself. During a college training exercise, which required that she work with another student she related:

> It was my turn ... suddenly I felt incapable of being present for her. I felt empty, almost numb, and very incompetent, not there. Normally, when in a tough situation, say arguing a surprise question of law in court, I would prevail through sheer willpower. Now I had none. I got through the session somehow, speaking, I felt, like a dummy. Others seemed not to notice much, but my expectations of myself are high, and I knew I had the ability. I sat unhearing through the comments, feeling as though the bottom had literally dropped away and I had no firm ground on which to stand. Back home, I felt my life was precarious. In my desperation I turned for the first time in my life to the Goddess, begging her not to kill me for my failure to ever

honour her and her divine power. I felt like prostrating myself physically but had no image before which to do so. The next day I ordered a museum reproduction of the great Goddess Uma, the consort of Shiva in Nepal. She sits in my entrance hall today and receives the light of candles, the sight of flowers and the scent of incense, offerings which serve to remind me of her power and divine presence in my life.

This woman 'just knew' what had to be done; because of her desperation, the power of the archetypal feminine could no longer be denied – it erupted into consciousness and required no justification besides its own numinosity.

Corbin (quoted by Avens, 1984, pp. 3–4) defines gnosis as a form of transformative and redemptive inner vision, corresponding to the world of the soul or psyche, which mediates, as the revealed God, between the hidden God and man's world, or between the material and spiritual worlds. I understand this to mean that the psyche stands between the unknowable Godhead and 'God' as experienced by human consciousness. The experience of the autonomous psyche produces such gnosis, which acts as a form of revelation, which is an 'unveiling of the depths of the human soul . . . an essentially psychological event' (CW 11, 127).

HOW DO WE KNOW: *VIA NEGATIVA* OR *VIA POSITIVA*?

Jungian approaches to intrapsychic Self images are sometimes said to be analogous to a positive theology, which traditionally sought to discover details about the nature of the divine and interpret them in the light of some authority. And there certainly is a danger in concretizing the meaning of a dream image, as if we could consider the dream analogous to a literal and permanent form of scripture. But this criticism betrays a fundamental misunderstanding about the way in which we deal with Self images. In his discussion of this question, Avens (1984, pp. 125–126) notes that Corbin actually relates the imaginal world to the *deitas absconditas* (hidden god) of apophatic theology, an approach which insists on approaching the divine by negation, or by a process of *not* knowing. This is because, Corbin notes, the Supreme Being of western theology is actually an idol, since the God of monotheism is only one of many manifestations of a hidden divinity which needs multiple images to reveal itself. Because none of these is adequate in itself, the hidden god is made manifest in 'an unlimited number of theophanic forms'; each theophany is appropriate to the soul's capacity to receive it (p. 126). Bearing this relativism in mind, emphasis on any individual intrapsychic image of the divine means that we must at the same time appropriate a *via negativa*, an apophatic theology which denies the value of conceptual thought or fixed ideas about the divine. This approach, again following Corbin, is not a simple polytheism, but a 'mystical kathenotheism' which holds that: 'the Divine Being is not fragmented, but wholly present in *each* instance, individualized in *each* theophany'. The reality of such events within the soul is highly individual, defined by the needs of the soul (Ibid., p. 126). This means that attention to intrapsychic or interpersonal experiences of the divine acts as a bridge between a divinity which is utterly transcendent and one which can be experienced. As Jung (CW 12, 4) said of the alchemists, certain people prefer to 'seek through knowledge rather than find through faith'. These are the psychological gnostics, in the sense that they are seekers of direct experience. Their spirituality is usually the outcome of a combination of personal suffering with a failure to find relief within traditional religious forms, while conscious that threads of meaning and presence do penetrate their lives.

THE NEED FOR A TRANS-ARCHETYPAL PSYCHOLOGY

Perhaps the greatest deficiency in the Western psychological traditions has been a neglect of the training of consciousness in ways analogous to the techniques of meditation found in Eastern religions. Such training requires a methodology which is distinct from that which enables us to study the contents of consciousness psychodynamically. These two different instruments provide different data. The Eastern traditions have preferred to try to understand the nature of consciousness itself, while Western methodology has turned to the contents of consciousness and the links between these contents. The meditative traditions have known for millennia that introspective study of the nature of mind reveals the mind's ways of constructing reality, and all meditation methods aim at deconstructing ordinary perception. With a few exceptions, Western psychologists have largely ignored this approach to the phenomenology of consciousness. Because of our lack of attention to the training of awareness, it is possible to be highly developed psychologically (the mythical 'well analysed' individual), or to be advanced in terms of Judaeo-Christian spirituality, but still to suffer from the effects of a scattered mind, prone to habitual, automatic action–reaction responses, without the focus on the clarity of awareness in the present moment stressed by Eastern traditions. It is equally possible to have a highly trained capacity for meditative states, but be quite emotionally immature and unconscious of one's own shadow. Some combination of Eastern and Western approaches to the psyche therefore seems desirable. For example, suppose that an individual is enraged because he is in the grip of a pathogenic complex that has at its core a father problem, or the negative aspect of the Father archetype. Dealing with this affective state, the Buddhist meditator is concerned with the detailed observation of the complex mind–body states associated with his rage, to which as much mindfulness and equanimity as possible are applied. He does not try to suppress the rage, but rather, with enough practice, the experience of rage is no longer a unitary one. 'Rage' breaks down into the fine details of its somatic and psychic components, felt as rising and falling wavelets of experience – muscle tensions, heart pounding, the urge to scream, images of attack and so on. Microscopic attention and equanimity are then applied to each of these elements in turn. Finally, rage is no longer felt as an undifferentiated, overwhelming flood. The meditator hopes that this process will lead him to a level of consciousness that is beyond that level that is possessed by rage. In this way, the meditator is freed from possession by the archetype at the centre of the complex; this is one meaning of the term 'trans-archetypal'. By contrast, the Western approach tries to understand the dynamic underpinnings of the rage, or the unconscious contents that gave rise to it, believing, correctly in principle, that this will dissipate the rage and eventually lead to its arising less easily. This approach also tries to free the person from possession by the archetype, but it does so by remaining within its transference and intrapsychic manifestations. On the surface therefore it seems that meditation tries to allow peace of mind regardless of the conditions one is in, while psychotherapy tries to alter the arrangement of one's internal conditions to allow peace of mind. It has been claimed that training the mind itself by means of meditation is helpful with the kind of emotional distress which western psychotherapy treats using interpersonal and intrapsychic techniques (e.g. Goleman and Schwartz, 1976). It is, however, clear to psychotherapists who have treated meditators that meditation alone can leave untouched serious emotional difficulties, or at times actually make them worse. Further study of the correct form of integration of these modalities within the psychotherapeutic setting is therefore needed.

A marriage of the training of awareness by means of meditation and standard depth psychological practice would deepen a religious approach to the psyche. This would be especially so if it led to the other meaning of the term 'trans-archetypal' psychology, by which I refer to the experience of levels of the objective psyche unconditioned by personal complexes. I envision this integration as a combination of modern depth psychology with traditional approaches such as the *Abhidarma* psychology of Buddhism, especially its treatise on meditation, the *Visuddhimagga* (see Goleman, 1988). This latter system is invaluable because of its sophisticated capacity to map altered states of consciousness which are beyond the grasp of psychodynamic theory. For example, the *Visuddhimagga* describes several levels of absorption or *jhanas*, which refer to states such as rapture or one-pointedness, leading to deeper levels such as no-thing-ness and states described as neither perception nor non-perception. But the psychotherapist also requires a psychodynamic grounding because the *Visuddhimagga* has no developmental theory and its practices presuppose a reasonable level of mental health on the part of the practitioner. The two approaches therefore complement each other. Without the training of consciousness, the psychodynamic practitioner may remain fixed on the analysis of content alone; without attention to psychodynamic factors, the meditation practitioner may not have a sufficiently healthy capacity for affect tolerance to sustain meditation without fragmentation.

There is no inherent difficulty about seeing these two approaches to the psyche as continuous with each other. The contents of consciousness are the preoccupation of traditional analysis, which deals with archetypally determined relationships, imagery and affects. But meditation allows us to move beyond the referents of the archetype within the personal sphere, into transpersonal levels of

226

Mind. Engler and Brown (1986) have shown that various stages of meditation represent definable developmental sequences which are alike across different traditions. If these stages indeed represent universal potentials for experience (Goleman, 1988) then these stages themselves may be archetypally structured pathways into levels of the psyche which are beyond image and complex. In other words, meditation allows the direct experience of the deep structures of reality itself, rather than only their images. But perhaps the most important overlap lies in a common goal. Meditation allows us to live fully in the awareness of the moment, experiencing it totally. This is the same goal as psychotherapy; when repressed and split-off aspects of the self no longer have to be repudiated, we can become filled with the experience of what is happening right now, without any internal alienation.

A CONTEMPLATIVE PSYCHOLOGICAL COMMUNITY: THE MONASTERY OF THE COMING ERA

Since the beginning of evolved religious life, there have always been people who have gathered together in order to live according to a particular, shared vision of reality, so that they could focus exclusively on what they considered to be sacred. I believe that the religious sensibility described in this book could lead to the development of centres dedicated to the study and experience of the numinosum and to a religious approach to the psyche. These communities will recognize that experiences of the sacred are indistinguishable from manifestations of the objective psyche. They will acknowledge that manifestations of the Self continue to evolve, producing new symbolic material and new demands for understanding the self–Self relationship that vary with the psychology of the experiencer. But above all, they will recognize that the Self can no longer be projected onto a particular figure; it must become personal knowledge. The purpose and goal of such communities will be to assist in the development of such modern-day gnosis as intensively as possible. Within traditional Christianity, monasticism developed according to a code of withdrawal from the world, including self-abnegation and asceticism, because it was felt that particular restrictions were necessary in order to serve God. These rules were applied to all members of the community. It now seems that we must foster the experience of the numinosum in individual ways, preserving where possible the authentic wisdom of the traditions but also taking into account the personal psychology of the individual.

Most people interested in the experience of the Self currently work within one or two psychotherapeutic modalities at a time, such as individual or group therapy, sand tray, body work, art, dance or other expressive forms. The activities of a centre dedicated to the experience of the Self would, however, enable the individual to participate in various forms of psychologically oriented activities, in the hope that simultaneous work at several levels of the psyche and body will lead to suspension of our usual defences against the numinosum and a deepening relationship to it. For work of this intensity to be carried on safely, the environment must be very supportive and understanding of the process, and the fragilities of the individual's character structure must be respected. But it is not suggested that these will be primarily treatment centres, although their results will be therapeutic in the real sense of the word. Given this caveat, participation in several psychotherapeutic modalities (approaches to the Self) at the same time, especially when carried out as a full-time occupation rather than at particular moments of the week, will concentrate the individual's understanding of his or her Self–self axis. All of this requires a setting which is conducive to introspection and psychological work, in which the ethos and values of the participants are based on a respect for the reality of the psyche and its religious function. Because of the psychological orientation of such a community, constant attention to problems which are so common in traditional religious settings, such as shadow projections, the abuse of personal power and sexual acting out, will allow these issues to be minimized or used as stepping stones for spiritual development.

As occurred in traditional monasteries, some individuals will choose to live in such a setting for long periods, as a permanent commitment to the contemplative way of life based on the experience of the Self in all its forms. Other people will choose to visit such a centre for varying periods, in order to retreat, study, work on personal difficulties or simply deepen their own individuation process. Whether these communities will develop distinct personalities, analogous to the various forms of monastic spirituality, remains to be seen. What is certain is that it is possible to characterize those individuals who may be attracted to such a place. They will be those who have traditionally been identified as interested in 'coming home', or being on the 'path of return'. These are people who are no longer primarily interested in narcissistic concerns such as making their mark in the world, being a mover and shaker, becoming famous, developing prestige and power or pursuing purely individual agendas. The path of return requires dedication to the life of the soul in its relation to spirit, to a life of understanding our interconnectedness, our rootedness within the Self, and to the experience of all of life as divine life. Only this attitude, based on experiences of the Self in innumerable situations, allows real compassion and insight into human nature.

APPENDIX

In his essay entitled *The Psychology of the Transference* (CW 16), Jung used a series of sixteenth-century alchemical woodcuts, the Rosarium Philosophorum, to illustrate the archetypal basis of some of the processes that occur in the therapeutic relationship. To do so was a part of his project to demonstrate that the alchemists were projecting intrapsychic dynamics into the apparently material operations of their laboratories. Jung interpreted these images in terms of the union of opposites, especially in relation to the anima and animus. Since then, these woodcuts have been reproduced many times in the Jungian literature, but I do not believe that they have ever been meaningfully linked to everyday clinical practice. One exception is Schwartz-Salant's (1989) attempt to use them to clarify certain dynamics of the borderline personality. He suggested that they represent a field of projective identification as experienced during therapy with such patients. However, I believe that this represents too partial a view. The motif of twoness and oneness, or the selfobject experience, is universal and not pathological.

It seems important to stress that some of the alchemists' imagery, which represented the search for the Self, was not simply the result of purely solipsistic preoccupations, but also reflected what the alchemists were experiencing in their relationships. I suggest that the idea of the self–selfobject tie is prefigured in the Rosarium, where the alchemists were able to illustrate this process in an imaginal form. The figures express a twoness that is at the same time subjectively felt as a oneness. But the heads of the figures are not joined, because consciously the participants know that they are separate – the merger is felt unconsciously. The participants are 'glued' together at the affective and intrapsychic levels. These figures illustrate both the archetypal basis of the selfobject relationship and the maintenance of a healthy sense of self by this means. The establishment of this type of relationship, whether developmentally or within the transference, is necessary for the experience of the *coniunctio*, or the joining of the personal selves within the encompassing field of the Self. Such union supplies or repairs what is missing within the personal self by means of joining with the other. The profound implication here is that all desire for union with others is fundamentally motivated by a desire for union with the Self, which is the psychological equivalent of saying that the desire for another person is at base a desire for union of the soul with God.

PHILOSOPHORVM.

Nota bene: In arte noſtri magiſterij nihil eſt Secretum
celatū à Philoſophis excepto ſecreto artis, quod artis
non licet cuiquam reuelare, quod ſi fieret ille ma
lediceretur , & indignationem domini incur=
reret , & apoplexia moreretur. ✠Quare om=
nis error in arte exiſtit , ex eo, quod debitam

C ij

Figure 1 'The King and Queen'
Source: McLean, 1980

ROSARIVM

corrũpitur, neꝗ ex imperfecto penitus secundũ
artem aliquid fieri potest. Ratio est quia ars pri
mas dispositiones inducere non potest, sed lapis
noster est res media inter perfecta & imperfecta
corpora, & quod natura ipsa incepit hoc per ar
tem ad perfectionẽ deducitur. Si in ipso Mercu
rio operari inceperis vbi natura reliquit imper
sectum, inuenies in eo perfectionẽ et gaudebis.

Perfectum non alteratur, sed corrumpitur.
Sed imperfectum bene alteratur, ergo corrup
tio vnius est generatio alterius.

Speculum

Figure 2 'Immersion in the Bath'
Source: McLean, 1980

CONIVNCTIO SIVE
Cortus.

Ⓞ Luna durch meyn vmbgeben/vnd fuſſe mynne/
Wirſtu ſchön/ ſtarck/vnd gewaltig als ich byn.

Ⓞ Sol/ du biſt vber alle liecht zu erkennen/
So bedarfſtu doch mein als der han der hennen.

ARISLEVS IN VISIONE.

Coniunge ergo filium tuum Gabricum dile=
ctiorem tibi in omnibus filijs tuis cum ſua ſorore
Beya

Figure 3 'The Conjunction'
Source: McLean, 1980

PHILOSOPHORVM.

CONCEPTIO SEV PVTRE
factio

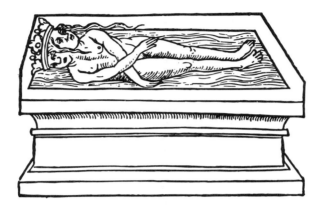

Hye ligen könig vnd königin dot/
Die sele scheydt sich mit grosser not.

ARISTOTELES REX ET
Philosophus.

Nquam vidi aliquod animatum crescere
sine putrefactione, nisi autem fiat putri∙
dum inuanum erit opus alchimicum.

Figure 4 'Death'
Source: McLean, 1980

ROSARIVM
ANIMÆ EXTRACTIO VEL
imp(r)ægnatio

Hye teylen sich die vier element/
Aus dem leyb scheydt sich die sele behende.

De

Figure 5 'The Ascent of the Soul'
Source: McLean, 1980

PHILOSOPHORVM

ABLVTIO VEL
Mundificatio

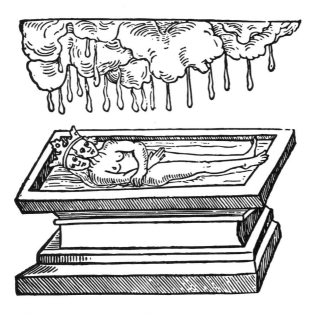

𝕳ie felt ber Tauw von 𝕳immel herab/
Vnnd wascht den schwartzen leyb im grab ab-

K iij

Figure 6 'Purification'
Source: McLean, 1980

PHILOSOPHORVM

ANIMÆ IVBILATIO SEV
Ortus feu Sublimatio.

Hie schwingt sich die sele hernidder/
Vnd erquickt den gereinigten leychnam wider-

L üÿ

Figure 7 'The Return of the Soul'
Source: McLean, 1980

PHILOSOPHORVM.

𝕳ie iſt geboren die eddele Keyſerin reich/
Die meiſter nennen ſie ihrer dochter gleich.
Die vermeret ſich/gebiert kinder ohn zal/
Sain vndötlich rein/vnnd ohn alles mahl·

Die

Figure 8 'Rebis'
Source: McLean, 1980

Figure 9 'The Risen Christ'
Source: McLean, 1980

The Rosarium woodcuts demonstrate an early intimation of various stages and vicissitudes of what we now call the selfobject relationship. Like all archetypal imagery, they represent deep intrapsychic processes of a fairy-tale or mythic-like quality, without any personal material present. For example, Figure 1, which Jung titles 'King and Queen', illustrates the initial encounter of the two participants still at the persona stage of the relationship. The descending dove indicates that the relationship occurs under the aegis of the spirit, stressing that their bond is ordered transpersonally; the subsequent Latin caption says 'spirit is what unites'. Figure 2, 'Immersion in the Bath', partly depicts what Kohut calls prolonged empathic immersion in the patient's material. The image illustrates the notion that the two participants share the same psychic field. What is not appreciated by personalistic psychoanalysts is that this field represents a very real third presence, the Self, acting as an objective Other, which contains the therapy and affects both participants. The water in which they sit is not circumscribed but is continuous with the water of Figure 3, 'The Conjunction'. At first this looks like an erotic, perhaps Oedipal, transference. It may also represent pre-Oedipal selfobject needs that have become eroticized because of their intensity. The overt sexuality in such situations covers deep yearnings for affirmation or idealization. Because these needs are still unconscious, the scene is depicted within underground water, also suggesting that the small bath (or the personal psyches) of the previous figure is continuous with a larger ocean. Figure 4, 'Death', also represents a 'Conceptio' according to the title, and the text suggests that this death will be followed by a new life. Thus begins the series of images with two heads and one body, suggesting the theme of twoness that allows the emotional sense of oneness. Perhaps this image represents the decay of old structures with the promise of a new sense of self. Figure 5, 'The Ascent of the Soul', may represent the painful state of 'soul loss' that occurs within relationships when the self–selfobject tie is disrupted, leading to despair and confusion. This is healed in Figures 6 and 7, titled respectively, 'Purification', a joyful state depicted as the grace of falling dew from heaven and 'The Return of the Soul', in which the re-establishment of the connection to the selfobject reanimates the relationship. The emergence of the 'Rebis' (Figure 8) indicates the development of a fully established self–selfobject tie – meaning intrapsychic wholeness or selfhood in the presence of a relationship with another. Within the alchemical metaphor, this stage represents a 'lesser' *coniunctio*, since further differentiation of the self is needed. The last picture of the original series (Figure 9), which was not used by Jung, illustrates the risen Christ. At this stage of mature selfhood, other selves are seen to be fragments of the Self, not essentially different from oneself. The lost or original Self of childhood, with which contact has been lost for a long time, is now resurrected as a conscious experience.

NOTES

2 PERSONAL SPIRITUALITY BASED ON CONTACT WITH THE NUMINOSUM

1 Jung used a series of sixteenth-century alchemical woodcuts, the Rosarium Phil-osophorum, to illustrate this interaction. The author of the Rosarium used male and female figures to depict a process in which elements of the two psyches involved mingle with each other at the intrapsychic and interpsychic levels, forming new elements. The bisexual imagery used by the alchemists led to Jung's describing the Rosarium pictures in terms of anima and animus, but this is too restrictive. Both our selfobject needs and the anima or animus connect us to the unconscious, so that anima and animus can be seen as carriers of selfobject needs or as special cases of the selfobject (Corbett and Rives, 1991. See Appendix.)

2 Here I wish to emphasize that Kohut's use of the term 'selfobject' is embedded within a totally different theoretical framework from that of Fordham (1976, pp. 20–1; 1985, p. 20) which is essentially an object relations approach. Although they use the same term they refer to very different subjective experiences which bear little resemblance to each other. Fordham uses the term to mean a part-object or a need-satisfying object such as the breast at a stage before the baby can symbolize. He contrasts the selfobject with early, bad or not-self objects. In his system, the selfobject is eventually destroyed in order to create a symbol. Or, the selfobject is used, in distinction from real objects, to perceive reality before the infant has reality testing.

3 It is noteworthy that Jung emphasized the search for meaning as a primary aspect of his therapeutic method. Perhaps his father's failure to provide an idealizable selfobject contributed to this aspect of Jung's psychological theory. He very much needed to find meaning because of this early lack. This kind of relationship between the personal psychology of the investigator and his theory helps to explain, but does not invalidate, his findings.

4 Because of the frequent absence of an idealizable father, many men have been drawn to the charismatic individuals who lead popular social movements. The danger of this situation has been that this idealization is fostered without such leaders realizing that the need for idealization represents a defect in the sense of self of their followers. This need is potentially easy to exploit. Idealization-hungry followers of charismatic leaders of all types do not have the opportunity to resolve their idealizing transference, since the nature of the relationship precludes its being analysed, and so they continue to search for an idealizable father substitute instead of developing an internal sense of direction.

3 THE TRANSPERSONAL SELF

1 Other transpersonal psychologists such as Assagioli have also made good use of the concept of a higher Self, as have philosophers such as Kant who distinguish between the empirical ego and the noumenal or real Self. However, I have remained with Jung's description for the sake of consistency, since other such concepts are embedded in their own theoretical contexts.

2 It is usual for Jung to refer to the personal centre of consciousness as the 'ego'; within psychoanalytic self psychology the term 'self' means the whole person, and is used to avoid any implied connections to drive psychology, which contrasts 'ego' with 'id' and 'superego'. Jung's use of the term 'ego' is not burdened with these implications, and so is roughly comparable to the psychoanalytic use of the word 'self'.

3 The Buddha denied the existence of self as a discrete entity, noting that personality is a composite of many parts; however (according to Coomaraswamy, 1943), he did not deny the existence of the Self in the sense of the Upanishads.

4 THE ARCHETYPE AS SYNTHETIC PRINCIPLE

1 Jung's argument places him within the tradition of Plato, Kant, and others who argue that there are two realms of reality. For these thinkers, the way the world appears is not necessarily the way it is in itself. We can only know the world as it appears to us, through our sense organs, as phenomena and not in terms of its deeper structures. Our knowledge is only the empirical knowledge of our experience, not necessarily knowledge of the underlying reality itself. (Modern micro-physics tends to support this view of things.) But there is also a long tradition of opposition to arguments that postulate two levels of reality, at least beginning with Aristotle, who argued that since we cannot talk meaningfully about categories that have no connection with experience, we should confine ourselves to the world of actual experience. In this vein, Hillman (1971) has criticized Jung's stress on the concept of the *unus mundus*, a level of unitary reality underlying our experience of the world as fragmented (see p. 137), on the grounds that this idea diminishes the vitality of the psyche, which is polycentric. He feels that to search for an underlying unitary plan prevents us from fully exploring each fragment of the psyche. It is important to Hillman that we not search for some referent beyond any given image itself, some deeper Platonic reality, because any attempt to amplify the image by reference to some other symbol system is dualistic. To his mind, the archetype is wholly immanent in its image, which portrays its own meaning as we immerse ourselves within it. Whatever we say about the archetype itself is conjectural and itself governed by an archetypal image (Hillman, 1974, p. 95n.). This view argues that: 'we perceive archetypes directly. They are *immediate* (non-mediated). They are not elsewhere, unknowable, noumenal, or uncertain; they are not . . . per se separable from the phenomenal environmental world' (Boer and Kugler, 1977, p. 149).

2 I mean only that we have lost the formal rituals characteristic of pre-technological cultures. Psychotherapy has its own ritual, which is not defined as such but which performs the same function of allowing safe contact with the numinosum. It is often complained that we have also lost our initiation rituals, but in fact any contact with the numinosum is initiatory. In a sense, therefore, the religious approach to the psyche is all about initiation.

3 For example, as Barrett (1986, p. 165) points out, there is a modern trend to see human consciousness in the light of computer models, in the spirit of Hume, as 'essentially additive and atomistic . . . [whose] function consists in combining one discrete datum or bits of data, with others; and mind itself is but an aggregate of such data'. In response, Barrett reminds us that each element of consciousness implies 'the more inclusive

structure of mind in which they are found .... The part has meaning only within the whole' (p. 109). Barrett (p. 75) points out the irony of a position that tries to desubstantialize consciousness; without mind, science could not exist. The often unconscious premise that the psyche should be studied as though it were divisible and amenable to statistical analysis is based on a particular concept of science.

5 MYTHICAL, SYMBOLIC AND IMAGINAL ASPECTS OF THE PSYCHE'S RELIGIOUS FUNCTION

1 It might be preferable to think of image as a manifestation of the psyche, or as a content or product of the psyche, which is the originating matrix of the image. The image is then not the psyche itself; we do not know the nature of that level of the psyche that is the matrix of image, since it is beyond image.
2 The squared cirle is a rather abstract Self symbol, suggesting the union of heaven and earth, or finitude and infinity.

6 A PSYCHOLOGICAL VIEW OF SOME TRADITIONAL RELIGIOUS IDEAS

1 In his attempt to understand the origin of this gap, Sherrard (1987, p. 104) has pointed out that there is a 'direct causal connection between the process of desanctification of the natural order and certain developments within Christian theology itself'. He traces the forced distinction between nature and the sacred to the assertions of theologians since Augustine, who radically separates the Creator and the created, to ensure that the experience of the spirit can only be experienced within the church, in the officially prescribed mode. Aquinas further widened the Augustinian rift between nature and grace by his assertion of a dualism between the natural and the supernatural worlds (Ibid., p. 108). Nature is then said to work according to natural laws, which can be recognized through man's capacity for reason. These laws operate without revelation or grace or need for faith because God himself is a rational being. Using this argument, St Thomas was able to maintain a synthesis between the idea that nature is an integral part of the divine order and the idea that it exists in its own right, autonomously. Sherrard points out that this thinking promotes the idea of a gap between God and man, does not allow the direct apprehension of spiritual reality, and neglects the 'possibility of man's personal participation in the divine' (p. 109). (This 'participation' of course is exactly the place of the psyche.) Later theologians totally severed the tenuous link St Thomas had retained between nature and the divine and stressed the autonomy of reason, removing any sense of the immanence of the divine in the world. The scene was then set for the scientific revolution and its mechanistic world view, in which modern personalistic psychology participates by also excluding any sense of divine participation from the material world and from the psyche.
2 It is important to acknowledge that James's work on the psychology of religion is a precursor of these ideas in other ways. James was aware that religious experience arises from the unconscious, and that religious history has been influenced by such experiences (1902/1958, p. 386). His notion of the 'divided self' corresponds exactly to Kohut's concept of vertical split within the personality. James also recognized that unification of such splitting may occur through religious or mystical experiences (pp. 146–147).
3 The methodological argument arises as to whether these texts are truly collective. That is, although the traditional theological understanding of the Old Testament is that it was revealed as a whole by God to man, modern scholarship suggests it is a composite

account of various authors. The New Testament is markedly influenced by the psychology of particularly influential individuals, such as Paul. It has also been heavily interpreted and edited, which presumably produced a major level of projection onto the text. Accordingly it is difficult to comment on the story itself without excursions into psycho-history or psycho-biography, both of which are fraught with the danger of misinterpretation because of insufficient information and because of our own projections onto the material.

4 Within Old Testament theology, the mythologem of redemption refers to payment to recover property sold in times of need (Lev. 25: 25), or payment to secure release from slavery (Exod. 21: 7–8). The underlying psychological determinant is a sense that, to reclaim or save something from misfortune, a price is required. In the New Testament, this mythologem evolved to include the idea of Christ as an intermediary; Christ is the redeemer in the sense that his blood buys man back from sin, as if he paid a ransom for mankind (Mark, 10: 45; 1 Cor. 6: 20). His death is therefore a sacrifice which redeems man from the old covenant by mediating a new one (Heb. 9: 15). This New Testament theme of sacrifice seems to continue an Old Testament practice; in both cases the shedding of blood is deemed essential, either for the appeasement of the deity or for the forgiveness of sins (Heb. 9: 22), which is brought about by the death of Christ (Eph. 1: 7).

5 For example, in St Paul's (Rom. 3: 23) words, 'All have sinned', and: 'Therefore as sin came into the world through one man and death through sin, and so death spread to all men because all men sinned' (Rom. 5: 12).

6 The patriarchy inexorably produces mother problems by devaluing women. Paul's misogyny, or that of the writer whose work is attributed to him, is clear in comments such as: 'and Adam was not deceived, but the woman was deceived and became a transgressor' (1 Tim. 2: 14). He wants women to: 'learn in silence with all submissiveness', and not be permitted to 'teach or have authority over men' but to 'keep silent' (1 Tim. 2: 11–12). He seems to be afraid of women, and perhaps of his own femininity.

7 Basch (1988, p. 78) makes a useful distinction between affect and 'feeling'. Feeling means the ability to relate an involuntary, raw affective reaction to a concept of oneself, by abstracting and objectifying the affect, as in 'I' am angry. In his schema, 'emotion' is a futher step in affective maturation and results from the joining of a feeling state to previous experience, so allowing one to give personal meaning to complex concepts such as love or hate. These are different usages of the term from those of Jung (CW 6, 681 and 724), who conflates emotion and affect, and views feeling as a value-endowing process.

8 It is impossible to know with certainty what these images are in preverbal babies, who clearly have a good deal of affect. Theoretically their imagery must be almost purely archetypal. That is, the baby is born with the potential for imagery and fantasy that is gradually filled in with human content. Kleinian theory concerns itself with this level in the baby, but it is difficult to be sure that the contents of the fantasies that this theory describes are not later developments. Klein's theory depends on the existence of endogenous fantasy, but here it is important not to confuse the potential for fantasy with the content itself; content is acquired, only potential is archetypal or innate.

9 This is a typical anthropomorphic projection onto the Self, which is hard to resist.

7 A DEPTH PSYCHOLOGICAL APPROACH TO THE PROBLEM OF SUFFERING

1 Jung suggests that other scriptures indicate earlier tendencies towards change in the collective God image, which tend to reparation of all the wrong done to man. These

are exemplified by the visions of Daniel, Enoch and Ezekiel which prefigure man's clearer knowledge of God, and the integration of wisdom and justice within the image of God found in the figure of Sophia, whose presence can revitalize and feminize a previously rigid God image.

2 Von Franz (1975, p. 174) notes that when Jung was asked how he lived with the knowledge he had expressed in *Answer to Job*, he replied: 'I live in my deepest hell, and from this I cannot fall any further.'

3 Jung's preoccupation with splitting reminds of the two very different personalities of Jung's childhood self, and how difficult it was for him to integrate them. While this problem may have stimulated his interest in wholeness, it does not invalidate Jung's observations on the subject.

4 Here I should again note that I prefer to avoid the word ego whenever possible, partly to avoid any implied connection to drive-defence psychology, and partly because by 'self' I include the whole person, not just the field of personal consciousness but also the body and the personal unconscious.

5 Incidentally, this view of gradual incarnation throughout life casts new light on the ancient theological debate about when the soul enters the body of the foetus or baby. Incarnation simply keeps increasing; as the body grows, and behaviour becomes more complex, so embodiment of the soul increases. This is a never-ending process that occurs *pari passu* with psychological development.

6 See note 2, p. 240.

7 I mean that they do not suffer from the weakness of theories that emphasize 'inner' vs. 'outer' worlds, or a radical subject–object split. They include the importance of the therapist–observer in determining the nature of the psychotherapeutic field.

8 The debate between Neumann and Fordham (see Samuels, 1985) about the mother as carrier of the child's Self vs. the idea of a primary Self within the infant is rendered moot here; both are included within the mirroring and idealizing poles of the selfobject.

8 SUFFERING

1 There is some loose correspondence here to Jung's typology, but I do not find that the two systems can be superimposed exactly even though some points coincide. As a rule, high levels of feeling predispose to devotional methods, thinking intuitives and intuitive thinkers enjoy enquiry, extraverted sensation types may employ service, introverted sensing types can use the body, and so on. Sometimes one is attracted to a technique that emphasizes the inferior function, because this allows the numinosum to enter.

2 By 'negative' I mean that men who have considerable fear of women are actually in thrall to the feminine aspects of the divine, or the Goddess, which they experience in her terrifying aspect. Anything female is numinous but deadly. Hence, the attempt to suppress Her.

3 *Karma* here refers to the consequences of an individual's actions in this or a previous lifetime, based on an inexorable law of cause and effect.

4 The idea that neurosis is purposeful is echoed in Kohut's notion of the selfobject need that manifests itself in order to obtain what is missing to restore the self.

9 SIN AND EVIL

1 Vertical splitting refers to the existence of sectors of the psyche which are conscious but which contain material whose emotional significance is not admitted. These sectors

are often at odds with the rest of the personality. Horizontal splitting is synonymous with repression, or a process of active forgetting which does not allow material to enter consciousness at all.

2 In the astrological myth, the planets, which represent archetypal components of the soul, may be arranged in harmonious or conflictual relationships with each other.

10 PSYCHOTHERAPY AND SPIRITUAL PRACTICE

1 Rizzuto (1979) has described the ways in which an intrapsychic representation of God forms as a product of developmental experiences. While there is no doubt that such experience affects the God image, I am also concerned with the divine, or the Self, as an organizing principle within the psyche prior to such representation.

2 I am indebted to Dr Paul Kugler for his discussion of these points with me.

3 These involve reports by people who have been clinically dead of typical experiences during attempts to resuscitate them.

4 The word 'client' was popularized by humanistic psychologists such as Rogers, as an alternative to the word 'patient', in order to remove psychotherapy from the hegemony of the medical model, which implied the patient's passivity and the doctor's authority. However, in some ways this change was a mistake. The Latin word *clinare* means to lean, implying that the client is in some way dependent on, or leans upon, the therapist. By contrast, the word *patiens* is derived from the Latin verb meaning to suffer patiently, clearly a preferable appellation for a person in psychotherapy. Further, there is a certain ethical protection in the role of patient that may not be present in the role of client.

REFERENCES

Adler, G. (1975) Aspects of Jung's Personality and Work. *Psychological Perspectives.* Spring, p. 12

Altschule, M. D. (1965) *Roots of Modern Psychiatry.* Grune & Stratton, New York.

Arlow, J. A. (1961) Ego Psychology and the Study of Mythology. *Journal of the American Psychoanalytic Association* 9: 371–393.

Asher, C. (1993) The Communitarian Self as (God) Ultimate Reality. Spring, 54: 71–99.

Avens, R. (1982) *Imaginal Body.* University Press of America, Lanham, MD.

—— (1984) *The New Gnosis.* Spring, Dallas, TX.

Aziz, R. (1990) *C. G. Jung's Psychology of Religion and Synchronicity.* SUNY Press, New York.

Barrett, W. (1986) *Death of the Soul.* Anchor Press, Doubleday, New York.

Basch, M. F. (1976) The Concept of Affect: A Re-examination. *Journal of the American Psychoanalytic Association* 24: 759–777.

—— (1983) The Perception of Reality and the Disavowal of Meaning. *The Annual of Psychoanalysis* 11: 125–154.

—— (1988) *Understanding Psychotherapy.* Basic Books, New York.

Bernoulli, R. (1960) Spiritual Development as Reflected in Alchemy and Related Disciplines. In: *Spiritual Disciplines, Papers From the Eranos Yearbooks.* Ed. J. Campbell. Princeton University Press, Princeton, NJ.

Blackney, R. B. (1941) *Meister Eckhart: A Modern Translation.* Harper & Row, New York.

Boer, C. and Kugler, P. (1977) Archetypal Psychology is Mythic Realism. Spring, Dallas, TX, pp. 131–152.

Bohm, D. (1980) *Wholeness and the Implicate Order.* Routledge & Kegan Paul, London.

Boisen, A. T. (1936) *The Exploration of the Inner World.* University of Philadelphia Press, Philadelphia, Pa.

Bowker, J. (1980) *Problems of Suffering in Religions of the World.* Cambridge University Press, Cambridge.

Brothers, L. (1989) A Biological Perspective on Empathy. *American Journal of Psychiatry* 146:1, 10–19.

Bruteau, B. (1974) *Evolution Toward Divinity.* Theosophical Publishing House, Wheaton, IL.

Buber, M. (1947) *Tales of the Hasidim: The Early Masters.* Schocken Books, New York.

—— (1952) *Eclipse of God: Studies in the Relation Between Religion and Philosophy.* Harper & Row, New York.

—— (1958) *I and Thou.* Chas. Scribner, New York.

Budge, E. A. W. (1969) *The Gods of the Egyptians.* Dover, New York.

Campbell, J. (1969) *The Flight of the Wild Gander.* Viking Press, New York.

Casey, E. S. (1974) Towards an Archetypal Imagination. Spring, Dallas, TX, pp. 1–32

REFERENCES

Christou, E. (1976) *The Logos of the Soul*. Spring, Dallas, TX.

Clark, S. (1986) *The Mysteries of Religion*. Blackwell, Oxford.

Cohen, J. M. and Phipps, J. F. (1979) *The Common Experience*. J. P. Tarcher, Los Angeles.

Coles, R. (1990) *The Spiritual Life of Children*. Houghton Mifflin, Boston, MA.

Coomaraswamy, A. K. (1943) *Hinduism and Buddhism*. Philosophical Library, New York.

Corbett, L. (1987) Transformation of the Image of God Leading to Self Initiation into Old Age. In: *Betwixt and Between*. Ed. L. Mahdi. Open Court, La Salle, Ill.

—— (1989) A Companion to Theory and Therapy. In: *Self Psychology: Companions and Contrasts*. Ed. H. Kohut and C. G. Jung, Analytic Press, Hillsdale, NJ.

—— (1990) The Archetypal Feminine. In: *Dreams in Analysis*. Chiron Pubs, Wilmette, IL.

Corbett, L. and Kugler, P. (1989) The Self in Jung and Kohut. In: *Dimensions of Self Experience: Progress in Self Psychology*, vol. 5. Ed. Arnold Goldberg. Analytic Press, Hillsdale, NJ.

Corbett, L. and Rives, C. M. (1991) Anima, Animus and Selfobject Theory. In: *Gender and Soul in Psychotherapy*. Analytic Press, Hillsdale, NJ.

Corbin, H. (1972) Mundus Imaginalis or the Imaginary and the Imaginal. *Spring*, Dallas, TX, pp. 1–9.

Corneau, G. (1992) Comme le Nuage Va, Comme L'Oiseau Chante. In: *Raisons de Vivre*. Les Editions L'Essentiel. Roxboro, Quebec.

Dallett, J. (1982) Active Imagination in Practice. In: *Jungian Analysis*. Ed. Murray Stein. Open Court, La Salle, IL.

Daniélou, A. (1973) *Hindu Polytheism*. Pantheon Books, Wheaton, IL.

Davies, B. (1982) *An Introduction to the Philosophy of Religion*. Oxford University Press, Oxford.

de Grouchy, J. W. (1986) In: *Jung in Modern Perspective*. Ed. R. K. Papadopolous and G. S. Saayman. Wildwood House, Middlesex, England.

DeVoogd, S. (1977) C. G. Jung: Psychologist of the Future, Philosopher of the Past. *Spring*, Dallas, TX, pp. 175–182.

Diel, P. (1980) *Symbolism in Greek Mythology*. Shambhala, Boulder, CO.

Dourley, J. P. (1981) *C. G. Jung and Paul Tillich: The Psyche as Sacrament*. Inner City Books, Toronto.

—— (1987) *Love, Celibacy and the Inner Marriage*. Inner City Books, Toronto.

Dunne, J. S. (1969) *A Search for God in Time and Memory*. Collier Macmillan, London.

Edinger, E. F. (1973) *Ego and Archetype*. Penguin Books, London.

—— (1984) *The Creation of Consciousness*. Inner City Books, Toronto.

—— (1987) *The Christian Archetype*. Inner City Books, Toronto.

Eliade, M. (1958) *Patterns in Comparative Religion*. Trans. Sheed, R. Sheed & Ward, New York.

—— (1964) *Shamanism*. Princeton University Press, Princeton, NJ.

—— (1974) *The Myth of the Eternal Return*. Bollingen Foundation, New York.

Emde, R. (1978) Emotional Expression in Infancy. In: *The Development of Affect*. Ed. M. Lewis and L. Rosenblum. Plenum, New York.

Engler, J. and Brown, D. P. (1986) The Stages of Meditation in Cross Cultural Perspective. In: *Transformations of Consciousness*. Ed. K. Wilber, J. Engler and D. P. Brown. New Science Library, Shambhala, Boston, MA.

Fairbairn, R. (1954) *An Object Relations Theory of the Personality*. Basic Books, New York.

Fordham. M. (1976) *The Self and Autism*. Heinemann, London.

—— (1985) *Explorations into the Self*. Academic Press, London.

Fox, M. (1981) Meister Eckhart on the Fourfold Path of a Creation Centered Spirituality. In: *Western Spirituality*. Ed. M. Fox. Bear Co., Santa Fe, NM.

Frazer, J. G. (1923) *Folklore in the Old Testament* Macmillan, New York.

Freud, S. (1915) *Instincts and Their Vicissitudes*. In: Freud 1960, Standard Edition, vol. 14, pp. 109–140. Hogarth Press and the 'nstitute of Psycho Analysis, London.

—— (1918) *From the History of an Infantile Neurosis*. In Freud 1960, Standard Edition, vol. 17, pp. 7–122. Hogarth Press and the Institute of Psycho Analysis, London.

—— (1927) *The Future of an Illusion*. In Freud 1961, Standard Edition, vol. 21, Hogarth Press and the Institute of Psycho Analysis, London.

—— (1930) *Civilization and its Discontents*. In: Freud 1960, Standard Edition, vol. 21, pp. 64–195. Hogarth Press and the Institute of Psycho Analysis, London.

—— (1933) *New Introductory Lectures on Psycho Analysis*. In: Freud 1960, Standard Edition, vol. 22, pp. 5–158. Hogarth Press and the Institute of Psychoanalysis, London.

Fromm, E. (1950) *Psychoanalysis and Religion*. Yale University Press, New Haven, Ct.

Frosch, T. R. (1974) *The Awakening of Albion*. Cornell University Press, Ithaca, NY.

Garrison, J. (1982) *The Darkness of God: Theology After Hiroshima.* Eardmans, Grand Rapids, MI.

Gerstenberger, E. S. and Schrage, W. (1980) *Suffering*. Trans. J.E. Steely, Abingdon Press, Nashville, TN.

Girard, R. (1979) *Violence and the Sacred*. Johns Hopkins University Press, Baltimore, MD.

Glover, J. (1988) *The Philosophy and Psychology of Personal Identity*. Viking Penguin, New York.

Goldbrunner, J. (1964) *Individuation: A Study of the Depth Psychology of C. G. Jung*. University of Notre Dame Press, IN.

Goleman, D. (1988) *The Meditative Mind*. Tarcher, Los Angeles.

Goleman, D. and Schwartz, G. E. (1976) Meditation as Intervention in Stress Reactivity. *Journal of Clinical and Consulting Psychiatry* 44: 456–466.

Govinda, A. B. (1977) *Creative Meditation and Multi-Dimensional Consciousness*. Mandala Books, London.

Hall, J. A. (1979) Religious Images in Dreams. *Journal of Religion and Health*. 18(4): 327–335.

Haule, J. A. (1986) Soul Loss and Countertransference: A Study in Restoration. In: *Carl Jung and Soul Psychology*. Ed. E. M. Stern. Harcourt Press, New York.

Heiler, F. (1985) Contemplation in Christian Mysticism. In: *Spiritual Disciplines*. Ed. J. Campbell. Princeton University Press, Princeton, NJ.

Henderson, L. (1967) *Thresholds of Initiation*. Wesleyan University Press. Middletown, CT.

Hick, J. (1966) *Evil and the God of Love*. Macmillan, London.

Hillman, J. (1971) Psychology: Monotheistic or Polytheistic. Spring, Dallas, TX, pp. 193–208, 230–232.

—— (1972) *The Myth of Analysis*. Northwestern University Press, Cranston, IL.

—— (1974) On the Necessity of Abnormal Psychology. In: *Eranos Jarbuch* 43. E. J. Brill Pubs, Leiden.

—— (1975) *Re-Visioning Psychology*. Harper Colophon, New York.

—— (1977) An Inquiry into Image. *Spring*, Dallas, TX, pp. 62–68.

—— (1979) Image Sense. *Spring*, Dallas, TX. pp. 130–143.

—— (1981) 'Appendix: "Psychology: Monotheistic or Polytheistic,"' in D. L. Miller, *The New Polytheism: Rebirth of the Gods and Goddesses*. Spring, Dallas TX.

—— (1983a) *Archetypal Psychology*. Spring, Dallas, TX.

—— (1983b) *Interviews*. Harper & Row, New York.

—— (1985) *Anima. An Anatomy of a Personified Notion*. Spring, Dallas, TX.

Hogenson, G. B. (1982), *Jung's Struggle with Freud*. Notre Dame Press, IN.

Horton, P. C. (1973) The Mystical Experience as a Suicide Preventive. *American Journal of Psychiatry*. 103: 3.

REFERENCES

Hostie, R. (1957) *Religion and the Psychology of Jung.* Sheed & Ward, New York.
Jacobs, L. (1973) *A Jewish Theology.* Behrman, New York.
Jaffe, A. (1971) *The Myth of Meaning.* G. P. Putnam, New York.
James, W. (1902/1958) *The Varieties of Religious Experience.* Mentor Books, New York.
Jeans, J. (1930) *The Mysterious Universe.* Macmillan, New York.
Johnson, C. L. (1981) Psychoanalysis, Shamanism and Cultural Phenomena. *Journal of the American Academy of Psychoanalysis* 9(2): 311–318.
Jung, C. G. (1965) *Memories, Dreams and Reflections.* Vintage Books, New York.
—— (1973) *Letters*, vol. 1. Ed. G. Adler, and A. Jaffe. Trans. R. F. C. Hull. Princeton University Press, Princeton, NJ.
—— (1975) *Letters*, vol. 2. Ed. G. Adler and A. Jaffe. Trans. R. F. C. Hull. Princeton University Press, Princeton, NJ.
—— (1976) *The Visions Seminars.* Spring Pubs, Zurich, Switzerland.
Kaufman, W. (1978) *Critique of Religion and Philosophy.* Princeton University Press, Princeton, NJ.
Kaufman, Y. (1978) Analytical Psychotherapy. In: *Current Psychotherapies.* Ed. R. Corsini. F. E. Peacock, Ithaca, Il.
Kohut, H. (1971) *The Analysis of the Self.* International Universities Press, New York.
—— (1977) *The Restoration of the Self.* International Universities Press, New York.
—— (1982) Introspection, Empathy and the Semi-Circle of Mental Health. *International Journal of Psychoanalysis* 63, 395.
—— (1984) *How Does Analysis Cure?* University of Chicago Press, Chicago, IL.
Kramer, S. N. (1972) *Sumerian Mythology.* University of Pennsylvania Press, Philadelphia, PA.
Krishnamurti, J. (1971) *The First and Last Freedom.* Quest Books, Wheaton, IL.
Luke, H. (1984) *The Voice Within.* Crossroad, New York.
McGuire, W. and Hull, R. F. C. (Eds) (1977) *C. G. Jung Speaking.* Princeton University Press, Princeton, NJ.
McLean, A. (1980) The *Rosary of the Philosophers.* Magnum Opus Sourceworks, Thames Press, Grand Rapids, MI.
Meier, C. A. (1967) *Ancient Incubation and Modern Psychotherapy.* North Western University Press, Evanston, IL.
Mindell, A. (1982) *Dreambody, the Body's Role in Revealing the Self.* Sigo Press, Santa Monica, CA.
Moore, T. (1983) *Rituals of the Imagination.* Pegasus Foundation, Dallas, TX.
Moustakas, C. (1990) *Heuristic Research.* Sage Pubs., London.
Mullahy, P. (1948) *Oedipus Myth and Complex.* Heritage Press, New York.
Murphy, J. M. (1964) Psychotherapeutic Aspects of Shamanism in St. Laurence Island, Alaska. In: *Magic, Faith and Healing.* Ed. A. Kiev. Free Press, New York.
Nelson, M. C. and Eigen, M. (1984) *Evil, Self and Culture.* Human Sciences Press, New York.
Neumann, E. (1969) *Depth Psychology and a New Ethic.* G. P. Putnam, New York.
—— (1973) *Origins and History of Consciousness.* Princeton University Press, Princeton, NJ.
Ogden, T. H. (1990) *The Matrix of the Mind.* Jason Aronson. Northvale, NJ.
Olson, C. (1970) *The Special View of History.* Oyez, Berkeley, CA.
Otto, R. (1958) *The Idea of the Holy.* Oxford University Press, London.
Panikkar, R. (1979) *Myth, Faith and Hermeneutics.* Paulist Press, New York.
Parrinder, G. (1970) *Avatar and Incarnation.* Oxford University Press, New York.
Perry, J. W. (1974) *The Far Side of Madness.* Prentice-Hall, Englewood Cliffs, NJ.
—— (1985) *The Self in Psychotic Process.* University of California Press, Berkeley, CA.
Peteet, J. R. (1981) Issues in the Treatment of Religious Patients. *American Journal of Psychotherapy* xxxv(4): 559–564.

Polanyi, M. (1983) *The Tacit Dimension*. Peter Smith, Gloucester, MA.

Prusak, B. P. (1979) Soul–Body Relationship. In: *Encyclopedic Dictionary of Religion*. Corpus Publications, Washington, DC.

Ranke-Heinemann, U. (1990) *Eunuchs for the Kingdom of Heaven*. Penguin Books, New York.

Rasmussen, K. (1927) *Across Arctic America*. Putnam, New York.

Rizzuto, A.-M. (1979) *The Birth of the Living God*. University of Chicago Press, Chicago, IL.

Rose, S. (1982) *Against Biological Determinism*. Allison & Busby, London.

Russel, J. B. (1977) *The Devil*. Meridian Books, New York.

Samuels, A. (1985) *Jung and the Post Jungians*. Routledge & Kegan Paul, London.

Sanford, J. A. (1982) *Evil, the Shadow Side of Reality*. Crossroad, New York.

Schneiderman, L. (1981) *The Psychology of Myth, Folk Lore and Religion*. Nelson Hall, Chicago, IL.

Schwartz-Salant, N. (1989) *The Borderline Personality: Vision and Healing*. Chiron Pubs, Wilmette, IL.

Segal, R. A. (1992) *The Gnostic Jung*. Princeton University Press, Princeton, NJ.

Sherrard, P. (1987) *The Eclipse of Man and Nature*. Inner Traditions. Lindisfarne Press, West Stockbridge, MA.

Sholem, G. (1961) *Major Trends in Jewish Mysticism*. Schocken Books, New York.

Soelle, D. (1975) *Suffering*. Fortress Press, Philadelphia, PA.

Spero, M. H. (1981) Countertransference in Religious Therapists of Religious Patients. *American Journal of Psychotherapy* xxxv(4): 565–575.

Stanner, W. E. H. (1984) Religion, Totemism and Symbolism. In: *Religion in Aboriginal Australia*. Ed. M. Charlesworth, H. Morphy, D. Bell and K. Maddock. University of Queensland Press, St Lucia, Queensland, Australia.

Steele, R. S. (1982) *Freud and Jung*. Routledge & Kegan Paul, London.

Stein, R. (1984) *Incest and Human Love*. Spring, Dallas, TX.

Stewart, L. H. (1987) Affect and Archetype in Analysis. In: *Archetypal Processes in Psychotherapy*. Ed. M. Stein and N. Schwartz-Salant. Chiron Pubs. Wilmette, IL.

Stolorow, R. and Atwood, G. (1992) *Contexts of Being*. Academic Press, Hillsdale, NJ.

Stolorow, R. and Brandschaft, B. (1987) Developmental Failure and Psychic Conflict. *Psychoanalytic Psychology* 4(3): 241–253.

Stolorow, R., Atwood, G. and Brandschaft, B. (1988) Symbols of Subjective Truth in Psychotic States. In: *Progress in Self Psychology*, vol. 3. Ed. A. Goldberg. Analytic Press, Hillsdale, NJ.

Stone, M. (1984) *Ancient Mirrors of Womanhood*. Beacon Press, Boston, MA.

Stoudt, J. J. (1968) *Jacob Boehme: His Life and Thought*. Seaburg Press, New York.

Tillich, P. (1948) *The Shaking of the Foundation*. Scribner, New York.

—— (1959) *Theology of Culture*. Ed. R. C. Kimball, Oxford University Press, London.

—— (1963) *The Eternal Now*. Scribner, New York.

Tomkins, S. S. (1962) *Affect, Imagery, Consciousness*, vols 1 and 2. Springer Pubs, New York.

von der Heydt, V. (1976) *Prospects for the Soul*. Darton, Longman & Todd, London.

von Franz, M. L. (1972) *Creation Myths*. Spring, Dallas, TX.

—— (1975) *C. G. Jung: His Myth in Our Time*. Putnams, New York.

—— (1980) *Projection and Re-Collection in Jungian Psychology*. Open Court, La Salle, IL.

Walker, B. (1983) *The Woman's Encyclopedia of Myths and Secrets*. Harper & Row, San Francisco.

Wheelwright, P. (1959) *Daedalus*. Journal of the American Academy of Arts and Sciences, American Academy of Arts and Sciences, Cambridge, MA, p. 360.

REFERENCES

White, V. (1960) *Soul and Psyche: An Enquiry into the Relationship of Psychotherapy and Religion*. Collins, London.

Wilbur, K. (1991) *Grace and Grit*. Shambhala, Boston, MA.

Wink, W. (1992) *Engaging the Powers*. Fortress Press, Minneapolis, MN.

Wolf, E. (1988) *Treating the Self*. Guilford, New York.

Woodruff, P. and Wilmer, H. A. (eds) (1988) *Facing Evil*. Open Court, La Salle, IL.

Zeigler, A. J. (1983) *Archetypal Medicine*. Spring, Dallas, TX.

INDEX